RICHARD
THE
LIONHEART

RICHARD THE LIONHEART

THE CRUSADER KING OF ENGLAND

W. B. BARTLETT

AMBERLEY

To Deyna and Miles,
with best wishes for your future life together.

First published 2018

Amberley Publishing
The Hill, Stroud
Gloucestershire, GL5 4EP

www.amberley-books.com

British Library Cataloguing in Publication Data.
A catalogue record for this book is available from the British Library.

ISBN 978 1 4456 6270 1 (hardback)
ISBN 978 1 4456 6271 8 (ebook)

Map design by Thomas Bohm, User design.
Typesetting and Origination by Amberley Publishing.
Printed in the UK.

Contents

Maps vi

Introduction 1
Prelude 3
1 The Third Nesting (1157–1167) 8
2 The Winter of Discontent (1168–1176) 26
3 A Family at War (1177–1183) 42
4 Crisis (1184–1188) 60
5 The Bitter Inheritance (1188–1189) 80
6 Long Live the King (1189–1190) 93
7 The Crusade Departs (1190) 115
8 Mayhem and Matrimony: The Journey Begins (1190–1191) 131
9 The Taking of Cyprus (1191) 156
10 High-Water Mark: The Siege of Acre (1191) 167
11 Arsuf (1191) 190
12 Facing up to Reality (1191) 212
13 The Forlorn Hope (1191–1192) 231
14 The End of the Dream (1192 246
15 Betrayal (1192–1193) 264
16 The Long Road to Freedom (1193–1194) 282
17 The Return of the King (1194–1195) 298
18 A Never-Ending War (1195–1198) 317
19 Last Rites (1198–1199) 339
20 Epilogue 353

Notes 372
Bibliography 390
Acknowledgements 394
Index 395

France and Britain at the end of the twelfth century.

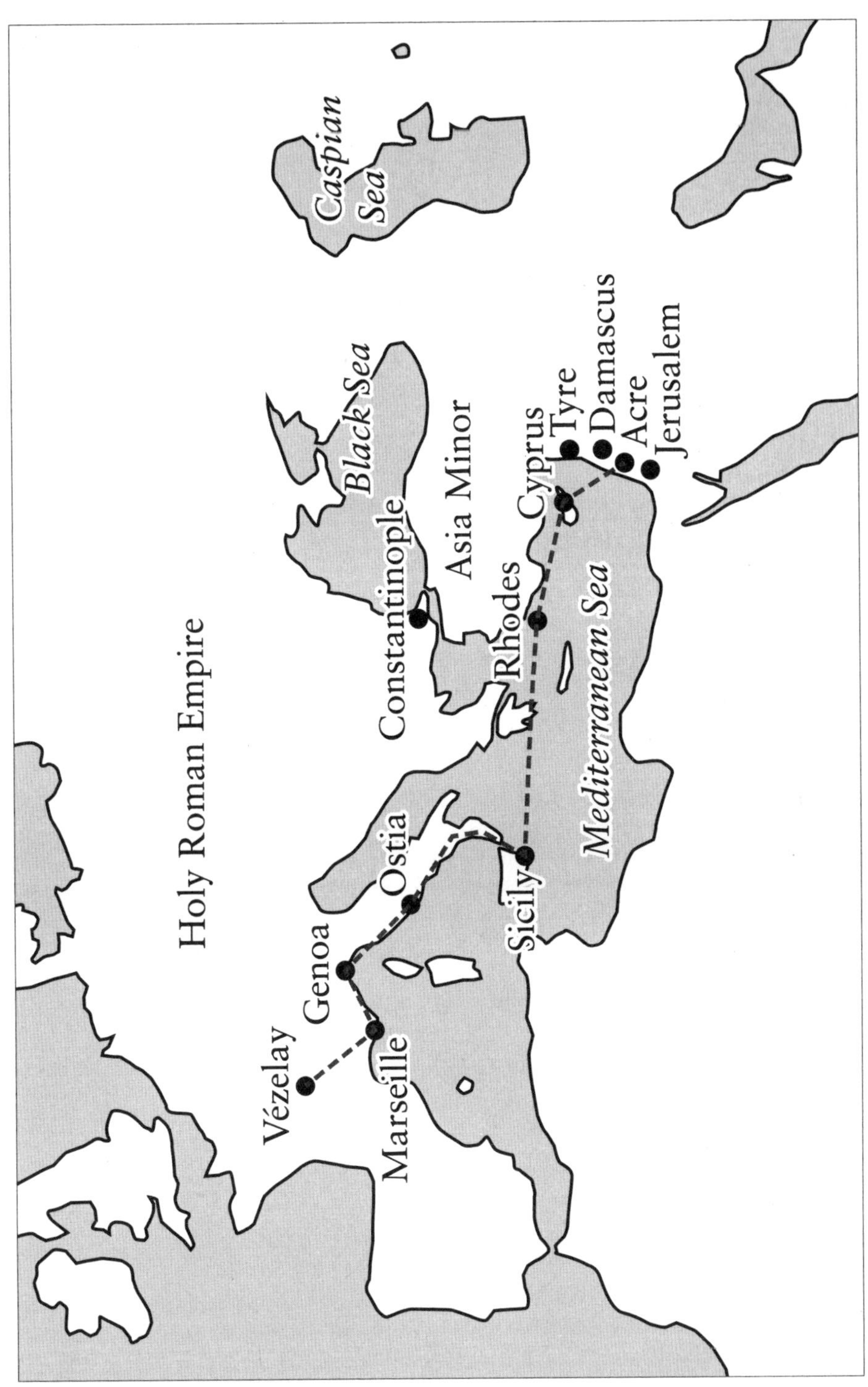

Richard's journey to the Crusades

Outremer at the time of the Third Crusade.

Introduction

Following in the footsteps of Richard in these strange times of Brexit and its uncertainties has been an interesting experience. In a world where we seem to be increasingly keen on emphasising our differences, travelling around France in particular has offered constant reminders of the similarities and connections that the British – or perhaps more specifically the English – share with their continental neighbours. But the journey around Richard's erstwhile possessions on the continent has also forcibly reminded me that Richard was a king of England and not an English king – two quite different things. Not all historians have made due allowance for the distinction in the past.

Going back a decade or so I was fortunate enough to travel around Syria and see some of the great crusader castles such as Crac des Chevaliers where, coincidentally, I was the only visitor along with a certain Boris Johnson. Poor, shattered Syria. Back in 2007 I was surprised to see how well Christian and Muslim communities had lived alongside each other for nearly 1,500 years, apparently with no tension or festering hostility beneath the surface. How wrong I was, and how fragile and transitory that illusion of peace. If nothing else, we should learn not to take peace for granted and instead nurture it gently and assiduously. If we don't, then it is all too likely to evaporate.

Richard was a man who crossed worlds, from Muslim to Christian, from French to English, from medieval to modern. You can feel him in France (where you can still follow the Route de Richard-Coeur-de-Lion around some of his Aquitanian haunts) and you could still feel his presence in Syria. Yet to understand him at all we must strip away our modern perceptions of what a king should be, of how he should think or act, for these are not fair or appropriate benchmarks by which to judge him. When we do this we find, perhaps surprisingly, that he did divided opinion in his own times much as he does today.

What we will see is that Richard did not have to seek far for enemies, not just from the Muslim world but also in fellow Christians who would criticise him, berate him, undermine him, imprison him and, ultimately, kill him. Even his own family did their best to keep him in his place.

The story of Richard is first and foremost a human one, of a man with flaws and virtues. He was a failed son, an uncommitted husband, a complicated and not always readable ally, an implacable and unforgiving enemy, an untrustworthy brother. He was driven by his ambition, his *superbia* (that is, his pride), his desire to be recognised for what he saw as his greatness, his zeal to be a chivalric and kingly paragon. However much the world today differs from that of 1189, Richard's story still has much to tell us about how it has evolved and, in some respects, how little it has changed.

Wayne Bartlett
Bournemouth
March 2018

Prelude

As the twilight of the day approached, the king made his way out of his tent and towards the small but defiant French castle that had been resisting his efforts to take it for far longer than he had expected. It irked intensely that this insignificant place had continued to frustrate him and his ambitions. By now it was much battered, but the pitifully small garrison still showed no inclination to accept the inevitable and surrender. The king was a proud man and also an impatient one, and he was increasingly irritated that the garrison continued to hold out against him – or, as he would have seen it, against the natural order of things.

One particular opponent more than any other was antagonising him. Within the castle walls, shattered in places but still strong enough to resist the efforts of the besieging force, was an impudent crossbowman who defended himself against Richard's archers and their bolts not with a shield but with a frying pan. The king now made his way toward the walls to assess for himself how much longer the castle was likely to be able to hold out and to see what progress had been made during the course of the day. He was virtually unescorted, for the garrison was small and no attack against his person was expected.

There was only the threat of the crossbowman to worry about; little else was going on. The king was confident that he would be able to move out of the way of any bolts that might be fired in his direction. He felt a grudging admiration for this man who refused to be cowed even by his great reputation. He was even moved to applaud him for his obstinacy. But surely no man would dare try to bring down a king.

He moved into range. The crossbowman took careful aim. Despite the lengthening shadows he had a clear shot. The bolt sped from his bow, carving its way through the air towards its target. Richard saw it coming and tried to take evasive action, but he was not quick enough. Perhaps over-exertion in battle through the years had taken its toll, or maybe too much good eating had slowed him down; whatever the reason, he was starting to turn fat. The bolt found its mark, embedding itself deeply in his left shoulder. Within days the target, Richard I, king of England, would be dead. A man who had won his name as the greatest crusader of them all was to die as a result of a squalid little engagement in a quiet and insignificant part of France. There could not have been a more inappropriate end to his life.

To his enemies, Richard was the greatest of foes. While Muslim writers regarded him suspiciously as a Christian warrior from the West, they nevertheless could not stop themselves from lauding his virtues, perhaps in an attempt to explain away the defeats he had inflicted on them. They praised him as the biggest military threat ever to face them. His showdown with one of their own greats, Saladin, fed the legend of the mighty crusader, imperious in battle and valiant beyond compare.

So marked was his impact that when, in our own time, Osama bin Laden preached jihad, he not only referred to the crusade that he felt was imminent but also reminded his audience that the crusades were not a new phenomenon. In the process, he referred specifically to some of the most notable crusaders of the past. High up the list of those named was Richard Coeur de Lion.[1]

Yet in recent times his own people have rejected Richard. Sir Winston Churchill, famous for his spellbinding narrative prose, while recognising Richard's formidable status as a warrior considered him to be a child in politics. While it would be a brave or foolish writer who would disagree with someone of Churchill's stature, this is a rather one-dimensional interpretation. It sees Richard in black-and-white terms although most people, even the greats of history, exhibit many shades of grey. Churchill may have had his Battle of Britain but he also had his Gallipoli. He may have built a deserved and outstanding reputation as a wartime Prime Minister but he also had the drubbing of the 1945 General Election on his CV.

Churchill, however, was not alone. The late nineteenth and twentieth centuries saw a number of historians critical of Richard as a king (though he had his supporters too, even then). If they were judging him from what was expected of a twentieth-century monarch, they were justified. The problem is that they were 800 years late in their judgement and what was expected from a king was very different when seen from a twelfth-century perspective. The twelfth-century benchmark is the one against which Richard should be measured; that is all he had as a comparator.

What follows is not just the tale of a king; it is the story of a family, the Angevins. This dynasty contained within its ranks some remarkable characters: a strong and dominant patriarch in the shape of Henry II; a wife and mother, Eleanor of Aquitaine, who was one of the most notable of all medieval women; and a brood of sons and daughters who would exhibit a remarkable range of strengths and weaknesses. It is, unfortunately, the brothers about whom we know the most because they are the ones the medieval chroniclers tended to write about, though we can frequently read between the lines about the sisters too.

The brothers were quite different characters. If we put one of them, William, to one side (he died while he was still in his infancy), there are four to consider. Two – Henry, the eldest, and Geoffrey, the second youngest – only feature in the early part of the saga, for they too died before their time, though not before they had played a prominent role in shaping the latter years of Henry II's reign and the early part of Richard's life.

It is the two surviving brothers, Richard and John, who feature the most in our tale. Richard became known as the crusader *par excellence*, though he is less remembered for other parts of his relatively short reign. The crusading period of his life covered the years 1190 to 1192, followed by a period of captivity until 1194 after he fell into the hands of his enemies – ironically not Muslims but fellow Christians and crusaders. This four-year period forms the main focus of attention for many, encompassing as it does the events for which he is most famous.

Yet the remaining thirty-eight years of his life give other insights into Richard and the twisted, tortured family relationships that defined him as a man. Modern sociologists would have a field day analysing the Angevins – a classic broken family, though one which should be seen through the prism of twelfth-century politics and society rather than twenty-first century paradigms. It is a complicated story not just of momentous events but also tangled familial relationships which were never better than complex and at some moments broke down completely.

Nowhere was this better evidenced than in the relationship between Richard and John, which oscillated violently. John, who became king after Richard's death, has become a byword for duplicity and faithlessness, the cowardly lion who is caricatured in Disney's cartoon version of *Robin Hood*. This book is concerned primarily with his elder brother, and historians, revisionists and counter-revisionists continue to argue about whether or not John's 'badness' has been overplayed. Regardless, his part in this story as it relates to Richard's life and reign cannot be ignored.

There are seven major chroniclers for Richard's reign; four of them were monks and the other three were secular clerks. Each of them had their own agenda and their own personal interpretation of Richard and the Angevin dynasty. Their accounts are all nuanced and cannot be regarded as black-and-white statements of fact.[2]

There are also many factual records that have survived the ravages of time. Record books may not be as exciting as chronicles, but they are generally more reliable sources of information. There was less incentive to exaggerate; falsifying accounting records could be a dangerous move with serious personal consequences for the fraudster. England's historical records are more comprehensive than those of most other nations, a gold mine for the historian, though the bureaucratic records of Richard's reign have been analysed less than those of some other monarchs such as that other warrior-crusader-king, Edward I.

There are good records too for Normandy, which had administrative similarities with England and formed part of the core territories of the Angevin rulers. In contrast, the records that survive for other parts of the Angevin territories – Anjou and Aquitaine in particular – are far less complete. But taken as a whole, this is a considerable body of evidence on which to construct a framework that lays out the key events of Richard's life and times.

What follows is the story of a fascinating man, a human being with great strengths and some significant weaknesses. There were virtues aplenty: courage, strategic insight and a strong grasp on administration – vital when the king was, to all intents and purposes, also the government, or at least its head. There were weaknesses too, as some of his opponents and rivals passionately asserted: pride, cruelty, duplicity, excess. What is not in doubt, though, is that Richard was, first and foremost, an extraordinary man, a human being far above the commonplace, and a king who won the admiration of many of his contemporaries and the disdain of others. Still, nearly a millennium on, Richard I, 'the Lionheart', divides judgement like few other characters in British history.

1

The Third Nesting (1157–1167)

'The eagle of the broken covenant shall rejoice in her third nesting'
The prophecy of Merlin as recalled by Ralph of Diceto

Where exactly to start the story of one of England's most controversial kings is a matter of personal choice, but a May day in 1152 in the cathedral of Poitiers in the south-west of France, a few years before Richard was actually born, would seem as good a time and place as any. It was Whit Sunday, one of the holiest days in the Christian calendar, but what was happening in Poitiers was more about secular power than religion. Those present in the cathedral had come to witness a wedding, one that would shake the structure of Western Europe to its foundations.[1] The aftershocks of this particular day would reverberate across the continent for the next three centuries.

The groom was one of the most powerful and eligible bachelors in Western Europe. Henry of Anjou (a territory that covered much of the Loire Valley) had inherited the title of that county the year before, on the death of his father, Geoffrey Plantagenet. Geoffrey ('the Handsome'), a man of charm and stunning good looks who in younger days was renowned for his golden-red hair, had himself enjoyed a stellar career. His territory in the north of France had expanded hugely while he was count, not least by the acquisition of Normandy.

But there was more to Henry, count of Anjou and duke of Normandy, than just this, for he also held a strong claim to the throne of England, a country that had recently been torn apart by a bitter and extended civil war in a time that was so evil it was said that 'Christ and His Saints slept'. Henry's claim to England had not yet been universally accepted – but it would not be long before it was.

Despite his immense wealth and significant status, in France Henry's powers were theoretically constrained as he was a subject of the French king, Louis VII. He therefore had to go through the motions of being a dutiful subject of Louis, though he would soon prove himself to be a stubbornly independent individual. The situation was something of a mirage, anyway: the territories held by Henry dwarfed those of the French royal demesne, the king's own lands, in terms of both size and wealth.

The bride was quite well acquainted with Louis too, having been his wife until just eight weeks before. She had been married to Louis for some fifteen years, having brought to the marriage Aquitaine, one of the jewels of France in the south-west, blessed by the sun and the grape. It was a wealthy and attractive region, if not always easy to control, and Eleanor, who inherited the duchy in 1137, had been a prize catch.

But the marriage to Louis had been little short of a disaster in almost every respect. The couple could not have been less compatible. Eleanor described her husband as a monk whereas she was vivacious, fun-loving and, according to gossips, an adulteress (with her own uncle no less, if those same wagging tongues were to be believed). Accusations of flightiness would follow her, and some contemporary gossips suggested she had once been the lover of her new husband's father.

While they were still man and wife, Louis and Eleanor had taken part in the Second Crusade, which journeyed to the Christian-held territories in Palestine with the aim of leading a fightback against a resurgent Muslim enemy. This was both a military catastrophe and a political fiasco. Louis's forces were decimated, along with those of his fellow crusader, the Holy Roman Emperor Conrad, while they were crossing Asia Minor. The surviving remnant of the army eventually made it to Jerusalem and launched an unsuccessful four-day attack on the city of Damascus, against the advice of most of the local barons of Outremer (the name given to the crusader territories in the Levant).

The reasons for this failure involved ineptitude of the highest order: although Damascus was a Muslim city, it was at the time one of the few non-Christian allies of Outremer in the region. Of course, that situation changed when it was attacked and the city was virtually forced into the arms of Outremer's Muslim opponents (widely referred to by Christian chroniclers of the time as 'Saracens').[2] The almost completely negative outcomes of the expedition were to set the tone for the response of Western Europe to crusade appeals for the next four decades, with disastrous results for the kingdom of Jerusalem in particular. It left many in Western Europe disillusioned and pessimistic about the likelihood of success of any future crusade, and interest in preparing one therefore dropped significantly.

The crusade was a personal disaster for Louis and Eleanor too. Before they set off, relations between the two were not good. During the crusade they disintegrated totally. It was said that Eleanor had become concerned about the close blood relationship between herself and her husband, which may have broken clerical law. This sowed the seeds that would ultimately lead to an annulment (what we would think of in modern terms as divorce did not exist; marriage was only dissolved if some technical bar to it could be proved, such as inappropriately close family relationships).[3] An uninformed interpretation of this situation might be that Eleanor was very much a God-fearing woman, anxious not to upset her Maker; a much more likely reason is that she saw this as a good excuse to escape from a failed, unfulfilling marriage.

After the couple had stayed for a time in Antioch, where Eleanor's alleged sexual dalliance with her uncle Raymond of Poitiers took place (though many historians think that this did not actually go beyond normal uncle/niece affection), Louis – previously almost childishly in love with his wife – became noticeably cooler towards her. When they subsequently spent time in Jerusalem together, Eleanor almost disappeared from view, as if under some form of house arrest. Unfortunately for her, this was a state of affairs that would become familiar to Eleanor.

Personal happiness was not really the prime requirement for married couples at the time, though of course it would be a welcome advantage. The main reason for marriage was to produce children, specifically sons, as well as to help secure and extend political power. It was just an extension of politicking and diplomacy. But after fifteen years of marriage, no sons had arrived to bless the union between Louis and Eleanor (though there were two daughters, Marie and Alix) and so an annulment was eventually sought. The Pope duly obliged, deciding that the couple were too closely related, though he also ruled that the daughters born from their union should be regarded as legitimate. It was a compromise solution, designed to please everyone.

Eleanor kept her substantial lands in Aquitaine after the marriage was annulled; Aquitaine was not at the time part of the royal French territories, and so Louis's claim to it died with the marriage. These lands, when added to those owned by Eleanor's new husband Henry of Anjou, covered a huge area. Through their union, a contiguous territory was formed which stretched from the English Channel in the north to the Pyrenees in the south.

Louis was greatly shocked when he heard of Eleanor's plans for her hastily arranged second marriage. The union threatened his position in France. The situation would not improve when, just two years later, the count of Anjou at last became King Henry II of England. This was another pivotal moment in European history, helping to shape a course of affairs between England and France that ended with what later became known as the Hundred Years War. The marriage, and its repercussions, also shaped the future life of Richard I. If Richard's legend was created by the crusades, then his life was moulded by the remarkable match entered into by his parents.

Eleanor's headlong rush into re-marriage upset a number of people. First and foremost, unsurprisingly, was Louis. Within weeks he was attacking Normandy in a very visible protest against the ambitions of Eleanor's new husband. Nor was Louis alone. There were disappointed suitors too, including Henry's own brother Geoffrey, who had even tried to kidnap Eleanor while *en route* to her wedding in Poitiers. Geoffrey sided with Louis in his retaliatory strike into Normandy, though this ultimately achieved very little. It would turn out that quarrelsome brothers were something of an Angevin trait.

The ceremony was a relatively low-key affair in contrast to Eleanor's first wedding in Bordeaux, where a thousand guests had been present. Given Eleanor's significance alone the match would conventionally have needed the approval of the king of France, but no such approval had been sought. It was not hard to see why; it was very unlikely that assent would have been forthcoming given the way that it would bolster the groom's already significant power.

Considering the immediacy with which the marriage was celebrated, it had probably secretly been in the planning stage for some time, very likely long before the annulment of Eleanor and Louis's marriage had been confirmed. Eleanor and Louis had paid a last visit to Aquitaine together just before the marriage formally ended. She had taken the opportunity to restore all the rights she had lost in Aquitaine when she married the French king. It is clear that Eleanor and Louis had both accepted that their conjugal alliance was about to come to an end some time before its final, formal denouement was reached.

Now Eleanor was married once more, and Henry no doubt wished to avail himself of all the power he could access in Aquitaine, a welcome addition to his own territories. There was something of an irony in Eleanor's second marriage. The annulment of the first had officially been granted because Eleanor and Louis were too closely related for the liking of the Church, but if anyone noticed that Henry was as closely related to her as Louis was then few seem to have bothered to mention it at the time.

Both bride and groom were remarkable people. Although their personalities did not always mesh well, they had enough in common to share a fascinating relationship. If anything, their intense ambition, their drive for greatness and their never-ending scheming suggested that they had rather too much in common to be able to live together in mutual harmony in the longer-term. And so it would prove; by the time the couple were divided by the death of Henry some thirty-five years later, they and their family had played out a drama akin to something in a modern soap opera.

A significant age difference (at thirty, Eleanor was eleven years Henry's senior) would suggest that this was a marriage of convenience rather than mutual attraction – though it would not have been something that necessarily seemed unusual to the groom, as his father was also eleven years younger than his mother. Henry was said to be ruddy and stocky, coming across as a robust, down-to-earth man in appearance, while the bride was described as being beautiful almost to a dangerous degree, seemingly a woman of great elegance and style, though more detailed descriptions beyond this general one have not come to light.[4] They made an impressive couple even if they were an unlikely match physically.

The union produced many heirs, providing plenty of circumstantial evidence that Henry and Eleanor shared a physical attraction, at least in the early years of their marriage. Their first child arrived just a year after the wedding and the last in 1166. The contemporary writer Gerald of Wales suggested that the couple were instantly attracted to each other when they had first met in Paris some time before, even though Eleanor was already married to Louis at the time. A child arrived on average once every two years during the first part of their married life. Eleanor's ability to survive the perils of medieval childbirth well into her forties would suggest that she was first and foremost a survivor.

Their first son, William, arrived in 1153, soon after their marriage. The arrival of a son seemed to be a very specific mark of divine approbation. The infant was soon made the count of Poitiers but he died of a seizure at Wallingford Castle in April 1156. However, a steady stream of sons followed. This contrasted vividly with the failure of Louis VII to produce a male heir in all those years of married life with Eleanor. These were tough times for Louis, when he was also deprived of some formidable advisers by their death; men such as the redoubtable Abbot Suger of St-Denis and the impressive Bernard of Clairvaux, two of the great personalities not just of the century but of the entire epoch in Western Europe. They died within a few years of each other at the start of the 1150s. Louis's star seemed to be waning while that of the Angevins rose ever higher.

The future King Richard I entered this world on 8 September 1157 in England at Beaumont Palace, close to the north gate of Oxford. Although virtually no trace remains of the palace now, it was a substantial building in its twelfth-century heyday. Its most outstanding feature was a great hall decorated with magnificent murals. There were two chapels and cloisters and a wide array of domestic buildings in which the queen and her entourage could find comfort. When the palace fell into disrepair, some of its stonework later found its way into Christ Church and St John's College, Oxford.

Beaumont had been built by a former king of England, Henry I, and it was here in 1133 that he had celebrated the birth of his grandson, the man who was to become Henry II, Richard's father. In hindsight, it was a somewhat inappropriate place for Richard to be born, this spot placed close to the heart of Middle England, for there was little to suggest that the country strongly commanded his affection in later life for anything but financial and political reasons. It was ideal for his father, though, being at the heart of well-stocked hunting lands which Henry often frequented. Henry also constructed a zoo there. By the standards of the time it was certainly exotic, including among its residents lions, leopards and camels. Richard would later house a crocodile there.[5]

Richard's birth strengthened the Angevin line of succession. Although he was not first in line, it was nevertheless important to have another son just in case, given the mortality rate of infants at the time (what in modern times is rather patronisingly referred to as a 'spare') as the early death of William, count of Poitiers, demonstrated. But some commentators marked the birth out for special mention. This was the era when the Arthurian literature industry was starting to gain momentum. Only a few decades previously Geoffrey of Monmouth had written his *History of the Kings of Britain*, which brought the mythical 'King' Arthur into public consciousness. It touched a nerve that generated enormous interest among those who heard the stories. Additions to the literary corpus based on the tales of 'King' Arthur soon proliferated.

One contemporary writer, Ralph of Diceto, was reminded of a prophecy from that mystical seer Merlin, Arthur's magus and close confidant. In a quote that would have done the cryptic Nostradamus proud, Merlin predicted that 'the eagle of the broken covenant shall rejoice in her third nesting'.[6] The 'broken covenant' could be attributed to the dissolved marriage between Eleanor and King Louis. The 'third nesting' was the third son Richard (though this ignored the fact that Richard had an older sister, Matilda, who presumably in those more misogynistic times did not count).

When Richard was born, there was a surviving elder brother, Henry, as well as the sister, Matilda. Further children would follow Richard: Geoffrey, Eleanor, Joanna and John. Most of these siblings were in one way or another to play a significant role in Richard's later life. From what we know, although there was a distance between noble and royal parents and their children in those days, Eleanor seems to have taken a greater interest in her offspring than most contemporaries. One historian has remarked, 'for no other noblewoman do we have similar evidence of such close contact with her children'. The same writer, though, also introduces a wise note of caution that surviving letters between mother and children 'should not be read as evidence of a close emotional relationship, but rather as evidence of her [Eleanor's] ongoing dynastic mission'.[7]

It was not the norm for an infant royal prince or princess to be raised by their mother, and a wet nurse was found for Richard. Her name was Hodierna and she had given birth to her own son, Alexander Neckam, on the very same day that Richard was born. She came from St Albans and in later life Alexander would enter the school of the abbey in that ancient city before studying at the University of Paris. He would go on to become abbot of Cirencester Abbey in 1213. He led a distinguished life and was an intelligent scientist who was the first in the West to work out that a magnet could be used as a compass.

The role of the wet nurse was an important one and it came with great responsibilities. Hodierna was in closer contact with Richard than anyone else during his formative years, including his parents. She shared her milk with the prince and her own child, though Richard latched on to her right breast as this was deemed to be where the richer milk flowed from. But the role of wet nurse could also be a dangerous one; in those days of high infant mortality, illness and death were never far away. In such cases, suspicion could fall on the wet nurse.[8]

Direct contact was lost with Hodierna in later childhood as Richard moved away from England, but it seems that he never forgot her. She would much later be awarded a pension of £27 per annum and was given land in West Knoyle, Wiltshire, in the parish that became known as Knoyle Hodierne. There were also grants of property at Rowden (between Chippenham and Bath) worth over £7 a year. From this we can assume that she was a dutiful woman who did her job well. Given her selection as wet nurse she was presumably already known to Richard's parents before his birth. She certainly seems to have held Richard's affection, and retained it in later life.

Richard's family antecedents on both sides were remarkable, in addition to his parents being extraordinary individuals in their own right. The Plantagenet dynasty that was now headed by Henry had a long history, though the title of Plantagenet was not formally adopted until the fifteenth century, when Richard, duke of York, leader of one of the parties in the mistitled Wars of the Roses, employed it. The name was supposedly taken from the common broom plant, *planta genesta*, a sprig of which was worn in the helmet of Geoffrey V, count of Anjou, Henry's father, to distinguish him in battle.

The Angevin dynasty, as it was alternatively titled, was named after the territory of France, Anjou, which was the family's heartland. Situated astride the Lower Loire, this was a fertile, productive land whose capital was at Angers. The counts of Anjou held an ancient and honoured title dating back to the late ninth century. Often playing a leading part in the affairs of the monarchs of France, the counts were important members of the nobility in what was a very fragmented country where the central power of the French king was often weak and regularly under threat from his powerful magnates.

For a while, the ruling Capetian[9] dynasty in France had to be content with holding the trappings of power rather than being able to wield it in a real sense. Their kings were placed at the apex of a formal feudal structure and played an important symbolic role, but they had to cope with powerful subjects who, while being nominally subservient to them, were difficult to control. However, this was changing by the mid-twelfth century, by which time Capetian monarchs were becoming more ambitious. The emergence of this new breed of rulers coincided with the greater prominence of the Angevins and led to a conflict of interests that would in the end have a seismic impact on Western Europe.

Perhaps one of the most influential counts of Anjou, certainly as far as the future Richard I was concerned, was Fulk, Geoffrey's father and Richard's great-grandfather. In another dynastic match that had a major impact on contemporary history, Fulk had married Queen Melisende of Outremer in 1129. Outremer – 'The Land Beyond the Sea' – was a series of small Christian kingdoms in the Levant established after the conquest of Jerusalem by Western European crusader armies in 1099.

Three separate states were subsequently established, based on Jerusalem, Tripoli (in modern Lebanon) and Antioch (in modern Turkey, close to the border with Syria). After that initial triumph, which was to many such an unbelievable victory against seemingly overwhelming odds that it could only have been a gift from God Himself, the newly established states quickly came under threat. Muslim powers in the region had been shocked by the fall of Al-Quds (Jerusalem) and a fightback against the crusader territories soon began.

Fulk had gone to Outremer on crusade in around 1119. A crusade was not necessarily a highly organised mass movement of tens of thousands of warriors; it was literally an armed pilgrimage and as such a very personal act, even though the pilgrims could and often did organise themselves into large groups, which was pragmatic in the circumstances. Many of the pilgrims were not warriors but civilians, young and old. The purpose of the pilgrimage was to complete the journey to Jerusalem, the holiest city in the Christian world (though it was also, as it still is in the twenty-first century, very sacred to Judaism and Islam). In theory, conquering Islam came second to completing the pilgrimage, though this was not how everyone saw it in practice.

Having completed this journey (though many would perish on the way through disease, malnutrition, shipwreck or violence) the pilgrim would be rewarded with an indulgence, a recognition by the Church that they had attained a sacred objective for which they would receive spiritual compensation in the hereafter and would therefore enter Heaven more easily; death en route was made more palatable by the awarding of this indulgence in such circumstances too. In a religious age, this was a significant incentive.

Many crusaders came to Outremer, visited the holy places of Jerusalem such as the Church of the Holy Sepulchre (the spot where Christ had died and been buried) and then returned home. In order to protect them during the last stages of their pilgrimage, military orders were set up to provide security for parties of pilgrims journeying to the Holy City. The most famous of them were the Knights Templar, although the Knights of the Hospital of St John of Jerusalem, the Hospitallers, were also to become important.

The development of these groups of what could be thought of as warrior-monks (for they were governed by strict religious regimes with rules that closely mirrored those of monasteries and other religious institutions) led over time to the formation of many other orders, less well known than the Templars and Hospitallers but still collectively forming a key part of the defence of Outremer.

On arrival in Outremer at the conclusion of his pilgrimage, Fulk joined the Templars, then a new body who were a long way from the heights of power that they would eventually reach (and ultimately fall from in spectacular fashion). Fulk quickly saw great personal opportunities in the new territories and over the next few years he took a close interest in the affairs of Outremer.

The second half of the 1120s saw the Angevin dynasty rise remarkably to its apex. Fulk had a son, Geoffrey, from his first marriage, and a match was arranged between him and Matilda, the daughter of Henry I of England, who lacked legitimate sons; Matilda was therefore heir to the throne of that kingdom. Matilda had been married to the Holy Roman Emperor Henry V; even when widowed and remarried she was still known as 'the Empress'. She was considered by some chroniclers (possibly misogynist critics who expected women to be quiet and submissive) to be haughty, proud and excessively aware of her status – all characteristics some would identify in her grandson, Richard. She was nevertheless an impressive and intimidating figure. It was from this match with Matilda that the Angevin claim to the English throne emanated, a claim which eventually led to Henry II being crowned.

It was an accident of fate – or in those days more pertinently the Hand of God – which laid the ground for these events. Henry I and his wife had a son, William, as a result of their union. But when William set out for England, coming back from France, on board a vessel known as *The White Ship* on 25 November 1120, their world was turned on its head. The weather was good for the time of year and a relatively straightforward crossing of the English Channel was anticipated.

But the ship was late setting out, there were stories of a party and it was alleged that the crew were drunk. Their vessel was driven straight on to rocks at the entrance to the harbour at Barfleur and quickly sank. There were only a few survivors and William was not among them. It was such a catastrophe that one modern commentator remarked of it that the loss of *The White Ship* created as much consternation in the twelfth century as the *Titanic* disaster did in the twentieth.[10] It turned the line of succession in England upside down.

The Angevins were the main long-term beneficiaries of this cruel twist of fate; after several decades of bitter warfare in England as the late king's daughter Matilda sought vainly to be crowned as queen in her own right, her son would become Henry II. Meanwhile, Fulk's own fortunes were rising to previously undreamed-of heights in Outremer. At the time, the kingdom was ruled by Baldwin II, who had no male heir and therefore named his daughter Melisende as his successor. But in the context of the times a husband was needed to strengthen and secure her position. Fulk was available; he knew Outremer well, and he was an experienced military commander with important status in the kingdom of France, the key guarantor of the Christian kingdoms in the East. He was an ideal candidate.

But Fulk exhibited that same ambitious streak that marked out his successors; he was not prepared to be merely the consort of a future queen. He held out for an arrangement that would make him co-ruler with his wife when she inherited the crown. And so it was arranged. The approval of the king of France was required for this arrangement, which was duly given by Louis VI, probably glad to ensure that a powerful vassal was more or less permanently resident in a region 2,000 miles away.

The marriage was duly celebrated in 1129, and just two years later Melisende became queen on the death of her father. Fulk therefore became joint-sovereign. He had already appointed his son Geoffrey as the new count of Anjou now that he would be spending little time in France. To be a count was a great thing but it paled into insignificance when compared to being a king.

Crusading interests were often linked to a family history of involvement in the movement. Given Fulk's activities in the East, it was always likely that future generations of the family would maintain family interest in the region, and so it proved for the Angevins. Henry II would often express concern for Outremer, though this was motivated more by political considerations than any real intention to visit. For Richard, the crusading movement would be his defining aspect, arguably of his life and certainly of his legend.

Strange supernatural tales had developed to explain the rise of the Angevin family. According to these, an early ancestor had married a woman by the name of Melusine, a mysterious but stunningly beautiful lady. Their marriage was happy and produced four children. However, gossips were jealous of the lady and looked for a flaw in her. They found one soon enough. Although Melusine regularly attended church, she invariably made her excuses before the Host was elevated at the start of the Mass and left early.

This was pointed out to the count and he had to agree that this was both true and strange. As a result, orders were issued to stop Melusine from exiting the church during the next service that she attended. When Melusine duly got up to leave she was forcibly prevented from doing so. At this, she took on an unearthly form and floated out through a window, never to be seen again. In the process, she took two of her children with her.[11] The mysterious Melusine was obviously of demonic ancestry.

This is an interesting story, though it should not be taken seriously. It is a nice mix of Greco-Romano classicism and Brothers Grimm fairy tale. One can imagine it being told on a winter's night in the shadowy, fire-lit great hall of a medieval castle. Presumably it provoked a smirk or a smile, particularly after a few draughts of wine or ale. It is a story that one or two of the Angevins themselves seem to have enjoyed very much. And indeed it was rumoured that they spoke jokingly of their origins; when someone later criticised them for their family infighting, they responded that because of their demon forefathers they could not help acting like devils.[12] For some, this extraordinary tale, folkloric as it might be, explained the volcanic fits of temper for which the Plantagenets became famous.

Although each of the men who became Angevin kings of England – Henry II, Richard I and John – showed differences in character, there were similarities between them too. One thing that all three

Angevin kings had in common was a volatile temper. It would mark the reigns of all of them in one way or another. For Henry, it would be through one of the most notorious acts of medieval history in the killing in his own cathedral of Thomas Becket, archbishop of Canterbury. John would become renowned for his violent moods, while Richard would show an uncanny ability to explode, to the extent that he completely lost control of his actions. No wonder St Bernard of Clairvaux, the greatest churchman of the twelfth century, would remark that 'from the Devil they came and to the Devil they will return'.[13]

The famous, not to say notorious, story of how Henry II fell out with his former friend Becket is one of the best-known tales of the Middle Ages. But in it we have some interesting clues to the character of the king and traits that were later to show themselves in the actions of his son and ultimate heir, Richard. The rift with Becket revolved around the authority of the king versus that of the clergy. Put simply, Henry wanted more power for the monarchy and Becket, once he was made archbishop of Canterbury, stubbornly resisted his efforts to gain it. One sees many faults on both sides and there was certainly some justice in the king's cause, which was centred on protecting royal rights that had been established by precedent. This involved discussion of problematic areas, such as whether the clergy should be subject to secular law and punishment for violent crimes that they committed.

Yet even Henry's largely sympathetic biographer W. L. Warren feels that he was heavy-handed in his actions and as a result unnecessarily alienated potentially friendly supporters. He was stubborn in terms of protecting the dignity and rights of the Crown even though as a human being he was seemingly not obsessive about the trappings of state. By his overzealous approach, potential allies were lost. This suggested a character flaw that would later be identified in Richard I on more than one occasion.

So much for the Angevins, but what of Eleanor and her antecedents? She was the daughter of William, the 10th duke of Aquitaine, who had died suddenly in 1137. The timing of his death was in some ways fortuitous for Eleanor as it was in the same year that she had married Louis, and she was therefore in a good position to find protection. It was very difficult indeed for a female heiress in such circumstances to fight off pushy suitors unless she was already married, especially when the lands in which she held an interest were so rich.

The dukes of Aquitaine included amongst their vassals the counts of Angoulême, La Marche and Périgord. By the acquisition of the vine-rich territories of Gascony and its great port of Bordeaux the position of the dukes had been strengthened in the recent past. As one contemporary English historian described it, Aquitaine's 'fields are fertile, its vineyards productive and its forests teem with wild life'.[14]

It was also on the major pilgrim route to Santiago de Compostella, in the north of Spain, so it was well known to many travellers of the time. The region though was volatile. The borders to the north abutted onto other powerful territories and the richness of Aquitaine tempted her neighbours from that direction. In the south the very different, self-contained Basque and Navarrese lands abutted Aquitaine, with their proud and independent people and their unique languages.

The people of the south of France were very different in temperament than those from the lands in the north. The south was full of life and colour whilst the people of the north were seen to be altogether drab and dreary in comparison. The south had its own language – the Langue d'Oc, after which a modern province in France is known, though it has morphed in modern times into Occitan. It also had very different cultural norms than the north, altogether more free-spirited and less restrained, so much so that it would later attract the enmity of the northerners which led in the early fourteenth century to the horrendous blood-letting that became known as the Cathar Crusades.

Yet there was paradox at the heart of Aquitaine. Whilst it was rich, it was not enjoying the thrusting economic development being witnessed in the north of France. And whilst Aquitaine had status, she did not necessarily have power. Her foundations were shaky. There were constant tensions with her neighbours, particularly the independently minded counts of Toulouse. The regional power enjoyed by the counts of Poitou, that is the Angevins, who came to rule the duchy of Aquitaine, has been compared to that presented by a rather shaky house of cards.[15] The power of the dukes of Aquitaine was always insecurely based.

An interesting point has been made by modern historians that, whereas some parts of the Angevin 'federation' had preserved historical attributes that made the power of the dynasty more secure, in Aquitaine this was not so. In England, the Angevins had inherited a strong monarchy that had retained its structural strength through the Norman Conquest; indeed, the Norman kings effectively took over the existing monarchical apparatus for themselves. In Normandy too, the power of the dukes remained strong. In Anjou, there were survivals in ducal powers that could be traced back to the Carolingian period over three centuries before. But Aquitaine was, in contrast, feudal, where the power of local barons had led to a great deal of what we would now call decentralisation, making it much more difficult for the dukes there to govern with absolute authority.[16]

At the heart of the paradox was the fact that although the soils of Aquitaine were perfect for cultivation of the vine they were less so for the humbler oats, barley and pulses that were driving demographic growth in the rainier north. Even a people as justly proud of their viniculture as the French cannot live on wine alone. The north grew incrementally as an economic power. Those from the south considered their northern neighbours to be uncouth, even barbarous, in comparison to the people of the Langue d'Oc. Differing perceptions had the south and north heading towards each other on a collision course. The two cultures would eventually crash into each other with horrific results.

Independently minded rulers of the major regions of France in the north such as Normandy, Anjou and Blois saw their power grow even as the Capetian monarchs sought to build their own centralised powerbase. Anjou in particular grew strong, with its position adjacent to the Loire and its main city at Angers, then, as now, a grey and imposing rather than beautiful city. The city spoke of austerity and control, and as such it represented something of the mindset of its counts, who wished to increase their power on the national and international stage. That said, the border regions with Normandy, facing both ways to England and France, and with the French Capetian monarchy, were always a potential flashpoint.

Henry II was, not untypically for those times, something of an absentee father to his children. His continental possessions took up a good deal of his time and energies; glimpses of him would have been a rare event for his family. When he returned to England in January 1163, he had been gone for four and a half years.[17] From early on, Richard was destined to be much closer to his mother than his father, with whom his later-life relationships would be, to say the least, complicated.

Although we do not know very much about Richard's early life, we do get an occasional glimpse. At the age of two his betrothal was discussed. His planned future bride was a daughter of Raymond-Berenguer IV, count of Barcelona. He was married to the queen of Aragon. The count was a rich man and his lands were positioned ideally to protect the southern borders of Aquitaine. Aquitaine was planned to be Henry's wedding gift to his son and future daughter-in-law. This proposed arrangement would never come to fruition but it is an interesting insight into the marital politics of the time.

Raymond-Berenguer would have been a useful ally in the ongoing tension between the counts of Toulouse and the dukes of Aquitaine. The latter had acquired a claim through marriage to Toulouse but the former resisted it. Sitting more or less on the sidelines was the king of France, who would move from one side of the argument to the other depending on what suited his interests at any given point of time. Toulouse could be a vital asset to the dukes of Aquitaine, helping to secure as it did the road (and the river routes) from the Mediterranean to the Atlantic. As such it was of prime strategic importance, hence Henry II's burning desire to add it to Aquitaine, even though this was nominally his wife's duchy rather than his own (Henry was never a man to pass up on an opportunity).

These references to Richard's early life tend to be mundane and short of colour but they do allow us to engage in some informed speculation. In May 1161, for example, Henry II was in Normandy. Here he was visited by Eleanor, accompanied by two of their children, Richard and Matilda;[18] clearly there were family reunions taking place where the family would meet up from time to time.

Henry II's family life would later become extremely complex. He eventually had four growing and competitive sons, Henry, Richard, Geoffrey and John, to take care of, each of them as they matured showing themselves to be ambitious and eager to get one step ahead of their siblings. The situation in France was particularly complicated as Henry's lands there were held as a vassal of the French king. Plenty of evidence would emerge to suggest that Louis VII felt that the Angevin monarch had rather too much power and he did not hesitate to try to take Henry down a peg or two if the opportunity presented itself.

The writer Gerald of Wales was resident in Paris in 1165. One night he was woken from his slumbers by a great commotion:

> ... through all the great city there was such a noise and clanging of bells, such a multitude of tapers kindled through all the open spaces of the town, that not knowing what such a racket and

> abnormal disturbance could mean, with such a blaze of light in the night, it was thought the city was threatened by a great fire.[19]

Calling out into the streets to enquire as to the cause of the great hubbub, he was told by two passing old ladies that the queen had brought forth a son. Revealing the gender bias of the times, one writer wrote that although the king had already sired daughters, he had now fathered a child of a 'more noble sex'.[20]

The monkish Louis had probably surprised everyone, perhaps even himself, by this great success. The contemporary French chronicler Rigord later gave the boy the moniker 'Augustus'. This was a clever play on words; it gave him the mark of Roman Imperial Majesty, merited in retrospect by the achievements of Philip's later life and the way in which the power of the French Capetian monarchy developed as a result of his achievements, but also referred to the month of his birth.

Philip was given another moniker, *Dieudonné*, 'God-given'. The desperate urge to produce a male heir is perhaps best remembered from the later example of Henry VIII of England, but in the medieval period the need to produce a son was considered crucial. The Salic law, which dated back to Merovingian times 700 years before, was later interpreted as debarring female succession to the French throne. This was an interpretation which was not without its controversy and led in part to the outbreak of the Hundred Years' War in the fourteenth century.

The example of Henry II's mother, the Empress Matilda,[21] showed how difficult it was for a woman to become a monarch. Following the death of his only legitimate son in the *White Ship* disaster, Henry I had made his barons swear allegiance to Matilda as his heir. But when he died, a number of them threw in their lot with her cousin, Stephen of Blois, something of an ironic comment on gender views of the time as Matilda exhibited far greater strengths than he did.

Chaos in England had been the outcome, resulting in a period known later as The Anarchy. This is evidenced by the fact that when Henry II was eventually crowned, one of his early acts had been to order the destruction of no fewer than 1,100 unlicensed castles, a truly stunning number.[22] These were unhappy and recent precedents, so the arrival of a male heir to Louis must have indeed seemed like a gift from God both to the king and to his people.

In his teens Philip would develop a serious sickness; this might have suggested at the time that if he lived to eventually become king he would prove himself weak and an easy touch. As it happened, nothing could be further from the truth. In early adulthood he would show himself to be a determined, stubborn and skilful opponent of Richard. After Richard's death, as Philip II, king of France, he would become the nemesis of the Angevin dynasty.

The year 1166 was important for the Angevins. They were deprived of their great matriarchal figurehead, the Empress Matilda, who died on 10 September. She was buried in Bec Abbey, though her remains were moved centuries later to Rouen Cathedral. Her epitaph stated 'Here lies Henry's daughter, wife and mother: great by birth, greater by marriage but greatest by motherhood'. This was a hugely significant moment for Henry II. Matilda had been the senior female figure in his political as well as his personal life. It left a void that his wife Eleanor was quick to fill.

As a happier counterbalance to this sad family news, another Matilda, Richard's older sister, was shipped off to marry her German prince, Henry the Lion. Although the marriage appeared happy enough from a personal perspective and she was a loyal lieutenant to him when he was absent for several years on crusade, there would be political problems about fifteen years later when they were forced into exile at Henry II's court in Normandy, where she would move back into Richard's orbit. Once again, an enormous age difference between bride and groom did not seem to matter too much; he was approaching forty, she was just twelve years of age.

These developments were all part of conventional family life; births, deaths and marriages; nothing out of the ordinary, albeit that this was a royal family. It was a strong family unit; a powerful father, a larger-than-life mother, a brood of lively, healthy children, and a series of politically useful marriages which helped to strengthen the dynasty. There was little to suggest that a family crisis was looming.

But there are moments in the lives of both individuals and families that with the benefit of hindsight appear to be seminal in terms of their impact. For the Angevins, such a moment arrived in 1168, a year in which decisions that would have massive repercussions – for Henry II, for Eleanor of Aquitaine, for Richard and for the family as a whole – were taken. Nothing would ever be quite the same for the Angevins.

2

The Winter of Discontent (1168–1176)

'Everywhere there was plotting, plundering and burning'
Contemporary chronicler Ralph of Diceto

The events that led to the disintegration of Henry II's family started in Aquitaine. The Aquitanians were stubbornly wedded to their independence. They did not like being told what to do by anyone and this, naturally enough, made them difficult to rule. Henry was largely an absentee lord, neither was he connected to Aquitaine by birth; both factors that weakened his hold over it.

Aquitaine was the country of those medieval songsmiths the troubadours, and Richard included amongst his own ancestors one such, his maternal great-grandfather Duke William IX of Aquitaine, a well-known crusader and troubadour. Some of William's poetry was designed to shock, being sensual, erotic and occasionally downright crude. His crusading exploits were ultimately disastrous, as his army was cut to shreds whilst crossing Asia Minor in 1101.

Henry was faced with several uprisings in Aquitaine, not major conflagrations but frequent sparks of dissent. They took time, money and effort to put down and were a distraction for Henry. The king at one stage thought about giving Aquitaine to his eldest son, also Henry, even though he had already been earmarked for England, Normandy and Anjou. The king now had a change of heart.

His new plan involved the return of Eleanor to Aquitaine. She would be accompanied by Richard, now around eight years old. Henry reasoned that if the Aquitanians felt that they had one of their own directly governing the duchy they would dampen down their rebellious tendencies. Although it was in practice to prove a difficult aspiration to deliver, it was an idea that certainly had merits.

In the event, the plan almost foundered before it began. On her way south, Eleanor was ambushed by a party led by Guy and Geoffrey of Lusignan. The Lusignans were relatively minor landholders at the time but their ambitions were virtually unlimited; they would play a significant part in the future history of the Angevins. Eleanor escaped, thanks in part to the bravery of a young knight who was in her escort. His name was William Marshal and despite initially limited prospects he would eventually rise to the loftiest heights in England outside of the royal family.

It was a violent assault in which Patrick, earl of Salisbury, Marshal's uncle, was killed. The ambush was a complete surprise and Eleanor's retinue seem to have been caught without their armour.[1] William Marshal was enraged and struck out violently, 'like a wild boar amongst the dogs' as one account vividly put it, but he was captured after being wounded with a lance that pierced his thigh and came out of the other side.[2] He had, however, earned Eleanor's gratitude and was later ransomed, though he was not well treated by his captors, who did little to attend to his wounds; the attack was not some chivalric escapade but a hot-headed outburst of violence.

Eleanor later took Marshal into her household, a sign of high preferment; the rest, as they say, is history. Marshal would move close to the heart of the Angevin dynasty, a position in which he remained for the next half a century. He would in a few years be given the responsibility for the military training of Henry and Eleanor's eldest son, Prince Henry, a meteoric rise in the context of the time. Marshal formed a deep affection for the latter, who he saw as the saviour of chivalry, which in his view was dying out: 'he revived chivalry which was then nearly dead' as one contemporary writer put it.[3]

The party survived the ambush and Eleanor and Richard took up residence in Poitiers. While Richard was later to be king of England, it was in the centre and south of France that his heart lay. This was a region of light and shade, of warm summers and mild winters. Here the wines were famous, and Aquitaine was also highly regarded – less well known now – for her salt.

Viniculture was a speciality of the region; Aquitanian wines contrasted markedly with those which were produced in England, of which one contemporary wrote that they were so bad that 'they could only be drunk with your eyes closed and teeth clenched'.[4]

Poitiers was a city with a long, illustrious history dating back to Roman times. It would be Eleanor and Richard's main base in Aquitaine. From the time of Eleanor's arrival in France, and quite probably before, a gap existed between her and Henry which progressively widened into a chasm. She looked fondly on her son, Richard, and he returned the sentiment. Given this, it was almost inevitable that he would side with Eleanor and she with him if an open breach with the king materialised.

It is quite possible that relations between Henry and Eleanor had been cooling for some time and this would naturally impact on Richard. The age gap between his parents was becoming significant. Eleanor was moving towards the end of her childbearing years and no more children would arrive after this date. Henry, on the other hand, was still close to the prime of life. He was renowned for his roistering ways and his strong libido. On its own this was probably something that Eleanor could live with: but from this point on they met less and less frequently and the gap between the two, and between Henry and the young, impressionable Richard, began to widen.

Henry sought to develop closer ties with King Louis, not for altruistic reasons but to help to cement his own position and that of his sons. Richard would prove a useful pawn in this game of international power politics. Now that the betrothal to Raymond-Berenguer's daughter had come to nothing, he was available for other politically beneficial marriage arrangements.

Negotiations to secure stronger ties between Louis and Henry had been going on for a while when in March 1168 they reached a critical stage. Discussions, which had so far been done through emissaries, now required Henry's personal presence. Under the terms of the agreement on the table, Richard would be declared duke-designate of Aquitaine and would marry Alice, Louis's daughter. Discussions were concluded by the Treaty of Montmirail in January 1169. It seemed a positive and significant step forward. In reality, a long-running soap opera had only just begun.

Alice was a product of Louis's marriage to Constance of Castile. In giving Alice life in 1160, Constance lost her own for she died in childbirth. Just five weeks later Louis married again, taking as his wife Adela of Champagne. The undue haste of the king's remarriage suggests a burning desire to produce a male heir, which was eventually sated a few years later when the future Philip II was born. At the time of Alice's betrothal to Richard she was passed over into the care of Henry. She was only eight years old but as time went on she would find herself at the epicentre of a royal scandal. It would be a long time before she left the orbit of Henry and his son Richard; arrangements would certainly not work out as planned.

Eleanor took over day-to-day control of Aquitaine, though she regularly travelled further north to Chinon and beyond to Normandy. Richard seemingly was regularly with her on these journeys.[5] In the process, he would see first-hand how politics worked and what it meant to rule, a valuable education. Eleanor and Henry superficially remained on good terms, formally polite and staying in touch with what was happening in each other's sphere of influence. But it was becoming more of a working relationship than a marriage.

Richard's betrothal was all part of Henry's plan to secure the succession. While Richard, the second surviving son, formally got Aquitaine as part of the arrangement, the eldest, Prince Henry, was to be responsible for those lands which Henry had brought to the marriage to Eleanor, namely Maine, Anjou, Normandy and England. Nor was it just Henry's male children who were to be married off. Negotiations also began for the marriage of his daughter, Joanna, to King William II of Sicily.

Henry's third surviving son, Geoffrey, was to have Brittany, which Henry had effectively added to his span of control by the deposition of Duke Conan in 1166. Conan's daughter and heiress was subsequently married to Geoffrey, who was to do homage to Louis for Brittany. Richard was to do the same for Aquitaine, where he would be designated duke. The marriage alliance between Richard and Alice would theoretically bring Louis and Henry's families closer together. They were already nominally close because Prince Henry was married to another daughter of Louis, Margaret. It suggested a plan to reconcile Henry and Louis, who had often been at loggerheads with each other in recent years. But whilst it looked good on parchment, ongoing practical barriers would reveal themselves before long.

The only problem with these seemingly generous settlements to his sons was that Henry intended that any transfer of power would be in name only. He would be the puppeteer pulling the strings whatever his sons thought. It was a situation that they would over time become unhappy with, resulting in a bitter family dispute that would threaten to shatter the dynasty into fragments. Henry had dangled a carrot or two in front of his brood: it would prove very difficult indeed to withdraw it again. All he had done was raise expectations that were not subsequently met.

In May 1170, Richard was formally installed as count of Poitou. The ceremony took place in the abbey of St Hilaire in Poitiers; a beautiful Romanesque building that came through the ravages of the French Revolution though not without the need for more recent restoration. Here Richard was presented with the holy lance and the standard of the man who was the patron saint of the city, Hilaire, its first bishop in the fourth century AD. The installation was followed by the normal round of celebratory feasts and tournaments. However, it would be several years before Richard would be formally installed as the duke of Aquitaine.

Prince Henry, his elder brother, was an incredibly handsome man, according to the contemporary writer Walter Map, just one step down from the angels. He was crowned as king of England in full pomp by the archbishop of York at Westminster in 1170, after which he became known as the Young King. The archbishop of Canterbury, Thomas Becket, was angry that it was not he who was presiding, as by tradition it fell to him to do so. Becket was in exile and had been forcibly detained on Henry's orders in Dieppe to prevent him from returning to make a scene. Becket and Henry had fallen out badly years before. The argument had festered and soured into a bitter feud that was beyond resolution.

The denouement of their vicious quarrel was approaching. The royal family, minus the Young King, spent Christmas at Bures, near Bayeux in Normandy; Richard was certainly present and the events that were about to unfold must have made a great impact on him. Peace had at last been brokered between Henry and Becket, and the latter had now returned to England. But as soon as he was back, Becket began acting in a high-handed manner, as was his wont. On Christmas Day, in a service at Canterbury Cathedral, he excommunicated all those bishops who had crowned the Young King. But three of these bishops, those of London, York and Salisbury, knew this was coming. They had already travelled to Normandy to tell Henry of Becket's plans.

This was to be a Christmas that would live long in the memory. Henry often organised family feasts at this season of the year (Whitsun and Easter were also popular times for such reunions), a time for fun and frivolity when he could be entertained by his favourite jester, Ralph the Farter, famed for being able to jump in the air, whistle and break wind at the same time.[6]

This Christmas would be one with a difference; there would be little festive cheer in evidence. Henry, famous for his extreme Angevin temper, erupted when he heard of Becket's continuing insolence. He berated those subjects who would not solve the Becket problem for him with direct action. 'Will no one rid me of this turbulent priest?' he is said to have uttered, though no contemporary chroniclers record these words. Four of his knights, hearing this, made their way surreptitiously from the court and back to England.

On 29 December 1170, the obstinate cleric was battered to death next to his altar in Canterbury Cathedral. This dramatic event had a catastrophic impact on Henry II and his reputation. In a classic display of Angevin anger, Henry had put a stain on his record that would never be expunged. It painted a vivid picture; the defiant archbishop before the altar like a sacrificial lamb; the martyr who refused to run from his would-be murderers within the confines of his cathedral; the murderers who scooped out his brains and spread them across the blood-soaked floor. Within decades the flawed Becket was made a saint of the Catholic Church. It was a public relations triumph for the Church and a disaster for the king.

Soon after Becket's death, Louis was writing of it in withering terms to the Pope: he talked of revolts against humanity and laid out what should be done in return in blistering fashion; 'such unprecedented cruelty demands unprecedented retribution. Let the sword of St Peter be unleashed to avenge the martyr of Canterbury.'[7] Some suggested that this was the worst event that had occurred in the world since the Crucifixion of Christ. Those responsible, suggested the archbishop of Sens, were even more evil than Herod or Judas. Such hard-hitting words hardly augured well for the prospects of improved relationships between Henry and the French royal family. They deteriorated still further in subsequent years and Henry's sons would be at the centre of the problem.

On 11 June 1172, Richard was at last formally installed as duke of Aquitaine. Dressed in silk and wearing a golden coronet, he was given the ring of St Valerie to wear (St Valerie was the first

Christian martyr of Aquitaine, beheaded in Roman times for her faith; it was said that after the execution she carried her severed head to the bishop who had baptised her). Richard's installation ceremony was symbolic of divine approval for the newly created duke of Aquitaine, who now became the leading man in a territory that would thereafter play a key role in his life.

If Christmas 1170 had been traumatic, that of 1172 was also significant for the Angevins. The family, including both Henry II and Eleanor, held court at Chinon, a favourite residence for Henry and a place that was to witness many significant and sometimes traumatic events that touched on the fate of the Angevin dynasty. It was in a wonderful spot, perched on steep cliffs above the river and the bustling town below. On the surface, as the family reunion began, all was sweetness and light. With their equally impressive patriarch and matriarch at the helm, the Angevin brothers met up. In hindsight, this occasion would appear to be one touched with nostalgia, a golden moment never to be repeated. Dark clouds were appearing; a storm was brewing that would break this cosy family set-up apart.

In February 1173, Richard was in Limoges with his parents and his eldest brother. Festivities were held there in honour of the kings of Navarre and Aragon as well as the count of Toulouse. Raymond of Toulouse had just pledged allegiance to the Angevins; this saved him from doing so to the king of France and demonstrated that relationships between those two men were not in the best of health. Given the traditional opposition of the counts of Toulouse to the dukes of Aquitaine, it was a very positive development for Henry II.

It built on other steps taken by Henry to strengthen his southernmost frontiers. In 1170, his daughter Eleanor was married to Alfonso VIII of Castile. She was given Gascony as her dower, to be handed over when her mother, whose lands these currently were, died.[8] Henry would be involved as an arbitrator in the affairs of the small 'Spanish' kingdoms to the south of the Pyrenees on several occasions and was actively involved in the politics of the region. Richard, too, would later be embroiled in them.

Richard, not yet sixteen years of age, visited King Louis of France in the spring of 1173. Louis made Richard a knight whilst he was in Paris, an important rite of passage for a young man for whom the concepts of chivalry and military glory would become important. The fact that the French king was knighting Richard also asserted a kind of hierarchical superiority over him. Louis may have sensed the ambition that coursed through young Richard's veins and went out of his way to encourage it. Anything that could discomfort Henry II was to be welcomed.

Now a young man, Richard was turning into a striking figure with a strong personality. Gerald of Wales described him as 'a hammer', speaking of his lusty violence and his tendency to often take the most decisive of actions when faced with a problem; this was rather like Alexander the Great solving the problem of the Gordian Knot by slicing it apart rather than bother to take the time to work out how to untie it. Physically Richard would strike an impressive figure, well over six feet tall and 'of elegant build'. He had long arms and hair that was somewhere between red and gold in tint, as described in a near-contemporary work called the *Itinerarium Peregrinorum*.[9] He also had his father's sapphire-blue eyes that seemed to see right into the soul of a man.

Richard's personality was complex. The troubadour Bertran de Born, at times a critic, at others an admirer, called him 'Richard Oc e No' ('yes and no'), possibly in reference to his laconic style of speaking and his desire not to use five words when one would do. This was the nickname by which he was frequently referred to during his life; 'Lionheart' did not appear until later on. On the other hand, 'yes and no' might refer to duplicity and untrustworthiness on Richard's part. Either interpretation is possible.

In 1173, Count Raymond V of Toulouse did homage for his county, first to Henry II, then to his eldest son Henry, the Young King, and last of all to Richard. The count had inherited his position at the age of fourteen and would retain it for nearly half a century. His county was vital in the context of France at the time. Its people had a well-defined sense of their independence and within its borders there were strong heretical tendencies evident in the form of the Cathars.

The Cathar movement – 'the pure ones' as its acolytes were called – had its origins in the East. In the Cathar view of religion there were two Gods – one good, one evil – the first of whom was associated with the New Testament of the Christian Bible and the latter with the Old. It was a controversial movement, very much at odds with the Catholic Church, and it would not be long before it attracted that body's violent enmity.

Toulouse was often on difficult terms with its near-neighbour Aquitaine and especially the latter's dukes. The demonstration of subservience to the man who was the duke of Aquitaine as well as the current king of England was therefore very welcome to Henry II. But it came against the backdrop of a very serious situation for him, for his family was by now in danger of fragmenting.

Ambition was at the heart of the problem, particularly that of the eldest son, Henry. He was now officially designated as king of England, but it was a title without real meaning. That Henry II still pulled the strings was made perfectly clear when he decided to give the castles of Chinon, Loudun and Mirebeau to his youngest (and currently landless) son John, 'Lackland'. The fact that they were in territory already theoretically held by his eldest son did not seem to matter much.

The Young King's response was predictably prickly. He refused to agree to the transfer without at least some real power being given to him in return. His father refused to budge; he had no intention of handing over real power to anyone. His disappointed son dutifully accompanied the king as he made his way north towards Chinon on the Vienne River. But beneath this submissive exterior he was seething. The moment his father's back was turned, young Henry fled. He made his way straight to Paris and the court of his father-in-law, King Louis.

It was not unheard of for ambitious royal sons to quarrel with their father. But this was not the only problem, for young Henry was not unaccompanied for long, as, soon after, he was joined by two of his brothers, Richard and Geoffrey. Only the youngest, John, far too young a child to play a part in these shenanigans, was not with them.

Matters quickly got out of hand. The chronicler Ralph of Diceto wrote that 'everywhere there was plotting, plundering and burning. And to take an omen from the seasons, the son took up arms against his father at just the time when everywhere Christians were laying down their arms in reverence for Easter.' He added, with grim admonition, that 'dissensions of this sort cannot end happily'.[10] How right he was.

Richard, like his elder brother, also felt that he did not enjoy genuine power. In Aquitaine, this was still exercised by his mother and father. He was really serving an apprenticeship in the role and like many young men of his age, felt the urge to wield greater responsibility and power. Henry II had occasionally tried to take complete control of Aquitaine for himself but this tactic had not met with much success as Eleanor tenaciously hung on to her rights.

This no doubt irked Henry; he was a man who was very fond of getting his own way and quick to anger when he did not succeed.

Henry had received a warning of trouble brewing not long before. It came from Raymond of Toulouse, his new-found ally, who advised him to beware of his wife and sons. Probably the count was quite happy to give the warning and cause Henry discomfort: his true allegiances in the affairs of this period are far from clear and he may have been playing a double game, encouraging Eleanor and her children to rebel whilst at the same time feeding information to the betrayed king.

The actions of his sons no doubt shocked Henry to the core. But the greatest shock of all came when it became clear who was the conspiratorial brain behind it all: no less a person than his wife, Eleanor. The plotting of a wife against her husband was considered the greatest form of betrayal; chroniclers of the time found plenty of precedents for sons betraying fathers, but not wives their husbands. In those times it was a wife's duty to obey her husband. Failure to do so was a crucial departure down the road to ruin as the contemporary tales of King Arthur and his wife Guinevere proved, for through her adultery the Round Table was destroyed.

The question to be asked is, why did Eleanor do this? Various suggestions have been made; for example, Eleanor's fury at the adultery of her husband with the famous 'rose', Rosamund Clifford, which had pushed her to the limit and beyond. This is a romantic idea but the truth was most likely rather more prosaic. Henry's attempts to directly control Aquitaine must have rankled. Eleanor was strong-willed and self-confident and her actions were probably motivated by this attempted downgrading of her duchy's status to just another bauble to be dealt with as Henry saw fit.[11]

There is little sign that Henry II and Eleanor had seen much of each other recently.[12] When considering the relative youth and inexperience of her sons, it is not hard to paint a picture that portrays her as the prime architect of all this dissent and dissatisfaction. Henry had done little to affirm her importance as an individual with powerful political ambitions of her own and, in so doing, he had seriously underestimated the personality and determination of his wife. Henry was a spider at the centre of a web, seeking to control his world. But those whom he wished to dominate refused to cooperate.

These defections came as a bitter blow for Henry II. Yet this was a strong king at the peak of his not inconsiderable powers regardless of the fall-out from the Becket affair. He refused to panic despite the scale of the opposition to him. He seemed unperturbed by his family's betrayal or by the fact that several key men in Aquitaine, including Count William of Angoulême and Geoffrey and Guy of Lusignan, supported Eleanor's rebellion against her husband. Many from Aquitaine seemed glad to be free of the excessive money-making efficiency of Henry II, who was known in those parts as 'The King of the North Wind'.

The antipathy of Henry II's sons towards him seemed complete. They took an oath in Paris not to make peace with their father unless Louis sanctioned it. Other prominent men took the side of Louis, including King William of Scotland and the counts of Flanders, Boulogne and Blois. This was a formidable coalition: Henry was surrounded by enemies on every side, yet he remained the master of the situation. He used his enormous financial resources to hire large numbers of mercenaries, money clearly being to his mind a stronger guarantor of loyalty than blood relationships.

When Richard and some of his allies invaded his father's lands in France in July 1173, Henry was ready for him. Philip of Flanders led the attack but it quickly ran out of steam when the duke's brother, Matthew of Boulogne, was mortally wounded by a crossbow bolt; the wound had only been to the knee but it festered and it was infection that ultimately took his life, showing how a lack of medical understanding at the time was potentially as big a killer as weapons were.[13] The attacks came to nothing and Louis was soon trying to broker a peace deal. Henry offered terms to his errant sons to encourage them to put down their weapons of war. Under Louis's influence, they refused.

In November 1173, Henry led a raid to the south of Chinon. A crushing blow for his enemies' cause followed, for soon after Eleanor of Aquitaine was taken captive. Some chroniclers said that she was dressed as a man when she was seized, emphasising in their eyes her cunning and duplicity. Only a few miles from safety when captured, her seizure would prove a terminal blow for the rebellion.

Richard and Eleanor were extremely close. Ralph of Diceto wrote of Richard that he was always inspired to do actions that would bring glory to his mother. Eleanor, it seems, felt the same in return. When she wrote of her youngest son John, she called him her 'dear son'; Richard was her 'very dear son' – a small enough difference perhaps but that extra word spoke volumes.

Given this, Eleanor's capture must have been a shock to Richard, but he did not show it. Instead he continued to lead the rebellion in Poitou, threatening the thriving new port of La Rochelle.[14] The nearby town of Saintes was on Richard's side, naturally enough as La Rochelle was an unwelcome new rival to its former local prominence.

But Richard was young and inexperienced. Soon after, at Whitsun, Henry launched a surprise attack on Saintes, catching it off guard, although Richard managed to make good his escape. However, he lost nearly 500 men and large stores of military supplies, seriously impeding his effectiveness. Henry at his peak was a formidable proposition.

It was the beginning of the end. Henry was more than a match for those who opposed him. On 12 July 1174, Henry had done public penance for the infamous uttering of the inflammatory words that led to the death of Thomas Becket. In an astonishing scene, the king walked barefoot through the streets of Canterbury. When he reached the crypt of the cathedral itself, each of the eighty or so monks there lashed him three times.[15] It was the ultimate humiliation for a king but one that Henry no doubt felt could not be avoided. With the shedding of royal blood, the crimson stains that had marked the ground where the martyr archbishop bled out his life just a few yards away were metaphorically expunged.

It did not take long at all for a reward for this penance to manifest itself. The day after, at Alnwick, close to the Scottish borders, the Scottish king, William, was taken prisoner by men loyal to Henry; it would have been strange if this had not been seen as a mark of divine forgiveness for Henry's submission to the chastising whips of the Canterbury monks. Henry was beside himself with joy when he received the news, tidings that were so amazing for him that he repaid the messenger who carried them with a generous grant there and then. The bells of London pealed in celebration. With the redoubtable Eleanor also in custody, Henry now held all the aces in his hand.

The completeness of his triumph was symbolised by the coterie of noblewomen, one might call them hostages, who had come to England with him when he had returned from France. Not only was there Eleanor but also Margaret, the Young King's wife and the daughter of Louis of France. Then there was Alice, another daughter of that monarch and Richard's betrothed, Constance of Brittany, engaged to Geoffrey, and Alice of Maurienne, from a strategically important territory in the north of Italy and promised to his youngest son, John. With a set of cards in his possession such as this, there was no doubt who was winning the game.

On 8 September 1174, Henry and Louis concluded an agreement known as the Treaty of Montlouis. It is notable that Richard, the rebellious son, was specifically excluded from it. Even the slippery Young King, the eldest son who had done much to foster the uprising, had come to terms with his father by now. Richard was now on his own and, as his father moved with his army towards him, Richard had no option but to retreat.

Richard, starting to run short of both men and resources, now realised that the game was up and reasoned that the best option was to submit to his father and seek forgiveness. This he did, entering King Henry's presence at Poitiers on 23 September 1174 with tears streaming down his face. These were very probably of the crocodile variety but a touching scene was played out nevertheless. Henry embraced Richard, giving him the kiss of peace. He gave way in terms of handing over more revenues to his sons, which he was well able to do given the vast resources at his disposal; Richard, for example, got half the revenues of Poitou and 'two castles from which he cannot harm me'.[16] On the more important subject, that of giving up some of his power, Henry in real terms budged barely an inch.

It had been a painful lesson for Richard, whose inexperience showed, although so too did his fighting spirit even at this young age. He had been caught badly off guard at Saintes, a military setback that the older Richard would have winced at. His father's resources and experience were so much greater than his that he had been in the end completely outmanoeuvred. But at least he had gained some additional monetary resources for his efforts. He was also back in position as the duke of Aquitaine. He was lucky. His mother, the supposed fermenter of all this trouble, would not be let out of her husband's sight. It was Eleanor's fate not to taste true freedom again for over fifteen years.

Richard, though, seems to have been rehabilitated, with his father seemingly not bearing a grudge against his errant sons in the same way that he did with his wife. Christmas was spent together at Argentan in Normandy, minus Eleanor, who was safely under lock and key on the other side of the English Channel. It must have been a strained atmosphere given recent events.

After Christmas, Richard returned to Aquitaine with clear instructions to stamp out any remaining embers of sedition. He did the job enthusiastically and, for one so young and inexperienced, very well. He took a number of castles including some that had only recently been built and in many cases, on the specific instructions of his father, destroyed them, depriving a potential opponent of a fortress; a measure that was often more useful and pragmatic than having to garrison it oneself.

Eleanor suffered badly for her rebellion and for a time there were even rumours of divorce, though they came to nothing. These surfaced in 1175 but the idea faded away, probably because it would compromise Henry's claims to Aquitaine, which was too valuable a prize to lose. But the suggestion was made that one of the reasons for these plans was that Henry would then be free to marry Alice, currently betrothed to Richard. A complicated *ménage a trois* was emerging.

Aquitaine remained volatile. The embers of rebellion had not been so thoroughly stamped down here after all. In 1176, the flames of revolt flared up once again, this time from a particularly worrying direction. At the heart of the uprising were the sons of the count of Angoulême and their half-brother Viscount Aimar of Limoges. This faction had in the past been mainly loyal to the cause of Henry II. They may have had strong cause to switch allegiance, to be found in events that took place after the death of Reginald, the earl of Cornwall, far away in England.

Why should these events hundreds of miles to the north have had such an impact? It was all to do with disappointed ambitions. The earl, who was an illegitimate son of King Henry I, held many lands and when he died he left three daughters but no sons. One of his daughters was married to Viscount Aimar. But Henry II, instead of distributing the lands in the conventional fashion amongst them, kept most of them for himself, or rather for his youngest son, John. The three daughters were given a token distribution of lands, far below what was expected.

Given this situation, it is slightly strange that Richard's finest modern biographer considers that these events were 'apparently unconnected to the war'.[17] Aimar must have seethed at the lost opportunity and it is not unlikely that the disappointed ambition gnawed away at him and incited him to rebel, along with his family. Soon the uprising was too hot for Richard to handle with the resources currently available to him. It is ironic that Aimar would be involved at the beginning of Richard's military career and that he would be there again at its very end.

Richard was forced to appeal to his father for financial assistance so that he could employ mercenaries to supplement his insufficient forces. It says much for the reconciliation that had taken place between Richard and Henry that the king was fulsome in his response. It would have been understandable if he had hesitated, afraid that Richard, so recently in rebellion, would use the money to cause yet more trouble. But Henry did not hesitate, and for the time being he clearly considered that whatever issues had led to Richard's rebellion had now been resolved.

Richard was seemingly a reformed character. He used the resources for their intended purposes and Aimar capitulated within a few days. Henry, the Young King, had joined his brother Richard and they set off on a foray into the county of Angoulême. Henry soon left, seemingly lacking the enthusiasm for warfare that Richard was demonstrating so clearly; he much preferred the chivalric make-believe of the tournament.

Undeterred, Richard laid siege to Angoulême itself. In less than a week it was his. An extravagant prize fell into his lap as a result: he captured an impressive collection of prisoners, including Count William of Angoulême, who surrendered many castles as well as his town. Limoges was taken after a siege that lasted just six days. A bevy of impressive captives was then sent to England to humiliatingly beg for mercy at the feet of Henry II. The king decided that he wanted nothing to do with them and promptly sent them back to Richard in Aquitaine.

In the summer of 1176, events were played out that were to resonate in Richard's life over a decade into the future. Henry II concluded negotiations for his daughter Joanna to marry William II ('The Good'), king of Sicily. She set sail from Southampton for France, having first met her mother, who had been allowed out of her royal prison at Sarum temporarily so that she could meet her.

Sarum was just outside of Salisbury and indeed had been the first site on which a cathedral had been constructed there. However, it was in a bleak, windswept position and water was in short supply so it was abandoned and the new cathedral at Salisbury was built early in the thirteenth century. Eleanor was to spend a good proportion of the following years in Sarum and Winchester. However, she appears to have been treated well. Records from the time show that the sheriff of Wiltshire spent significant sums on her maintenance between 1175 and 1180, and clothes for Eleanor and her household were regularly sent from London.[18]

Joanna made her way across France to the south, where she took a ship across the Mediterranean to Sicily; her brother Richard accompanied her for much of the last stage of the French journey when she crossed his lands. She married William in Palermo Cathedral the following February. The ceremony was a splendid one, attended by the good and the great on the island. Joanna was sumptuously dressed and was formally crowned queen. But afterwards she led a secluded life, her husband having adopted some of the more exotic practices of the East, including the maintenance of a harem.[19] Such were the risks of marriage for a woman in the twelfth century and Joanna would later find out from her brother Richard just how little human emotions came into it when a woman's worth in the marriage stakes was being discussed. They were an extremely valuable and tradeable commodity on the marriage market.

Peace had been made between Richard and his father and normality had returned, or so it seemed. But the wounds inflicted on them in the 'great war' ran deep and the reconciliation would prove to be temporary. Henry and Richard were now walking a tightrope from which either man could at any moment plunge into an abyss. If the legend of Richard is shaped in the main by his crusading activities, the story of his life was shaped by these next turbulent years.

3

A Family at War (1177–1183)

'He cost me much but I wish he had lived to cost me more'
Attributed to Henry II on hearing of the death of his eldest son, the 'Young King'

Richard was in Bordeaux for Christmas in 1176, unusually holding court himself whilst his brothers were with their father in Nottingham. The festive season seemingly inspired him with energy. Soon after, he launched his forces on a whistle-stop raid around the south-west of France. Between Christmas 1176 and 9 January 1177, the towns of Dax and Bayonne had been taken and he had reached the borders of Spain. This was a spectacular feat; no one expected such a burst of activity in winter. It had the desired effect. Henry II had been worried about the dangers faced by pilgrims passing through the region on their way to Santiago de Compostella but now the disorderly peoples there, including the ferocious Basques, sent envoys to Richard asking for peace.

These were wild frontier lands on the periphery of European Christendom, with the country to the south still in Muslim hands beyond the small Spanish kingdoms. They were characterised by the gnarled Pyrenees, rocky fastnesses where robber barons could disregard instructions from their nominal overlords with impunity. No doubt from time to time they dreamed of acting as independent principalities, a vision that for some in the Basque country has still not gone away. Richard's successes meant that that particular genie was put back in the bottle for the time being.

Unfortunately, there were problems after the campaign was declared to be a 'mission accomplished'. A number of Richard's troops were mercenaries, notoriously difficult to control and loyal to no one but themselves. Those from Brabant (now in Belgium), who were often employed by Henry and Richard, were particularly notorious for their misbehaviour. They engaged in 'utter destruction in every quarter; sparing neither age, nor sex, nor rank, nor the religious profession; on the contrary, as it appeared, aiming at the perpetration of homicide, sacrilege, and rapine alone'.[1]

Now that their usefulness was over and they were let go, they created havoc. Although they were professional fighters, their uncontrolled excesses outraged the local population so much that they rose up and slaughtered them in what became known eloquently as 'the Butchery of Malmorte' after the place where they were brought to account. Such brutal excesses from these mercenaries, followed by an equally and deservedly brutal reaction against them from an angry local population, were typical of the times.

Richard's willingness to use mercenaries was pragmatic but rather contradicted the efforts he assiduously made to portray himself throughout his life as a patron of chivalry. It was the knight who was at the heart of the concept, not these ruffians. Chivalry was all about a code and following rules; mercenaries basically had none. They were a scourge on the lands through which they passed and from time to time those who had first employed them later found themselves going out of their way to wipe them out, as had been the case here. However much Richard played to the gallery when talking of chivalry, he also had a ruthlessly pragmatic streak.

The use of such mercenaries was counter-productive in the long term. The Angevins needed to build support for their dynasty across a wide range of territories and the extreme actions of the mercenaries, whilst quelling uprisings in the short term, bred resentment and resistance beyond it. Aquitaine, however emotionally attached Richard might feel to it, would be a thorn in his flesh throughout his life. He would give a quarter of a century of his life in efforts to subdue it and he would never achieve this on a permanent basis.

The employment of military force in Aquitaine was something of a blunt instrument. It is noticeable that during the latter part of Richard's life, almost all his major officials and witnesses on legal documents were English or Norman. Very few names appear from Aquitaine or Anjou and it appears that Richard's efforts to build political links here were more tenuous. This seems a political mistake for if more men from these territories had been advanced in Richard's jurisdiction perhaps greater unity and security might have been achieved across the Angevin federation.

Richard, though, rose in his father's favour. His position contrasted with that of his older brother. There is some evidence that the Young King had been doing his best to take on more of a role in government within the territories that were nominally his. He had been busily accompanying his father not long before as he travelled around England. But a careful reading of the record suggests that by now he had given up. From this point on (at around the end of 1176 or the early months of 1177) he seems to have dedicated himself to the more interesting challenges of life on the tournament field.[2]

Later in 1177 Henry sent a delegation to Paris demanding that Louis should fulfil certain agreements made when his daughter Margaret was married to the Young King and when Alice had been betrothed to Richard. This was a bit rich considering that no further steps had been taken by the English king, who had Alice safely in his custody, to go ahead with her match with Richard. Louis responded by producing news of an interdict prepared by Pope Alexander III threatening religious sanctions against England; this was to be made active within a year if Alice's marriage to Richard did not take place.

Shown to be somewhat shifty, Henry II decided that he now had to demonstrate some proactivity and a conference with the French was arranged, at which ongoing disputes concerning land in Berry and the Auvergne were to be hammered out. The wedding of Alice and Richard was to proceed quickly and both Henry and Louis were to set out on crusade shortly afterward.

The backdrop to this was that there were persistent rumours that Alice had by now become Henry II's mistress. The *Chronicle of Meaux* even states that she bore him a son and a daughter, who subsequently died.[3] If Alice were indeed in such a situation then any reluctance on Richard's part to marry her would be understandable at a personal level, especially as her alleged lover was his father.

There had also been a major international development, for there was trouble brewing in the crusader kingdoms of Outremer. The Muslim forces in the region had grown increasingly powerful under their great leader Nur al-Din. He seemed to be unstoppable. He achieved the significant feat of uniting Muslim Syria and Egypt under one man. This was a strategic hammer-blow to Outremer.

It meant that the crusader kingdoms there were now trapped between two powerful states which historically had been far too busy scheming against each other to unite. It would now be much easier to combine forces against the enemy from the West.

The threat level felt in Outremer rose exponentially. No doubt much relief was felt by her rulers when Nur al-Din died in 1174, as he seemed to be the cementing force behind Islam's revival in the region. There had been, almost inevitably, a succession dispute after his death, which seemed to hint at imminent disunification for the Muslims in the region again. An ambitious man in his late thirties was the ultimate victor in the squabbles that followed the death of Nur al-Din. His name was Ṣalāḥ ad-Dīn Yūsuf ibn Ayyūb. His Christian opponents would simplify this to the name by which the West still largely knows him – Saladin.

Of Richard's activities in 1178 we only catch a few glimpses, although we know that he spent Christmas at Angers with his father and two eldest brothers in 1177. Christmas was not just a time for fun and feasting though. Again, the family would discuss more serious matters and set the agenda for the following year; Christmas was, in other words, a time for politics as well as festivities. Given the extended territories that the dynasty was collectively responsible for, time together was limited and when such an opportunity to put plans in place came along it could not be wasted.

After Christmas, Richard returned to Aquitaine and the surrounding regions, engaging in the local politics and occasional skirmishing that was often the lot of a contemporary duke. There were still too many signs of rebellion for comfort in Aquitaine. Richard launched an attack early in 1179 against the castle of Pons, which played a significant part in supporting the interests of the dissatisfied elements of the local aristocracy. But he was in for a disappointment. Perhaps anticipating the siege, supplies in the castle had been stockpiled. The defence was vigorously and stubbornly led. By Easter, Richard realised that there would be no quick win here and, leaving a force behind to carry on the siege, he went with some of his men to look for alternative opportunities.

Pons and other castles at Richemont and Taillebourg were in the possession of a particularly troublesome baron, Geoffrey de Rançon. They held a crucial strategic position, dominating the routes between Bordeaux, Saintes and La Rochelle. Geoffrey was always difficult to keep under control, a 'perpetual rebel' as a modern French historian described him.[4] He was a constant thorn in the flesh, always springing up like a jack-in-a-box when least expected.

The failure at Pons must have frustrated Richard. But any frustration he felt was soon to be counteracted by what we should judge, in military terms, to be Richard's first brush with greatness. High above the River Charente stood the seemingly uncrackable fortress of Taillebourg, 'fortified both by artifice and nature'.[5] Richard knew the castle well; he had found refuge there when in rebellion against his father. It was only approachable on one side, the other three sides being impregnable because of the sheer cliffs that surrounded it. A small town had developed around the walls of the citadel, perched on the banks of the Charente.

Richard now attacked Taillebourg. He launched missiles from his siege engines against the walls of the town. He then sent his men to ravage the surrounding area, home to lush fields and rich vineyards; this was not a chivalric war but a harsh campaign where the local population suffered more than anyone. The garrison, seeing their lands being destroyed before their eyes and noticing how close Richard's camp was to the walls, were enraged and charged out of the gates. But he was more than ready for them. A fierce counter-attack was launched. Richard's men forced their way through the open gates. The garrison managed to reach the relative security of the castle but, their will to fight gone, they gave up after three days.

They were not alone. The commander at Pons, hearing the news, surrendered at once. Richard decided that, rather than try to garrison the captured castles, he would destroy them. The walls of Angoulême soon followed suit. Richard had earned a great triumph and had in the process exhibited outstanding personal bravery, throwing himself into the hottest part of the battle at Taillebourg. It was, it has been said, the actions of a man who was becoming 'an acknowledged expert in the vital art of siege warfare'.[6]

Yet it was also something that desperately needed to be done to restore credibility. Richard's initial failure at Pons cast doubts on his ability to enforce his rule across Aquitaine. One of the main purposes of medieval castles was to tie up resources; bodies of men were forced to lay siege to untaken castles, diverting them from other campaigning, and this the fortress at Pons had done admirably. In the meantime, rebellious forces elsewhere could assert themselves and the impact of the Angevins' superior resources could be diluted.

To restore prestige something spectacular was needed and the taking of Taillebourg certainly fitted into that category. Richard, no doubt ably assisted by more experienced warriors including mercenaries who were to all intents and purposes professional soldiers, had fought the perfect campaign, depleting the surrounding lands of foodstuffs, destroying property, striking fear into the besieged. He and his lieutenants had also managed to persuade the garrison to make the cardinal mistake of sallying out of the town and not retreating back in time. It was a masterful example of how to successfully wage a short, sharp, decisive siege. An unfortunate blot on Richard's reputation brought about by the indecisive events at Pons had been decisively expunged.

Richard returned to England soon after to be greeted by his father as a hero. Ralph of Diceto said that Richard 'was received with great honour by his father'.[7] No doubt the twenty-one-year-old milked the glory for all it was worth. If he did, he was justly proud for he had come of age. He had shown both military talent and considerable political acumen. Henry II too must have gloried in his son. Perhaps in the occasional quiet moment, the all-action Henry sat and wondered what the future of England and the Angevin lands in France would be if only Richard was his heir. These were heady days for father and son; in the years to come they would become a dim and distant golden age.

Richard had done a magnificent job in increasing the power of the duke of Aquitaine. He had been given the foundation of that power by the marriage of his father to Eleanor. Henry's 'empire' was now extremely large and diverse, and given the many tensions that would have to be faced it was too big for one man to govern alone (some historians do not consider that the lands were homogenously ruled and prefer the term 'federation' to 'empire').[8] Richard's performance had been full of promise and energy, and at this stage loyalty too, which must have been a relief to Henry after recent problems.

On 1 November 1179, Richard attended the coronation of Philip, son of Louis of France. Louis had recently suffered a stroke which had effectively ended his reign to all practical intents and purposes, though before he had been completely incapacitated he had managed to make a pilgrimage to Canterbury and the shrine of

Thomas Becket (the first time that a French monarch had set foot in England).

There was concern in France when Philip was taken ill but he pulled through. His coronation ceremony took place at Rheims, the traditional site for such events, and after it Richard, who was present, paid homage for the lands he held in France, as did his brother Geoffrey. Philip was only fourteen years old at the time and was unprepossessing in appearance. He was dour and serious but this belied a flinty interior which showed itself in a gritty, determined personality, as the Angevin princes would find out to their cost.

Louis VII died soon after. On the accession of Philip, there was a change of course in French politics. Louis had forged close relationships with the house of Champagne but after Philip's coronation their fortunes quickly went into decline. Louis VII's widow, Adela of Champagne, was sidelined and she successfully sought the support of Henry II in response. Henry played a surprise hand as a mediator in the dispute, with the result that relations between Philip and Adela were restored. But the new regime clearly had its own agenda in France. Young though Philip was, he would be no pushover.

For several years after, there was peace in Aquitaine. Some of the leading barons in the region set off on pilgrimage to Jerusalem, no doubt relieved to get away from the sight of the ruined walls of their fortresses, a permanent reminder of their collective emasculation at the hands of the young duke.

However, there were suggestions that Aquitaine was still far from subdued in reality. Chroniclers such as Ralph of Diceto tell how Richard was hated by some of the barons of Aquitaine, who saw him as little more than a despot who was anxious to trample down their rights at every opportunity, a perception that was probably correct. The Dean of St Paul's heard tales that Richard was oppressive and frequently employed violent measures in asserting his rights, something that chimes with Richard's actions in later life.

Worse tales still were written down by the chronicler Roger of Howden, which describe Richard as little better than a sex-driven monster. There were stories of beautiful women being carried off to satisfy Richard's lust before then being given to his men to enjoy. This sounds like malicious gossip but an overall oppressive attitude from Richard is far from unlikely, particularly as his father wanted stronger centralised control in Aquitaine.

Modern critics of Richard make much of his alleged ruthlessness, overlooking the fact that his opponents were often equally as savage. They even criticise him for his enjoyment of the bloodthirsty sport of hunting[9], extraordinarily overlooking the fact that this was a very normal pursuit for royals and nobles at the time. Henry II was famed for his love of the chase, as was Richard's younger brother John in later life. Richard should be judged by the standards of his own time, not ours.

In 1181 trouble flared up in Aquitaine again, once more fuelled by a succession dispute. Count Vulgrin of Angoulême died, leaving only an infant daughter. Local custom dictated that the brothers of the dead man should have a share of the inheritance as well as his young daughter. But Richard wanted the daughter to inherit virtually everything; as he would have custody of her whilst she was still a child, it was not hard to see why. It was a stance that closely echoed that taken by Henry II on other occasions, an effort to change traditional rights to the advantage of the Crown. This was a trait that Richard had seemingly inherited from his father.

Vulgrin's brothers were unsurprisingly extremely irritated by this unwelcome assertion of ducal power. They joined forces with Aimar of Limoges and other leading nobles and soon the shadow of rebellion loomed over Aquitaine again. The fuse would be lit by King Philip II, who had formally taken the throne of France on the death of his father on 18 September 1180. Another key player in Richard's story had stepped on to the stage. He would rarely be off it for the remainder of Richard's life.

A well-known troubadour of the time, Bertran de Born, was a prime motivator in the problem that developed in Aquitaine and at this stage was a fierce critic of Richard. He was a colourful figure, once condemned to suffer in Hell by none other than Dante. His words stirred up violent emotions and he had plenty of ammunition to utilise. However much Richard's biographers might present his actions as those which were to be expected of any assertive nobleman of the period,[10] his heavy-handed intervention, so typical of his father in some ways, was a clumsy attempt to change the traditions and conventions of Aquitaine in a way that was bound to alienate those involved.

And therein lay the problem. In England, Henry II would probably have got away with it. But this was not England, it was Aquitaine, a land with its own traditions and customs which her barons protected jealously – at least as far as their own rights were involved. Henry's 'federation' was a complex network of loosely linked territories whose only overall connection was that at the apex of the pyramid of power was Henry II. It was widely dispersed and as such it was always going to be difficult to keep under control. Henry would only be as good and as effective as his sons ruling their respective parts of the federation were.

Each part of the federation kept its own traditions and style of government to an extent, and when any one of the Angevins tried to change this and replicate what they were doing in other parts of their domains there was often resistance. There was, for example, no common coinage in place across all the territories. The ability to control Church appointments, crucial back then, varied across different parts of the federation. The division of territories amongst Henry's sons has been likened to attempts to ensure the sustainability of a 'family firm' rather than the ruling of a coherent empire.[11]

A spectacular problem was about to arise. Henry II was in many historians' opinion a great king. But he was much less successful as head of the family. Not to mention the fact that his wife had now been under lock and key for the best part of a decade, there was about to be a fall-out between his two eldest sons, Henry and Richard, a situation that Geoffrey, another brother, would also be drawn into.

There were many cases in those times when a father divided his inheritance amongst several sons: William I had left his conquests in England to his second son, William II, for example. There was even a name for it; *parage*. The word comes from the Old French, which reveals the origins of the idea behind it, and it passed into Middle English, which says something about the transference of the idea across the English Channel.

In the classic structure of *parage* there was one son more dominant than the others, the chief executive of the 'family firm', to continue the analogy. Henry the Young King, the oldest surviving son of Henry II, was this prominent figure and the other brothers were to an extent required to doff their caps to him, though they also held lands of their own with Richard nominally in control of Aquitaine (passing the mother's inheritance to a second son was not unusual). It was a fine theory but in this case it would not work out well in practice, largely due to character flaws in the personalities of Henry and Eleanor's bloody-minded brood.

The eldest son, Henry, was a man of frivolous tastes, poorly suited to the demands of kingship. He may have complained on occasion of a lack of real power but the reality was that any time he was asked to take an interest in government he showed no inclination to do so. He lived for the tournament, those mock battles where the fantasies of chivalry could be played out and men could win fame and, if they were lucky, fortune too in a completely unreal world.

The tournament was very different fr the organised and somewhat sanitised events that a Hollywood-painted image of modern times would portray. Rather than a well-regulated contest on neatly manicured tilting lawns such as we might expect, at this time it was typically a cross-country chase with limited supervision, a free-for-all brawl far better defined as a mêlée. Men hacked indiscriminately at their immediate opponent, occasionally bringing them down and holding them for ransom before they were released. In the pell-mell nature of these occasions, lives were sometimes lost even from the very highest echelons of society. No wonder then that the tournament was currently banned in England and knights had to make their way to the Continent to participate, leading to suggestions from some Frenchmen that the English were keener on drinking and boasting than fighting.[12]

For those involved in such tournaments, and indeed those who fought in real-life wars, this was a way of earning a living of sorts. Such a life particularly appealed to younger sons of the nobility whose prospects were otherwise limited due to their lack of access to the legacies or lucrative marriages that would flow to older siblings. Such men, of which the finest example was the ultimately famous William Marshal, would aspire to join the coterie of cavalry that was attached to kings and great nobles, a set-up known in the language of the time as the *mesnie*. Such men would often wear the uniform of their lord, giving them a personal and symbolic linkage to the man to whose cause they were attached.[13]

The so-called Age of Chivalry was beginning to get into full swing. The younger Henry was caught up in its dreamy landscapes, its escapism, its unreality. In that respect Richard could not have been more different. Why have mock battles when real fighting was available? Why aspire to make-believe power when real acts of government were within your grasp? Richard may have later been portrayed as a paragon of chivalry but he was also a hard-headed and determined pragmatist.

That said, certain things were expected of him in the context of chivalry. This undoubtedly affected the way that people saw him at the time for in many ways he played his part well. A paragon of chivalry must act in a certain way. He was required to be a perfect knight with the qualities of prowess, loyalty, largesse and courtesy. He should be a mighty warrior with strong martial skills and a generous spirit.[14] On occasion – though not on every occasion – Richard was very capable of exhibiting these qualities.

For Henry II's scheme of governance to work, each son had to play the part allocated to him in it properly. The land of Aquitaine abutted on to the borders of Anjou. In Henry II's perception of the federation of power that he had built up, this was its strength. From Normandy in the north to Aquitaine in the south, with Anjou in between, there was an unbroken bloc with his two eldest sons in charge. This should in theory make for peace and stability – but only if both the Young King and Richard bought in to the idea.

In practice, the young Henry and Richard did not see eye to eye – they saw themselves as rivals. In the late summer of 1182 the young Henry started to agitate for greater powers in Normandy. What he really wanted was not to govern but to have access to greater sources of wealth that he could finance his chivalric fantasies with. There was a fall-out and the Young King took himself off to Paris in a huff. The matter was patched up soon after but Henry II would delay his return to England for two years due to the unpredictability of his eldest son.

Although Henry II was no longer the exuberantly energetic young ruler of twenty years ago, he still retained much of his political astuteness (during these years he strove to intervene positively in the affairs of France and thereby get closer to the young King Philip) and he sensed that there were disturbing undercurrents about which could bring his federation tumbling down.

Christmas 1182 was spent at Caen in Normandy and it was to be a real family gathering again as Henry was joined by his three eldest sons, Henry, Richard and Geoffrey. Richard's sister Matilda was also there accompanied by her husband, the German prince Henry the Lion. There were also 1,000 knights from across Normandy present. Whilst this splendid festive gathering was by no means unusual – though this was a splendid Christmas celebration even by Angevin standards – what followed was, as Henry and his sons then spent some time journeying around the surrounding region, travelling to Le Mans, Angers and Mirabeau.

Matters were about to come to a head. On the north-east border of Poitou was Clairvaux. The territorial limits between Aquitaine and Anjou around here were not clear but for a long time Clairvaux had been regarded as belonging to the latter. Of course, it should not have mattered as both territories were under the control of Henry's sons. However, Richard had decided that he should build a castle here. Not far away, and definitely in Anjou, was the crucial fortress of Chinon and the strong castle that Richard built at Clairvaux looked like a counterbalance to it. It did not make a great deal of sense unless Richard expected trouble from his elder brother's direction.

There were good reasons though why he would be wise to expect exactly such a threat. Matters in Aquitaine were still in a state of flux. At the heart of the conspiracy against Richard which was now brewing was Aimar of Limoges, but other prominent agitators included William and Adémar of Angoulême, Elie the count of Périgord, and Geoffrey of Lusignan. They seem to have found a sympathetic listener in the Young King. It is highly probable that Richard's elder brother had been encouraging rather than dampening dissent in Aquitaine. No wonder that Richard was on his guard.

The matter was brought up in conversation with the brothers by the king. Henry II suggested that Clairvaux should be given directly into his hands to resolve the dispute. Richard was reluctant to accede to this but eventually agreed. Sensing trouble in Aquitaine, the king summoned the barons of the duchy to meet with him in Mirabeau so that their grievances could be heard.

This was progress but there was a third element to the deal that Henry II had brokered which proved to be the spark that lit the fuse. The three brothers, Henry, Richard and Geoffrey, were required to take oaths to support each other. The two younger brothers were also instructed to swear allegiance to the Young King for the lands that they held.

This is where the problem arose, for Richard insisted – with some legal justification – that allegiance for Aquitaine was not due to his elder brother but was part of his mother's territories and was therefore owed to the king of France. On the other hand, the practice of *parage*, by which younger sons recognised the seniority of older brothers, was well established in France and Richard was not being asked to do anything particularly innovative or revolutionary; but it is understandable that someone with his pride would not want to go along with it.[15]

Naturally this did not mean that Richard was anxious to be subservient to the king of France, rather that he was not keen to be subservient to his elder brother. Nevertheless, a compromise of sorts was worked out but the Young King refused to accept it. Soon after, Richard dutifully handed Clairvaux over to his father. But the Young King was using the situation as a cover for greater grievances and the tension was palpable. The meeting broke up soon afterwards and Richard rushed away to Aquitaine, expecting trouble and readying his castles for action. The Young King persuaded his father to let him go to Aquitaine to calm the barons and bring peace to the region; Geoffrey was already there. Henry accepted the offer and his eldest son made his way south to the duchy. The denouement was imminent.

Henry II followed on closely after his sons. What he found when he arrived in Aquitaine was a mess. When he reached the citadel at Limoges, he was fired on from inside the walls (or what was left of them, for Richard had pulled most of them down not long before). It was explained that this was all a big mistake and that the garrison had failed to recognise him but every time that he re-approached, the king was fired upon. His negotiators were treated to abuse. It was clear that those inside had no intention of letting him in and that they were in league with the Young King and Geoffrey against Richard.

The citadel of Limoges was not in a great state to defend itself and hasty fortifications of earth, stone and wood had been erected. But it was clear that those inside planned to resist Henry II and his assertive son. Father and son did not yet have enough men to hand to do much about this state of affairs so they took up residence in the town that surrounded the citadel. However, there was some fighting and in one incident the king's horse was struck by an arrow that narrowly missed hitting him. Roger of Howden wrote that if the horse had not changed direction at the last minute and so took the blow itself, Henry would have been struck in the chest.[16] Henry took himself off to Richard's castle at Aixe, where they discussed their next move.

The situation at Limoges was all down to the Young King, who was in league with some of the rebel barons in Aquitaine; they sensed he was a 'soft touch' compared to the more assertive Richard. Because Henry II had been careful not to allow the Young King too many men, he was not able to do much damage on his own. But his younger brother Geoffrey did have access to men from Brittany and was coming to his aid. Even now a large band of mercenaries was on its way to invade Poitou. The family was splitting in two. To make matters worse, King Philip of France had also sent men to fight against the Angevin king and Aimar of Limoges had summoned up forces, described as being little more than brigands, to also fight against Henry II and Richard.

It is not clear who was really the driving force behind this move. While the Young King was undoubtedly the senior partner when compared to Geoffrey, he comes across as a weak, indecisive and vacillating character, unsuited to life outside the tournament field. In contrast, there seem to have been hidden devious depths in Geoffrey, if contemporary chroniclers are to be believed.

Gerald of Wales, who certainly had a poisoned quill when the mood took him, went overboard in his description of Geoffrey, describing him as 'overflowing with words, smooth as oil, possessed, by his syrupy and persuasive eloquence, of the power of dissolving the apparently indissoluble, able to corrupt two kingdoms with his tongue, of tireless endeavour and a hypocrite in everything'.[17] Roger of Howden was equally unimpressed, calling Geoffrey 'that son of perdition'[18] and 'that son of iniquity'.[19]

This is hardly a flattering picture and it is known that Geoffrey was in Aquitaine during the previous year. It is easy to imagine late-night plotting during 1182, sensing that several important men in the duchy were not happy with Richard's aggressive assertion of his rights. It was an ideal opportunity to stir up trouble and set up alliances in advance of decisive action. Certainly in 1183 Geoffrey was quick to get involved when matters heated up in Aquitaine.

Philip's men committed several atrocities as they advanced and parts of Aquitaine were soon under heavy attack. It was the first sign, perhaps, that Philip did not like the great power that the English king enjoyed and would do anything he could to chip away at it. It was the start of an antipathy towards the powerful Angevin dynasty that would never be far away for the next quarter of a century.

The Young King was soon under siege in the citadel of Limoges with Viscount Aimar. The rebel prince's main problem was that he was now deprived of funds so it was difficult to finance the men in his force. A painful process of attrition followed. The siege ground on and the Young King decided to escape from the confines of the citadel and stir up more resistance further afield. The rest of the garrison stayed put. The weather was wet and cold and the besieging forces became demoralised. Eventually the siege was called off.

It was a serious blow to Henry II, Richard and their joint credibility (though it is not clear that Richard was actually present in the later stages of the siege and he may have been campaigning elsewhere by this time). More reinforcements rushed to join the cause of the rebels, though some too for the English king and his son from Alfonso II of Aragon. The kings of Aragon were long-term rivals of the Counts of Toulouse and were a useful counterbalance to their ambitions.

However, despite initial successes the Young King, Geoffrey and their allies had bitten off far more than they could chew. Henry II played his political part masterfully. Firm instructions were sent back to England to ensure that potential sympathisers of the rebels should not come out in their support. They did not. In the meantime, Richard launched a blitzkrieg against those in arms against him. The reports that survive suggest that he was savage against those taken in arms, drowning, butchering or blinding them; few prisoners were taken in what was a brutal campaign waged by a man, Richard, who was furious at the turn events had taken.

The campaign ended in complete humiliation for the Young King. When he sallied out of Limoges he was not allowed back by the citizens when he later returned. They could now see that there was a gulf between chivalric idealism and military and political pragmatism. The Young King might have cut a dash in a tournament but he was out of his depth on a military campaign. He was also denuded of funds, so much so that he resorted to pillaging religious shrines, such as the famous site of Rocamadour, to obtain funds, along with other religious establishments such as that of Grandmont, significantly sites often sponsored by Henry II.

The younger Henry then made a desultory *chevauchée* around Aquitaine in an attempt to break the deadlock. It did not have any clear objective and the hardships of life in the field started to take their toll, the exertions of the siege and the lack of proper nutrition starting to grind him down. The biggest killer of medieval warfare in Europe, certainly at this stage of its development, was disease, especially dysentery, the 'flux of the bowels'.[20] The Young King was soon suffering from it.

Urgent messages were sent to his father telling him of the illness. But the king did not trust his son, who had let him down before, and, sensing a trap, he refused to visit him. But the news was genuine and Henry was at least moved enough to send his ailing son a large ring, once owned by Henry I, as a sign of his affection.

Soon after, at Martel to the south of Limoges, the young Henry put on a hair-shirt covered by the garments of a crusader. He lay on the floor on a bed of ashes with a noose around his neck, the mark of a penitent. He gave his cross to William Marshal to carry to Jerusalem in his stead; the two men had only recently been reconciled after an unseemly fall-out from an alleged affair between Marshal and Queen Margaret.[21] The next news that the older Henry got was that the Young King was dead.

Marshal fulfilled his pledge and duly travelled to Jerusalem. Perhaps he had been reminded of his own mortality by witnessing the painful demise of the Young King. This was an interruption to his career but he did not neglect his future planning completely. Before departing he took his leave of Henry II, probably to gauge what his prospects with the king were. Henry gave his blessing to the journey and was probably impressed by Marshal's dedication and loyalty. Marshal would be able to slip smoothly into the direct service of Henry II on his return from Jerusalem (where he bought some expensive silk which he planned to use to make his shroud when he died).[22] He would prove invaluable to Henry and his successors as kings of England.

Henry II was quick enough to forgive the Young King and his other sons for many of their errant deeds. Roger of Howden recorded that when he got the news of his eldest son's death he was overcome with grief, falling to the floor in tears and devastated at the loss.[23] Blood on this occasion was much thicker than water. The king followed his dead son's cortege back to Rouen. It was later said that Henry II remarked that his son had 'cost me much but I wished he had lived to cost me more'.[24]

Following the burial customs of the time, the Young King's brains and entrails had been extracted and buried at Grandmont. The remainder of his corpse was salted to preserve it. It was then wrapped in bulls' hide and lead before being taken to Rouen. Roger of Howden tells how, when the cortege reached Le Mans, the citizens demanded that the Young King be buried there, in some ways a very appropriate choice as this was also where Geoffrey Plantagenet, his grandfather, lay. Henry II, who shortly afterwards receive an angry delegation from Rouen laying claim to the body, was furious. He demanded that the body be disinterred and moved to Rouen.

Bertran de Born eulogised over the Young King. Bertran was at the same time symbolic of all that was best and worst in chivalry.

It would be wrong to say that he lived for chivalry; he lived for warfare, one of its major elements, and he did not seem to mind who suffered because of it. He worshipped the Young King for his fighting spirit and said of him 'you would have been the king of the noble and emperor of the brave, lord, if you had lived longer'.[25]

News was sent to Eleanor, the Young King's mother, who was still at Sarum. She received the news stoically; she said she had foreseen his death in a dream. In this she had seen a sapphire ring on his finger, the recent peace offering from his father. It was a brave performance but, in all probability, an act: years later she told a Papal legate that she had never stopped being tortured by the memory of the younger Henry.[26] Perhaps there is a hint in the reaction of both father and mother that the Young King held a special place in their affections, greater than that for any of their other sons. Despite his many faults, he cut a dash as a chivalric leader and this was maybe what made it so easy to forgive his excesses.

The best eulogy for the Young King came from Walter Map who counted himself a friend but was also able to see his faults clearly. He spoke of the Young King's handsomeness – it was Walter who likened the late Henry to the angels – and his virtues in war. But he also said that he applied his talents to evil ends. He recalled, in keeping with the literary fashions of the times, a prophecy of Merlin, who told of a lynx who would threaten his own kind with ruin.

Walter berated Henry for his patricidal tendencies towards his father. Yet it is perhaps significant that the harshest comments were related to the Young King's feelings towards his brother Richard. Caustically Map remarked that 'knowing his death made Richard, who he loathed, his father's heir, he died raging mad'.[27] It is a significant comment which gives an insight into the extent of the dislike between the two brothers.

Why this dislike, so deeply felt that it might almost be termed hatred, existed must be a matter of speculation. But on his deathbed perhaps the Young King could see the ultimate triumph of his brother, and in that triumph he foresaw that the substance of Richard was far, far greater than the chimera that he offered in comparison. Young Henry was all about chivalry; glory as it might now be termed. Richard was also about substance and practical achievement. Perhaps Henry could see in his last, laboured breaths that it was his younger brother who would enter into legend and not him.

The weather that accompanied the funeral cortege, contemporary chroniclers observed, was pleasant, in contrast to the mood of the older Henry. There was still some bridge-building required with his sons. Geoffrey sought, and of course received, forgiveness soon after at Angers. The rebellion in Aquitaine was over, apart from the retribution that Richard continued to exact in the duchy from those who had finished on the wrong side. Viscount Aimar surrendered Limoges on 24 June. The hurriedly erected temporary fortifications were pulled back down once more to again emasculate the citadel.

For the ambitious Richard, there was slightly less grief at the death of his brother. He was now in pole position to inherit everything. New vistas had opened up. Richard had proved himself again, this time at the side of his father. Though Henry II was shrewd enough to realise that Richard was far from flawless he would be forced to rely more than ever on him now. It is debatable whether or not the Young King would ever have matured into a competent monarch. Now, anyway, that conversation was completely hypothetical.

4

Crisis (1184–1188)

'O Lord, show unto us thy mercy'

From a crusader prayer of 1188

The premature demise of the Young King opened up the prospect of a glorious inheritance to Richard. His elder brother had been without doubt the *primus inter pares*, already a crowned king of England – if without real power – and the duke of both Normandy and Anjou. A great prize was now seemingly available to Richard. Yet rather than new doors being opened, they were instead slammed in his face. The reason for this was down to the idiosyncrasies of two men; Richard himself and his father Henry II.

Perhaps after all they were too much alike; stubborn, suspicious, distrusting; even, and especially, of their own kinfolk. They shared more in common than they would like to admit, both fiercely protective of their rights. Richard may have been regarded then and since as a 'mother's boy', something which would only have made Henry II even more watchful of him as Eleanor remained under close guard. But Richard was perhaps closer in temperament to his father than either man would willingly concede.

Henry was careful not to give too much away after the death of his eldest son. There may be several reasons for this. Firstly, he had a great depth of feeling for the late Young King, perhaps more than for any of his other sons, even John. Richard did not seem to have had the same hold over him. Perhaps, too, Henry sensed in Richard a greater danger to his authority than had ever come from the ambitious but feckless Young King. That previous experiment had not ended well; as one man remarked, the Young King had caused his father 'endless troubles by his unrighteous and vexatious conduct'.[1]

Specific problems between Henry and Richard are referred to in the works of modern historians. The French writer Jean Flori suggests that Henry distrusted Richard for 'his quick temper, his fits of rage and his independent temperament'.[2] It was also true that he had not always been loyal, but then neither had the Young King. Richard had at least buckled down and more recently had sought to further his father's interests and had proved a loyal lieutenant to him. He had performed very effectively, far more so than his late brother had. And perhaps this was the secret of Henry's mistrust; Richard was too much of a threat.

Then there was Eleanor's situation to consider. In a family that was split down the middle, Richard was in his mother's camp. Maybe handing over all the late Young King's rights seemed too much of a concession to the opposition. This would have been a very natural and human calculation on Henry's part given his frosty relationship with Eleanor. He might also have regretted handing over so much notional, if not actual, power to the Young King and saw this as an opportunity to claw some of it back. Even in the death of his eldest and most loved son, the king, considered by some to be as cunning as a fox, saw an opening.

We should not overlook Richard's character either. His pride had already been seen in his stern treatment of the rebels in Aquitaine. Power needed to be exercised wisely, even on occasion with tact. In his crushing of rebellion in the duchy, Richard had exhibited little of that. Perhaps now there was the danger that too much power would rush to Richard's head and as a result make him uncontrollable.

It was a difficult calculation for Henry; a quarrel loomed and it was a struggle for power that initiated it. Henry's youngest son, John, had been designated king of Ireland. This sounded a rather grander and more substantial title than it actually was. Ireland was not firmly integrated into Henry's federation as it was far from conquered.

Henry was not the last monarch to find out that the conquest of Ireland was rather more straightforward in theory than it was in practice. Beyond 'The Pale', the area around Dublin, and a few other settlements, much of the island remained stubbornly resistant to any suggestion of subservience to Henry. It soon became apparent that taking and subduing Ireland would be a very long-term assignment with absolutely no guarantees of success.

The death of the Young King gave Henry the chance to find another role for John instead of this rather ambitious one. John's nominal claim to be king of Ireland was dropped and it was decided that he would instead make an ideal duke of Aquitaine. The trouble with this splendid plan was that there was already one of those in place and he showed no intention of giving up his title. Richard said he would think about the proposal but then fled from Henry's court at the first available opportunity.

Missives sent after him by Henry were responded to with defiance. Richard clearly had no intention of meekly handing over a region which he had fought long and hard over. Henry even told John to go and claim it for himself, though he did not provide him with the wherewithal for an army to do this. Nevertheless, after Henry had returned to England in 1184 John combined with his brother Geoffrey of Brittany and went on the offensive.

It was like poking a stick into a hornet's nest. Richard was already mature enough to expect such a move and had prepared for the eventuality. This included the hiring of mercenaries, amongst them men led by a captain named Mercadier who would play a prominent part in Richard's later career. Presumably Mercadier was well paid by Richard for his help but later he would develop a strong personal loyalty to him, something for which mercenaries were not generally well known. Geoffrey soon found that Brittany itself was under attack from Richard. Henry was now alarmed and summoned all his sons to England so that matters could be sorted out. He still had enough remaining authority for them to obey but a patched-up reconciliation did little to dispel the tension.

Henry was now in his fifties and ageing, overweight and looking his years as well as being left with a limp after a hunting accident. He had not yet named a successor. The concept of primogeniture was not yet decisive and there had been recent cases of succession disputes on the death of a king, such as those which followed the demise of William the Conqueror or Henry I. This ambiguity probably suited Henry quite well as it kept his shrinking brood of quarrelling sons on some kind of a leash.

However, one thing did emerge soon after in a tantalising comment in the chronicle of Roger of Howden that Normandy was to be put under the guardianship of Geoffrey of Brittany. In a geographical sense, this was not unreasonable as Brittany and Normandy were adjacent. But it is also hard not to see this as a warning to Richard that he should not now assume that all the territories which had once been notionally under the rule of the Young King would ultimately pass to him. He had been required to toe the line on Aquitaine and had singularly failed to do so.

The ongoing delay in the marriage of Richard and Alice, which by now was reaching ridiculous proportions, re-emerged as an issue. Philip was keen to move matters to a definitive conclusion. At a meeting between the kings at the castle on the Norman border at Gisors in December 1183 this inevitably was one of the topics of discussion. Here Henry introduced an intriguing idea; why not marry Alice off to John? Given the fact that she was such a prized catch, this must have set off further alarm bells with Richard, perhaps even alerting him to the danger that John would be named heir to some of Henry's territories rather than him.

There was, nevertheless, a public reconciliation between the quarrelling brothers at Westminster in late 1184. On 30 November, the whole family was reunited. Henry's sons came together and even Eleanor, by now enjoying more exposure to public life though still closely watched, was there. As well as family matters, the selection of a new archbishop of Canterbury was also one of the items on the agenda.

Richard's marriage possibilities were still a point of discussion, even though he was betrothed to Alice. Philip's half-sister flits in and out of the picture during these years though she does emerge from the shadows occasionally; for example, we know that she was residing in Winchester at this time. A delegation (led by the archbishop of Cologne) from the Holy Roman Emperor Frederick Barbarossa offering his daughter as a prospective wife for Richard aroused Henry's interest; it would certainly unsettle Philip of France, though it came to nothing because the potential bride-to-be died not long after.

Eleanor's presence at the discussions was most likely to get her acquiescence to Henry's plans for Aquitaine. Henry asked Eleanor to give Aquitaine to John. She refused. Neither did she stand alone. The new archbishop of Canterbury, Baldwin of Forde, supported her, as did several other leading lords. Faced by this opposition and the fact that Eleanor would probably be backed by Philip of France in any dispute, Henry was unable to force the issue and backed down.

Just before Christmas, Geoffrey was sent to Normandy to keep an eye on the duchy for Henry, another snub for Richard. This led to speculation that Geoffrey might be named Henry's heir.[3] This must have infuriated Richard and fuelled his suspicion of his father. A further deterioration in their relationship was now highly likely. Christmas that year was kept at Windsor with the rest of the family. Soon afterwards, Richard returned to Poitou.

On the horizon an international crisis was looming that threatened to move the attention of the West eastwards. Since the capture of the Holy City in 1099, the kingdom of Jerusalem had progressively seen its power decline. After an initial few years of conquest and consolidation, the kingdom had been under increasing threat. Its high-water mark had ironically arrived not long after its great initial triumph at Jerusalem.

The threats were now reaching crisis proportions. The neighbouring Muslim territories of Syria and Egypt were united under one leader for the first time in centuries, under the control of the ambitious and politically astute Saladin. Jerusalem on the other hand was ruled by a young, inexperienced king, Baldwin IV. He was suffering from that most awful medieval malady, leprosy. His efforts to overcome the worst effects of this terrible curse were valiant and determined; no one could accuse the king of being a coward or lacking persistence. But his life could only be eked out for a few years and there was no obvious successor to replace him. In these circumstances, the long-term prospects for the kingdom were gloomy.

Heraclius, the Patriarch of Jerusalem, made his way to Western Europe in 1184. Little meaningful support had come from there to the threatened kingdom for nearly four decades. Help was urgently needed and Heraclius had a clear idea of where he might get it. One of his main targets was England, though he also visited Italy and Paris, meeting both Frederick Barbarossa and Philip of France in the process.

Reaching England, Heraclius first met Henry II at Reading. There were further meetings in London. Whilst he was there Heraclius consecrated the Temple Church, now hidden away in a prestigious legal district just off the Strand in London. Over the door there is still a Latin inscription noting his visit and its purpose.

Heraclius came accompanied by a letter from Pope Lucius III which was blunt in its assessment of the parlous situation facing Outremer. It spoke of a 'time when peril or even extermination is dreaded as impending over the Christian people', that Outremer was 'being now trampled under foot, and hemmed in by the pressure of a perfidious and most abominable race, it stands nodding to its downfall'.[4] Nature was also supportive of the notion that something sinister was abroad; there were famines, earthquakes and frequent eclipses of the moon and the sun according to one chronicler, all suggesting that there was something amiss in the balance of nature.[5]

Heraclius came carrying the keys of the city of Jerusalem and those of the Church of the Holy Sepulchre (on which, appropriately enough, the Temple Church was modelled). He presented these to Henry, inviting him to take up the responsibilities of the king of Jerusalem (it was said that a similar ritual had also been played out in Paris with Philip of France). There may have been some tugging at the heartstrings here, for Henry's grandfather had once been so, and many prominent crusaders were driven to make their vows by family tradition. Henry had also made a pledge to go on crusade as part of his penance for the murder of Thomas Becket.

Yet the timing could not have been worse. Henry was struggling to keep control of his strong-willed sons and God alone knew what would happen if he departed the scene and left them to their own devices. He nevertheless discussed the matter with his baronss at the Council of Clerkenwell, a meeting that lasted for days before they recommended that he should not take up the offer, no doubt to his great relief. They said that his first responsibility must be to his own people, also probably sensing that if Henry were to depart then the Angevin federation would quickly start to disintegrate.

Neither did Heraclius make a universally good impression. Some of the more conservative West Europeans who saw him and his entourage were shocked at the expensive jewellery and the lavish trappings of power that they ostentatiously displayed as they processed around the region, as well as the fumes of the incenses that betrayed their presence as they passed through the courts of kings and emperors.[6]

Henry would not go, and neither would his sons. With extensive lands to rule including Aquitaine, Anjou, Normandy, Brittany, England and Wales, and potentially Ireland too, and with his sons an essential part of the system of government, they could not be spared. Instead Henry made generous monetary gifts to help support the kingdom of Jerusalem. It may have salved his conscience but it was not what Heraclius or the kingdom needed.

In the words of Gerald of Wales, the Patriarch left England to return east, muttering that 'all the world will offer us money, but it is a prince we need; we would prefer a leader even without money, to money without a leader'.[7]

That said, many did ceremonially take the cross. Those that did so included Baldwin, the archbishop of Canterbury; Walter of Coutances, the archbishop of Rouen; Hugh, the bishop of Durham, and some knights from England, Normandy, Aquitaine, Brittany, Anjou, Maine and Touraine.[8] Impressive though this list was, it was one thing to take crusader vows, quite another to fulfil them.

The times continued to be inauspicious, with the year 1185, when Heraclius returned to Jerusalem, marked by bad omens. A serious earthquake struck England, badly damaging the church at Lincoln; Heraclius was still in the country at the time. That same month, May, 'a total eclipse of the sun was seen, which was followed by thunder and lightning, and a mighty tempest; from the effects of which men and animals perished, and many houses, being set on fire thereby, were burned to the ground'.[9] These were harrowing times and it was easy to interpret such portents as a sign that God Himself was angry.

The intransigence of Richard regarding Aquitaine continued. Henry might not have had the spring of youth in his step anymore but he was still more than capable of standing up to an errant son. In 1185 he appeared in Normandy with an army, planning to march with Geoffrey and bring Richard to book. But he also came armed with a cunning plan. As Richard had himself pointed out on occasion, Aquitaine was really Eleanor's and Henry II saw this as the ideal moment to release her from custody and demand that Richard hand Aquitaine back to her. He told Richard bluntly that if he did not comply, then Eleanor herself would lead an army against him.

It was a stroke of brilliance and completely wrong-footed Richard. He lay down his arms and Aquitaine reverted to Eleanor. She herself found her public position improved, for a time at least, which is presumably why she went along with the plan even though it disadvantaged Richard. However, for Henry and his relationship with his eldest living son, the damage had already been done and was now terminal. Henry continued to calculate that ambiguity regarding the succession would be a key safeguard of his position. This must have infuriated Richard still further.

Nevertheless, Richard at last toed the line, at least in public. Whilst he gained a reputation for obstinacy he again buckled down, perhaps because of his closeness to his mother rather than any respect for his father or, equally as likely, because he felt his cause was best served for waiting for the right moment to strike: revenge is a dish best served cold. Henry and Richard, in the meantime, decided that the thorny issue of Toulouse needed to be resolved. Count Raymond of Toulouse had supported the rebels in the recent uprising in Aquitaine and should be punished for his temerity.

Philip of France did not stay on the sidelines for long and threw another issue into the melting-pot in 1186. Probably encouraged by Geoffrey of Brittany, he started to again put pressure on Henry for the marriage of Alice and Richard to go ahead. As the betrothal had been announced in 1161, and since Alice had been in Henry's custody, this did not seem unreasonable. There were issues at stake far above domestic happiness though. As part of her maritagium, or marriage settlement, the key frontier territory of the Vexin on the borders of Normandy had been given to Henry.

It was embarrassing and harmful to the image of the French Crown that no marriage had taken place a quarter of a century after the betrothal had been announced. Therefore, Philip wanted the marriage to proceed without any further dissimulation or delay. There were also rumours that Geoffrey had been negotiating privately with Philip to take over the rule of Normandy after laying it waste in a large raid from Brittany.

The year 1186 turned out to be crucial for the Angevins in several ways. On a positive front, the new kingdom of Ireland was at last recognised by the Papacy, there being a special protocol for such matters. A crown adorned with peacock feathers was sent in recognition though the reality was that the military campaigning that had taken place on the island towards the end of the previous year had done nothing to secure the English hold over Ireland. This step was really a cosmetic one. It was an initiative launched by the new Pope, Urban III, who had recently taken the place of Lucius III and wanted to establish a strong relationship with Henry.

But then Henry II suffered a further blow. His son Geoffrey was a keen participant in tournaments just as the late Young King had been. Taking part in one such event in Paris in August, the over-enthusiastic Geoffrey was fatally injured (other less dramatic versions of his end say he died of a fever; but Roger of Howden said unambiguously that he died 'from bruises which he had received from the hoofs of horses') .[10]

Despite the fractured family relationship that Henry and his wife and children enjoyed, this was a further shock for the king, though he did not grieve for Geoffrey in the same way that he had for the Young King. Of the five sons born to him and Eleanor, three were now dead. This left just the increasingly assertive and hard-to-control Richard and the young, inexperienced and previously unsuccessful John. Henry needed a counterbalance to Richard and his ambitions and it must have been concerning to him that he was now forced to rely on John for this, despite his insignificant experience and chequered track record.

Increasingly Henry and Richard were at loggerheads. There was respect from Henry to his eldest son from time to time but there was little in the way of loyalty from either side. This probably reflected as much as anything the way that the family unit had broken down. Richard and Eleanor's closeness is well known and, given the fact that she had nurtured him for many of the formative years of his life, is unsurprising. The long-term imprisonment of Eleanor must have rankled with Richard.

There was a sadness at the heart of the family and the contemporary writer Gerald of Wales wrote a story that eloquently portrayed it. It concerned a brightly coloured chamber in Winchester Castle. Here there was a blank space on the wall, waiting to be filled by order of the king. He later did so with a creation of his own design. On it was painted an eagle. Four young eagles were perched on the parent bird. Two were on its wings and a third on its back, all pecking at it. The fourth was pecking at its eyes.

In case there was any ambiguity about what this disturbing symbol meant, Henry explained it plainly. The four birds on the parent eagle were his sons who would not, the king said, 'cease persecuting me even unto death'. The youngest, the king sagely suggested, the one who he embraced 'with such tender affection', would turn on him and 'afflict me more grievously and perilously than all the others'. It spoke of a tragic bitterness at the heart of this dysfunctional family.[11]

The death of Geoffrey came as a strategic blow to Henry; it compromised his plans to play off his sons against each other. It also coincided with a worsening of relations between him and Philip of France. These events were not unconnected. Philip was close to Geoffrey, or at least participated closely with his scheming; it was said that he was so moved at Geoffrey's burial that he had to be physically restrained from throwing himself in his grave in the choir of the unfinished cathedral of Nôtre Dame in Paris. Geoffrey had been a useful counterbalance to the ambitious and threatening Henry. Now he was gone. So too was the Young King, on the whole unthreatening, a dreamer, no real threat to Philip in France and easily manipulated by his father.

Philip was quick to stake a claim to Brittany, which he was formally overlord of anyway. Geoffrey's widow was pregnant at the time of his death and some seven months later, on 29 March 1187, Constance gave birth to a son. He was named, with optimism, Arthur, for Brittany was much connected to the Arthurian legends. His life though would be short and tragic, brought to a premature close when he was just a young man because he posed too great a threat to the claims to the English crown of his uncle, John. Constance was now taken under the protection of Philip, along with the two daughters born to her and Geoffrey previously. It was no doubt kind of Philip to assume this role but it is likely that it was the political advantages that it gave the French king that were prominent in his mind.

Looking after Geoffrey's heir was a consideration more for the future than the present. For Philip, this left just Henry II, his son Richard and the increasingly significant John to worry about. John seems to have resembled most closely his late brother Geoffrey. He had physical similarities to him, being thick-set with reddish hair and he too was a lover of extravagance. Like his father, he was obsessive about the hunt too. He was also, in the opinion of some, lazy and indolent. Whatever could be said of Richard, these were faults that could not be laid at his door.

Henry and Richard posed a much greater threat to Philip. For some years, Henry and Philip had been, on the surface at least, on good terms. In the early years of the decade, this suited Philip's purpose. His position in France was far from secure and he needed allies against powerful vassals inside the country; Angevin help was useful as a counter-balance. But in 1186 that all changed. Philip once again demanded action on the marriage of Richard and his sister Alice. But Henry continued to prevaricate. Richard by this stage had completely lost interest in the plan too – if indeed he had ever had any. By this time he was looking at an alternative bride, Princess Berengaria of Navarre.

A marriage with Berengaria would benefit both parties. The Angevins would gain an ally on their southern Aquitanian borders, able to act as a counterbalance to the Counts of Toulouse. On the other hand, the small kingdom of Navarre would receive a powerful ally against the neighbouring kingdoms of Castile, Leon and Aragon. Navarre was in an important strategic position, on the Pyrenean borders of what is now France and Spain and astride the important pilgrim route to Santiago de Compostella. The royal family could claim an illustrious heritage going back to the valiant and renowned hero El Cid.[12] Politically, this was a match that made a lot of sense.

Some chroniclers suggested that Richard had met Berengaria some time before. Although she is first mentioned in the chronicles only in 1191, Ambroise and the writer of the *Itinerarium Peregrinorum* suggest that Richard and Berengaria had met some time previously. One suggestion is that this was at a tournament, though this is not wholly convincing; Navarre was not a hotbed of tournament activity and there is little evidence that Richard frequently participated in such events. A much respected early twentieth-century biographer of Richard, Kate Norgate, believes that discussions could be dated as far back as 1183. However, she believes that it is likely that these discussions were kept secret for several years.[13]

Bertran de Born was delighted when Richard chose Berengaria as his bride rather than Alice in a poem that some have dated (though there is not unanimous agreement on this) to 1188. It is not at all unlikely that Richard and Berengaria might have met at some time in the past. Given the position of Navarre, next to Richard's territories in the south-west of France, it is by no means improbable that he would have visited the court there on diplomatic business and on one such visit he might well have met Berengaria.[14] However, a romantic attachment from early on seems unlikely given the course of their future relationship.

In the ideals of the time, at least as imagined in the make-believe world of the writers of chivalric romanticism, such a union should involve love. Richard's own trouvère, Blondel of Nesle, wrote that 'my lady is like water and fire; and she can inflame me or extinguish me'.[15] There is no convincing evidence that Berengaria ever did anything to ignite any flame in Richard; quite the opposite in fact.

The dilatory efforts taken by Henry and Richard as far as Alice was concerned were probably evidence that they did not perceive this to be the best match that could be made given other potential suitors. Conversely, a ready-made excuse was at hand for Philip to stir up trouble whenever he could take advantage of it. He now felt that such a moment had arrived.

Philip demanded that Richard remove himself from the county of Toulouse, where he had recently intervened with an army. He had no legitimate interest there, the French king asserted. If he did not do so, then Philip would attack Normandy. As much as anything this was a sign of a young king who was finding his feet and was prepared to face up to his powerful Angevin vassals. He had not yet decided to definitively take them on but he was flexing his muscles. His opposition to the Angevins would continue to grow.

The problem in Toulouse had occurred because the count had taken advantage of the disunity of Henry II's family to seize several Angevin-held castles there. After Richard temporarily patched up his difficulties with his father, he took a force of mercenaries financed by Henry II to sort things out. In typical fashion, he did not limit himself to reconquering the lost castles but also took others that had not been held by the Angevins previously.

Alarmed, the count of Toulouse had appealed to Philip for redress and it was in response that the French king had issued his demands to Henry II. Discussions were held and a temporary and insecure truce was agreed. Neither Henry nor Philip wished to push the point at this moment in time. Nevertheless, they both gathered their forces in a show of strength.

Matters came to a head when the two large forces faced each other at Châteauroux. Open conflict seemed possible but the two kings had drawn back from the brink. Philip had already pushed his forces into Berry, an area where there were tangled relationships with both Angevins and Capetians in possession of some of the key places. However, open battle was rare at this stage of medieval warfare: the outcomes were too uncertain. Sieges and skirmishes, bluster and negotiation, were more the norm. Even a famous warrior like Richard fought few major battles in his life.

There were stories that at Châteauroux divine intervention played its part. It was said that one of Richard's mercenary soldiers was so upset when he lost a game of dice in the town square that he threw a stone carelessly in the general direction of a statue of the Virgin. It struck the arm of the Christ Child that she was holding, which duly started to bleed.[16] Due to this miraculous sign of divine disapproval, open conflict was avoided as those present were overawed by these events.

There were, no doubt, many prospective crusaders who were becoming frustrated at these internal squabbles. The news from Outremer was discouraging and suggested an urgent need for help from Western Europe. These delays seemed immoral to some; while we may be cynical about the morality of crusading from a modern perspective, to the medieval crusader it was undoubtedly seen as a moral act. Not only did this infighting hold back the departure date of any potential crusade, it also depleted the funds available for it.

Philip, an astute politician, had detected a chink of weakness in the Angevin position in the shape of Richard. At Châteauroux he had attempted to split him away from his father. He had not at the time succeeded but he had seen enough prevarication to try again at some point in the future.

When Richard returned south, the count of Flanders came to see him as an envoy. He carried a message from Philip, suggesting that Henry was going to disinherit Richard and marry off Alice to John. There was enough conviction and credibility in what he said to feed Richard's insecurities. Shortly afterwards, he visited Philip in Paris. Here they formed such a close relationship that they even shared a bedchamber at night, though for the sake of clarification when looked at from a modern perspective and later stories about Richard's sexuality this was by no means conclusive evidence of a homosexual relationship.[17] Far more worrying to Henry was the suddenly close political relationship between Philip and Richard.

Much has been made of those words of Richard and Philip sharing a bed. To one historian, they confirmed that the two men became lovers.[18] What has not been talked about so much is the terminology that chroniclers employ to describe the strength of the relationship, using the word *vehementer*, which suggested a deep intensity. Henry was dumbfounded, reading Roger of Howden's words not so much by the fact that a friendship had formed but at how intense it seemed to be. As one historian remarked, 'it hardly suggests mere mateship'. Whether sexual or not, there clearly seems to have been something very deeply felt going on here. This may help to explain the bitterness that ensued when the relationship later disintegrated.[19]

Richard had decided that the time for revenge against his father had now arrived. From Paris he made his way to Chinon. Here he took as many arms from the arsenal as he could find and moved back south to Poitou, where he fortified his castles. Messengers arrived from his father demanding that he come and explain himself. Richard was not at this stage ready for an open breach. He acceded and once again matters were patched up, but this was a truce in the intra-family conflict and an absence of war in this case definitely did not equate to peace. It was only a matter of time before problems flared up once more.

By 1187, Philip was completely exasperated with the continuing insincerity of Henry and demanded that the English king hand back to him both his sister Alice and her dowry, the Norman frontier lands of the Vexin. That same year Philip's wife gave birth to a son and heir, further strengthening the self-confidence of the French king.

And then a hammer blow was launched from the East. The dire warnings of Heraclius now came home to roost with a vengeance. The gallant but cursed Baldwin IV did indeed succumb to his leprosy shortly after Heraclius returned without the manpower or the prince that was desperately needed. That said, according to Roger of Howden there was 'an immense multitude of men-at-arms and other pilgrims' who came to Jerusalem on pilgrimage. But they did not stay long and did not provide a long-term solution to Outremer's problems.[20] The leper king was replaced on his death by a young boy, Baldwin V, but he did not survive long either.

This left no immediate heir to the kingdom. The next surviving person in the royal line was a woman, Sibylla (who was Richard's cousin), and she could not rule without a king. However, her husband, Guy of Lusignan, was not popular and the barons of the kingdom did not want to serve him. Nevertheless, it was he who became the new king of Jerusalem. The Lusignan family emanated from Aquitaine and as such were vassals of Richard as the duke of the duchy. This was a fact that would within a few years assume great significance.

Guy's hawkish policies were a disaster for the kingdom. Saladin launched a huge invasion of Outremer, with tens of thousands of troops from across his lands. Guy assembled a substantial army in response, the largest that the kingdom had ever put together. The best policy was for Guy to stay on the defensive. It would be difficult for Saladin to keep his army supplied in the parching summer heat.

In Guy's army were most of the men from the garrisons of the major cities of the kingdom. The Military Orders, the Templars and the Hospitallers, contributed large numbers of men in support. The huge size of this force fuelled euphoria; such an army, marching under the sign of the Cross (literally, for a fragment of the relic known as the True Cross was carried before them), was surely invincible.

A kind of hysteria descended on the crusader army. The king, who needed to prove himself, allowed himself to be convinced that the army should go on to the attack. So he led his men out into the barren, largely waterless lands that led east towards Saladin's mighty force.

This was a gift to Saladin. Within a few miles, sniping attacks were launched by highly mobile Saracen cavalry. But this was not the greatest enemy. The fierce heat of the summer sun sucked the life out of the men as they marched. It was only a matter of time before they began to run short of water. Men started to fall out, in ones and twos at first and then in much larger numbers. By the evening of 3 July 1187, the army could at last see water in the distance in the form of Lake Tiberias. But a far more terrible sight also met their eyes; between them and the water was Saladin's massive army.

Guy's men, exhausted and dehydrated, soon found themselves surrounded. Through that long and weary night they could hear the exultant celebrations of Saladin's army, who were confident of victory. Their confidence was not misplaced: this was the last night of the kingdom of Jerusalem. The following day the Saracens attacked with a ferocity that was fuelled by the certainty of success. Guy's army was destroyed, being overwhelmed at last around two hills known as the Horns of Hattin. The king was captured and every single Templar or Hospitaller warrior who was taken alive was executed. Worst of all perhaps, the relic of the True Cross was lost; the bishop of Acre, who accompanied it, did not survive the battle. It appeared to be the death knell of the kingdom of Jerusalem.

What happened next did little to dispel the impression. With insufficient manpower and still less hope, city after city was taken. Acre, later the site of a massive and extended siege when Richard arrived on campaign a few years later, was lost to the crusaders less than a week after Hattin. Sidon and Beirut fell to the north, whilst Ascalon, a key frontier town, was taken in the south.

In October came the heaviest blow of all. With no possibility of rescue, Jerusalem itself, Al-Quds, the Holy City, surrendered. This was as a result of a negotiated settlement and as the Muslim forces, ecstatic at their triumph, entered the city there was no blood-letting, no massacre, in vivid contrast to what had happened there when the first crusaders had captured Jerusalem in 1099. Those who could paid a ransom and the rich and well-connected made their way out of the city and westwards towards freedom, amongst their number the Patriarch Heraclius. For thousands of poorer citizens a life of slavery beckoned.

Many traces of Christianity were removed from the city. According to Roger of Howden, the Cross was pulled down from 'the Temple of our Lord', the Dome of the Rock, built on the spot from which Muhammad made his miraculous night journey into Heaven. The Cross was then, he said, ceremonially beaten for two days, Muslims rejecting the concept of the Crucifixion on theological grounds. The building was also washed and purified with rosewater, both inside and out.[21]

Communication in those days was by nature slow but when the news reached the West the reaction was one of overwhelming shock, disbelief even, fuelled by a sense of guilt that the West had nothing to help prevent this catastrophe, even after Heraclius's plea for help in 1185. The chronicler Ambroise summed up the sense of grief: 'through this great disaster all people, throughout the world, of high or low estate, were afflicted and could scarcely be comforted'.[22]

The loss of Jerusalem was such a shock that Pope Urban III died as soon as he heard of it. His successor, Gregory VIII, fared no better; he became Pope on 21 October 1187 and was dead by December of the same year, being succeeded by Clement III. In his short pontificate, Gregory had written to the kings and great men of the West in terms of barely concealed incomprehension; there were several long, rambling letters that spoke of a man who was tortured by the burden that had suddenly been placed on him; 'both we and our brethren have been put to confusion with terror so extreme, and afflicted with sorrows so great, that it did not readily suggest itself to us what we were to do, or what indeed we ought to do'.

The flesh of the servants of God had been fed to the vultures of the desert whilst that of the saints had been given to the beasts of the earth, he said. In Gregory's opinion, it was 'dissension' amongst Christians that had led to such an unbelievable state of affairs and the 'iniquity of sinful people' had led God to turn His back on His flock.[23] It was now time for this to stop. In his brief but significant reign, he also issued a formal Papal bull, the *Audita Tremendi*, which was the formal call to arms in response to the news of Hattin.

For many, the loss of Jerusalem required a decisive and instant response. Richard took the vow of a crusader almost as soon as he heard the news in November 1187. He did so in Tours Cathedral, only recently rebuilt after being burned in the wars between Henry II and Louis VII just two decades before. He was following in the footsteps of his great-grandfather Fulk of Anjou, who had headed out east earlier in the century to become king of Jerusalem. There were many instances of family history encouraging later generations to become crusaders; other examples can be found in the Counts of Champagne in France or the Montferrat family from what is now Italy. These families were to play key roles in the crusade that now loomed.

Now the reality of the parlous state of Outremer hit home. As one historian has put it, 'pious promises and conscience-salving donations were at last replaced by the armies of the Third Crusade'.[24] The business of crusading was soon to be characterised by a new phrase, the *negotium sanctum*, 'the holy business'. This was all very well but the key question was, was it too little, too late?

The immediacy of Richard's reaction suggested that the news touched a particular nerve. Here was a chance to win renown. Some historians see impetuosity in his quick reaction and this may be so. But an alternative interpretation is that this was a display of decisiveness, the seizing of an opportunity to be at the forefront of the crusade. He was after all not a king, he had not yet even been declared heir. The crusade offered him a chance of glory and through this recognition.

Henry and Philip were slower to respond. Henry had sent money in response to the Patriarch Heraclius's appeal during his visit to the West in 1185, some of which had probably gone towards financing the army that had been annihilated at Hattin. There had even been some Englishmen fighting there such as Roger of Mowbray and Hugh of Beauchamp; Beauchamp, as he lay dying, came up with the excruciating pun that he had never been in beau champ (i.e. paradise) until today.[25] Now something more was expected of the king.

Richard's taking of the cross, probably in advance of the receipt of the Papal bull, greatly perturbed his father.[26] It was an act of huge political and financial significance and Henry was dismayed at Richard's decision. He locked himself away for four days in a state of shock. His reaction evidenced an ongoing resentment between father and son. But Richard may well have acted out of frustration. Henry was showing no obvious signs of weakening and could be king of England for years into the future. On the other hand, Heraclius had been in London just a couple of years before offering the throne of Jerusalem to either Henry or one of his sons. With the precedent of his great-grandfather Fulk of Anjou before him, perhaps this was an irresistible lure for Richard at this precise moment in his life. Rather than piety driving his response, ambition seems a more likely motivator.

Philip was not happy with Richard either. Richard could use his decision as yet another excuse to delay his marriage to Alice. Philip was not going to tolerate this and, accompanied by another large force, set out for Gisors to meet Henry again. They met in a 'great and lovely meadow' on a beautiful sunny day in January 1188[27] but this was to be no convivial picnic in the pristine French countryside. Here they were preached at by the archbishop of Tyre, who urged them to bury their differences and concentrate on preparing a large expedition to the East.

Sensing that the tide of public opinion was flowing against them, Henry and Philip both took the cross, becoming *crucesignati* as it was known. They were joined by many knights who were so overwhelmed by emotion that some of them collapsed. A truce was agreed between the warring kings that was supposed to last for seven years.

It was said, in one of the classic *topoi* of the time, that a cross could be seen in the sky, a mark of divine approbation for the decision made by the two monarchs. This mirrored a similar incident in the previous year at Dunstable, England, when the clouds opened and a cross could be seen, with Christ nailed to it, His feet and His side scarlet but His blood not falling from the sky.[28]

Special crusader prayers were written asking that God show mercy on his people. 'Save thy people, O Lord. Be thou to them a tower of strength. Let not their enemies prevail against them'. The Pope and his cardinals, in the prayer they wrote for the peace and deliverance of the land of Jerusalem, begged that God might forgive His people their sins and that He should not cast them off forever.[29]

Henry now called on his substantial administrative resources across his territories to impose a heavy tax which became known as the 'Saladin Tithe'. This was to be collected based on an assessment of 10 per cent of the value of movable property and revenues.

This was no 'light touch' collection process. The 200 richest men in London and the 100 wealthiest in York (with men from other cities in proportion to their population) were summoned to personal hearings where their stores of wealth were examined and the assessment on them was confirmed. Any who appeared 'contumacious' in their response were put in irons and locked up in prison until they saw the error of their ways. Jews were subjected to similar treatment. Henry even tried to extract the tithe from King William of Scotland, though with limited success.[30]

The Tithe was not popular, not so much for the amounts involved but rather for the dangerous precedent that it set. In France, where it was also imposed, it was so unpopular that Philip had to withdraw it, though no such thing happened in the territories of Henry II, demonstrating the greater degree of control that the latter enjoyed in his territories at the time. That said, there is evidence from the reign of his son Richard that further south in places like Poitiers and Limoges even the Angevins had trouble raising the tax and had to secure papal support in their efforts to collect all the amounts due.[31] But soon money was flowing from out of the coffers to towns involved in procuring supplies for the crusade; 200 marks to Bristol, 2,500 marks to Gloucester, 5,000 marks to Southampton.[32] (A mark equated to two thirds of one pound, though it was a unit of accounting and not an actual coin.)

Archbishop Baldwin famously went on a recruitment drive in Wales. Details of this were later written up by Gerald of Wales. It was said that Baldwin forced his entourage to walk rather than ride up the steep Welsh valleys as a form of physical training for their forthcoming exertions in Outremer.[33] Gerald himself took the cross in Radnor (though like many clerics he never subsequently actually made the journey east). Rather than a spontaneous gesture triggered by Baldwin's eloquence and genuine crusader emotion, this was all part of a pre-arranged plan by which others present would be emotionally moved to also become *crucesignati*.[34] It was all very well stage-managed.

It would be some time before the crusade was ready to set out. Not only would it take a while to collect all the taxes due but there were many logistical arrangements to be made to provision such a large army. The route of the expedition also needed to be agreed and transport arrangements made. Politics too played their part; both Henry and Philip would want to ensure stability in France before they left. There was a deep distrust between the two men;

each wanted to ensure that their plans were co-ordinated so that no skulduggery could take place if Henry left in advance of Philip or vice-versa.

It was decided that those marching under the banner of the king of England would wear white crosses, those from France red, and the expected contingent from Flanders green (the latter a form of recognition of the power of the very autonomous count of that region). Men who took the cross would be exempted from the Saladin Tithe, not unreasonably given the risk that they were taking and the cost of their own personal crusading plans. Crusaders would be given some exemptions on their debts while they were away.[35]

The spiritual benefits obtained from crusading were probably still a prime incentive for many. Those involved were to be given indulgences. When men and women confessed their sins, they were required by the practices of the time to undertake defined penances. The indulgences issued by the Church acted as remissions of these penances. It might seem a fine academic point to the modern mind but such things were keenly felt in the twelfth century.

There was no further reason to prevaricate; the clock was ticking and with each passing day the West's tenuous foothold in Outremer became less secure. But despite the euphoria and regardless of the bravado, time passed and nothing happened. So great was the distrust between Henry and Philip that excuse after excuse followed. And in the background Richard's frustrations grew, a build-up of volcanic emotions that was about to erupt and blow apart the Angevin dynasty. Richard was on the verge of a decision that would obliterate the last vestigial residue of affection between father and son.

5

The Bitter Inheritance (1188–1189)

'The lord Yea and Nay has been burning and shedding blood'
Bertran de Born, the Occitan troubadour,
on the actions of Prince Richard

However impulsive he might seem to be, Richard had no intention of leaving for the East without resolving the situation concerning his inheritance. Richard rightly feared that John would attempt to take advantage if anything happened to his father whilst he was away. Henry now suggested that he himself would accompany Richard on crusade. As he had vowed to go nearly two decades before after the death of Becket and had not yet done so, it is likely that few believed him.

Richard also had unfinished business in Toulouse to sort out. Shortly before, some traders from Aquitaine were badly treated by Raymond of Toulouse (an understatement: depending on which account is to be believed they were either put in prison, castrated, blinded or killed). Richard now stormed into the region with an army to seek retribution. Once more, the gains from his subsequent conquests far outweighed the wrongs committed against him with seventeen castles being captured. The region known as the Quercy came under his control, a dominance reinforced by the installation of a garrison at Cahors.

Richard fought an extremely fierce campaign. He 'entered the territories of the count of St Gilles [the count of Toulouse] with a great army, laid it waste with fire and sword, and besieged and took his castles in the neighbourhood of Toulouse'.[1] At one stage, even the city of Toulouse itself was threatened. The count of Toulouse once more sought protection from Philip. The French king did not want to alienate Richard so tried to gingerly walk a middle path. He demanded that Henry II bring a stop to Richard's depredations, threatening to drive a wedge between father and son. But if some contemporary stories are to be believed Philip was secretly financing Raymond of Toulouse.

Not wishing to antagonise Philip further, Henry ordered Richard to rein in his raids. Richard refused to co-operate. Philip then invaded Berry, occupying a crucial strategic position between Normandy and Anjou in the north and Aquitaine further south. Several important towns including Châteauroux surrendered to Philip. Seeing that Loches, a key town in Anjou, was under threat, Henry decided to meet force with force. Large numbers of mercenaries were raised to face up to the threat from Philip.

Philip's response was to withdraw to Berry. This enabled Richard to recover a good proportion of the territories that had been lost. However, Châteauroux held out against him and in an attack on it Richard was thrown from his horse in a skirmish. He barely escaped, allegedly only with the help of a humble butcher – hardly a chivalrous withdrawal.

Richard was involved in personal combat with a French knight, William des Barres, during the fighting. William, who had won a fine reputation on the tournament fields of Western Europe,[2] lost and was captured. He was released on parole which he broke shortly afterwards. He then claimed that he had been unfairly beaten by Richard, who had killed his horse when he saw that he was losing; 'gamesmanship' as we would now call it was as much a feature of medieval tournaments as it is of modern football.

There were intermittent mêlées between the forces of Philip and Richard but no full-scale confrontation. More negotiations were arranged to put a stop to the fighting. The English and French kings again met at Gisors at the beginning of July 1188 to try to resolve the situation. Here there was an ancient elm tree, beneath which the kings of France and the dukes of Normandy had often met in the past to talk peace.

The negotiations started badly and got progressively worse. It became clear that Philip was in no mood to concede on virtually any point. But neither was Henry prepared to budge; the irresistible force against the immovable object. Tempers started to fray and then were lost completely. Philip ordered that the great elm tree be cut down in a decisive symbolic act; he and his entourage were outraged because they had been left standing in the sun whilst the Angevin party sheltered in the shade of the tree's branches.

The gloves were off but why had Philip been encouraged to take such a strong line? The answer was clear enough; there was an undermining influence in Henry's camp. Richard, still not declared Henry's heir, had had enough of his father's prevarication. He was moving closer to an alliance with Philip in an effort, still at this moment clandestine, to protect his inheritance. For some time he had had a foot in two camps, playing a double-game with potentially explosive ramifications.

On the surface, Richard was still acting as if he was supporting his father. Henry soon after launched an invasion of Philip's lands. The main attack was preceded by incendiaries, men tasked with setting fire to as much of the territory in front of them as they could. The *Chansons des Lorrains* describes the situation graphically:

> Soon all is in tumult. The peasants, just come out to the fields, turn back, uttering loud cries. The shepherds gather their flocks and drive them towards the neighbouring woods in the hope of saving them. The incendiaries set the villages on fire and the foragers visit and sack them. The terrified inhabitants are either burned or led away with their hands tied to be held for ransom. Everywhere bells ring the alarm; a surge of fear sweeps over the countryside. Wherever you look you can see helmets glinting in the sun, pennons waving in the breeze, the whole plain covered with horsemen. Money, cattle, mules and sheep are all seized. The smoke billows and spreads, flames crackle. Peasants and shepherds scatter in all directions.[3]

This was the reality of medieval warfare, not brightly caparisoned knights fighting in tournaments in make-believe tales of chivalry. In this kind of total war, the masses were the very deliberate target for they provided the lifeblood through which kingdoms survived. This was pre-planned, cold-blooded murder; destroy the flocks, the crops and the people who tended them and the region would grind to a halt. It also made the king look weak; he could not protect his people and therefore his credibility was compromised. But in this case the tactics did their job. Not only was Philip forced onto the back foot, Richard soon after presented himself to his father and promised him his loyalty.

One man was overjoyed at this turn of events. Bertran de Born was now firmly in Richard's camp and would remain there from now on. He had apparently been a beneficiary of Richard's largesse; 'I cannot help but spread the song around, since the lord Yea and Nay has been burning and shedding blood, because a great war makes the miserly lord generous'.[4]

Philip sought another conference. War was not in his interests at this time and the imperative to organise the crusade could only be put aside for so long. Henry, Richard and Philip met at Châtillon-sur-Indre though the discussions remained tense. Philip demanded that Richard give up his recent conquests in Toulouse, whereas Henry may have wanted to be more flexible on the issue. Soon after, Richard approached Philip directly to see if they could reach an accommodation of their own.

The plot thickened further when another round of three-way negotiations was arranged at Bonsmoulins. Again the discussions started off badly. They were not helped when Richard arrived in the company of Philip, making clear the direction in which his allegiance was headed. Over the course of three days matters once again deteriorated. By the third day, members of the respective delegations were on the verge of drawing swords on each other. The fire was fuelled as Philip demanded that Richard and Alice's wedding should proceed and that Richard should be formally declared Henry's heir; in all likelihood, a plan of action agreed between Philip and Richard as a negotiating strategy in advance.

Henry stared back stony-faced. He has been well-described as 'a compulsive hoarder when it came to power, reluctant to let a single ounce of authority slip from his grasp'.[5] He would not be held to ransom. Richard then stepped forward and demanded in person that his rights as heir be recognised; a moment of truth had been reached, the time for equivocation had passed. There was no answer from his father; his silence spoke more eloquently and decisively than any words could. A pause, heavy with threat, followed as father and son stared into the eyes and soul of each other.

After what seemed an eternity, it was Richard who broke the silence: 'I can only take as true what previously seemed incredible'. Then he took off his sword and knelt before Philip. Richard swore allegiance to him for Aquitaine and Normandy. Then he asked Philip to help deliver him his rightful inheritance. At this point Richard and Henry walked away from each other and the conference broke up. It was a deliberate public humiliation directed at the English king.

Faults on both sides had led to this parting of ways. Richard had been arrogant and demanding. In response, Henry had kept his cards close to his chest, rather too close as it turned out. He had done little to discourage stories that he was thinking of making John his heir. Richard was not a patient man and, not getting what he wanted, had struck out. Henry now found himself entangled in a web of his own making.

One last attempt at reconciliation was made. Allegedly on the advice of William Marshal, now a close adviser, Henry sent a message after Richard to try to get him to return to discuss the issues directly. But when William, who was delegated to fulfil the task in person, reached Amboise, Richard's last known location, he was already gone. Those there said that they had never seen Richard in such a hurry to call up his forces and prepare himself for a fight.

The episode at Bonsmoulins looks like a pre-arranged deal where Richard would throw in his lot decisively with Philip in a public gesture that could not be misconstrued. This was the end of the double-dealing; Richard was frustrated beyond endurance with his father's dissimulation. Ambition had won out over family loyalty. This time the situation was beyond recall.

Henry was wearying. He was now in his sixties and had suffered on and off from illness since 1182.[6] He threw his diminishing energies into preparing the defences of Anjou and Aquitaine. This was an alarming development, particularly for the crusade that was supposedly being prepared. Instead of building up their forces against Saladin, the kings of England and France were planning to fight each other with another potentially key crusader, Richard, also heavily involved. Attempts were made to hold yet more negotiations but they came to nothing as Henry had now been taken ill. Philip, thinking this yet another of the wily old fox's tricks, did not believe the news when he received it.

There was a hint of change in the air. Henry's achievements in keeping his federation largely intact throughout his reign were significant. The way he had achieved this had been masterful but it relied on his considerable energy and guile. But he was now visibly flagging. His vassals in France sensed weakness and were not slow to react. When Henry held his Christmas court at Saumur in 1188, a major occasion when he expected as many as possible of his prominent barons to attend, most of them were conspicuous by their absence.

Richard, though, still had distractions elsewhere to concern him. There was yet another uprising against him in Aquitaine in 1188. There was a certain wearying consistency in the names of the chief plotters; Adémar of Angoulême, Geoffrey de Rançon and Geoffrey of Lusignan. It was even said that Henry II was secretly funding Geoffrey of Lusignan. An ambush from the latter in which one of Richard's confidants was killed led to a violent reaction.

Richard's response was predictably fierce. Castles were taken and demolished, cities burned, plunder seized, even fruit trees were ripped up. Once again the rebellion was brought to a violent halt. Richard's conditions for peace were stern and designed to ensure that the revolts stopped, at least for a while; the chief rebels were to set out on crusade. Geoffrey of Lusignan did so almost immediately, probably encouraged by the thought that in Outremer he could support his brother, Guy, who was certainly down on his luck.

Christmas 1188 was a devastating time for Henry. In the past, family differences had largely been put aside at this time of year. Dissenting brothers would bury their differences, even though a pragmatist like Henry would have realised well enough that a cessation of war on a temporary basis did not mean much.

Now though it was just him and John holding court together. Richard was at his throat, his other legitimate sons were dead, his wife was a long-term prisoner at his own behest. This was a fractured, failed family. And to cap it all Henry's health was getting worse.

Soon after, there was rebellion against Henry's overlordship in Brittany. The duchy was, true to the Celtic blood that flowed prominently through the veins of its people, fiercely independent. It did not like the subservience to neighbouring Normandy that had been forced on it in recent times. Sensing that Henry's powers were waning, the Bretons took full advantage to rise in rebellion. Henry sent a number of messages to Richard to try and restore their damaged relationship but it was too late. There was a deafening silence in response. The chronicler Gervase of Canterbury said that Richard simply did not believe his father anymore.

Henry tried a direct approach to Philip. William Marshal was sent to lead the negotiations but when he reached Paris Richard's envoys, led by William Longchamp, were already in deep discussions with the French king and the mission came to nothing. Shortly after Easter 1189 Philip launched raids on Henry's territory with the help of Richard and men from Brittany. A papal legate, John of Anagni, worried that the crusade would never set out, managed to get the two parties to talk.

Philip spoke on behalf of both himself and Richard. The marriage of Alice and Richard was to go ahead, he insisted; it was now pushing three decades since their betrothal. Richard should have his inheritance honoured and John was to go on crusade. Richard interrupted and made clear that he would not be going to Jerusalem unless John went with him. Henry made a counter-offer, according to Roger of Howden, and suggested that John replace Richard as a prospective groom for Alice. This can only have made Richard even more suspicious of his father's intentions.

Cardinal Anagni's objective was clear enough; stop the petty arguments of the ruling dynasties of England and France, get them to bury their differences and set out on crusade. The cardinal saw Richard as a major stumbling block to this plan. He threatened his lands with an interdict if Richard would not budge. This inflamed Richard. He berated the cardinal for his nerve and even unsheathed his sword, threatening to attack him. His entourage managed to intervene, convincing him that it was only the cardinal's desire to have the crusade set out for Outremer that had led to his tactless comments. It was not the last time that Richard would find himself in opposition to the Church.

The discussions with Henry were again not going well. Richard failed to see that Philip, a master negotiator even at his young age, was trying to drive a wedge – very successfully – between father and son. The negotiations broke up. Shortly afterwards, Philip and Richard attacked the nearby castle of La Ferté-Bernard, about 25 miles north-east of Le Mans.

Worse was to follow for Henry, who was by now clearly seriously ill. Le Mans, the place of his birth, was attacked. It was a special place to Henry; the great cathedral which still figures prominently in the landscape of Le Mans had been dedicated by him in 1158 in much happier times, and his father lay sleeping the sleep of eternity within it. The city was well protected with strong walls enclosing an imposing citadel.

On the morning of 11 June 1189, William Marshal was leading a scouting party outside the walls. It was a misty start to the day but as the fog lifted Marshal saw before him an immense army. He rushed back to the city to call its people to arms. They resisted the attack vigorously but a fire broke out, allegedly lit on the instructions of Stephen of Tours, the seneschal of Anjou, as a defensive measure. But it blazed out of control and soon the city was aflame.

There was a fierce battle on a stone bridge (the only practical way in and out of the city) during which many men from both sides lost their lives. Many of Henry's army fled into the city but this allowed French soldiers, intermingled with them, to enter it too. Soon it became clear that Le Mans had fallen. The idea of a retreat inside the city's citadel was discussed but quickly dismissed. Henry, along with 700 of his knights, made his way northwards towards Normandy and safety in what was quickly turning into a chaotic retreat. They could not miss the plumes of smoke that billowed up behind them. Hundreds of Welsh mercenaries who were in Henry's army were killed in what was rapidly becoming a rout. Richard, sensing victory, chased after the panic-stricken survivors.

Henry's party soon realised that they were being pursued. Some of his men, led by William Marshal and William des Roches, turned to face his pursuers and allow him to make good his escape. Perhaps Marshal swallowed hard when he saw leading the pursuing group none other than Richard. Marshal charged straight at him, lance lowered. He caught him by surprise and Richard, who was not dressed for conflict, came off worse. Richard, isolated now from the rest of the group, pleaded with William not to kill him as he was not protected in the absence of armour; he also only carried a sword whereas Marshal held a lance.

William replied that he would not kill Richard; he would leave that task for the Devil. He struck down his horse instead so that Richard could not continue the pursuit; for a knight like Marshal who had been trained how to use a lance since he was a teenager, a process in which he had obtained thousands of hours of experience, hitting a target as big as a horse was an easy assignment. This may be, it has been suggested, a tale improved upon by William Marshal himself, for it was he who related it.[7] In any event, it stopped further pursuit by Henry and his party and the ailing king was able to escape.

Henry drove himself and his men hard but he was fading fast. Suffering from an anal fistula, the journey was excruciating. As twilight descended, he and his escort were near Alençon, the front door to Normandy and relative safety. But now Henry did something extraordinary. He did a 180 degree turn and headed south towards Anjou, back towards danger. He made for Chinon, though the roads were too closely patrolled by Philip and Richard's men for him to take a direct route. As one modern historian has suggested the most likely reason for this seemingly illogical response was that he was returning to Chinon to die.[8]

Tours and its treasury fell to Philip and Richard on 3 July. The French chronicler Rigord, who wrote a biography of Philip, credited the French king with this success. He said that he used his local knowledge to point out a fordable crossing of a nearby river. Miraculously, as they crossed the river the water levels dropped. Even God, it seemed, was on their side.

A few miles away at Ballan a parley was arranged between Henry and Philip, to take place the very next day. The latter could see when Henry arrived that his claimed illness was no trick; he had to be supported so that he did not fall off his horse. Richard was there too. The tide had turned decisively against Henry. Many of those who might in the past have supported him had seen the way that it was flowing. Henry's time was fast running out.

It was a poignant and pathetic scene, made more ominous by a lightning bolt that struck the ground between the two kings.[9] This alarmed the two men, who drew back from each other, and before long a full-blown thunderstorm was raging, a perfect backdrop for the tragedy that was being played out. Philip, seeing that Henry was genuinely ill, offered him a cloak on the ground to sit on. Henry, imperious to the last, replied that he had not come to sit but to learn the price of peace. It was significant that this gesture of pity came from the French king and not from Richard, whose heart was now seemingly completely hardened against his father. Any flickering vestige of familial loyalty between the two men had long been extinguished.

The terms were laid out by Philip: Alice to be handed over to a guardian and then married to Richard on his return from crusade, Richard's rights to inherit to be publicly recognised, an indemnity of 20,000 marks to be paid to Philip. Henry was too weak and too tired to argue. At the end of the ceremony he gave his rebellious son the kiss of peace. Even as he did so, he whispered in his ear that he hoped that God would restore him to health so that he would be able to take his revenge for this treachery.

This was the denouement of a tragic family breakdown. As Henry gave that false embrace to the son who had betrayed him – the kiss of Judas in reverse – it was the final act in a broken father-son relationship. Those words, motivated by a burning desire for vengeance, were the very last uttered between Henry and Richard.

Only Gerald of Wales related this story of the muttered words of vengeance whispered into Richard's ear by his betrayed father. Some historians consider it a 'strange story'.[10] Perhaps it is the impact of being conditioned by too many modern soap operas but the tale does not seem at all strange. Henry could see his world slipping through his fingers, all his plans unravelling at a rate of knots, and the main reason for this was his son, a prince who refused to be ruled by his father. It was little wonder that Henry felt betrayed and thirsted for revenge.

Henry was now too ill to ride and he was carried back to Chinon on a litter. He was taken to his chamber. A list was soon after received of all those who had been disloyal to him. He was unable to read it himself, so he commanded his servants to do so for him. There was some reluctance on their part but when he insisted they started to read. At the top of the list was his youngest son John, the prince he had nurtured and protected. Here was the ultimate betrayal.[11] As soon as the bearer of these terrible tidings, Roger Malcheal, the keeper of the king's seal, uttered John's name, the king told him to stop; 'you have said enough'.[12]

It was a blow from which Henry would never recover. Although it is perhaps too melodramatic to say that he was dying of a broken heart, it would nevertheless be understandable if he was losing the will to live. He slowly turned his face towards the wall of his chamber and refused to speak to anyone. He was turning his back on the world. Delirium took over and from this point on moments of lucidity became increasingly rare. Eventually he was carried to his chapel and laid in front of the altar. His life ebbed away as he lay in penitence, praying for forgiveness of his sins. Richard had been told that his father's last moments were imminent but refused to believe it, thinking it a trick. There was not one atom of trust left between them.

Henry died, surrounded by only a small entourage of loyal servants. He cursed both the day he was born and his sons, wrote Roger of Howden.[13] Estranged from his wife, as he had been for nearly two decades, and deserted and betrayed by Richard and John, he expired on 6 July 1189. Only one son stood by his deathbed and he, ironically, was illegitimate; he was also named Geoffrey. Henry reportedly said of him that he was his only true son; it was the others who were bastards.

Richard, when he became king, made Geoffrey the archbishop of York, the second most important ecclesiastical post in the country, which had been vacant since 1181. It was a position which had supposedly been promised to him by the late king in his last days according to Gerald of Wales.[14] Soon after, Richard and Geoffrey would be at odds with each other; this Geoffrey possessed the same quarrelsome nature that the other son of Henry II with the same name had. Perhaps it was after all an Angevin trait.

Henry II was moody, impetuous and capable of extraordinary outbursts interspersed with long, sullen silences. Yet for all that his achievements were immense. Only in the last years of his reign did his 'federation' start to unravel. Perhaps that was a function of age and tiredness; or, alternatively, the increasing ambition and impatience of his sons. It was probably a combination of all these, along with an ever more assertive and maturing opponent in the shape of Philip of France. Whatever the reasons leading to the trauma of these last few years, he deserved a better end than this.

The quill of the contemporary chronicler Roger of Howden, normally a matter-of-fact and measured writer, was dipped in acid when he wrote of these events. He had performed several services for the late king during his life and therefore knew him well. Roger wrote that, 'after his death, having plundered him of all his riches, all forsook him; so true it is that just as flies seek honey, wolves the carcase, and ants corn, this crew followed not the man, but his spoils.'[15]

But tragic though the final days of Henry were, maybe there was an element of karma in all this too. When Henry's father, Geoffrey of Anjou, lay dying some years previously, he ordered Henry not to bury him until he had handed over some of his inheritance to his younger brother. Henry had had no intention of doing so. Even after Geoffrey died, he refused to comply. Only after Geoffrey's body had started to decompose did Henry relent. This was the harsh reality of the world in which Angevin ambition sought to advance itself.

Henry's body was carried in regal procession (or as near as could be mustered in the circumstances: most of the expensive items he had with him were pilfered on his death) to the nearby abbey of Fontevraud. Here he was buried in 'the choir of the nuns' as Roger of Howden calls it; Henry had wanted to be buried at the abbey of Grandmont, which he had helped to rebuild, but the summer heat was already doing its work and made this an unrealistic possibility.

Richard came to pay his respects at Fontevraud soon after. The loyal William Marshal, whose fidelity had not wavered in those awful last days, was keeping vigil over the late king when he arrived. Richard knelt briefly beside the body of the father with whom he had experienced such a difficult relationship. It has the appearance of a perfunctory act, performed because it was expected of him. Richard had played a huge part in his father's death by his actions in the last few years. But now he had a whole new world at his feet.

There was a story told by Roger of Howden that, as Richard approached his father's body and wept, it bled at his approach, a sure sign that the corpse was in the presence of a murderer. This is another classic topoi of the time which we would see as being a tale of superstition and the supernatural. But it was in its own way an appropriate story, speaking eloquently of the complete disintegration of the relationship. So successful in his early decades, the last days of Henry II were an unmitigated family tragedy that was almost Shakespearian in its pathos.

It is worth reminding ourselves that parental relationships were different in the twelfth century than they are in modern times. It has been said that 'the chief purpose of the father in the medieval period was not to be loved, but to protect and provide, to school and to dominate'.[16] Henry had certainly tried to dominate; the problem was that his sons, and Richard especially, would not accept this.

Although Richard had not been nominated Henry's successor, it would be a brave or foolish person who would resist him now that the throne was vacant. He had a proven, impressive record and his achievements contrasted markedly with those of the inexperienced and, so far, unsuccessful John. But being a prince was one thing, becoming a successful king was another. The fortunes of his peoples would sink or swim depending on how he acted next. Richard was now the ruler of a far larger and more diverse group of territories than he had ever been before.

He certainly acted as if his succession was beyond contestation. He gave orders that his late father should be buried with all due pomp and ceremony; whatever his personal feelings toward Henry, it was important that all the required majesty and grandeur of a royal burial was forthcoming. He then turned to William Marshal and ordered him to follow. Marshal did so and soon threw himself behind the new king. If Marshal was not about to argue with Richard's claim to the throne, then it was very unlikely that anyone else would.

Richard duly came into his inheritance but what a bitter, tainted inheritance it was. There was little mourning or sign of regret in evidence as Richard turned to the business of governing his vastly expanded territories. He had spent very little time in England since his early days but she was the main source of his power as this alone was where he was king. Some time now needed to be spent there. There was a great deal to be done and, to cap it all, he was about to set out on crusade. It was time for Richard to prove himself as at last the scene was set for the drama that would write his name on the pages of history.

6

Long Live the King (1189–1190)

'A new day-star ascending'
Roger of Howden on the accession of Richard I

The heady taste of power was now Richard's to enjoy. This would be the first undisputed royal succession in England since the Norman Conquest, an irony as Richard had not been officially declared Henry's heir. In fact, he did not feel the need to hurry back to England and would not even arrive in Normandy until three weeks after his father's death. Here he met Baldwin, the archbishop of Canterbury, and Walter of Coutances, archbishop of Rouen, to discuss his plans. He was then invested with the sword and standard of the duke of Normandy, which he now was, at Rouen.[1]

William Marshal had been a loyal supporter of Henry II; loyalty would turn out to be his strongest suit. It was possible, given his resilient attachment to the late king, that Marshal's career was now over.[2] But Richard saw things differently. If Marshal's loyalty could be won for himself, then Richard would be making a very important ally. William was offered the hand of Isabel de Clare, heiress to rich estates on the borders of Wales. The match was so valuable that it had to be awarded by the king. Henry II had promised to do so to Marshal but never did. Richard was now quick to follow through with the bargain, which was duly made.

This followed what might have been a difficult interview. According to the man who penned the biography known as the *History of William Marshal*, Richard was inscrutable when meeting Marshal at Fontevraud. His eyes, said the writer, gave nothing away; it was impossible to tell whether the new king was joyful or grief-stricken. Richard was playing a part, a role which required that he did not reveal his true feelings, and he was playing it well.[3]

Not long before, Marshal had killed Richard's horse under him when the then prince had been in hot pursuit of his father. Now Richard accused Marshal of threatening his life. This claim was easily rebuffed by the knight; he rightly pointed out that his arm was true and his aim straight and, if he had wanted to kill Richard, he would have done so. Richard accepted the point and from them on Marshal would be a loyal supporter of Richard as he had previously been of the Young King and Henry II.

Richard was quick to order the release of his mother. Eleanor had been kept in confinement for most of the past one-and-a-half decades. But by the time that William Marshal arrived in England to arrange for Eleanor's freedom her situation had already been sorted out. She had already demanded that her keepers release her, no doubt reminding them that their positions might be reversed when Richard came to England. With typical energy, remarkable for a woman of nearly seventy who had spent years in prison, she indefatigably moved from city to city and castle to castle around England, building up support for the new king.[4]

When, soon after, a number of other prisoners were released by Richard, she said that she knew how joyful the feeling was. The fresh air of freedom tasted sweet. Those prisoners who had been held on the command of only the late king or his justiciars without being tried by county or hundred courts were singled out as they appeared to be victims of arbitrary justice.[5] Several populist measures were quickly taken. Those who had broken Henry II's unpopular and draconian forest laws were particular beneficiaries. Henry's enthusiasm for hunting had led to him inflicting harsh punishments against those who had broken the laws of the forest.

Eleanor's financial resources were soon after substantially increased by Richard, allowing her to live well and with independence. She would be a great asset given her political acumen and vast experience. Richard had unofficially appointed Eleanor as his regent until he arrived and William Marshal came armed with strict instructions that her word was to be law. She now busied herself preparing England to receive her son. She ordered that every freeman in the country should swear fealty to the new king. Some attended a ceremony at Westminster where she accepted their pledges of loyalty in the presence of the archbishop of Canterbury.

William Marshal quickly returned to England. So excited was he by the rich match that had been promised him that he almost fell off the gangplank when he hurried on to the ship taking him back. Romantics might hope that this was because of the attractions of his wife-to-be (he was forty-three, she was seventeen) but far more likely the wealth that went with the marriage was the main reason. That said, the marriage was very productive. Isabel was pregnant before the year was out and the union would go on to produce ten children.[6] With a symmetry that chimed well with Marshal's general good fortune and sense of equilibrium, there would be five boys and five girls. There was no rumour of Marshal having extra-marital affairs during their long marriage, so there were good indications that it was generally a happy one.

This decision was a clever move on Richard's part as Marshal would gain important territories on the Welsh borders as a result. At the time, parts of Wales were still stubbornly independent. Henry II's attempts to subdue the country had nearly met with disaster. The combination of bad weather, the difficult terrain and the ferocity of the Welsh guerrillas who lurked in the mountains and on the moors had proved a formidable obstacle that Henry had never overcome.

In the west of Wales Rhys ap Gruffydd, or Rhys of Deheubarth as he is also known, was one of the most assertive of the Welsh princes to ever take on domineering English would-be overlords. Born in 1132, by 1189 he was past the peak of his powers but he was still a great threat in Wales. He had made an agreement with Henry II that he would recognise him as his liege lord but there was little doubt that he would use the occasion of the late king's death to consider the agreement null and void. True to form there would indeed be an uprising in West Wales soon afterwards and several castles were taken by Rhys's forces. But at least Marshal would be on hand to ensure that trouble did not spread too far east.

Marshal's rise was a spectacular one. Born in 1146 or 1147, Marshal's father was a minor noble, who has been described as having the financial resources of 'a prosperous minor baron'.[7] As a younger son, he would be left nothing in terms of lands when his father died, so he had to make his own luck. He had been sent to Normandy to train as a knight when he was twelve, spending time in the castle of his mother's cousin. Tales of his bravery followed as he grew to manhood.

Marshal earned a reputation, as well as worldly wealth, following a great deal of success in tournaments, being a strong knight and a canny operator on the tournament field who was not above using underhand tricks to win. He entered Henry II's service in 1185 and became a loyal supporter of the late king even in his final days when he was abandoned by most others.

Now Richard had plans for Marshal whilst he was away on crusade. Richard had decided to place him on the council that would be responsible for the government of England in his absence. It turned out to be an astute move. Marshal's loyalty to Henry II, and before that the Young King, had resonated with Richard as the sign of a man of honour who could be trusted. That loyalty went deep; after his elevation by Richard, Marshal founded an Augustinian religious house at Cartmel in Lancashire. As part of its endowment, he gave funds so that prayers could be said for the soul of 'my lord' – not Henry II, nor even Richard, but the Young King.[8]

Marshal was an extraordinary man in several ways. He played key roles in the reigns of four English kings (if the Young King is excluded from the list); Henry II, Richard I, John and Henry III. But we also know more about him than most, for shortly after his death a biography (in the form of a poem) was written about him: the only biography of a secular Englishman other than a 'royal' from the twelfth and thirteenth centuries that is known.[9] From this we get a unique insight into the mind of a powerful baron of the time and of some of the key events of Angevin history.

Richard could not stay out of England for too long. He needed to be invested with the crown through the solemn ritual of his coronation, his formal anointing, after which no Englishman could in conscience reject Richard's right to rule. Arrangements were duly made and both Richard and John made their way back to England, though on different ships. This might well have been a security measure given the dangers of the crossing – the tragedy of the *White Ship* was only two generations back – but it was also a way of ensuring that nothing distracted attention away from the new king.

Richard arrived at Portsmouth on 13 August 1189, having crossed over from Barfleur, and was greeted with enthusiasm. Two days later he was reunited with his mother at Winchester, and with his brother, John. In Rouen, John had just been made the count of Mortain in Normandy and was often subsequently referred to as such.

Richard was in his prime, just past thirty years of age, but already a renowned warrior. He could defend himself and his rights, and it was hoped that he would do the same for his kingdom. Some may have reflected that he had been as responsible as anybody for the tragic last years of the late King Henry's reign but perhaps they did not care overmuch about that. Anyway, news from France in a largely non-literate society outside the rarefied world of the clerisy would have been patchy and was unlikely to mean very much to those below the ranks of the nobility. This was still a society where travel for most people was a journey to the nearest village or town and where France seemed like the other side of the globe.

Roger of Howden waxed lyrical about the welcome that was given to Richard. He referred to him as 'a new day-star ascending' who would 'bring a time of prosperity by a sudden change at sunrise'. Richard was 'the flower of chivalry, whose word has a truth that comes from the heart, whose tireless munificence cannot be exhausted but when he has given much thinks he has given little'. Great things were expected of Richard, not least by Roger; 'the son became greater and greater, enlarged the good works of his father, while the bad ones he cut short.'[10]

These were glowing words but it is doubtful that his English subjects were so immediately won over. After all, they had barely seen Richard for two decades as he had been in France for most of the time. The main thing that would recommend him to them was that he was not his father. Whilst Henry II had inspired respect, and on occasion fear, this was quite different than affection. Henry had been remarkably good in extracting taxes, hardly something to commend him to his people.

Sensing a public relations opportunity, Richard had Stephen of Tours, one of his father's most unpopular administrators, accompany him to England – in chains. He was eventually released after Richard 'took ransom of him to the uttermost farthing'.[11] It cost Stephen 30,000 crowns and by the time he was released he was 'emaciated with woeful hunger and broken with the weight of his irons'.[12] It was a welcome symbolic assertion that the harshness of his father's years was over, or so at least the people of Richard's territories thought.

Richard did not generally penalise those who had been loyal supporters of Henry II. It was those who had betrayed the late king who suffered; they could as easily be as disloyal to Richard as they had been to his father. Several important barons in France, Guy de

Laval, Ralph of Fougères and Juhel de Mayenne, were kept under close watch by Richard; they were all turncoats against Henry II in the last years of his reign and had therefore proved that they could not be trusted.

Further sad family news marked these days. Matilda, Richard's sister, also died at around this time. The last decade of her life had been difficult. She had spent many of those years in exile with her husband, Henry the Lion, in Normandy. At one time, the couple had been allowed back to Saxony by the Holy Roman Emperor, Frederick Barbarossa. But Barbarossa then reversed his decision shortly before setting off on crusade.

Henry and Matilda had gone back into exile, this time to Brunswick. Matilda died just months later, on 28 June 1189. But it was not all sadness; her daughter, also named Matilda, was married to the heir to the county of Perche by Richard at around this time. On the borders of Normandy, a crucial part of Richard's French territories, the gaining of an ally in the region was an important step. The politics of marriage often played as important a part in the securing of Richard's territories as military enterprise did.

Once back in England, Richard ordered a stocktake of his father's treasury. A great deal of gold and silver was found. When counted and valued, its worth was well over 100,000 marks.[13] Preparations were then put in train for Richard's coronation. It would be a splendid ceremony, to be led by Baldwin, the archbishop of Canterbury, who would be supported by the archbishops of Rouen, Treves and Dublin and the bishops of Durham, Lincoln, Chester, Hereford, Worcester, Exeter, Bath, Norwich, Chichester, Rochester, St Davids, Saint Asaph, Bangor and others. Nearly all the abbots, priors, earls and barons of England would also be present. It was a veritable who's who of the Establishment.

Exactly a month after landing in England, Richard was crowned at Westminster. The abbey was a very different building then than the one we see now. It had not undergone that magnificent transformation overseen by Richard's nephew, the future Henry III, let alone the Gothic Revival towers for which it is now most immediately recognisable, which were added in the eighteenth century. The church was then in the Romanesque style, the form in which it had been built by Edward the Confessor, saint and king, in the mid-eleventh century. Since Harold Godwinson, every English king had been crowned there. It was steeped in both history and sacred symbolism.

Roger of Howden wrote a detailed description of the coronation that helps breathe colour into the event.[14] The bishops, abbots and clergy led the procession into the abbey wearing silk hoods. Preceded by cross-bearers and censers they led Richard to the High Altar. William Marshal carried the sceptre and William Fitzpatrick, earl of Salisbury, a rod of gold. David, earl of Huntingdon and brother of the king of Scotland, was there, as was Robert, earl of Leicester, to whom Richard had recently restored lands that had been taken from him by Henry II a long time before. William de Mandeville, earl of Essex, carried the crown.

Richard was escorted in procession by Hugh, bishop of Durham, on his right and Reginald, bishop of Bath, on his left. Four barons carried a canopy of silk above him, raised high on spears. During the ceremony, Richard picked up the crown of state and handed it to Baldwin, the archbishop of Canterbury, who ceremoniously put it on the king's head. The archbishop had to be helped by two barons to support the crown as it was so heavy. The air was heady with the sweet smell of incense and heavenly music echoed through the church.

The most symbolically significant part of the ceremony took place when the king was anointed with the holy oil. Richard was stripped of most of his clothes and then, dressed in only his shirt and breeches, the oil was applied to his head, his chest and his hands (it had been handed to the archbishop by the Dean of London, Ralph of Diceto, a chronicler of the times). This act sanctified the king and signified the divine approval of God which no man could defy without putting his immortal soul at risk. Solemn oaths were sworn by Richard, to repeal bad laws and only introduce good ones. He was instructed to be a good king to his people, to show mercy and exercise justice in his acts and his decisions. After the harsh efficiency of Henry II, people hoped for a lighter touch.

This sacred act over, the king was re-dressed. Spurs which had been carried during the ceremony by John Marshal, William's brother, were placed on him. Richard ascended the throne and sat there imperiously while Mass was celebrated. He now held the sceptre in his right hand and the rod in his left. It was an awe-inspiring event, steeped in history and tradition. The precedent for such ceremonies, though not the specific details, could be traced back to the Bible and the coronation of Roman emperors. The particular version in use for Richard, the so-called Third

Recension, was a combination of the old Anglo-Saxon rite and that used to crown the Holy Roman Emperor.

Eleanor was there, no doubt looking on with a great deal of merited pride. She and Richard had ridden through streets decorated with tapestries and flowers and strewn with scented rushes on their way to the abbey. She was arrayed in sumptuous clothes, including a cape made of silk. John was there too, no doubt feeling decidedly less generous towards the new king and wondering whether or not one day he might be the centre of attention at such a grand ceremony.

An illustration in the *Chroniques de Saint-Denis* shows Richard wagging his finger, almost in a threatening manner, to the archbishop, although as it dates to a period of time at least 150 years after the coronation took place it is unlikely to be realistic in every respect. Richard, beardless, appears young and almost effeminately beautiful, though there is more than a hint of regality in his look. Such an impression seems entirely appropriate in terms of setting the scene for Richard's future reign.

But next to the ceremony portrayed in this illustration flames can be seen dancing from the windows of a tower. Whilst the great feast that followed the coronation was being held in the nearby Palace of Westminster, a party of Jews tried to enter bearing gifts for Richard, against the instructions of the king who had ordered that they should not attend the coronation. At the time of many crusades, violent anti-Semitism often showed itself. During the march of the armies that marked the setting out of the First Crusade in the last years of the eleventh century there had been frequent massacres of Jews along the way to Outremer.

Anti-Semitism had been experienced in France more recently when, in 1182, King Philip had the Jews expelled from his country. Rigord, the French chronicler, said that at the time they owned half of Paris. They were accused of mocking Christianity and of buying precious chalices and drinking out of them. Philip was brutal in his persecution of the Jews, burning ninety-nine of them alive for their alleged insulting of Christianity. They were a wealthy, convenient scapegoat for the ills of society as they have been in so many times. When Philip threw the Jews out of France he was widely applauded for his actions (though in time the finance that they allowed him to access forced him to bring them back again). Some sought and found sanctuary in England. Now the unreliability of such sanctuary, the barely concealed resentment of the 'other' so often exhibited against them over the centuries, was about to ignite once more.

Though Jews were often despicably treated in Western Europe – in England, in France and in parts of what we would now call Germany for example – it was not the case everywhere. The small kingdom of Navarre, birthplace of Berengaria, Richard's future wife, was a good example. The kings of this small country (in fact, the 'kingdom' was new and its rulers would not officially receive 'kingly' status from the papacy until later on in the century) sponsored Jews in several important positions. These not only included commercial occupations, for which the Jewish communities in many countries became well-known, but also others like doctors. Some important Jewish figures came from the region such as the famous Benjamin of Tudela, a noted traveller who hailed from Navarre and lived from about 1130 to 1173 and Abraham ibn Ezra (1089–*c.*1167) who was a widely respected philosopher and poet.

At the coronation, a riot broke out when the crowds outside the gates of the palace saw the Jewish party seeking entrance. Taunts soon turned to violence as mob rule took over. Some of the Jews there were killed, others injured, though a few escaped 'by the kindness of their Christian friends'. From this initial spark a greater conflagration grew, in this case literally. The trouble spread into the City of London and houses were plundered and burned and more Jews killed.

The chronicler Richard of Devizes wrote of the massacre in terms that suggested that he was an enthusiastic supporter of it (he also wrote a story of a young Christian boy being killed and eaten by an evil Jew in Winchester).[15] His words are particularly chilling; 'a sacrifice of the Jews to their father the devil was commenced in the city of London, and so long was the duration of this famous mystery, that the holocaust could scarcely be accomplished the ensuing day'.

One word leaps out of this phrase; 'holocaust', a combination of two Greek words, *holos* ('burnt') and *kaustos* ('a sacrificial offering to a god'). It was the first known use of the word in the context of a massacre of the Jews and we have of course become uncomfortably familiar with it since. The chronicler told how the Londoners, in a great demonstration of faith, 'despatched their blood-suckers with blood to hell', his words and tone giving a chilling insight into contemporary mentalities.[16]

Not everyone, even in England, agreed with these actions though. Ralph of Diceto stated emphatically, 'let no man believe that wise men rejoiced at the dire and dreadful slaughter of the Jews, for it is written in the Psalms of David which come frequently to our ears, slay them not'. It was an enlightened attitude which sadly was not shared by many of his countrymen.[17]

Whilst all this was happening, Richard was the centre of attention in the great feast being held in the palace. He had exchanged the heavy robes and crown used in the coronation ceremony with lighter versions of them. The records known as the Pipe Rolls, so called because the parchment on which they were written were rolled up in a pipe-shaped form, tell us that 1,770 pitchers, 900 cups and more than 5,000 dishes were bought for the feast, an insight into the size of the celebration that was taking place inside while slaughter was taking place outside.[18] The feast went on, according to the chronicler Ambroise (who seems to have been present), for a full three days.[19]

Richard was furious when he heard of the damage done by the outbreak of violence and three of the rioters were hanged for their part in the outrage, though Roger of Howden suggests that this was because of the Christian property that they had destroyed and not because of any outrage committed against Jews.[20] A Jew who had become a Christian when faced with the choice of conversion or death was encouraged to return to his faith by Richard. Instructions were sent out across England warning his subjects that there must be no repeat elsewhere in his kingdom, followed by similar warnings issued in Normandy and Poitou.

But it did little good for there were more anti-Semitic outrages elsewhere; at Norwich (6 February 1190), Lincoln and Stamford (7 March) amongst others and, in March 1190, at York. At Stamford, it was suggested that ostentatious displays of wealth by members of the Jewish community incensed would-be crusaders who were short of money due to their plans to journey east. Only Winchester was singled out for avoiding the excesses of the atrocities; 'the city always acting mildly, spared its vermin'.[21]

York was a key city in the North. It was described by Richard of Devizes as a place that 'abounds in Scots, vile and faithless men, or rather rascals'. Just to even it up, the writer suggested that Chester, Hereford and Worcester should be avoided because there were too many 'desperate Welshmen' there. Bath was 'placed, or rather buried, in the lowest parts of the valleys, in a very dense atmosphere and sulphury vapour, as it were at the gates of hell'. Ely was 'putrefied by the surrounding marshes'.[22]

Now York became famous for something else. There was a small but significant Jewish community in York; one of their number, Benedict, had been badly wounded in the riots that marred the coronation feast. It was he who had been forced to convert to Christianity (he took the 'Christian name' of William), only to return to Judaism with the tacit support of Richard. When Benedict died soon after at Northampton neither Jew nor Christian would accept his body in their cemeteries. Roger of Howden betrayed his own anti-Semitic prejudices when he said that Benedict had 'like a dog, returned to his vomit'.[23]

The Jewish community incurred the enmity and envy of some of the citizens of York because of their wealth and, stirred up by anti-Semitic emotions, some of them tried to burn down Benedict's house, for he had been the wealthiest member of the Jewish population. Allegedly the rioters had been egged on by some of the leading men of York who owed significant sums to Jewish money-lenders in the hope that any evidence of their debts would be destroyed as a result.

The Jews found protection for a while in the royal castle, where Clifford's Tower now stands in the city. They barricaded themselves in. Outside, an incensed hermit urged the rioters to exterminate the Jews within. When he was killed by a falling stone, the blood of the mob was up. Many Jews trapped inside, seeing no escape, killed their families and then themselves. A gruesome scene was played out as men slit the throats of their wives and children and then cut their own. The wooden keep was torched and a pall of acrid smoke soon choked the lives out of those who still lived.

A few of them tried to take advantage of assurances that if they gave themselves up and converted to Christianity then they would live. This was a lie for as soon as they handed themselves over they were killed. The mob then marched to the Minster where they made a bonfire of all the records of the debts they had seized so that they were expunged, showing what this atrocity was really all about.[24]

When Richard heard what had happened, his blood was up once more. The city was heavily fined for what had happened though no individuals were personally punished for their part in the pogrom.[25] However, Henry Longchamp, brother of William (later to become chief justiciar and chancellor of England), who had been sent to York to punish the ringleaders, was unable to do so as most of them had fled before he got there.

In claiming to protect the Jewish community, Richard was continuing a policy that had been instituted by Henry II. Jews were relatively numerous in the country at the time; the restrictions on lending with interest that were applied to Christians, which were seen to be an immoral practice known as usury, did not apply to the Jewish community, who were therefore often useful sources of funding.

Richard had many matters to attend to before he could set off on crusade. He had to ensure that the key positions in terms of governing England were all filled before he left. John would not be going with him, despite Richard's assertions in the not-too-distant past that he would not travel east without his brother; presumably the situation had changed now that Henry II was dead and Richard was king. It has been suggested that Eleanor was not happy with the prospect of both brothers being away at the same time and given the lack of a clear heir from a dynastic perspective this made sense.

Nevertheless, John would need to be watched. He was given very generous grants of lands across England; in Cornwall, Dorset, Somerset, Derby, Nottingham, Lancaster and the castles of Luggershall and Marlborough, as well as those of Bolsover and Lancaster.[26] The grants were so liberal that some men at the time said that Richard had no intention of ever returning to England.[27] John was also given the hand of Isabel of Gloucester. Archbishop Baldwin protested against this, as they were second cousins and too closely related to be married.[28] He was ignored; but when John, a decade later, looked for a way out of his marriage he quickly found one in the closeness of their relationship and was soon after granted an annulment.

Some historians have criticised Richard for being too open-handed with John but this seems unfair. Quite what else Richard could have done to try to gain his brother's loyalty is not at all clear. In the longer term, the policy failed but partly only because of an unforeseeable sequence of events. John was at least not given ultimate power and Eleanor effectively acted as Richard's eyes and ears when he was absent, though she was only part of a larger ruling body and was not his official regent.

It is also notable that the majority of John's landholdings lacked real strategic clout. The territories in the West Country, for example, were a long way from the mainstream of the contemporary political scene and offered more in the way of hunting opportunities than they did military influence; there is still a King John's Hunting Lodge at Lacock in Wiltshire, for example, which commemorates his passion for the pastime as well as at least one King John's Inn, located in his former hunting grounds in the West Country. They were also largely in regions where Richard had strong support and John could be watched. Further, in some cases royal castles in these territories were kept in the king's hands. Given this, the granting of these lands might suggest an attempt to neutralise John rather than be over-generous to him.

Some have asserted that Richard should have locked up John whilst he was away in the same way that Eleanor had been incarcerated by her late husband or as Henry I had done with his brother Robert at the beginning of the twelfth century, when the latter could be considered a rival for the throne.[29] This really put Richard in the 'damned if you do, damned if you don't' camp. It is very likely that Richard would then be accused, possibly by largely the same group of critics, of tyranny, of which this would be considered a prime example. The problem of the troublesome brother, and Richard himself had been such a figure in the past, was a difficult one and Richard could not win whatever he did.

But this also came at an exorbitant cost. Richard was giving away royal lands that Henry II had assiduously assembled during his reign; the way in which he restored the royal patrimony after the disaster of Stephen's civil wars was one of the greatest achievements of the late king's reign. Recent research has shown how dramatic was the effect on royal incomes of Richard granting these lands to others; from £21,000 in 1188 the income then dropped to around £11,000. These might not appear to be large sums by modern standards but they made a huge dent in Richard's revenues. Some modern historians have even referred to Richard's 'ravaging of the royal lands'.[30] To compound the issue, this was also a time of high inflation, with prices doubling between 1180 and 1220.[31] The general economic backdrop to the period of the Third Crusade was grim.

A council was held at Pipewell Abbey in Northamptonshire. Its aim was to put in place the infrastructure for how the Angevin territories would be governed while Richard was away. The abbey was later demolished after Henry VIII's Dissolution of the Monasteries three-and-a-half centuries later and by the eighteenth century it was very hard to tell that it had ever existed at all. But during September 1189, shortly after Richard's coronation, it became the focus of attention for the great men of England. Roger of Howden records who was there in a long list of archbishops and bishops and most of the great magnates of the country.

Some key decisions needed to be made before the king's departure. The king's main minister was the chief justiciar, a position of great power, the holder of which was often regent in the king's absence. The chief justiciar was also head of the Court of the Exchequer which looked after the royal finances and was responsible for auditing them. The post was currently held by Ranulf de Glanville, its incumbent since 1180; there were widespread allegations that he had been pilfering funds for his own benefit ever since. He had been a loyal lieutenant of Henry II and was at one stage Eleanor of Aquitaine's custodian in Winchester Castle. He was subsequently imprisoned and forced to pay the enormous ransom of £15,000 for his release.[32] He then took the cross, a major commitment on his part as he was now around seventy-seven years old, and would die during the forthcoming crusade.

Richard replaced Ranulf with not one man but two. One was William de Mandeville, earl of Essex. He already had crusading experience, having accompanied Count Philip of Flanders on an expedition to Outremer in 1177, though he returned to England soon afterwards. He managed to make the transition from Henry II to Richard well, if only briefly. He was present when Henry died at Chinon and then carried Richard's crown during his coronation. However, he would have no time to make an impression as justiciar for he died on 14 November 1189 at Rouen.

The other chief justiciar was Hugh de Puiset, a vastly experienced politician who was consecrated as bishop of Durham in 1153. He was the nephew of the late King Stephen and as such not a natural ally of the Angevins but he had since walked a narrow tightrope without falling off it, even managing to stay neutral in the dispute between Henry II and Thomas Becket. Nevertheless, at one stage he had lost Henry's trust during King William the Lion of Scotland's invasion of England. Despite this he had managed to survive and retain a position of influence: Henry did not want another fall-out with a prominent cleric to explain away.

It was not unusual for a bishop to also play a prominent political role in politics at the time. In Hugh's case, this was partly because of where he was. The north-east of England was in an exposed position, close to the border with Scotland and often subject to raids from the country to the north. Because of this, the bishop of Durham was known as a prince-bishop, a man with vital secular as well as ecclesiastical authority in the region, especially in times of war.

De Puiset paid £1,000 for the post of justiciar. He also had to buy himself out of his crusading vow so that he could stay in England. He paid another £2,000 for the positions of earl of Northumbria and Sheriff of Northumberland and gave 600 marks for the purchase of the manor of Sedbergh. The bishop was clearly a man of worldly ambition and not a little wealth, a perception that was reinforced by his extravagant tastes and general ostentation.

Even at the time these actions caused comment, William of Newburgh arguing that a bishop should not also be justiciar. De Puiset was soon at odds with the replacement justiciar who was appointed after the death of William de Mandeville, William Longchamp. Richard's appointment of two men who disliked each other intensely in a situation where their respective roles were poorly defined proved to be a mistake.

Longchamp had risen from humble stock to be Richard's chancellor in Aquitaine and had recently become bishop of Ely. He was not much to look at; he had a limp and a stammer and the caustic Gerald of Wales described him as looking like a hairy ape. Richard of Devizes suggested that he was small of stature.[33] Of Norman background, he had little respect for anything or anyone English. The English returned the compliment and he was widely detested for his arrogance.

Below these men, Richard appointed co-justiciars to support them and do much of the spadework required. These associates, known as *appares*, included William Marshal (whose brother Henry was to be the Dean of York), Geoffrey fitzPeter, William Brewer and Robert of Whitfield. Apart from Marshal, these were men with previous administrative experience who would not need to be shown the ropes. Their roles provided a mundane contrast to Richard the crusader but they were a key part of his plan for government whilst he was away. They were soon struggling to stop Longchamp from getting out of control; before long he was falling out with many people, including the Marshals.[34]

On another lower branch of the tree, though still important, were officials such as the sheriffs around the country and the constables of the royal castles. Here Richard exercised his patronage in a different way. These posts tended to go to the highest bidder. In the process, many existing incumbents were replaced; of thirty-one sheriffs rendering accounts in 1189, only six were to be kept in office.[35] It was not unnatural that Richard should try and maximise revenues by doing this, particularly as royal income was down due to his gifts to John. But the move potentially created local tensions. Richard guarded against this by generally appointing men to these posts with local knowledge who should understand the areas they were responsible for, warts and all. On the other hand, it was hard to make the sheriffs accountable for the funds that they collected and some considered that the post was a heaven-sent opportunity for them to make money corruptly.[36]

During the few months that he was in England, Richard – in true Angevin fashion – was extremely busy. The archbishop of York's throne was free and had been for a time. During the resulting interregnum, Hugh de Puiset had amassed even more power in the north-east. Richard wanted to fill the post and had someone in mind for it. The major problem was that the man he had identified did not want the job.

Geoffrey, his illegitimate half-brother, was Richard's choice. Some suggested that Geoffrey harboured designs on the throne. There were stories that on one occasion he had played the fool with the lid of a golden bowl on his head, asking his friends if he would not look good in a crown? This may have been mere play-acting, though if so it was a dangerous game he was playing. After all, the taint of bastardy had not prevented William the Conqueror from becoming firstly duke of Normandy and then king of England. But if Geoffrey were to become a cleric that would effectively rule him out of the equation. It was a neat solution to the problem and probably for that reason Geoffrey resisted it.

In fact, he had 'form' in doing so. In 1181, he had refused the post of bishop of Lincoln when he was offered it. He had been fulsome in his excuses; he was too young and not qualified enough for the task. He would be better suited serving his father, Henry II, in a military capacity and 'to refrain from interfering in episcopal matters',[37] so his reluctance to accept Richard's offer probably did not come as a shock.

The canons of York were also unhappy with the proposition, sharing the view that the slippery Geoffrey was an inappropriate choice as their religious leader. But Richard was not to be refused. He put pressure on all parties to drop their opposition, which they duly did. Geoffrey was installed in post, though from the start he took a contentious path on most of the issues that came his way. Another long-running soap opera had begun.

Moving Geoffrey to York had several useful benefits for Richard. Geoffrey's main sphere of influence was in France. By moving him to Yorkshire, where he would be surrounded by men who were largely known to be loyal to Richard, he would be neutralised. But Geoffrey was soon showing open opposition to Richard. He was unhappy at several appointments that Richard made to York and he sought to receive the *pallium*, the robe which the Pope gave to recognise new ecclesiastical appointments, without going through the king as was conventional. Richard was furious and fined him heavily.

Geoffrey was also soon falling out with several important members of the Church at York too, including his dean, Henry Marshal, brother of William. A dispute arose because Henry and Bucard, the treasurer at York, had started a church service without Geoffrey. When Geoffrey later entered, he ordered that the service should stop at once. But Henry and Bucard ignored him and carried on as if he was not there. However, most others in the church stopped and the archbishop began the service again. At this, the treasurer extinguished the candles, effectively bringing the service to a premature end.

The archbishop soon after suspended Henry and Bucard from their posts. It was an unseemly spat and the archbishop followed up by excommunicating the men. In the event the dispute between Geoffrey and Bucard would rumble on and the latter would eventually go to Rome to claim, and receive, absolution from Pope Clement. It would be a reasonable assumption that Geoffrey had had his nose put out of joint by the recent rapid elevation of the Marshals (not just William had benefitted from a change of family fortunes, though perhaps he was the rising star whose illuminating presence had encouraged Richard to promote others such as his brothers). The fall-out was certainly to do with politics rather than religious principle.

Richard also made other important ecclesiastical appointments. William Longchamp, Richard's chancellor, was appointed bishop of Ely, Godfrey de Lucy the same at Winchester, Richard fitzNeal at London and Hubert Walter (the nephew of Ranulf de Glanville) at Salisbury, the latter a post that had been vacant since 1184. The promptness with which these appointments were made contrasted favourably with the deliberate prevarication of Henry II in such matters; he preferred to wait and pocket the revenues from vacant posts for himself. Richard also filled other appointments at religious establishments around the country, including those at Glastonbury, Sherborne, Selby, Feversham and Evesham.[38] By so doing, he lost himself a lot of potential revenue. This was one area where he was much less ruthless in extracting money than his father.

There was another religious controversy yet to be tackled. For several years the monks of the cathedral priory at Canterbury had been at odds with their archbishop, Baldwin of Forde. Baldwin was a vastly experienced cleric who was seemingly destined for a religious life from the start as his father was an archdeacon and his mother had later become a nun. He had studied at Bologna and then earned a reputation as a clerical judge who was involved in some high-profile activities, especially during the bitter dispute between Thomas Becket and Henry II. He later became abbot of the Cistercian house at Forde Abbey on the borders of Dorset and Somerset.

He had been a loyal supporter of Henry II and in his last days had tried to negotiate between the late king and Richard when they were at each other's throats. He had been recognised as a reliable supporter by Henry, who insisted on his election as the new archbishop of Canterbury in 1184. It was a move that was resisted by the monks of the cathedral priory but to no avail and the English bishops duly confirmed Baldwin in the post.

Problems followed soon after. The Cistercian Order was renowned for its austere way of life, whereas the Benedictine monks at Canterbury were suspected of enjoying rather too comfortable an existence, financed by the considerable proceeds that were being gleaned from the burgeoning cult of Thomas Becket. They felt particularly aggrieved when Baldwin announced that he was planning to construct another church in Canterbury dedicated to Becket and St Stephen.

Although the cathedral where the archbishop had been killed would no doubt remain the major point of focus, the proposed new church at Hackington would deprive the monks there of income. It was an unmistakable attempt by Baldwin to establish an element of competition. The impact of the income earned by pilgrimage activities was considerable. It is noteworthy that just a few years before, in 1184, Glastonbury Abbey had been badly damaged in a fire. Miraculously, the tomb of King Arthur and Queen Guinevere was discovered there later, in 1191, leading to a major boost in abbey funds. Becoming a centre of pilgrimage was a very effective economic move.

This discovery at Glastonbury would suit Richard rather well. Some said that Arthur, the king of legend, had not died but was just sleeping, pending a reawakening when his people needed him most. This led to some of Richard's Celtic subjects believing that one day the Norman kings of England would be expelled and the rightful line of Ancient Britain restored. Finding 'Arthur's' dead body (as well as that of his wife Guinevere) nicely proved that there could be no reawakening. But Richard was also interested in the legendary Arthur and would later take a sword named Excalibur on crusade with him; he would make a present of it to Tancred of Sicily at an opportune moment.

That was all in the future and the current controversy concerned Canterbury. The monks there appealed to the Pope to intervene on their behalf. Henry II had previously involved himself in the dispute but only succeeded in adding to his reputation for double-dealing in the process. The monks ended up virtually confined within the priory and were even forced to rely on the provision of food from the local community (including the Jewish element of it) for sustenance.

Richard could not leave this situation unresolved while he was away on crusade, not least because Baldwin would be going too. The archbishop had already taken the cross in January 1188 along with Henry II. Soon after, Baldwin had gone on a memorable preaching tour in Wales, drumming up support for the crusade. Some suggested that he was partly responsible for the harshness of the Saladin Tithe. Now Richard wanted Baldwin to play a role on the crusade but this messy situation needed to be resolved before their departure.

Richard called the monks together, urging them to accept arbitration. They would not do so unless two demands were met. Firstly, work at the rival church at Hackington must stop. Secondly, they demanded the removal of their recently appointed prior, Roger Norreys. Roger had only been in post since October 1189, having been appointed by Baldwin. Although originally one of their own, having been persuaded to support Baldwin in the dispute, he was considered by the monks to be a traitor to their cause. He had escaped the confines of the priory the year before by crawling through the sewers, no doubt considered a very appropriate escape route by some of the brothers.

Tense negotiations followed. Baldwin would not accept the monks' conditions. But at last arbitration from the archbishop of Rouen was accepted and all the disputing parties were called together to hear his judgement. He ruled that Baldwin had the power and the right to appoint whoever he wanted as prior; he could not be prevented from building new churches wherever he felt inclined to do so. In the gathering gloom of the chapter-house the monks were crestfallen. Baldwin's rights had been re-asserted. The monks were forced to kneel before Baldwin and ask for forgiveness.

But then came a remarkable conclusion. Baldwin accepted their contrition and offered his own, asking for their forgiveness in return. It was then agreed that all parties should go and hear a Te Deum in the church and exchange the kiss of peace. Before they did so, a further announcement was made. Work on the church at Hackington was to cease – Baldwin would build one at Lambeth instead – and prior Norreys was to be stood down (he would receive the abbacy of Evesham in compensation for his loss). It was an unexpected compromise solution to a dispute that had festered like an open sore for far too long.[39]

The probable role of Walter of Coutances, the archbishop of Rouen, should not be overlooked. He was renowned as a fixer in such disputes. But neither should that of Richard. He had put subtle pressure on both parties to move from their inflexible positions, not in a display of bullying or Angevin anger but in the application of much more discreet influence. It all contrasted rather positively with the interventions of his late father. But in the process, Richard managed to offend his old rival, Cardinal John of Anagni, who had been kept waiting whilst the negotiations at Canterbury were going on. He had crossed the Channel hoping to bring about a reconciliation and he was greatly offended when he arrived only to find out that everything had been sorted out without him.

In October, Richard received a delegation from Philip of France, telling him that he planned to be at Vézelay the following Easter and urging him to be there also; soon after, Richard confirmed to Philip that he would be (though there would subsequently be a delay). The following month, William the Lion, king of Scotland, arrived in England. He was welcomed by Geoffrey, archbishop of York.

After paying his respects at Bury St Edmunds on 20 November (it was Edmund's festival day and the king regarded Edmund as one of his favourite saints), Richard journeyed on to Canterbury. William made his way to join him there. He was ceremoniously given back the key border castles of Roxburgh and Berwick whilst doing homage to Richard for his lands in England. Richard also confirmed Scotland's independence, though he was given the princely sum of 10,000 marks in return. Although Richard kept some theoretical claims to the Scottish Crown they were not emphasised with much force. This was a welcome contrast to the Scots compared to what had happened during the reign of Henry II; he had tried to increase his influence over their country after the capture of their king.

This naturally enough ingratiated Richard to many Scottish historians, though the sentiments were not necessarily echoed by their English counterparts. The reality was that Richard had many other distractions to cope with and needed to at least neutralise the threat of trouble in his absence from north of the border. Not only was there very little in terms of a legitimate claim to Scotland to base a case on but Richard needed to avoid any trouble from there whilst he was away. He already had an extended set of territories to oversee, including England and half of France. Ireland was also an ongoing problem. In such circumstances, it would have been foolish to lay claim to Scotland too.

The move paid dividends. Scotland did not attempted to take advantage of the chaos that loomed when Richard failed to return home after his crusade. Richard's strategy in this case must be considered a diplomatic success. Neither did most of the semi-autonomous princes of Wales cause problems during his absence.

There was one striking exception to this situation of general stability around England's frontiers, in the form of Rhys of Deheubarth. Richard had feared trouble from his direction and it duly arrived. Rhys succeeded in capturing the castles of Laugharne and Llanstephan in the west of Wales and then laid siege to Carmarthen, a pivotal town in the region. Prince John, who had just been made the lord of Glamorgan, was sent to deal with him. He brought Rhys back to Oxford to talk face-to-face with Richard but the king refused to see him; there were rumours of a private pact being made between Rhys and John.

This seems like a miscalculation on Richard's part, even if the accusations of the secret treaty were true. It would have been more statesmanlike for Richard to have dealt with Rhys one-on-one. In refusing to see Rhys, Richard ensured that he returned to Wales an angry man. He was soon in arms again and would continue to cause trouble in the west of the country for some time.

Richard took other measures to protect the borders of England and Wales. Not only was William Marshal given responsibilities there, so too were other men that he could trust like Henry Longchamp, William fitzAlan and William de Beauchamp. Richard remitted debts owed by William de Braose so that with the money saved the baron could prepare the castles of Llawhaden, Carmarthen and Swansea against any attacks that might come from the direction of Rhys, whose lands were close by.[40]

This, though, was all in the nature of preparatory work. Such events were necessary to ensure that Richard's main focus, the crusade he planned to lead, could be undertaken with reasonable confidence that he would not be forced to hurry back because of problems at home. This would prove to be a very optimistic hope in the light of subsequent events. But the time for waiting was coming to an end. Money had been raised and the troops were assembling. Richard prepared to cross back over the Channel and meet up with Philip. It would not be long before the crusade would at last set out.

7

The Crusade Departs (1190)

'Even those divided by inveterate hatred were recalled into goodwill'

The writer of the *Itinerarium Peregrinorum* on the mood as the crusade departed

The shock engendered by the news of Hattin three years before had barely abated in the West. With each day that passed before the crusade set out, the sense of shame and grief grew. Moralists had a field day looking around for scapegoats to blame. High up the list were the 'Franks', the *Franj* as they were known to their Islamic neighbours, those West Europeans who had settled in Outremer.

The loss of Jerusalem had been such a catastrophic moral blow that in the West it was almost inevitably seen as a punishment from God for the sins and decadence of the *Franj*. The writer of the *Itinerarium Peregrinorum* did not pull his punches about them, claiming that 'it would take a long time to describe their murders, robberies and adulteries' or their 'immoral behaviour, disgraceful lifestyle and foul vices'. He assumed that 'the Lord saw that the land of His Nativity, the place of His passion, had fallen into the filthy abyss' and had therefore turned His back on His people, allowing Saladin to conquer them.[1]

The *Itinerarium* is a key work, particularly for Richard's actions on crusade. It was long thought to have been composed by Geoffrey de Vinsauf, a poet who was probably born in Normandy but spent some time in England; he was a well-known wordsmith of his time. However, more recently opinion has moved towards believing that Richard de Templo, a canon of Holy Trinity in London, was the main author.

The background to the *Itinerarium* is a complex story in itself. There are some fifteen versions currently surviving. There is an account that is believed to be the original version; this is widely known as IP1. Then there is a longer version (IP2), the one believed to be written by Richard de Templo some years later. This takes the original IP1 and adds in a significant amount of detail from other chroniclers, particularly Ambroise who we will also hear a good deal from. It has also been suggested that the writer of IP2 added his own details, hinting that he may himself have been an eye-witness to some of the events he describes. This compilation of several sources is believed to have been written in around 1220 (i.e. about three decades after the events described).[2]

A caveat about both the *Itinerarium* and the chronicle of Ambroise, which is also important in describing the events of Richard's life, is appropriate here. Both works are written in a style that eulogises Richard. They are composed in the same way as the great Arthurian romantic epics of the era. They also reflect other semi-legendary works such as the famous poem that extolled the virtues of Roland, Charlemagne's greatest warrior and one of the most popular of contemporary literary pieces: Roland died in the cause of honour fighting a hopeless rear-guard action in defence of his king and had become renowned for it.

The poem that spoke of Roland's virtues was only the most popular of a whole raft of such works, known collectively as the *chansons de geste* ('songs of deeds'), which talked up the prowess of the greatest knights in Christendom. In this respect, Richard had to be extolled to be the *primus inter pares* of such men.

Ambroise and the author of the *Itinerarium* tell collectively how Richard would charge an enemy single-handed, kill dozens of the enemy on his own and display their heads as proof of his valour. How much of this is literally true is very hard to tell and we should therefore be cautious before accepting either work at face value. The primary purpose of these chroniclers was not to record historical fact but to build up their main subject, Richard, in a way that mirrored the great heroes of the Age of Chivalry. The *Itinerarium* even has a story of the later King Richard taking on a huge wild boar in single combat in a manner that would have done Sir Gawain or Sir Lancelot proud.[3]

Religious fervour in Western Europe demanded that Jerusalem must be restored to Christendom. Some men who appeared reluctant to enlist were sent gifts of wool and distaffs, suggesting that they were more suited to women's activities: a twelfth-century equivalent of the White Feathers of more recent times. Even priests had taken up arms to participate in the crusade.[4] Passions were high and the blood was up. Given this, it became increasingly difficult for either Richard or Philip to delay any longer.

Richard planned to transport his army to the East by ship. This contrasted with major crusades of the past which had typically marched overland to Outremer. This approach became much more difficult soon after the heady success of the First Crusade, which ended with what seemed like the miraculous capture of Jerusalem. This had only been possible because of the disunited state of the Muslim powers in the region when the crusader forces arrived from Western Europe.

This situation changed dramatically soon after. When armies – mainly from Germany, France and the Low countries – set out on the so-called Second Crusade in 1147–48, they were decimated as they crossed Asia Minor. This made a sea-crossing attractive in comparison. It was highly probable that more men would arrive safely, that provisions would be in greater supply, and that the journey would be quicker. Richard planned to go by sea. This, however, looked like a change of plan. During the last years of Henry II's reign, the late king had written to Frederick Barbarossa and King Bela of Hungary asking permission for Richard to lead a crusading army across their lands.

A sea-crossing still presented challenges. Even short crossings of the English Channel could end in disaster, as the tragedy of the *White Ship* had demonstrated. A crossing of the Mediterranean was a major undertaking. The frail ships could founder in storms, or be lost in a different sense by going off-course. There were practical difficulties too; ships had to be conscripted or built from scratch. The Cinque Ports, those famous towns which provided England with much of its seapower during the medieval period, alone provided thirty-three ships.[5] Contributions were also required from across Richard's continental territories.

The cost of this was massive. The fleet would have to be manned during the many months that Richard was away. The price to be paid for the vessels and their crews was substantial. Richard paid wages of 2*d* per day to the sailors, with steersmen of the ship receiving double that (this money to be paid a year in advance).

He probably paid two-thirds of the cost from royal resources, with the crusaders travelling with him providing contributions to make up the rest. Other supplies were also huge in scale; for example, 50,000 horseshoes from the Forest of Dean. Enormous sums of money were involved.[6]

Richard did not have enough resources immediately to hand to pay for all this. He needed to raise more funds and resorted to draconian measures to do so. The expedient of the Saladin Tithe had been a one-off. It was considered a heavy burden by those who paid it and even Richard, with his absolutist tendencies, saw that a repeat could do him great harm. It had raised £60,000, a useful sum though some of this had been wasted on the wars subsequently fought between Henry II and Philip of France. But it had been deeply unpopular: the slightly later chronicler Matthew Paris said of it that 'this forcible extraction had angered clergy and people alike; because although called a charitable donation, it was pure and simple robbery'.[7] Something different was needed if Richard were to bridge the financial gap.

One measure taken was to sell off some of the properties held by the Crown. The wealthier sections of English society were happy to buy into such opportunities. In return for their initial investment, they would receive long-term revenues from what they had purchased. For those that we might now call 'cash rich', this was an excellent chance to secure a regular income stream for years. Famously Richard was even reputed to have said that he would sell off London if he could find a buyer for it.

Richard also issued several new fines to help finance the crusade. He was adept at identifying opportunities to penalise those who had offended the royal authority, however accidental or tangential such offences were. Rarely had a king been so solicitous in identifying such breaches; for example, when the Jews of York were slaughtered, the fines Richard issued were an attempt to redress the wrong done them but also put money into the royal coffers. As Richard of Devizes caustically remarked, 'the king readily disburdened all whose money was a burden to them'.[8]

These expedients were in the main one-offs and Richard could be criticised for losing out on revenues in the longer-term by his short-term measures. They were akin to privatisation in modern times; the family silver can only be sold once and then the regular income streams that should have flowed from it longer-term are lost. But in Richard's situation, it was also one-off expenditure that he was trying to finance, so these measures made a degree of economic sense. And they were certainly successful in terms of their impact, raising £31,000 in 1190,[9] more than enough to replace the lost revenues from his generous allocation of royal lands to others.

But this did not go down well with everyone. These measures were concentrated on a small cross-section of society, namely the rich who held the lion's share of the country's wealth. Gerald of Wales described Richard as 'a robber permanently on the prowl, always probing, always searching for the weak spot where there is something for him to steal'.[10]

Throughout Richard's reign, the short-cross penny remained the basic unit of currency in England, as it was until 1247. It was a sign of the times perhaps that, during his reign, Richard's portrait did not appear on the penny. Instead that of his father, 'Henricus', continued to be used (this was also the case for much of the reign of his brother and successor, John), although this was not the case for coins issued in his French possessions.

Perhaps this was because Richard only spent a few months in England when he was king. It might also reflect the fact that the currency was now increasingly mass-produced. In the past, local moneyers had regarded the coins they produced as a source of pride. But examination of the coins of Richard's reign suggest that the quality was much diminished from that of late Saxon and early Norman times.[11]

Whatever else might be said of the wisdom or otherwise of Richard's measures to raise as much finance as possible, one thing can be said of them: they worked. Sufficient funds were collected to enable the crusade to go ahead. Further, so significant were they that they allowed Richard to be the major partner in the expedition. If the ends justified the means, then Richard was right to do what he did.

But his hard-hitting measures allow some historians to assert that Richard was so obsessed with his crusading obligations that he bled his country dry for no good purpose. However, these accusations come from a modern perspective, not that of the twelfth century. At the time, there was nothing more important than the recovery of Jerusalem, the loss of which was widely deplored. It was a disgrace to the whole of Christendom and it became the issue of the day, both for the Church and for secular society. The significance of Outremer was further inflated by Richard's family connections with the kingdom of Jerusalem. Given his background, and the sense of shock that followed the news of the Battle of Hattin, it was only to be expected that Richard's immediate priority was Outremer.

Reactions were probably also shaped by a sense of guilt. For years, there had been warnings that Outremer was under threat. In 1181, Pope Alexander III had written to the kings of Western Europe in unequivocal terms, stating that a response was urgently needed to the threat; 'therefore let the zeal of the Lord move you, and let not the Christian religion sleep in its sorrow over such mighty evils as are threatening that land; but on the contrary manfully defend all those places which our Saviour and Redeemer has sanctified by His bodily presence, and despise the nations which reject the Lord, and strive to sweep away the Christian name from off of the earth'.[12] These dire warnings, along with the more recent pleas from the Patriarch Heraclius, had largely gone unheeded.

As well as Richard and Philip of France, the Holy Roman Emperor Frederick Barbarossa was leading a massive force eastward. Unlike them, Frederick was taking a land route, planning to cross Asia Minor, modern Turkey. He was an experienced emperor and a forceful leader and he led a large army. Given the combined forces available to the three rulers, this was a massive crusade that was about to set out.

So confident was he of success that Frederick had sent a letter to Saladin, telling him bluntly to 'flee from Jerusalem'. Saladin would soon, he warned, 'become acquainted with the rage of Germany'.[13] Saladin was perturbed enough by the emerging threat that he sent out messengers to assemble as many reinforcements as possible. These included men from as far away as Irbil and Mosul in modern Iraq (Saladin was of Kurdish stock) as well as Baghdad.[14] In the other direction, he also sent pleas for help to Muslim rulers in the Maghreb in North Africa and in Spain.

Frederick left in advance of Richard and Philip. He was a formidable figure; when the Byzantine Emperor sought to outwit him en route, the latter found himself on the verge of a humiliating defeat until he backed down. At one stage, an attack on Constantinople looked likely and was only narrowly averted: instead Barbarossa had his army shipped across to Asia from a camp he had established at a place called Gallipoli. There was skirmishing with the local Seljuk Turks as the army advanced but it survived largely intact and reached Christian lands, ready to descend on Saladin.

'Barbarossa' means 'red beard'; a contemporary description describes him as a man of 'slightly above average height, with gold-red hair and red beard both mingled with grey-white; prominent eyebrows, burning eyes, cheeks short but wide; his chest and shoulders were broad; the rest of his appearance was also manly'.[15]

An intimidating visage was matched to a range of other striking characteristics; organisational capability, military might and a larger-than-life charisma. Now nearly seventy years of age, he had been a ruler for nearly four decades, so he had vast experience. It seemed that a decisive confrontation now loomed.

But then, from the Muslim perspective, Divine Intervention played its part. Frederick got into difficulties crossing a swollen river in Asia Minor; some chroniclers suggest that he was not a strong swimmer. No one knows for sure what happened: he either drowned (though the Muslim chronicler Ibn al-Athir suggests that the water where he perished was not even waist deep)[16] or simply had a fatal heart attack, which was not improbable for a man of his age crossing a fast-flowing river months into a hard campaign. In any case, he was gone.

His body was subjected to gruesome treatment. It was boiled and the flesh, brains and entrails were buried in the city of Antioch. The duke of Swabia, Barbarossa's son, ordered that his bones should be carried, wrapped in linen, with the army to Outremer, where they were eventually buried at Tyre. When the Muslim defenders of the city of Acre, then under siege from a crusader force, heard the news, their joy was uncontainable. They shouted over the walls to their attackers, taunting them at the loss and with it, they hoped, the destruction of any realistic hopes for reinforcements for the crusaders.[17]

The fight went out of the German army. Some wanted to return to Northern Europe at once, others soon lost heart even though they stayed on for a little while. Although a small remnant arrived in Outremer, most of the army drifted away. As a result, the German contribution to the forthcoming Crusade would be hugely diminished, diverting increased responsibility onto the forces of Richard and Philip as a result.

Even though he was suffering from a fever, Richard crossed from Dover to Calais on 12 December 1189. He moved from here to Normandy, accompanied by Philip, Count of Flanders, who had met him on his arrival and escorted him along the way. With him were Cardinal Anagni, Walter, archbishop of Rouen, and the archbishops of Bayeux and Evreux. Richard held his Christmas festivities at Bures in Normandy. Eleanor was still with him there in February 1190 and he was also joined by other members of the family.

Richard then met up with Philip at Nonancourt. There was much to discuss. There were logistical arrangements to finalise and the crusade needed to be properly co-ordinated. The two kings also needed reassurance that their respective kingdoms would be protected during their absence. Although many prominent men were going on crusade, others would be left behind, more than capable of making trouble in their absence; Philip's father, the late Louis VII, had been threatened by the actions of his brother who stayed in France whilst he was involved in the catastrophic Second Crusade as one example of what could go wrong.

Richard and Philip's own personal relationship also entered the equation. It was complicated. At times they had been allies, at others they had been leading armies against each other. Their own personal interests dictated their actions from a day-to-day perspective and there was little depth in their relationship, which was fuelled first and foremost by self-interest. If that self-interest required a change in strategy, they would not hesitate to change tack. With very good reason, neither Richard nor Philip trusted each other one iota.

The terms of the treaty now made had important though subtle undercurrents that hinted at future problems. The two kings were referred to in quite different ways: 'I, Philip, king of France, shall hold Richard, king of England, as my friend and faithful man. I, Richard, king of England, shall hold Philip, king of France, as my friend and lord'.[18] The phrasing is suggestive, demonstrating that Philip was the senior party in terms of his status.

Nothing demonstrated the level of underlying insincerity more than the oaths that both men now took not to take advantage of the other's absence on crusade for their own personal benefit. This was a common enough vow for crusaders to take but if often did not stand the test of time. Nowhere was this to be more spectacularly demonstrated than by Philip's actions, when Richard was later prevented from returning home from Outremer. Rather than being united beneath the sign of the Cross, Richard and Philip took their domestic quarrels with them on crusade and carried on playing out their differences on the far side of the Mediterranean.

Not that Richard can be exonerated from the charge of insincerity. He was still, after nearly three decades, betrothed to Alice, but even though he could now take his own decisions the marriage seemed as far away as ever. The rumours concerning Berengaria of Navarre stubbornly continued. When Eleanor of Aquitaine had become de facto Richard's regent for a time, she reaffirmed that Alice should be kept in confinement. She had little reason to like Alice, especially if the rumours of her relationship with her late husband were true. When Richard later journeyed to France en route to the crusades, Alice also crossed the Channel, but was then kept under close watch in Rouen.

What was Richard thinking as he set out? Was he inspired just by thoughts of glory or did he also have religious motivations? Fulk of Neuilly, a preacher who later played a key role in the Fourth Crusade that took place after Richard's death, accused him of fathering three daughters; Pride, Avarice and Sensuality. Richard, a clever man who possessed a sharp wit, replied that he had given his Pride to the Templars, his Avarice to the Cistercians and his Sensuality to the Princes of the Church.[19] It was an intriguing comment, perhaps not reflecting just Richard's sense of humour but also a jaundiced view of the Church.

Yet not too much should be read into this statement. Richard enjoyed good relationships with the Templars when he was in Outremer and would often be in their company; when he was later captured on his way back from crusade he would have a small escort of their knights with him. He was also a known benefactor of the Cistercian Order, as the chronicler Ralph of Coggeshall, who was himself a member, noted. Richard made gifts to other Christian Orders such as the Premonstratensians. They were renowned for their austere ways and were a favourite Order of that later warrior-king of England Henry V. The Cistercians too, still then a relatively young Order, were also famed for their austerity and for building their abbeys in beautiful, remote locations (though the fact that they were also good for sheep-farming, which underpinned much of the Cistercians' wealth, also helped). Perhaps this should be read as a hint into Richard's own austerity, a soldier's view of the world, giving us a glimpse into the window of his soul.

Given the situation with Alice, Richard's view of marriage is significant. This was a pragmatic one, hardly unique in the context of the times. Marriage then was rarely a question of love or sexual attraction, though that did not mean that a strong sense of attachment might not follow. It was more a question of politics and social advancement. Richard's sponsoring of various matches to some of his key supporters reinforces this. William Marshal's match has already been discussed; another beneficiary was a Poitevin noble, Andrew de Chauvigny, Richard's second cousin. He was married at Salisbury to an heiress from Berry, Denise de Déols.

De Chauvigny and Marshal had been rivals in the last days of Henry II. In a fight between the two, de Chauvigny was unhorsed, as a result of which he broke his arm. The lands held by de Chauvigny's bride included crucial border territories between Anjou and the royal French demesne including the town of Châteauroux. Richard was giving responsibility for key strategic areas to loyal supporters and proven warriors though de Chauvigny would set out on crusade with Richard.

Richard appointed seneschals to protect his interests in Normandy, Maine, Anjou and Aquitaine whilst he was away. Most of them would perform good service in what would be an extended absence though the situation in Normandy would later become a problem. The fact that Richard's position in France did not completely collapse when he subsequently became a prisoner is testament to the fact that his appointments there when he set out on crusade were broadly sound.

There would be one major exception to this general rule in the shape of William Longchamp. Longchamp, bishop of Ely and one of Richard's senior justiciars, was sent back to England to look out for Richard's interests there and accelerate preparations for the crusade. One of his first actions when arriving back was to order that a moat should be built around the Tower of London. He later took delivery of horses from the major cities of the kingdom as well as from the abbeys and manors of England.

Richard continued to exercise a great deal of caution as he continued his preparations for the crusade even when he reached France. Neither was Philip in a hurry. It was finally agreed that they should set out together; this could be interpreted as a sign of unity but it much more likely reflected a lack of trust. Philip had some very valid reasons for delaying. His queen, Isabella, was heavily pregnant. In fact, an awful family tragedy was looming. On 15 March 1190, Isabella gave birth to stillborn twins, losing her own life in the process. She was buried soon after in the new church at Nôtre Dame in Paris. Philip could easily have used this as an excuse for an extended delay but did not take the opportunity to do so.

The challenges facing Richard in terms of securing his French territories in his absence should not be underestimated. His northern French territories were adjacent to the French royal demesne and Normandy and Anjou had both been under threat from the French king in the recent past: just because Philip was away with Richard on campaign did not mean that his supporters who stayed behind might not try to take advantage of the English king's absence.

His southern French territories were also a problem. One prominent French baron had conspicuously not taken a crusader vow: Count Raymond of Toulouse. The possibility of his misbehaviour in Richard's absence had to be guarded against. The areas that abutted Navarre and the Basque region, on the southern fringes of Aquitaine, were a problem too. They were notorious for their lawlessness. The busy pilgrim route to Santiago de Compostella, one of the most significant in Europe, passed through them.

The Basques and Navarrese were notorious for extorting money from passing pilgrims, a lucrative trade given how many of them there were. A contemporary guide for pilgrims described the peoples of these lands in extremely hostile terms, describing them as 'malignant, dark in colour, ugly of face, debauched, perverse, faithless, dishonourable, corrupt, lustful, drunken, skilled in all forms of violence' and so on.

The guide was a description in many words of the Basques and the Navarrese, most of them negative. It was as if the writer wanted to utilise every piece of vocabulary possible to denigrate the inhabitants of these lands. A Basque or a Navarrese would kill a Frenchman for a penny, the writer noted.[20] Mindful of the flexible views that existed regarding law and order there, Richard took the opportunity to lay out a few ground-rules before he left, though whether these independently minded people would honour any commitments they made to behave themselves in Richard's absence, only time would tell.

Richard found time before his departure to journey far south, to the region of the Pyrenees. Here, the lord of the castle of Bigorre had been engaging in banditry against passing pilgrims on their way to Compostella in Spain. Richard would not tolerate this and decided to make an example of someone, to 'encourage the others' whilst he was away. The unruly lord duly met his end hanging from a rope; a useful if brutal message to other warlords in the region to behave themselves.

A counterbalance to these threats in the region was the renewal of an old alliance between Richard and King Alfonso II of Aragon, frequently a rival of Toulouse. This also strengthened the links between Richard and King Sancho VI (El Sabio, 'The Wise') of Navarre, who was on good terms with Alfonso. Despite Richard's extended betrothal to Alice of France, there had already been rumours of a match with Sancho's eligible daughter, Berengaria. It is likely that now discussions on that point took a decisive turn. With Richard planning to set out on crusade, with all the attendant personal risks which this entailed, the need for a wife and an heir assumed vital political significance.

In the light of these considerations, a conference held by Richard in Normandy in mid-March assumes seminal significance. Several bishops were present at this, along with Richard's brothers John and Geoffrey, who were both cajoled into taking an oath not to return to England for three years. This clearly shows what Richard thought of their potential reliability in his absence. Eleanor of Aquitaine was also present. Most remarkably of all perhaps, Alice was there at the conference but she would soon afterwards find herself returning to confinement in Rouen.

What went on behind closed doors is largely unknown but the heavy-hitting nature of the delegation suggested it was something highly important. It could have been held just to finalise crusading arrangements and the pressurising of John and Geoffrey to stay out of England was significant in its own right. Yet given events concerning Berengaria and Alice later that year, it is probable that more personal matters were also on the agenda.

Richard was later persuaded to change his mind regarding the travel restrictions he had placed on John, possibly through the intervention of Eleanor. This was to prove fortunate for Richard: when John later began to stir up trouble in England, Eleanor and other key supporters of Richard could limit the damage: this would have been much more difficult to do if John was on the other side of the Channel.

There would be no reprieve for Geoffrey though. He was not Eleanor's son and she had no reason to feel any sympathy for her late husband's illegitimate offspring. He was installed as archbishop of York at Tours but was not allowed to return to England to take up office there. The ban would subsequently be breached by Geoffrey, leading to some dramatic complications at a later stage.

In addition to Geoffrey, Richard and John had another half-brother, William Longespée, born in 1176. William was the son of Ida de Tosny, a royal ward who became the mistress of Henry II.[21] Ida was subsequently married to the earl of Norfolk and several children followed. Too young to go on crusade with his brother, William would later fight alongside Richard in Normandy. William would subsequently be given a good match by Richard when he was married to Ela, countess of Salisbury. He would become a staunch supporter of John when he became king. He died in 1226 and was the first man to be buried in the new Salisbury Cathedral.

Richard at last felt ready to depart. He journeyed to Chinon where he issued orders concerning the discipline of his troops. These ordinances were tough. They stated that if a man killed another whilst at sea, then he was to be tied to the victim's body and both should be thrown into the waters together. If the killing took place on land, then the murderer should be buried alive with the corpse. If a man even drew a knife against another, then his hand was to be cut off. A thief apprehended aboard ship should be tarred with boiling pitch and feathered and put ashore as soon as possible.[22]

On 24 June, Richard bade his farewells to Eleanor at Chinon. He would be required to rely on her in his absence, though the extent of this reliance was not yet fully apparent. Subsequent events would reveal that Eleanor was the vital bedrock on which Richard's tenure of the English crown was based. Neither mother nor son can have had any idea just how much water would flow under the bridge before Richard eventually returned to his territories in England and France.

Richard journeyed to Tours to prepare himself personally for what was to come, for a crusade was essentially an act for the benefit of an individual's soul, even if that individual was a king. Richard was given the scrip and staff of a pilgrim, which was exactly what a crusader was. Roger of Howden wrote that when Richard leant on the staff it snapped under his weight; not a good omen at the beginning of the crusade. By 2 July Richard had reached Vézelay, where the body of Mary Magdalene was believed to lie. Here he met up with Philip who was with his army and some of his key lieutenants including Hugh, duke of Burgundy, and Philip of Alsace, the count of Flanders.

The writer of the *Itinerarium* paints a vivid picture of the scene; of vast numbers of pavilions, so many of them that it was as if they formed a city. The elite of the young warriors of Western Europe were present, so numerous that they seemed to form an invincible army. Military discipline and common purpose were the secrets of ensuring that the army was successful, reasoned the author. An absence of these qualities was all that could defeat them, or so the writer intimated. In those early, euphoric days, so typical of the early days of so many wars over time before the harsh reality of conflict becomes apparent, it seemed that nothing stood between the crusade and the re-establishment of God's lost kingdom in Outremer.[23] The two kings seemed to be on good terms with each other. At the start, the mood music as we might now call it was encouraging.

An agreement was brokered between the two kings. This stated that all conquests made during the crusade were to be divided equally between them. There was some ambiguity about exactly how this was to be interpreted in practice, a confusion that was to create significant problems later. But Richard and Philip at this stage found some semblance of common ground. Henry II had before his death agreed to pay an indemnity to Philip, amounting to 20,000 marks: Richard now paid this over plus another 4,000 marks, a generous gesture that was potentially useful in securing good relations between the two men.

Philip and Richard led their armies south, leaving Vézelay on 4 July, the third anniversary of the disaster at Hattin. They made for the coast and their respective fleets. Richard was headed for Marseille and Philip for Genoa (the French king did not like sea voyages and was keeping them to a minimum); they would re-join each other at Messina in Sicily. The two men may have aspired to be equals in terms of their roles but they created a vastly different impression on observers; to Bertran de Born, Richard seemed like a lion, Philip a lamb. His impression of Richard was justified, his observation of Philip far less so, for he had hidden depths as Richard would find out.

Gerald of Wales also referred to Richard's leonine qualities and the attribution soon stuck with further references along these lines being made in other accounts of Richard's life that appeared in the thirteenth century.[24] The comparison with the lion seemed to sum up the king's character rather well; on the one hand, fierce in battle and respected for his fighting qualities, on the other someone to be feared.

On reaching Lyon, the two kings separated. The spirit of the armies was good, though the womenfolk who bade goodbye to their men were often in tears as they said their farewells.[25] However, practical problems were already emerging. The land through which the armies were passing struggled to provide them with sufficient supplies though many of the inhabitants rushed out to give them water and were ecstatic at the wonderful sight. Some of the chroniclers' descriptions may be hyperbole, though they sound remarkably similar to the euphoria that has greeted the start of other, more recent wars.

Disaster was narrowly averted when a narrow wooden bridge collapsed under the weight of the men crossing it; however, although 100 fell into the water, only two men were lost. But this caused a delay; the only way that the army that was stranded on the wrong side of the Rhône could be brought over was in small skiffs, which clearly took a long time given the number of men involved.[26] According to Ambroise, it took three days to complete the crossing.[27]

Richard had many more men with him than Philip; records show that the French fleet in Genoa had been contracted to provide sufficient transport for 650 knights and 1,350 squires and their horses – though these figures understate the contribution of the French to the crusade as many had journeyed east independently in advance of Philip.[28] Many French crusaders had already arrived in Outremer where the crucial seaport of Acre, which had fallen into Muslim hands after the capture of Jerusalem, was the centre of a massive siege, which was widely seen as a symbol of Outremer's fightback and a barometer of its chances of success.

Richard's army was subject to a greater degree of centralised control than Philip's. Richard's ordinances showed that he intended to keep a tight grip on his men, to control them with a rod of iron. Yet Richard had never fought a campaign on this scale before and the crusade would be a massive learning experience for him. He was a proud man and a prouder king; just how merited any claims to greatness were was about to be tested.

This was the greatest force that England had ever contributed to the crusades, though it must be emphasised that there were also many non-Englishmen in it from Aquitaine, Anjou and Normandy in particular. The English participants were noted for eating three times as much bread as anyone else in the army and drinking a hundred times more wine.[29] While there had been English involvement in previous crusades, the English had in the past been very much the junior partners when compared to soldiers from

France, the Low Countries and Germany amongst others. Now that was going to righted.

Men were marching off to war, with that heady and intoxicating cocktail of fear, excitement and a sense of adventure and anticipation that often characterises such expeditions, particularly when the participants do not really know what they are letting themselves in for. For the king of England too, the adrenaline was flowing. It was a wonderful chance for Richard to make his mark on contemporary opinion and on the course of history.

The chroniclers wrote enthusiastically of a new sense of purpose that was abroad. One of them said of the initial reaction to the calling of the crusade that 'songs were silent, dainty dishes and luxurious clothes given up; disputes laid to rest; a new peace formed between old enemies; legal actions terminated in settlements; and whatever the case, even those divided by inveterate hatred were recalled into goodwill because of this recent development'.[30] Given the bitter acrimony between Henry II, Richard and Philip that had been present in the build-up to the crusade this was a rather rose-tinted view of reality. The full extent of the goodwill between Richard and Philip was about to be tested to breaking point and beyond.

8

Mayhem and Matrimony: The Journey Begins (1190–1191)

'A fine lady, both noble and beautiful'
Ambroise on the Lady Berengaria

The eleventh century had been an age of extreme violence. Society teetered on the edge of a precipice, threatening to tumble into oblivion. Famine stalked the land and some chroniclers wrote of the practice of cannibalism in times of extreme shortages. There was also an absence of strong centralised authority in Europe. Local warlords took what they wanted and those who dared resist were crushed underfoot. Some of the offences against humanity perpetrated included the seizure of property from, and violence against, the Church.

It was partly because of this seemingly uncontrollable violence that the Catholic Church developed an idea that, if morally highly dubious (even to some at the time), nevertheless had a ruthless pragmatism about it. One of the early exponents of the idea of redirecting violence against the enemies of Christendom, Abbo of Fleury, who wrote in the late tenth century, said of the warlords 'let them not make war within their mother's bosom, and turn their efforts rather to extirpating the enemies of the holy Church of God'.[1]

About a century later, Pope Urban II latched on this concept to come up with the idea of the crusades; sanctified violence against the enemies of Christ. Men could now go and fight without the need to feel guilty as a result; in fact, they were doing the work of God. It was an idea that worked brilliantly in meeting the aspirations of both Church and warlords; the latter could now do what they liked best and serve the interests of the former in doing so. Everybody was happy – except for those on the receiving end of the crusades.

Societal upheaval nevertheless continued in Europe into the twelfth century. Generally, these years saw a significant strengthening of monarchies and as a result centralised power, in England particularly so during the reigns of Henry II and Richard I after the chaos of Stephen's civil wars. France had lagged behind but then Philip began to close the gap significantly. Indeed, within the first two decades of the thirteenth-century England was falling apart again and France presented the stronger image of a powerful monarchy.

Recruitment for the crusades was driven by two major factors. Firstly, this was a religious age and the remittance of sins which participation in a crusade offered was no small reward given the threat of harsh judgement in the world that was to come. But it was also a militarised society. Henry II had issued decrees concerning the weapons that were to be held by members of the various sections of society. Holders of a single knight's fee were to keep a cuirass (armour covering the torso), a helmet, shield and lance. Freemen were to keep a gambeson (a long, padded jacket), an iron head-piece and a lance.

Further rules dictated that no weapons were to be held by Jews. There were restrictions on carrying arms out of England without the king's permission, as well as selling them. On the death of those in possession of these arms they were to be bequeathed to their heirs.[2] This meant that men were equipped to fight at short notice, which was invaluable at times such as this.

Richard, now the beneficiary of this recently forged centralised monarchical power, was one of many drawn in by the prospect of both glory and religious reward offered by the crusades and he now set out enthusiastically to redeem his pilgrim vows. He and his entourage made their way to Marseille, expecting to meet the English fleet there. This was some 100 ships strong. The fleet was well provisioned. Most of the ships (excluding the larger 'busses') could carry forty trained battle horses, forty horsemen, forty foot-soldiers, fifteen sailors and enough food for a year, animals included (the 'busses' could carry twice as much).[3] But the fleet was behind schedule. When Richard scanned the horizon as he reached the Mediterranean coast, he looked in vain. The fleet was late and was only just about to pass through the Straits of Gibraltar.

The fleet, mainly composed of snacks or snekkars, long, thin, oared transport ships of Scandinavian type,[4] had put into Lisbon on its way down to the Mediterranean, having set sail from Dartmouth. It was under the command of Richard de Camville and Robert de Sablé.[5] On reaching Lisbon, which had only been captured from Muslim forces not long before, they at first proved helpful, assisting King Sancho I in driving off a Muslim attack (parts of the Iberian Peninsula were then still under Islamic rule).

But the situation soon deteriorated. Some of the crusaders were offended by the presence of Muslims and Jews moving freely about the city; this outraged their Christian sensibilities. Other elements of the fleet were little better than common criminals. They molested women, stole whatever they desired and pillaged all the vineyards in the vicinity, 'not leaving so much as a grape or a cluster'. The citizens of Lisbon were incensed and fought back. Lives were lost on both sides. Sancho shut the gates of Lisbon, trapping many crusaders inside, and 700 of them soon found themselves locked up.[6]

There were several features here that were common to many such military expeditions in the medieval period. It was very hard to keep control of a large body of men who had been cooped up in ships for a time, never much liking military discipline and with too much time on their hands. This was a recipe for trouble and frequently led to it. This would be shown with horrific effect when the Fourth Crusade sacked Constantinople just fourteen years later.

There were also different views of the world in play too. In regions where many Muslims, Jews and Christians were present there was a need to find a way of living together. A degree of tolerance, of 'live and let live', was necessary. This was true in Iberia, it was also true in Outremer. Crusaders from other regions could not understand this. Egged on by crusading sermons that inflamed the emotions and priests who travelled with them to remind them of the evil nature of the enemy, this tolerance seemed contradictory, hypocritical even. This was almost bound to lead to violence.

Nevertheless, Sancho managed to patch things up with the crusaders. A truce was brokered and the crusading fleet soon after sailed away, no doubt much to the relief of the people of Lisbon. The fleet then sailed past a great mountain that jutted out into the sea. This was Cape St Vincent, which was 600 years later to be the site of one of Nelson's greatest triumphs. They then cruised past what is now Cadiz and through the Straits of Gibraltar, or the Straits of Africa as they were known then.

Then it was on past Malaga, Almeria – famous for its silk – Cartagena and Valencia. All these places were then in Muslim hands. They then passed Christian cities, the property of the king of Aragon, including Tarragona and Barcelona. Next it was the picturesque port of Collioure and Narbonne and the mouth of the Rhône. But by the time the fleet reached Marseille, then part of the territories of Aragon, Richard had gone. From here, with a fair wind, it was only fifteen days sail across the Mediterranean to Acre.[7] The fleet stopped at Marseille for eight days to carry out running repairs and then pushed on to Messina, hoping to catch up with Richard there.

An advance party had already set out from England for Outremer. This included Baldwin, the archbishop of Canterbury, and Ranulf Glanville, the former justiciar of Henry II. They reached Tyre in Outremer on 16 September 1190. However, John, the bishop of Norwich, was not with them even though he had started out in their party. He had stopped off at Rome and been absolved from keeping his crusader vows by the Pope and then returned to England, having been robbed of everything that he was carrying whilst passing through Burgundy. Richard was angry and fined the bishop 1,000 marks.[8] Perhaps he was so annoyed because this was part of a wider trend; many prominent clerics took a vow to go on crusade but only Baldwin and Hubert Walter actually fulfilled it (though many men of the cloth of lower standing did take part and played various important roles in the crusade).[9]

Richard made his own way at a more leisurely pace. Before he left Marseille, he was joined during August by someone of vital importance to our understanding of Richard's reign. This was Roger of Howden (or Hoveden), a place in the east of Yorkshire. Roger was a justice of the forests in Yorkshire, Northumberland and Cumberland. Henry II had used him as an ambassador on several occasions so he was clearly a man who enjoyed royal confidence.

His main claim to fame though is as a chronicler. He wrote a history of Henry II and Richard I (the *Gesta Henrici II et Gesta Regis Ricardi*) which was later incorporated into a monumental work, his *Chronica*. This covered the period from 721 to 1201. Much of the early history in this is from other sources so it adds little to our knowledge of those periods. However, Roger's account of the reigns of Henry II and Richard I is a goldmine, especially as Roger was with Richard when he eventually reached Outremer.[10]

Roger returned to England before the crusade was over and the latter part of his chronicle concentrates mainly on ecclesiastical matters, especially a fall-out between Geoffrey, the archbishop of York, and his canons, with whom he was in violent disagreement in a dispute that seemed to go on forever.

Another crusader chronicler was Ambroise. He was probably a cleric, and he may well have been present at and taken a part in the coronations of both Richard I and, later, John. His language was Norman, which suggests that the duchy was his place of origin. He is quick to praise the Norman warriors on crusade and denigrate those who were French. His account was written after Richard's return from crusade in 1194 but before his death in 1199.[11] Little is known about Ambroise's life story and only a single version of his chronicle remains in the Vatican. It was long overlooked by historians but is an important document, giving us the first-hand account of an eye-witness to many of the great events of the crusade.

Richard had grown tired of waiting for his ships at Marseille. As well as the diversion at Lisbon, they had earlier been held up by storms in the Bay of Biscay (then known as 'The Spanish Sea'); the seas had been mountainous and the crews aboard had despaired of their lives. They had only been saved, they later said, by a vision of Thomas Becket; ironic given his dispute with Henry II.

They eventually arrived in Marseille on 22 August 1190; Richard had left there over two weeks before. He had hired ten large ships and twenty galleys and made his own way along the French coast and then down the Italian peninsula. He kept close to the shore, as was customary for ships of the time, passing close to Nice on the way; just after here was the border between the kingdom of Aragon and those of the Italian territories. Soon after, he arrived at Genoa, the departure point of the French fleet, only to find that Philip of France was still there, ill and bed-ridden.

Philip asked Richard for a favour, the loan of five galleys. Richard responded with a counter-offer of three but this was not sufficient for Philip who turned it down. This did not augur well for future co-operation on the crusade. It presumably would have been easy enough for Richard to find the two extra ships from somewhere and he did not make the effort to do so. On the other hand, three galleys were better than none and Philip's response seemed churlish.

Whilst here, Richard also held discussions with Grimaldo Grimaldi, a prominent statesman who had been consul of the city several times. Following on from these talks, Grimaldi's son Frederick joined Richard's army as Master of Crossbowmen. If this was a plan to forge close links between Richard and the Genoese, it failed. The Genoese would later throw in their lot with Philip and the French when there was a falling-out with Richard. The Grimaldis continue to play a role in modern Europe as their descendants form the ruling dynasty in Monaco.

Richard then set off down the Italian coast. He stayed at Portofino for a few days and then moved on to Pisa, where he was reunited with Walter of Coutances, the archbishop of Rouen, and John, bishop of Evreux, who was ill. Richard made no attempt to visit Pope Clement III even though he stopped at the mouth of the River Tiber, close by the ancient ruins of the Roman port of Ostia. An envoy was sent to him from Clement to encourage him to visit but Richard showed no intention of doing so, having little time for the Papacy and regarding it first and foremost as a money-making operation. In fact, it was said that he equated Clement with the Anti-Christ, which helped to explain his reluctance. But he found plenty of time, several weeks in fact, to stop in Naples and Salerno. There was no sense of urgency; that said, he may have wanted to spend some time with the famous doctors of Salerno to seek advice as to how to improve his frequently poor health.

Whilst in Salerno, he received word that his fleet had been sighted and was not far off Messina, the rendezvous for the English and French fleets before setting off to Outremer (though some crusaders had made their way independently through ports such as Genoa, Venice and Brindisi).[12] Richard now hurried up. He made his way more quickly down the Italian Peninsula, stopping overnight in abbeys and castles that he passed on the way. By 22 September 1190, he was in Sicily.

He had to cross the Straits of Messina from mainland Calabria to get there, a region which at the time formed part of the kingdom of Sicily along with most of the southern part of the Italian peninsula. Sicily had been conquered in stages by the Norman lord Robert Guiscard and then his brother Roger; the current kings of Sicily were descended from them. Robert had also taken the islands of Corfu (where, Roger of Howden said, the traitorous Judas Iscariot had been born), Crete and Rhodes though some of these had later reverted to Byzantine rule.

The last part of the journey to the Straits of Messina was an overland one. Richard was travelling virtually without an escort. The fact that the king was heading across a strange and unknown country with so little support is an example of Richard's personal rashness, in contrast to his strategic and tactical caution. Another illustration of this soon followed. Shortly after leaving Mileta Richard passed a cottage, inside which he saw a majestic falcon. To Richard this was not a bird for rustics but for nobility and kings so he helped himself to it.

Not knowing who he was, the householder came at him with a knife. Richard defended himself, striking him with the flat of his sword, which promptly broke. He only escaped by hurling stones at the assailant and his friends as they came at him. An ignominious end for the mighty crusader was only narrowly averted. The whole situation had brought about by Richard's lack of tact and excessive sense of his self-importance. It was not the last time that he would be in trouble because of this particular character trait.

Having crossed the Straits of Messina (then called the 'river Del Far')[13] and spent his first night on the island of Sicily in a tent close by a stone tower, Richard arrived at Messina on 23 September 1190. He found that Philip was already there, having made a quiet entrance into the city, which was then ruled by King Tancred.

The island of Sicily was a fascinating and unique cultural melting-pot. When the Norman conquerors took over they found an ancient mix of cultures there. There was a Roman influence but also an even older Greek presence there, as well as evidence of Carthaginian occupation. Later Byzantine conquest accounted for the fact that there was a strong Orthodox influence too. The island had also been subject to Muslim colonisation.

The Norman invaders, rather than seeking to obliterate such cultural foundations, let them be and what resulted was an amazing hybrid, evidenced by the glorious architecture of places such as Monreale Abbey, a fascinating mixture of West European, Orthodox and Muslim building styles. But not everyone was impressed. Ambroise was blunt in his assessment of the city that Richard had arrived at: 'Messina was full of comforts, but we found them an evil people'.[14]

Messina was at the extreme north-east corner of the roughly triangular island. It stood on one side of a very narrow crossing over to the mainland of Italy; so close is the island here to the mainland that in modern times there has been regular talk of building a bridge across. In the distant shadow of Mount Etna, and as such at the mercy of frequent seismic upheavals, Messina was one of the main ports of an island that was astonishingly fertile, renowned for its olives, its grapes and its wheat production (in former times, it had been the bread-basket of the Roman Empire).

Philip had entered Messina without ostentation. Despite the shortness of the crossing, he had a rough passage across the Straits of Messina from the mainland and food, wine and other supplies had been thrown overboard to increase the stability of his ships; no doubt, this did nothing to improve Philip's view of the benefits of seafaring. He had been put up in the palace of Tancred who was a usurper, having claimed the kingdom after the death of King William II. The late king had played an important part in Outremer after Hattin, sending a fleet that helped to save Tripoli after Joscius, archbishop of Tyre, had arrived on the island carrying the terrible tidings.

Philip's arrival could not have contrasted more markedly with that of Richard, who was determined to put on a show. With a large fleet of what were described as 'innumerable galleys', draped in bright colours with flags flapping in the breeze and the sound of trumpets rending the air, the ships of Richard's fleet hove into view. They included *dromonds*, galleys that were bulkier than the sleek *snekkars*, aboard which Richard's warhorses were carried.

It was an impressive sight and the people of Messina flocked to see it. One man literally rose above it all; Richard had positioned himself on a raised platform so that as many people as possible could see him. He clearly wanted to be noticed. He was dressed in his best, eager to make a strong first impression. He did not disappoint, though not everyone was impressed, particularly Philip; and some of the local population also felt that Richard had overdone it. The English chroniclers on the other hand thought this show of strength and magnificence completely appropriate and exactly what was needed to project authority in contrast to the rather mean entrance made by Philip.[15]

Richard now met Philip again. On the surface, all was sweetness and light. But the real feelings of Philip can best be gauged by the fact that he tried to sail away from Messina that same day, only to be forced back by a contrary breeze. Tensions soon bubbled to the surface, partly because of the rough behaviour of some of Richard's uncouth soldiers. Some of the locals were probably reminded of the fact that only a century or so before Sicily had been conquered by Norman adventurers of similar racial origin as some of Richard's army; hardly a happy precedent.

Ambroise spoke of barely concealed contempt from some of the local population; of fingers pointed in the street, of insults, of curses muttered under the breath, even of crusaders murdered and their corpses thrown into latrines.[16] Richard of Devizes stated that they were killed in their 'forties and fifties' whenever they were found unarmed, though this is hard to take at face value as a much less measured response would surely have been launched by Richard if this had been true.[17]

An atmosphere of mutual distrust quickly developed. Some of Richard's men behaved inappropriately towards the women of the city, as they had done in Lisbon. There were tensions over comparatively minor issues. Ambroise spoke of a woman called Ame who came into the camp to sell her bread for prices that the crusaders thought extortionate. There was a violent verbal altercation which then turned physical and one of Richard's followers was badly beaten-up. Disputes over alleged profiteering are hardly unique in wartime but it marked another deterioration in relations between the locals and the crusading army.[18]

Richard tried his best to restore order; after all, he had issued those fearsome ordinances before leaving on crusade. Then a further problem raised the tension another notch. Richard's sister Joanna was the childless widow of the late king of Sicily, William II.[19] Tancred had treated her shabbily and kept her as a captive. This situation quickly changed when Richard arrived with a large army; Tancred may have been ambitious but he was not a fool. Joanna was released shortly after Richard's arrival.

Tancred was now in a difficult position. When William II died, his heir was his aunt, Constance. She was married to the son of Frederick Barbarossa, Henry. Pope Clement III was terrified at the prospect of being surrounded by Germans and therefore gave his support to Tancred, an illegitimate cousin of the late king. He did not seem to have a lot going for him. Physically he was completely unprepossessing. His opponents, and there were many of them, said that he was so ugly that he looked like a monkey with a crown on its head.[20]

Matters now got more complicated. The recently widowed Philip set eyes on the newly released Joanna and liked what he saw. Rumours of a potential marriage quickly developed but Richard was not interested and they came to nothing, though Philip did not drop the idea for several years. Soon after arriving in Messina, Joanna was taken to the Italian mainland and holed up temporarily in the priory of La Baniare, where she was watched by a strong guard.

That left the small matter of Joanna's large dower, which should have been handed to her now that she was widowed. William II had also left a sizeable bequest in his will to Henry II, including money, gold, huge quantities of grain and wine, and a vast fleet of 100 galleys. Tancred considered that the death of Henry II meant that this obligation no longer stood; Richard, as Henry's heir, not unnaturally took the opposite view and demanded that Tancred honoured the arrangement.

Richard, always on the lookout for an opportunity to make extra money, was unlikely to let this chance go and soon increased the pressure on Tancred. Early in October 1190 he took over the monastery of St Saviour and used it as a base for building up supplies. To some it looked like a precursor to the conquest of Sicily. There were further brawls between Richard's men and the citizens of Messina whilst French troops were allowed to come and go into and out of the city as they pleased. Richard sensed collusion between Tancred and Philip. It was hardly likely to keep his short-fused temper under control.

The crisis point was reached on 9 October, when Richard held a conference with Tancred and Philip to soothe the situation. Even while they were talking, violence flared up again and rioters attacked Richard's camp. Richard asked Philip for help to restore order but none was forthcoming. Richard then stormed out and told his men to prepare for battle; it is tempting to assume, so rapid was the response, that Richard had anticipated such a situation and had told his men to be ready for it in advance.

The fighting that followed was not without its challenges. The townsfolk had the advantage of high ground and threw down stones onto the soldiers attacking them but this did not deter Richard from charging uphill, even though he was significantly outnumbered. Three knights who broke into the town but were then cut off without support were killed and their bodies thrown back over the walls.[21]

On the other hand, his men included seasoned troops, which gave them an advantage. Although some of Richard's men were lost – five knights and twenty men-at-arms were killed – the outcome was decisive. His archers caused chaos; 'the walls are left without guard, because no one could look out of doors, but he would have an arrow in his eye before he could shut it', as one commentator put it.[22] Richard's men broke open the gates of the city with a battering ram. They soon took Messina and a limited sack followed. Some of the ships in the harbour were burned. According to Ambroise some women were 'acquired', which sounds ominous for them.

Richard's banners were soon flying over the walls. The flying of these pennons was not just a symbolic gesture. It represented the fact that in Richard's eyes the city now belonged to him. Philip was peeved at this and wanted his own standard to be hoisted over the city so that he could have a share of the spoils; this despite the fact that he had not long before refused to get involved. But a deal of sorts was agreed by which the Templars and Hospitallers took over the city, which defused the situation for the time being, though Ambroise says that the dispute rankled so much with Philip that it eventually had far-reaching implications.[23] But this was not the end of it. Richard soon built a wooden castle, dominating the city. It was called 'Mategriffon' – 'Kill the Greeks' ('Greeks' being the pet name given by western crusaders to Sicilians).[24]

Richard appointed ambassadors to treat with Tancred. They included Hugh, duke of Burgundy, and Robert of Sablé, a trusted lieutenant of Richard and one of his fleet commanders; he would later become Master of the Knights Templar.[25] There was tension for a time and supplies were cut off from Richard's army though he had sufficient stores with his fleet to keep his army adequately provisioned. Tancred soon realised that he was losing the game and came to terms with Richard. He hung on to Joanna's dower but paid Richard 20,000 ounces of gold for the privilege; the English king was still showing considerable fund-raising skills.

On top of this another deal was struck and this one was even more remarkable. Tancred had a young daughter – 'a talented and attractive girl'[26] in contrast to reports of Tancred's appearance – and it was agreed that she should marry Arthur, Richard's young nephew, though as he was only two years old at the time it would be a while yet before the marriage could take place. Tancred would pay another 20,000 ounces of gold for Arthur's hand, though Richard would have to pay this back if the wedding did not subsequently take place.

As part of this arrangement, Richard would designate Arthur his heir in the absence of any son of his own. This bypassed any claim that his brother John might have. The terms of the agreement with Tancred were unambiguous on this point: it talked of Arthur 'our nephew, and if perchance we die childless, our heir'.[27] Such an agreement could only undermine the self-confidence of John, in a way that Richard would have understood only too well after his own treatment by his late father. Indeed, if the roles had been reversed then it is likely that Richard would have acted in the same way as John later did.

That said, the agreement, which was recorded in detail by Roger of Howden, was hedged about with caveats; about what would happen if either king died before the deal concerning Arthur's marriage was fulfilled, or if Arthur himself proved recalcitrant (though given his age, this was ridiculous), of what sanctions would come into play if the terms of peace between the two men were breached in the future. In other words, what comes across is a deal that smacks of expediency, with a significant possibility that its terms would at some stage in the future be reneged upon. But it did at least give Richard a nice sum of money in his pocket for his very high travel expenses.

The effect of these negotiations, led by William, archbishop of Monreale; William, archbishop of Reggio; and John, bishop of Evreux, was to change Tancred from a hostile opponent of Richard to a potential ally. This would be useful to Tancred as well as the English king, for his claim to Sicily was vigorously contested by the Holy Roman Emperor, Henry VI. Henry had already tried to take Sicily and had indeed captured Salerno and then laid siege to Naples on his way to attempting to do so. But Henry's army had then been decimated by disease and the emperor almost died. He retreated to Milan but there was little doubt that the kingdom of Sicily was unfinished business as far as Henry was concerned.

The terms of the agreement required Richard to come to Tancred's aid should he be attacked, though significantly only if the king of England was in Sicily at the time. For Richard, the alliance against Henry VI would have disastrous future consequences. Richard and the Angevins were traditionally opponents of the Holy Roman Emperor whilst Philip was friendly towards him. The tangled power politics of Europe were a vital backdrop during these years and Richard would later find himself in deep water because of them.

Full details of the arrangement were then sent to the Pope so that he too would be aware of them. Matters in Sicily improved, though Ambroise's hint that occasionally miscreants were hanged or killed for their actions suggests that not all was plain sailing even now.[28] All these negotiations were done at a distance it would seem, for soon after Tancred and Richard met for the first time at Catania; the Sicilian king had previously stayed in Palermo.

There was for the time being a thawing of relations with Philip, though these improvements would prove to be temporary. Richard made an important concession, ceding a third of what he had received from Tancred to Philip. They also agreed on pricing arrangements for goods supplied by Sicilian merchants; these had previously been excessive in many people's eyes. Bread prices were fixed at a penny a loaf and the price of wine was also stabilised. No merchant was to make a profit of more than 10 per cent on any particular deal.

There were also restrictions placed on gaming, which had led to trouble when those who had lost were unable to pay their dues. In future, common soldiers and sailors were banned from games of chance in the absence of their officers who were presumably supposed to limit any excesses and act as an arbiter in the case of a dispute. Any soldier who broke this rule was to be whipped through the camp for three days running whilst any sailor was to be keel-holed daily over the same period.

To show that even on crusade social discrimination carried on regardless, these restrictions did not apply to knights or members of the clergy who could wager up to 20 shillings (£1) per day. If they exceeded this amount they were to be hit with a large fine; no whipping or keel-holing for them. It almost goes without saying that the kings were exempt from these restrictions.[29] There were indeed some strange restrictions in place at the time of crusades; these included some issued at Le Mans in 1188, when Richard was in attendance, which put an injunction on the wearing of beaver furs and that meals should be restricted to two dishes.[30]

There was friction in the ranks. Many complained at the costs they had incurred, so much so that Richard felt obligated to make generous gifts to them. Silver chalices and gilt cups were distributed freely and women from Outremer who had been dispossessed were also given presents.[31] Richard was free-handed with his support, as was King Philip. Such generosity was a prime requirement of chivalrous knighthood as well as kingship.

Something extraordinary happened to Richard whilst in Sicily. Crusading was often an intensely emotional experience for those involved; after all, these were religious pilgrimages for the men and women taking part. The challenge of the journey undertaken, across heavy seas and to the other side of the known world, added to the intensity. Many of those taking part had vivid religious experiences; some claimed to see visions of saints and even of Christ Himself, or of the Virgin urging them on. These were not limited to clergymen; a whole range of crusaders claimed to experience such visions.

Richard now went through a deeply personal religious experience. He publicly expressed his shame at his past conduct. He confessed that he had been subject to excessive lust in the past or, as Roger of Howden put it, of 'being sensible of the filthiness of his life'. But now, he said, 'the thorns of lustfulness had departed from his head'.[32] He repented of his base emotions and actions. He threw himself naked at the feet of his bishops and asked for forgiveness. He stated that from now on he would act in a completely different way, living his life in the service of God.

Quite what motivations led to this extraordinary scene must be a matter of conjecture. To some historians this is a mark of repentance for his homosexuality and the sin, as it was at the time, of sodomy. But this is not the only plausible reason. Richard's actions had been critically remarked upon by chroniclers previously but in terms that castigated him for his immoral treatment of women rather than men. This too is a possible reason for his very public penitence, particularly as now Richard was on the verge of committing himself to life as a husband as Berengaria was on her way to join him. It was likely that his wife-to-be knew of these stories and would welcome Richard's commitment to turning over a new leaf.

Richard was visited on Sicily by a famous Christian prophet, Joachim of Fiore, the abbot of Corazzo. Nearly eighty years of age, he was well known for his fire and brimstone approach to Christianity and specialised particularly in interpretations of the Book of Revelation, the apocalyptic last chapters in the Bible that foretold the end of the world.

His interpretation of Chapter 12 of Revelations struck a nerve with Richard. Its cryptic verses told of the Last Age of man before Christ returned to reclaim the earth. These verses spoke of a seven-headed dragon which stood by a heavily pregnant woman about to give birth with the intention of devouring her offspring as soon as they were born. Joachim interpreted the seven heads of the dragon as being the seven great enemies of the faith, including such tyrants as Nero and Herod, as well as the Prophet Mohammed. He regarded Saladin as the sixth enemy and it was Richard's destiny to strike off his head.

A series of complicated calculations had suggested to Joachim that the Last Age would come between 1200 and 1260. In this period the infidels who had taken over the Holy Land would be wiped out and Richard – Joachim was quite specific about this – would be the instrument of their destruction. But this did not actually mean that the end was nigh even then, as the seventh and worst persecutor of the Christians, Anti-Christ, was still to make himself known; he had recently been born in Rome. However, his rule would be brief, only lasting for three-and-a-half years. Then the time of the Saints would come, when there would be no more need for the Church of Rome (presumably the Papacy was not very keen on this prophecy) and God would rule the world in peace and harmony.

We tend to gloss over such beliefs in our modern secular era but to do so ignores the fact that Richard's value systems were very different than ours. Medieval Christianity could be frightening. Churches were decorated with wall paintings that constantly reminded a largely illiterate audience of their own mortality and of the fact that they were doomed to judgement, which would often be harsh. Preying on these fears was one cause of the crusading phenomenon whereby pilgrims would receive remittance of their sins.

Roger of Howden was fascinated by these discussions, which he probably witnessed personally; he devotes over ten pages of his account to an analysis of them.[33] Jean Flori, the modern French historian, explains in a remarkably lucid and convincing piece how he feels Richard would have been touched by Joachim's revelations. It reveals a side of the warrior-king that is often overlooked or ignored, even though it was a core part of who Richard was. This gives an insight into a deeper-thinking crusading prince which is not often recognised in modern times.[34]

Time hung heavy over the Sicilian winter. Given the inclement weather in the Mediterranean at this time of year and the vulnerability of the ships, there was no prospect of completing the passage to Outremer until the spring. Roger of Howden records a thunderstorm on 14 December that was so great that a bolt struck a ship in the harbour at Messina and sank it, whilst also levelling some of the walls of the city.[35]

Christmas was spent at Messina and it was not a time of peace and goodwill for all men. After Richard and Philip had feasted together at Mategriffon, a splendid occasion when only gold or silver tableware was used and both kings were extravagant with their gifts, there was a violent altercation between sailors from Pisa and Genoa and Richard's galleymen. Sicily, given its position, was at the centre of a crucial Mediterranean commercial hub and Pisa and Genoa, along with other ports such as Venice, were at the heart of a trading boom which was making the twelfth century world much smaller. Even as the Middle East was in uproar international trade was reaching heights that had not been seen since the heyday of the Roman Empire. This had some negative side-effects with tensions between Italian maritime city-states being one of them.

Lives were lost on both sides and try as they might Richard and Philip were unable to bring a stop to the fighting, though nightfall halted it temporarily. The next morning, trouble broke out again when a Pisan sailor knifed and killed one of Richard's men in a church. General fighting broke out once more and 'multitudes were slain on both sides'.[36] Only by deploying large numbers of men were Richard and Philip able to bring a halt to the brawling. If fellow Christians were this violent towards each other, then heaven help the enemy.

With time on his hands, Richard ordered that his ships should be repaired after being hauled ashore; their timbers were being attacked by worms. There was also time to prefabricate siege engines that could be reassembled once the army reached Outremer. With the French and English armies living on each other's nerves, and their kings increasingly rivals, occasional flare-ups between the two forces who were allies in name only continued to occur. In one such fall-out in February 1191, Richard came off worse in a confrontation with William des Barres, an old rival from his days in France.

It was all something of a nonsense. A peasant had brought some canes into Messina and Richard, William and others used these for an impromptu joust. A strike from William broke Richard's head-piece. This set Richard's short fuse alight and he charged recklessly at William in retaliation. But try as he might Richard was unable to best his opponent. This hurt his pride greatly and he insisted that Philip banish des Barres from his entourage, which he eventually did, reluctantly. Tales such as this gave credence to stories of Richard's short temper and excessive pride; the chroniclers were given a good stock of raw materials to work with when painting pictures of Richard's character.

Richard and Philip were natural rivals, given that Richard wanted to strengthen his power in France whilst Philip aimed to reduce it. But they were also different in temperament, which drove them still further apart. Richard was outgoing, extrovert, haughty and excessively aware of his own importance and status. Philip was quiet, introverted, understated; the two men had very little in common.

They were about to have one less thing in common. For several decades, Richard had been committed to being Philip's future brother-in-law through his betrothal to Alice. The whole idea had perhaps become a longstanding joke by now but it was about to assume deadly serious proportions; it now became obvious that Richard was at last about to get married, but not to Alice.

His prospective bride, Berengaria of Navarre, had been collected by Eleanor of Aquitaine, a senior delegation being required to act as the escort accompanying a princess on her way to her marriage. Although some accounts say that Eleanor met Berengaria at Bordeaux a modern biographer believes that, based on contemporary evidence, Richard's mother crossed the Pyrenees to Navarre to collect her.[37] The match would bring valuable protection to Richard's southern borders in France.

The princess of Navarre was in her mid-twenties, not young for a bride in those days. The chronicler Ambroise, who saw her in Sicily, described her as 'a fine lady, both noble and beautiful, with no falseness or treachery in her'.[38] William of Newburgh and Roger of Howden praised her for her beauty but Richard of Devizes said that she was more accomplished than beautiful.[39] But he probably never saw her himself and we should bear in mind the memorable phrase of one modern writer that he comes across as 'a malicious old gossip-columnist' who sees Berengaria (from a second-hand viewpoint) as 'an unattractive bluestocking'.[40]

Berengaria was a well-educated woman who spoke several languages.[41] But from the start, it seems clear that Eleanor took the opportunity to remind Berengaria who was the senior woman in Richard's life. Berengaria is almost anonymous to the chroniclers and stays in the background, almost obediently, as if ordered to stay there. The same cannot be said of Eleanor and in this case the stereotype of a domineering mother-in-law may not be so far off the mark. In any event, accompanied by a large escort provided by

King Sancho of Navarre, Eleanor, with Berengaria in her train (for it was assuredly not the other way around), set off to rendezvous with Richard in Sicily.

For the bride-to-be, there may have been mixed feelings as she headed for the island. Berengaria's aunt, Margarita, had married William I, king of Sicily. His nickname was 'William the Bad' and while not all historians agree that the title was merited, he certainly had a difficult reign. From their marriage, a son was born who would become King William II, the late husband of Richard's sister, Joanna. Margarita had been regent until her son was of age and had had a difficult time. The track record of Navarrese queens in Sicily was not promising.

Jean Flori summarises the view of medieval aristocratic marriage (of which that of a king was the ultimate example) as 'a social contract, the union of two houses rather than of two persons, its prime purpose to assure peace through family alliances and its sole aim the procreation of an heir'.[42] Another commentator writes that 'companionate marriage was not unknown in the Middle Ages but it appears to have been accidental rather than habitual'.[43] Little room for love here then, more a question of political realities and alliance-building.

Love did of course exist then, as it always has done, but concepts of it were developing in a very specific way. This was through the ideal of courtly love, conceived in the vivid minds of lovers of romantic literature such as Chrétien de Troyes and Marie of France, the countess of Champagne (Richard's half-sister, the daughter of Eleanor of Aquitaine and her first husband, Louis, king of France). But this love was all too often not between a man and his wife but between a man and someone else's wife. Simplistic analysis of the literature suggests that part of the prime requirements for the woman in this *ménage a trois* was that she should always remain unobtainable. Yet despite this, boundaries were sometimes crossed and disastrous consequences ensued, such as in the case of Lancelot and Guinevere, the wife of his friend and lord King Arthur.

The role of women in such relationships was largely a subservient one. Gender historians have assessed their part in relationships in the following way; what was expected of them was 'chastity, humility, modesty, sobriety, silence, work, charity, discipline'.[44] Women were essentially pawns on a political chessboard, to be moved around largely on the instruction of men. While they might have real power in their own households, it was much more difficult to be politically independent. Even the great Matilda, 'Empress Maud', was remembered through the epitaph on her tomb as a daughter, wife and mother, not for her own achievements.

Richard was not made of stone and there are enough stories to suggest that he enjoyed sexual encounters, possibly with members of both sexes. He was notorious when younger for enjoying the wives of the lords of Poitou. Men of the time were not ice-cold asexual machines, such as might appear to be the case in the slightly later development of the paragon of chivalric virtue Galahad in the Arthurian corpus. They were probably more typically like that supposed real-life example of knightly perfection William Marshal. He was accused of having sexual relations with Margaret, the wife of his late lord, Henry the Young King (who would, soon after being widowed, marry King Bela of Hungary). The vocabulary leaves little doubt as to what allegedly happened:

> But that is the pure truth.
> That he is screwing the Queen.
> And it is a great shame and a great scandal.[45]

Quite possibly this was a scurrilous accusation brought on by envy at Marshal's exploits and prominence but it threatened to do him great harm. And it did not have a lot to do with courtly love.

Sancho, Berengaria's brother, may have accompanied his sister on the first stage of her journey, though we cannot be sure of this.[46] A journey from the Pyrenees and across the Alps in winter was a potentially terrifying ordeal. Perhaps Eleanor, not long free after being under close watch for the last decade and a half, welcomed the adventure. Eleanor and Berengaria reached Italy where they were eventually met by Philip of Flanders, a leading crusader and one of the greatest of all counts of that land.[47] It was now only a matter of time before Richard's secret marriage plans became very public.

On the way down through Italy, a perilous journey as the party did not have safe conducts and some of the regions that they passed through were rife with bandits, they met the Emperor Henry VI and then moved on to Pisa before proceeding to Naples after they failed to find a ship to take them straight to Sicily.[48]

Richard sent galleys up to Naples to ferry the women down to Sicily but these missed the party as they had already made their way to Brindisi; Philip of Flanders had stayed behind and used the galleys himself to reach Messina. Sensing trouble, Tancred said that the delegation could not complete its journey across the Straits of Messina as the island was incapable of providing the requisite luxurious welcome for them as it was already overwhelmed with other royal delegations. Richard for once played the part of diplomat, plying Tancred with gifts, including a sword said to be the famous Excalibur. But Tancred was not taken in by his sudden generosity and continued to hold his ground.

It transpired that one of the major reasons for Tancred's reservations was that Philip had suggested that Richard was plotting against him, though he was probably also worried about the recent meeting between Berengaria's party and the Emperor Henry, his bitter rival. If English chroniclers are to be believed (French chroniclers do not mention this story) Philip had presented forged documents 'proving' Richard's involvement in a conspiracy. Richard convinced Tancred that this was not true. Tancred now decided to side with Richard.

Richard and Philip had an impromptu meeting shortly after at Taormina, a short distance south of Messina.[49] Given the general situation, it was an unsurprisingly frosty encounter. On the one hand, Richard believed that Philip had been conspiring to turn Tancred against him; on the other, he was about to publicly reject, and as a result shame, Philip's sister after a ridiculously long betrothal.

Philip was enraged at the rejection of Alice, stating, 'if he does put her aside and marry another woman, I will be the enemy of him and his so long as I live'. As is often the case, money found a way and for 10,000 marks (2,000 yearly for the next five years) Philip agreed to cancel the betrothal following the intervention of the count of Flanders.[50] Yet this must have been a major public humiliation for Philip. Roger of Howden states that 'on that day the king of France and the king of England were made friends'.[51] If Roger really believed this, he knew little of human nature. If Philip's future actions are any guide to his feelings, from this moment on Richard was an enemy for life.

It had been widely stated that Alice was no longer a suitable match because of her alleged infidelity with the late Henry II. This must have stung Philip to the core. In the search for a political answer to explain why Philip and Richard had such a strong mutual antipathy, especially in the future, it would be a capital mistake to ignore the personal. After all, Henry II and Richard had been playing off Philip and his father Louis for decades, treating Alice as nothing more than a pawn in a political game. Now Richard had decided that the game had come to an end, on his own terms and in a way that could only cut Philip to the quick.

Philip was probably further annoyed by the terms that Richard set for Alice's release back to him. Richard insisted that this should not be done until both kings had returned from crusade. Perhaps even now the breakdown of trust between both men was so absolute that Richard deemed it highly unlikely that Philip would be hanging around for very long in Outremer and wanted to keep Alice as a hostage for his good behaviour in France if he returned before Richard.

It would not help to soothe Philip's feelings that Eleanor was also arriving in Messina; this would really rub salt into an open wound given the way that she had so publicly humiliated his father in the past. He pressured Richard to sail east with him in March but Richard resisted. Philip left on 30 March 1191, reaching Acre on 20 April. It seems highly unlikely that it was a coincidence that he left just a few hours before Eleanor and Berengaria reached Messina. One can hardly blame Philip for not wanting to be present at the imminent royal wedding given the shame involved. Richard sailed next to him for the first few hours of the journey before returning to Sicily; if this seemed to be a friendly gesture, it barely hid some strong undercurrents of antagonism.

In the meantime, the situation in England was already becoming problematic. Eleanor was confident enough to leave the country for a while but there were risks in doing so. William Longchamp was already making himself unpopular and John had also returned by now; Richard of Devizes records that the first meeting between him and chancellor Longchamp took place in Winchester on 4 March 1191.[52]

Longchamp was widely reviled and his aversion to women led to implications that he was homosexual.[53] Roger of Howden was clearly no fan of Longchamp; he wrote of him as being oppressive and haughty, seeing himself as being above all other men, even John. He laid claim to castles, estates, abbeys, churches and other rights of the king as if they were his personally. He travelled around with a great retinue, not just of men but of horses, hawks and hounds, and with such extravagant tastes that if he were to stop overnight on his travels it would take the place three years to recover financially.

Did this 'wretched man', Roger wondered, not think that one day he would have to account for all this excess before the Almighty? Longchamp's humble beginnings also seemed to count against him in Roger's eyes, rather as in the reign of Henry VIII those of Cardinal Wolsey and Thomas Cromwell also registered a black mark against them.[54] Trouble was already brewing.

Soon after, Richard received disturbing news. A delegation reached him complaining of the excesses of William Longchamp who was at loggerheads with Prince John, as well as many other important men in England. Richard was disturbed enough at these allegations and the possible unrest that they might lead to to send William of Coutances, the archbishop of Rouen, back; a proven trouble-shooter to help deal with the potential problem. The co-justiciars who had been left behind were already fearful that Longchamp was running out of control and needed to be replaced. Trouble was already brewing in England and the crusade had barely begun.

Berengaria and Eleanor were taken to the priory of La Baniare. Here Eleanor met Joanna. It was the first time that mother and daughter had seen each other for fourteen years. But they were not together long. Berengaria was left in the company of Joanna on the Italian mainland, the start of a companionship that would last for many years. Eleanor on the other hand was brought over to the island of Sicily to meet Richard; they had a lot to discuss and her advice would be invaluable.[55]

In contrast to Philip, Richard seemed in no hurry at all and took his time before leaving Sicily. Some of his men complained at the delay; their funds were limited and they saw the extended stop in Messina as a waste of both time and money. But Richard would not be pushed and continued to wait. He calmed his men down by his generosity, well able to do so given the funds that Tancred had helpfully given him.

Eleanor barely stopped to draw breath and began the journey back to England on 2 April; she had fulfilled her mission and there was little reason for staying on particularly given evidence of problems back home. Before she left, she showed a mother's touch by helping Richard to purchase suitable clothes for his forthcoming marriage. With her would go a number of those with the expedition who were not up to fighting though they were to leave their money and any arms they had with them behind.[56]

Eleanor journeyed to Salerno and then on to Rome to see the Pope. However, Clement had not long to live and would die at the end of March, something that no doubt was welcome news to Richard who despised him. By the time that Eleanor's party arrived in Rome on Easter Sunday, 14 April 1191, he had been succeeded by Celestine III.

Eleanor mentioned her concerns about Longchamp to the new pontiff. Longchamp was the papal legate in England and Eleanor managed to advance the interests of Walter of Coutances, archbishop of Rouen, ahead of him; this was not too difficult as Longchamp's position as papal legate had notionally expired on the death of Pope Clement. Shortly after, Celestine met with the Holy Roman Emperor Henry VI, a difficult meeting as neither man trusted the other (with good cause). European power-politics was about to get yet more complicated.

For Richard and Berengaria there would be no instant marriage for this was Lent and such actions were prohibited during this holy period; the ceremony would have to wait until a more suitable time later. The issue of sexual relationships was a complicated one during a crusade. Many Christian clerics argued that sex at such times threatened the attainment of spiritual benefits on the part of participants (what has been called 'the Delilah factor').[57] The church's conservative, and on occasion paranoid, views on sex were behind this thinking. There were also practical considerations too; women did not fight and therefore were not only a distraction but also in effect an unproductive extra body to feed and provide for. And the tittle-tattle surrounding the actions of Eleanor of Aquitaine during the Second Crusade provided another good reason in the eyes of some to keep women well away from the warzone – even queens.

But with the coming of spring and better weather, there were no further excuses for Richard to delay. With affairs in Sicily sorted out satisfactorily and his bride-to-be now with him and the season for sailing at hand, it was time to go. Richard and his army now set out on the next leg of their journey. It would not be long until they were face to face with Saladin's army in Outremer. But there was to be another diversion along the way.

9

The Taking of Cyprus (1191)

'Like a shower upon the grass did the arrows fall on those who fought'

Roger of Howden on Richard's attack on Cyprus

Richard did not stay long in Messina after Berengaria's arrival. He left on 10 April, the same day that the man who he thought of as the Anti-Christ, Pope Clement III, died in Rome. He took with him not only a bride-to-be but a castle, for his prefab fortress Mategriffon was dismantled and put aboard ship, to be called into use again at some future time. Richard was said to be delighted with Berengaria; the chronicler William of Newburgh suggested this was a good thing for it would be a distraction for Richard against the evils of extra-marital fornication, another hint concerning Richard's energetic sexual exploits in the past.

But the Mediterranean weather was unreliable. The fleet had planned to put in at Crete as a staging-post on the way east. Crete, with Mount Ida dominating the view, was said by the sailors with the fleet to be halfway between Messina and Acre. Richard's flagship hoisted a lantern as a beacon for the other vessels, over 200 of them by now, to follow, 'as the mother hen leads her chicks to food'.[1] It was no easy task as the ships were of different construction and therefore journeyed at a varying pace. They were soon widely dispersed.

The ships were supposed to stay within a trumpet call of each other but the weather had other ideas. Ironically, it was on the holiest of days in the Christian calendar, Good Friday, that the storm broke, on 12 April, just two days after leaving Messina. Soon the ships were being tossed around on the choppy surface of the waters with great rollers and violent waves creating panic.

The helmsmen gave up trying to steer as it was a useless task. Many men felt more seasick than terrified, so bad was the effect of the motion. Eventually the wind eased off but now the fleet was all over the place. Although most of the ships made it to Crete, twenty-five snekkars did not, much to the fury of Richard. Two were particularly important; one carried Richard's treasure and the other his wife-to-be and his sister Joanna, who were travelling separately from him; they had set out in advance in ships that were slower than his but stronger.

While Richard moved on to Rhodes, with the winds still gusting and the waves still high, other ships were despatched to look for those which were missing. It was a worrying time; many of what we now call the Greek islands were at the time bases for pirates. Richard did hear that Philip had arrived at the Siege of Acre but for ten days there was no news of the missing ships.[2]

On 1 May, Richard at last learned that the ship carrying Berengaria and Joanna, the *Buza di Luna*, had been found, anchored off Limassol in Cyprus. Two other ships had sunk nearby. Amongst those who had been lost was Richard's Vice-Chancellor, Roger Mauchat. Mauchat's body had been pulled from the sea with the royal seal still suspended around his neck.

The local Cypriots had pillaged the wrecks. This was not altogether surprising in those days; Richard had only recently cancelled his right to wrecks that were thrown up on the shores of his territories. Ironically, one of the recovered seal's uses in Sicily was when Mauchat witnessed a document that confirmed this action.[3] Now on Cyprus survivors had been taken prisoner, useful hostages and a further way of raising money; again, not unusual for the times. Others had been killed. The ruler of Cyprus, Isaac Comnenus, had invited Berengaria and Joanna to disembark but they had wisely resisted the bait; they would have made the most valuable hostages of all.

Isaac resorted to trickery to lure the women ashore, sending them gifts including presents of Cypriot wine, said to be the best in the world.[4] He was painted by some writers as the ultimate villain, 'the most wicked of all bad men. He surpassed Judas in faithlessness and Gamalon in treachery', which seems like something of an exaggeration, however underhand his tactics were. Some chroniclers even said that he was in league with Saladin and the two had drunk each other's blood as a mark of their friendship.[5]

An intriguing prospect has been raised by some historians,[6] namely that Richard had always planned an attempt on Cyprus. Possibly Richard had already seen both the importance of Cyprus and its vulnerability to attack given the fact that the position of Isaac Comnenus was far from secure. It is an interesting speculation, even if an unproven one.

When he received news of Berengaria and Joanna's whereabouts, Richard moved into action, although he was now ill again. A fleet sailed across the Gulf of Antalya, considered to be particularly dangerous because of the strong currents there in a location where several different seas met. Before long they were off Cyprus.

Isaac was a usurper. He had taken advantage of the declining fortunes of the Byzantine Empire to seize Cyprus. He proved to be an unpopular ruler. On his arrival off Limassol on 6 May 1191, Richard predictably demanded that Isaac release his prisoners. The Cypriot king (Isaac called himself Emperor, but of exactly what was unclear) equally predictably showed that he had no intention of doing so. The matter would be decided by force.

According to the chroniclers, Isaac's reply to Richard's messengers was extremely discourteous. Those who knew Richard understood that this must lead to an aggressive response. The Cypriots had a military advantage as they held the shoreline. Amphibious operations are always a risk in any age and when Richard's ships hove into view the beachhead was strongly defended against them.

The assault would require the attackers to transfer to small rowing boats from their ships and make their way ashore in these. It was not an attractive proposition. Those in the boats would be exposed to missiles from the shore. The Cypriot forces had set up ramshackle barricades, behind which they prepared to drive Richard back into the sea. Richard ordered his archers to unleash their volleys and soon their arrows were streaking across the sky; 'like a shower upon the grass did the arrows fall on those who fought' Roger of Howden wrote.[7]

Richard had immense forces with him – one commentator has suggested that the fleet of 200 ships and more was probably carrying 17,000 men[8] – and although they were probably not all with Richard on Cyprus he certainly had a large force present to call upon. The eye-witness Ambroise put it very well: 'we had the worse hand, for we were coming from the sea, in tiny little boats, exhausted by the storms, crippled by the waves, weighed down with our arms and all on foot. They were on their land. We, however, better understood the business of war'.[9] And so indeed it would prove.

Galleys sent out to stop the crusader's boats were met by a hail of crossbow fire and were soon taken, with many of the men aboard jumping into the sea rather than be captured. As Richard's boats moved closer to shore, his men plunged into the waters, eager to close with the Cypriots. At their head was Richard, allegedly the first into the sea at the head of his army like a latter-day Alexander storming ashore on the beaches of ancient Troy. The position held by the Cypriots might in theory be strong but when they saw the cream of Richard's army heading for them they opted for flight rather than glory. They rushed panic-stricken back into the nearby town but in such a haphazard way that it was easy for Richard's men to follow them into it, particularly given the fact that it was unwalled.

Once inside, the crusaders started to help themselves to anything of value that they could find; particularly satisfying was the seizure of large stocks of corn, oil, wine and meat. Inevitably there was some confusion when Richard's men broke in, and it is probably a safe speculation that they were also distracted by the prospect of booty. In the chaos, Isaac Comnenus made good his escape on the back of a swift-footed steed called Fauvel.

Richard chased after him, demanding that he stop and give battle, again rather as Alexander the Great had done at the decisive Battle of Gaugamela when the Persian king, Darius, was fleeing from him nearly 2,500 years before. Both Richard and Alexander had been unsuccessful in their challenge and one modern historian suggests that Richard probably was not even heard in the din of battle and that this was nothing more than a piece of 'ritual sabre-rattling'.[10] Isaac was able to regroup with some of his men just a few miles away and prepared to confront Richard in battle once more.

In the meantime, Richard ordered his horses to be brought ashore. They were unsteady on their feet, having spent some time at sea; it would take a while for them to find their 'land legs'. They would not have long to recuperate as Richard planned to use them on the next day. Isaac's men slept in their hastily established camp in an olive grove that night, perhaps fearing the worst for the battle which was likely to come when the sun rose on the following morning.

In the event, they would not have to wait that long. Richard had now been joined by Berengaria and Joanna. He smelt the scent of fear amongst Isaac's men and was determined to take full advantage of it. That night, seemingly informed by spies of Isaac's whereabouts, he launched a surprise attack on his camp, which was completely unprepared to receive it. Richard and his men fell on the Cypriots 'like ravening wolves'.[11] It was a rout. Disoriented by the ferocity of the attack and the enveloping cloak of night, the Cypriot army fell apart.

Once more, the faithful Fauvel did his part, bearing Isaac away to safety. But the camp contained much of the king's treasure and with its loss to Richard a great deal of his remaining power went too. His gilded standard was captured, a great symbolic blow for him to compound the material losses he had suffered; Richard would later make a gift of it in honour of the Anglo-Saxon king and martyr, Saint Edmund.

More mundanely, Isaac's bed was taken along with cloths of silk and scarlet dye. A plentiful supply of food was seized too: oxen, cattle, pigs, goats, capons and cocks, fat mules bearing embroidered cloth, good doublets, elegant, beautiful clothes and good horses.[12] It was a hammer-blow to Isaac's cause and it was only a matter of days before many of the nobles of the island were deserting him and submitting themselves to Richard's mercy.

Many of those Cypriots with horses managed to escape to the mountains; the foot-soldiers in Isaac's army were either killed or captured and lines of the latter blocked the roads. Soon after, on 11 May, three ships hove into view. They came from Outremer and on board one of them was her disenfranchised king, Guy of Lusignan. He was accompanied by his elder brother Geoffrey, who Richard knew well from his days in Aquitaine.

Guy, captured at Hattin, had been released when his wife Sibylla handed over Ascalon in exchange for his freedom. On board with him were also some of the other leading men of Outremer, such as Raymond of Antioch, Bohemond of Tripoli and Humphrey of Toron. Richard was about to come face-to-face with the realities of the politics of the crusader kingdoms of the East. Having said that, he probably knew a great deal about them already. The arrival of an advance party of English crusaders in the region some time before, led by Archbishop Baldwin supported by Hubert Walter, would have given Richard plenty of opportunity to find out what was going on on the ground in advance of his arrival.

Guy's position was desperate. He had been taken prisoner by Saladin during the closing moments of the disaster at Hattin. Saladin had treated him well, as befitted a king. He had offered the devastated Guy a goblet of water cooled by snow from the mountains to refresh him against the heat of the mid-summer sin, a crucial gesture as the offering of hospitality to a captive was a sign that he was now under his captor's protection. This was a chivalric move, fully in line with Saladin's reputation for courtesy and honour.

It had contrasted rather markedly with some other actions of Saladin at the end of the battle. Among the many men captured was an arch-enemy of his named Reynald de Chatillon. Reynald was a violent adventurer who had committed many great crimes against Islam, including attacks on pilgrims on their way to Mecca. He had also allegedly outraged Saladin's sister when she had fallen into his hands, a stain on the Muslim leader's honour that could never be forgiven. When Reynald was captured, he was brought before Saladin and executed. It was said that Saladin himself had personally struck his head from his shoulders.

Guy was then taken off into captivity; his survival was not just a chivalrous act but also one of realpolitik. He was too valuable a bargaining chip to be removed from the scene. He was of great use to Saladin. In the aftermath of Hattin, much of Outremer fell to Saladin, most famously Jerusalem and the great seaport of Acre. Apart from Tripoli and Antioch in the north, every other place of note was lost to the crusaders, or the *Franj*, as the western settlers in the area were known.

Or, to be accurate, every other place but one; the port of Tyre. Saladin had been dilatory in laying siege to it, seen by many historians as a critical mistake on his part, for the delay was Tyre's salvation. Saladin had moved on Jerusalem, a crucial prize from a religious and political perspective, but its fate was already decided. It would fall, sooner or later, provided that Saladin could keep his army together. If Tyre had fallen, then every major port on the coast would be denied the crusaders, making any attempted landing by a fresh wave of crusader reinforcements extremely difficult. Jerusalem could be left to wither on the vine; cut off from supplies it must fall.

Jerusalem was, though, a huge symbolic prize. It was retaken by Saladin on the exact anniversary of the day on which Mohammed was said to have ascended into Heaven from the city. The timing was perfectly stage-managed and Saladin's place in history was assured by this one conquest alone. It also meant that his men were inspired to stay by his side whereas a long, tedious and unglamorous Siege of Tyre could well have seen thousands drift away. Saladin had taken a calculated gamble by concentrating on Jerusalem but it did not work out as he had hoped.

Even as Tyre was contemplating surrender, a ship arrived. Aboard was an Italian adventurer who had made his name in Constantinople. This was Conrad, Marquis of Montferrat. The Montferrats had married into the highest levels of imperial Byzantine society but they had fallen on hard times recently. Conrad was fleeing a charge of murder. He was cynical, manipulative, devious and untrustworthy. He was also the saviour of Outremer.

Conrad had left pretty much everything behind in Constantinople and therefore had little else to lose. Sometimes desperation drives men on to extraordinary things and now was such a moment. Conrad breathed new life into the defence of Tyre through his determination and energy. Those who had before been without hope came to see Tyre as a rallying point and those who still had the stomach for a fight made their way there. It was a glimmer of hope that revived the dying body of Outremer.

Saladin was not without his critics, even amongst fellow Muslims. Ibn al-Athīr said of him that 'he never evinced real firmness in his actions. He would lay siege to a city, but if the defenders resisted for some time, he would give up and abandon the siege'.[13] He realised too late that Tyre needed to be taken but try as he might it was now determined to resist. Conrad's father, an old man by the name of William, was Saladin's prisoner, having been taken at Hattin. He was brought before the walls of Tyre. Saladin threatened to kill him unless Tyre was surrendered. Conrad – *al-Markish* as the Muslims called him – took up a crossbow and offered to shoot him himself. Saladin, his bluff called, desisted.

He had then tried another tack. Conrad did not seem the sort of man who would meekly put Guy of Lusignan back on the throne. He was intensely ambitious and probably saw himself as the next king of Outremer. So Guy was then released by Saladin in a move that he hoped would spread dissent and disunity amongst the *Franj*. It was a clever ploy but it did not work in the way intended for one very surprising reason. Guy, the loser of Hattin, was about to act completely out of character.

This eventual result was not at first obvious. On his release, Guy had made his way to Tyre to re-establish his leadership of the kingdom of Outremer. Conrad was having none of this; he had not put in so much effort just to restore the throne of a discredited ruler. Guy was not allowed into Tyre and his hopes for a restoration were dashed. Guy it seemed had struck rock bottom.

Guy's reputation had suffered irreparable damage through the disastrous Hattin campaign, which had effectively destroyed Outremer. In modern times, some historians say that his incompetence has been over-emphasised and that he has unfairly been made a scapegoat for everything that went wrong in 1187. It is certainly true that other, far more experienced, men played their part too; Reynald de Chatillon and Gerard de Ridfort, Grand Master of the Templars, had both exerted pressure and their actions had also contributed to the catastrophic decision to march into Saladin's pre-arranged trap at Hattin.

That is true enough; but what is also true is that Guy was king and as such the ultimate decision lay with him. A stronger man, Richard for example, would have resisted the foolish advice offered and stayed put. Guy did not do so.

But having been rejected by the people he claimed to lead, Guy then did something extraordinarily decisive, even though at the time it seemed foolish. Acre was the crucial seaport that needed to be taken back from Saladin if there was to be any real hope of revival in Outremer and Guy had moved to lay siege to it after being turned away from Tyre. It seemed a pointless gesture as he was outnumbered and out-resourced.

Guy took up a strong position. He did not have enough men to break through the towering walls of Acre but he could not be driven off either. Soon, crusaders came to see Acre as the place where the fightback would begin. Conrad's efforts at Tyre had provided a powerful symbolic moment but they were essentially a defensive action. At Acre, Christendom was going onto the offensive.

And so a great siege had been established at Acre – in many ways one of the greatest set-piece sieges of the Middle Ages in terms of both its duration and its violence. It kept Guy tenaciously hanging on as a player in the politics of Outremer. Guy's position had been further weakened by the subsequent death of his wife Sibylla. This was a constitutional disaster for Guy as his claim to the throne came from the fact that he was her husband; he had no entitlement to be king in his own right. This complicated matters further.

Now he had come to Cyprus to seek Richard's help. There was good reason to think he could get it, for after all the Lusignans were vassals of the dukes of Aquitaine and could therefore hope for a sympathetic ear, however rebellious they had been in the past. When he reached Cyprus, Richard greeted Guy with enthusiasm. He was happy to support Guy's claims to be reinstated; it would do him no harm to have someone who was nominally his vassal as the king of Jerusalem and there was even a distant family relationship between the two men. Richard made a generous gift of 2,000 marks and twenty expensive goblets, two of them of pure gold; much needed as Guy was now 'poor and destitute'.[14] But there were other matters to be attended to on Cyprus before Guy's cause could be more actively supported; the battle for the island was not yet over.

On 12 May 1191, a day which many who knew Richard must have doubted they would ever see at last arrived. On this day, the Feast of St Pancras, Richard was married to Berengaria, who was then about twenty-six years of age, in the Chapel of St George in Limassol by Nicholas, Richard's chaplain. Records have survived which tell us what he was wearing; a rose-coloured tunic made of samite, a rich silk fabric. He also wore a mantle (a cloak) threaded with gold crescents and silver suns. On his head was a bonnet decorated with gold beasts and birds, while he also wore buskins (boots) with gilded spurs.[15]

Roger of Howden, who described the king's coronation in copious detail, gives us the merest scraps of information about the wedding ceremony; and while telling us what the groom wore, not a mention is made of what the bride was dressed in. The whole event was in keeping with Richard's love of extravagance: records also show him buying several expensive (and striking) scarlet robes for the king.[16] Richard was clearly no hair-shirted pilgrim.

The chronicler Richard of Devizes noted that the bride was 'probably still a virgin';[17] possibly because this contrasted the pure Berengaria which the much dishonoured or abused (depending on the observer's point of view) Alice. This helped to justify Richard's abandonment of Alice. Berengaria was at once crowned queen of England by John, the bishop of Evreux. The prevarication was finally over. All this was in stark contrast to the way in which Alice had been dealt with during a largely humiliating three decades. Philip of France would not have been human if he had not noticed the difference in treatment. It can only have jaundiced him even more against Richard.

Richard went through the required formalities in honouring his bride. It may even be that he set up an Order in her honour, the delightfully named Order of the Blue Thong.[18] But this was in many ways a formulaic response of a man and a king doing what was expected of him and no more. There would be few signs of real closeness, let alone intimacy, in their future married life.

Negotiations between the competing parties in Cyprus had in the meantime been ongoing, brokered by Garnier of Nablus, Master of the Hospitallers. Isaac Comnenus was now suing for peace. He offered the sum of 20,000 gold marks as compensation for his mistreatment of the shipwrecked crusaders. He undertook to provide troops for the crusade and indeed to take part in it personally. He would also swear homage to Richard as his liege lord and would hand over several of his castles as security.

This was exactly what Richard wanted and Isaac visited his camp to agree terms. But then for some unknown reason he had a change of heart and, whilst the camp was enjoying a siesta, he rode off; possibly the terms that he had been discussing with Richard had been so harsh that it drove him to take precipitate action. There was a brief skirmish when he left but he managed to make good his escape.

Richard of course was not likely to let this go and anyway probably preferred an unconditional surrender from Isaac; he might even have made it deliberately easy for Isaac to make his getaway. He led his men after him and caught Isaac holed up in a castle. One of Isaac's advisors plucked up the courage to suggest that the best thing he could do was surrender. Infuriated at this advice, Isaac struck him with a knife and cut his nose off. Not surprisingly, the mutilated adviser escaped from the castle as soon as he could and made his way to Richard, where he became his ally.

Richard's strategy for the taking of Cyprus involved splitting his army. One part was to be led by Guy of Lusignan; a good opportunity for the man whose family had been troublesome rebels in Aquitaine to prove his loyalty now. The second sailed around the island to attack from the other side. The fleet was led by Robert of Turnham. The two forces re-joined at Famagusta, where Richard had ordered that a close watch should be kept to prevent Isaac from escaping by sea.

While he was there, Richard was confronted with a delegation from Philip who was now at Acre. It was led by Dreux of Mello (later constable of France) and Philip, bishop of Beauvais, the latter a man that Richard would come to despise. Ambroise and the writer of the *Itinerarium* both suggested that they were far from diplomatic in their language; their message was purely and simply to tell Richard to hurry up and make his way as quickly as he could to Acre. They went as far as to suggest that the king was a coward and should not be wasting time fighting other Christians when there were Muslim armies to take on. They got a suitably blunt reply from Richard 'Oc e No' who was greatly angered at their tone and the nature of their mission.[19]

Richard then moved on Nicosia, the main town on Cyprus. An attempted ambush laid by Isaac with the support of 700 men achieved nothing. Although it was said that he fired two poisoned arrows at Richard, they failed to bring him down.[20] Richard attempted to charge Isaac but was unable to catch him. Isaac sped to safety again on the back of the fleet Fauvel. Nicosia, which had recently been sheltering Isaac, was taken and the men of the city were deprived of their distinguishing beards. This greatly offended the proud but impotent Isaac Comnenus, who mutilated some of his captives in response.

Richard stayed at Nicosia for a short while as he was still feeling unwell; mentions of such illnesses frequently appear in the accounts of the chroniclers and suggest that he was prone to bouts of poor health. Once Nicosia was taken the end was nigh as far as Isaac was concerned as his remaining support started to melt away. The great castles on the north of the island, like Buffavento, Kantara and the stunning St Hilarion ('Didemus'), held out, sentinels astride the entrance to the mountains, but these were only final places of refuge and not those from which a counter-attack could be launched.

Isaac's daughter, a young girl, was taken captive at Kyrenia when it fell; Guy of Lusignan oversaw the successful operation. She prostrated herself before Richard when taken before him and was well treated in return. Some suggested that Richard became inappropriately intimate with her. Later, she was sent to stay with Berengaria who may well have been expected to play a role in her education as this was the way in which young ladies of the aristocracy were taught in those days with formal learning often denied them.[21] Shortly afterwards, Buffavento was under siege. Isaac was soon blockaded at Kantara but the loss of his daughter broke his resistance.

Isaac was still understandably reluctant to surrender; as he told Richard through his envoys, he had no wish to be a captive in iron chains. Richard promised that he would not be so shamefully treated so Isaac duly gave himself up. Richard kept his word;

the chains that Isaac was led away in were made of silver. Some thought this a clever trick, not without its amusing side in a 'black humour' kind of way. But it is also evidence of a cruel streak.

Isaac was a man with many faults. He was a usurper and he was not much loved by his people who were quick to abandon him when the time came. The Byzantine chronicler Niketas Choniates was scathing of him as a man with a volcanic temper. Yet for all this there is no reason to doubt that he felt a genuine and deep affection for his one and only child. There were stories of a brief and tearful reunion between father and daughter but the reign of Isaac Comnenus was over. His moment in the sun had been short-lived. Born into the Byzantine royal family, though not close to the centre of power as he was a minor relative, he now faced an uncertain and, as it transpired, tortured future. Perhaps he pondered on the words of the biblical prophet Samuel as he was led away: 'how are the mighty fallen'.

The fight for Cyprus was over and all the important nobles on the island surrendered to Richard. Two of Richard's supporters, Richard of Canville and Robert of Turnham, were appointed to govern it on his behalf. Shortly afterwards the island was sold to the Knights Templar for 100,000 Saracen bezants, to be paid in instalments.[22] It was a crucially important strategic gain given its position just off the coast of Outremer. If the crusaders could attain supremacy at sea, then supplies and men could flow through the island and on to the crusading battlegrounds. It was in a prime position both to keep Outremer provisioned and for launching attacks on the coast of Muslim-held territory in the region. The Templars, guardians of the Christians in Outremer, should theoretically be reliable custodians of the new acquisition.

The terms of the final settlement were harsh for the people of Cyprus; empire-building and conquest back then being a question of exploitation as it always has been. A 50 per cent capital tax was levied on the Cypriots. There was even cultural humiliation to endure; Greeks were to shave off their beloved beards and be clean-shaven in the Western fashion. Some refused to submit and one prominent rebel, a relation of Isaac Comnenus, was captured and hanged by Robert of Turnham.

A huge amount of plunder was taken in the capture of the island. Ambroise said that when Richard examined what he had seized, 'he found that the towers were stocked with treasures and riches, with pots and pans of silver, great vats, cups and bowls of gold, spurs, bridles and saddles, rich and precious stones, which were powerful against infirmity, cloths of scarlet and of silk (I have not seen any like them anywhere else I have been) and all other riches appropriate to the high and mighty; the king of England conquered all this in the service of God and to take His land'. These were of course hugely welcome; but so too were the substantial supplies of barley, wheat, sheep and cattle that could be brought from Cyprus to the crusading army in Outremer.[23]

The situation in Cyprus had presented Richard with a glorious opportunity that he had taken full advantage of. He had added a significant prize to his territories and boosted the prospects for Outremer too. But that was not all. He had had the chance to forge an alliance with a man who was his vassal back in Aquitaine in the shape of Guy of Lusignan. He would therefore already have a strong position when he arrived in Outremer, not just against Saladin but also against his longer-term rival, Philip of France. And he would be able to present the French king with a *fait accompli* on the marriage front too.

Philip of France soon after suggested to Richard that, as Cyprus was conquered whilst on crusade, the spoils taken should be divided equally between them. Richard responded that the deal made at the start of the crusade only applied to gains made in Outremer, though he had already surrendered some of the spoils he had taken at Messina which weakened his negotiating position. It is highly unlikely that Philip was satisfied with this answer though he was in no immediate position to do anything about it. He stored up the perceived duplicity of Richard as yet another on his rival's part. One day, he would take his vengeance on him; it was just a question of waiting for the right moment to do so.

The fall of Cyprus can only have raised Richard's prestige still further. It was an important achievement for both him and for the crusading movement. He had completely outmanoeuvred Isaac Comnenus in his blitzkrieg on the island. Richard's reputation as a warrior had risen again. But this was only the beginning. Not far away, across the short stretch of water that separated it from the mainland, was the vital port of Acre, under siege as it had been for several years. It was to this even more crucial prize that Richard turned his attention next. Three and a half years after impulsively taking the cross, Richard was at last about to arrive in the Holy Land.

10

High-Water Mark: The Siege of Acre (1191)

'The Christian glories in the death of the pagan, because Christ is glorified'

St Bernard of Clairvaux

Acre: it was here on the Mediterranean coast of Outremer that Richard was to first taste crusader glory. The siege of the city and its consequences would shape his kingship, his life, his reputation. Here he would lay the foundations of his legend. Here events would be played out that would make the breakdown of relationships with Philip of France irreparable. Here an ill-timed moment of pique would lead to cataclysmic personal consequences when he fell out with Duke Leopold V of Austria. And here, in the aftermath of the capture of the city, would be played out the darkest and most controversial event of Richard's life which still resonates now, nine centuries on. After Acre, nothing would be the same again.

Richard already had experience of siege warfare, though nothing on the scale of what he was about to face. Philip had less experience to call on. Both men though were keen students of military strategy and in particular the renowned Roman writer on the subject of siegecraft ('poliorcetics' to give it its formal name), Vegetius.[1] The depth of their learning was about to be fully tested.

Richard set sail from Cyprus on 5 June 1191, accompanied by Guy of Lusignan and other new-found allies. Berengaria and Joanna sailed for Outremer too, though on different ships, which was a trifle odd as this was effectively a honeymoon period for the newly married couple.

Richard did not make straight for Acre though. Travelling in the galley *Trenchmere*, he stopped first at the mighty crusader fortress of Margat (or Marqab), just a couple of miles inland from the Mediterranean coast, where he deposited Isaac Comnenus for safekeeping. Margat was widely considered to be impregnable and had been one of the few castles left to the crusaders after Saladin's conquest of Jerusalem; it would not be easy for the deposed king of Cyprus to escape from here.

Richard sailed past Tortosa and Tripoli. Then it was on to Tyre and a most unwelcome turn of events. When Richard arrived here, he was refused entry on the orders of Conrad of Montferrat and his new-found ally, Philip of France. This was hardly the unified start to the crusade that was needed. Richard was forced to spend that night in tents outside of the city.

Richard did not delay there any longer but made his way down the coast to Acre, the centre of the ongoing conflict with Saladin and his 'Saracen' army. After Guy had initially laid siege to the port a couple of years before, positioning his force around a small hill known as Tell-Fukhkhar to the south-east of the city, they themselves had been subject to a counter-attacking force that had then laid siege to them; the besieged were themselves besieged in other words.

But neither party had been strong enough to push on to a decisive victory; Ambroise said that when he first arrived Guy had with him 400 knights and 7,000 foot-soldiers, not enough to defeat Saladin's army though far from a token force.[2] On the other hand, Saladin was generally dilatory in his response, perhaps underestimating the size of the challenge that he faced. The crusaders could not take Acre, and the counter-attackers could not drive them off. A war of attrition followed.

Inevitably in these hot and insanitary conditions, the greatest enemy of all medieval armies had a field day; disease. It was this which had taken off Queen Sibylla as well as her children and many others. But the bold move of Guy of Lusignan to lay siege to Acre in the first place had inspired others and he had been joined by new crusader arrivals from Flanders, Denmark and Germany, as well as Philip's forces; for example, in September 1189 a Danish-Frisian[3] fleet of about fifty ships including a famous knight and hero of the tournament field, James d'Avesnes, and men from the marches of England along with a Cornish contingent, had joined them.[4]

Everywhere men and women fell to the ravages of pestilence: the author of the *Itinerarium* describes them as martyrs: 'no small number of them died soon afterwards from the foul air, polluted with the stink of corpses, worn out by anxious nights spent on guard, and shattered by other hardships and needs'.[5] For a time, Acre was the centre of the world; as one writer said, with only a certain amount of hyperbole, 'Acre will certainly win eternal fame, for the whole globe assembled to fight for her'.

Guy and his force had faced an enormous challenge. The walls of the town were massive and he simply did not have enough men to encircle them completely.[6] Food was also in short supply; when a horse was killed during the siege, it was soon surrounded by men and women desperate to eat parts of it; even the head and the intestines were considered edible. Men were reduced to eating grass. In one story of the time, two men bought thirteen beans with their last coin. When one of the beans was found to be inedible as it was riddled with maggots they walked miles back to the vendor to argue successfully that he should give them a replacement.[7]

In terms of supplies, the defending Muslim garrison inside Acre had up until now had an advantage. They had managed to keep control of the sea which meant that they had been able to ship supplies in from along the coast. This meant that one of the most effective weapons in a besieging army's armoury, the ability to starve the enemy out, had been denied to the crusaders so far.

The Muslims had frequently launched deadly attacks on the besiegers, who were forced to defend themselves by digging deep ditches with sharpened stakes in the bottom with which they hoped to impale careless attackers.[8] The chroniclers gloried in the details of this. It gave them a chance to liberally sprinkle accounts of miracles and fantastic events in their writings; of a man whose armour had been pierced by a crossbow bolt but whose life had been saved when a flimsy piece of parchment with the name of God on it stopped it from going through to his heart; of a 'Turkish' emir who set fire to his own genitals when he dropped a container of Greek Fire; of a 'Turk' who was shot dead with a crossbow bolt even as he urinated on a crucifix.[9]

Philip had already been in Outremer for two months and he had done his best to prosecute the siege. He had ordered the construction of siege engines to batter away at the thick walls of Acre and had also arranged for the erection of siege towers to attack the city. This was very much needed; earlier attacks to take Acre had only made a limited impression because they lacked the stone-throwing petraries that were necessary to make a breach.[10] But Philip did not have enough men to take the town and his ships were too few to set up a blockade and deprive the garrison of supplies.

But it seemed to some that Philip's arrival was an anti-climax. The Saracens knew he was coming and had been told to expect a substantial army. However, the force he arrived with was much smaller than anticipated and rather than fear, it was a sense of relief that the garrison of Acre felt. Richard, though, was on his way with a much larger contingent. At last, he was about to step centre-stage into the crusade. He arrived nearly one year after his nephew, Henry of Champagne, had done so (he had been made commander of the crusader army for a time) and several months after Philip of France. Richard had certainly not been in a hurry to get there.

Richard and his force were anxious for a fight now though, and had already had some useful practice in the gentle arts of warfare whilst travelling from England; Lisbon, Messina, Cyprus – it was already an impressive rollcall. As men from his armies began to pour in, they could scarcely believe the sight that met their eyes. To some of those who witnessed it, such as the chronicler Ambroise, the numbers involved in the battle seemed to run into the hundreds of thousands.[11] This does not mean that we should take this number literally; merely that this was by contemporary standards a very large siege.

A scene of epic proportions met their eyes when the newcomers arrived. The siege had assumed a life of its own. The crusaders had dug themselves trenches, not just to shelter from the garrison inside the city but also against counter-attacks from Saladin's encircling Saracen forces that tried to drive them out. The sky was streak-marked by huge boulders flung from massive siege engines to batter against the cracked walls of Acre. Return fire came from those inside.

From time to time, the besieging crusader forces would launch raids on the city but never with a great deal of success. Both sides were committing huge resources to the fight. Saladin had placed one of his most valued commanders, by the name of Baha' al-Din Qaragush, in command. He was a eunuch of Armenian origin and greatly experienced in the construction of fortresses, bridges and palaces.[12] With these skills in his armoury, he was the ideal man to maximise the defensive potential of Acre.

Much heroism and stoicism was demonstrated on both sides. There were women as well as men in the crusader camp. In a tale that touched the hearts of many, a story was told of a woman who was fatally wounded in the battle. Even as she lay dying, she asked that her body should be thrown into the ditch that surrounded Acre to enable the attacking crusaders to cross it more easily.[13]

The hardships endured by the besiegers had been great. There were sometimes desperate shortages of food. It was said that a loaf of bread, which could normally be purchased for a penny, at one time of famine had risen to a price of sixty shillings.[14] The Church sometimes intervened and made provision as far as it could for the poor and hungry, but were themselves constrained by shortages of provisions. Only the fact that the crusaders occasionally received supplies by sea allowed the siege to be viable.

The fighting was visceral in its intensity. Whilst the crusaders brought up scaling ladders to their trenches, the Muslim defenders would sally out and attack them. Bitter hand-to-hand fighting would then ensue in the trenches as each side sought vainly to gain an advantage. Greek Fire, that nasty incendiary device that was almost impossible to put out once aflame, was thrown down onto the crusaders. In the bitter combat that followed, heroes had been born such as Geoffrey of Lusignan, Richard's Aquitanian vassal, and English knights who had arrived in advance of the main army such as Ralph de Tilly.

After one particularly vicious fight, the river at Acre was almost clogged with dead bodies that had been thrown into the river (deliberately on Saladin's orders, according to Ambroise). Soon the smell of death almost suffocated the besiegers as the bodies started to rot in the fierce sun. Those who were able to buried as many corpses as they could but still the stench was unbearable and men avoided the area for months.[15] From time to time, the bodies of captured crusaders who had been executed by the garrison were hung from the walls to taunt the besiegers and break their spirit.

Nor were the atrocities one way. When a Muslim galley was captured, the crew was assaulted by a party of women who first of all yanked their hair and then cut off their heads. This only seemed to make the garrison of Acre even angrier for thereafter they attacked with renewed vigour, in their thousands, in hordes like flies according to Ambroise. He described them as being a 'hideous black people' which may have been not only a derogatory term but also an allusion to the fact that some of the garrison may have been Nubians who had very dark complexions.[16]

Roger of Howden drew up a long list of those who died at Acre in 1190. They included Queen Sibylla and her two daughters, Heraclius, the Patriarch of Jerusalem, and Baldwin, the archbishop of Canterbury. Four other archbishops died there too, including the archbishop of Nazareth, and four bishops. A long list of abbots, priors and prominent secular nobles and knights was also included. It should be noted that Roger says that these people 'died' at Acre. He separately notes those nobles who were 'slain' in battle, of whom there were noticeably fewer.[17]

All in all, Roger names about fifty prominent individuals who died at Acre that year. Medieval life was always fragile, hanging by a tenuous thread that could be snipped at any minute. But the intimation here is that the rate of attrition was alarming. It is notable that both Richard and Philip fell ill shortly after arriving at the siege in 1191. The rate of loss due to factors such as malnutrition and the disease that thrived in the insanitary conditions of a medieval siege camp could be terrifying.

The winter of 1190/91 had been a particularly trying one for the besiegers. It rained incessantly and those besieging Acre, with minimal cover in many cases, were half-drowned. Soon the noise of hacking coughs permeated the camp. Legs and faces swelled up. Teeth fell from the gums of the suffering, probably as a result of scurvy due to a deficiency of Vitamin C in their diet. At one stage, a thousand people lay dead.

Death was the constant companion of the crusaders. As well as the better-known crusaders who died in Outremer, such as Baldwin, the archbishop of Canterbury, English records tell of a number of lesser-known men who never returned to their home shores after setting out. They included Roger le Pole, a knight in Hubert Walter's entourage, Simon of Odell from Bedfordshire, Richard of Clare, who died in October 1190, and Geoffrey Hose, a Wiltshire man.[18]

Roger of Howden mentions some of lesser note from Yorkshire and Lincolnshire who died during the crusade, presumably men that he knew personally as they might otherwise not have received a mention.[19] We should assume that these known individuals are just the tip of a rather large iceberg. It is easy to be cynical about crusading motivations; but for many the decision to make the journey turned out to be a death sentence.

For the poorest participants of the crusade it would have been virtually impossible for them to pay their own way. The cost of crusading was simply beyond their reach. They would almost certainly have been there because they were in the service of their lords or alternatively they may on occasion have been acting as proxies for other men who had taken the cross but had been unable to fulfil their pledges. Whether such men were spiritually motivated or not is an irrelevance; such virtuous motives would have been insufficient on their own to allow them to make the journey without some form of funding or support.[20]

Conrad of Montferrat came in for much criticism as he was believed to be hoarding food in Tyre. Before Richard's arrival, there was even evidence of desertion from the crusader army to the Muslim side, some renouncing their faith in return for food and survival. Ambroise suggested that there was enough food to go around but that merchants were holding it back to benefit from profiteering. He told with glee how a Pisan merchant, who hoarded food so that he could sell it at an exorbitant price, lost it all when the place where he was storing it caught fire.[21]

The port had become a symbol for both sides, the battle for it a fight that could not be withdrawn from without enormous loss of face. Huge resources had been thrown into what had become a battle of attrition. Acre 1191 was in its way the medieval equivalent of Verdun 1916, where the combatants were so fiercely committed to the fight that strategic objectives soon got lost in the mists of war. And, just as in that much later battle, for a long time stalemate ensued. The hope was that Richard and Philip would be able to break it.

Richard had only just arrived in the region of Acre when a glorious opportunity for him to make a strong first impression in Outremer presented itself (Ambroise specifically places this incident near Beirut). At this stage of his life, Richard seems to have been endowed with a generous stock of good luck, though of course he needed skill and verve to benefit from the opportunistic openings that presented themselves, one of which was imminent. As his fleet kept watch off the coast, a large three-masted ship hove into view, said by some chroniclers to be the biggest ever seen except for Noah's Ark.[22] It was flying the French flag but something about it was suspicious. A small boat was launched to go and investigate. As it got closer to the large ship, it was suddenly greeted with volleys of Greek Fire.

This was a highly flammable concoction of chemicals; the only practical defence against it was wood or leather soaked in vinegar, urine or sand.[23] It even burned on water. The use of this terrifying substance confirmed that this was no friendly vessel but that it was undoubtedly up to no good. It was in fact a Muslim supply ship from Beirut trying to break through with provisions. As the English ships approached, they were also greeted with a hailstorm of arrows from those aboard the vessel.

The fleeter English vessels quickly surrounded the becalmed enemy ship, which was allegedly carrying 200 poisonous snakes for the defenders of Acre to throw down on the besieging forces. There were large numbers of crossbows, other weapons and a great stock of food aboard. But there was a problem; although Richard's ships could outpace the enemy, it was very difficult for them to attack it directly as it towered over Richard's galleys. Divers were therefore sent down to disable the rudder. Attempts were then made to board but the defence was vicious. Some men managed to climb the cables hanging from the ship and a vicious hand-to-hand fight broke out on board deck with arms and hands hacked off, men decapitated and their bodies thrown into the sea.

The initial tactic was seemingly to try and take the ship, with all the goods it had aboard, intact. But it became clear that this was not going to be possible. Eventually, Richard's galleys rammed their 'beaks' into the sides of the surrounded ship, quickly splintering the timbers and stoving its sides in and water began to pour through the gaps. Before long, the ship was sinking (though Muslim chroniclers suggested that it was deliberately scuttled rather than let it be captured).[24] Many of the defenders jumped into the sea to save themselves but most of them were drowned or killed even as they struggled for life in the water. Richard ordered some of those captured to be drowned anyway; all those taken in fact, except for thirty-five emirs and engineers who were more valuable alive than dead.

It was a morale-boosting moment and Richard's stock soared. In contrast, Saladin was said to have pulled his beard in anger and frustration when he heard of the loss of the ship.[25] Even the normally critical French chronicler Rigord was impressed.[26] While it was a great fillip for the besiegers, it was equally a bitter blow for the Muslims inside the walls as they realised that their position had taken a serious turn for the worse. Not only had a vast amount of supplies been lost, so had 800 fighting men who could have made a considerable difference to the vigour of the defence.

This victory was not only significant in a tactical sense, it also marked a decisive change in the balance of naval power. Although there had been an attempted blockade of Acre at an earlier stage, there had not been enough ships to enforce it. Resupply from Egypt across the sea or from Beirut to the north had still been an option up until now. But now this particular door had been slammed firmly shut. The arrival of Richard's fleet was as important as the army that he had brought with him. In fact, the situation was far worse than the garrison yet knew for all that had arrived so far was an advance force of twenty-five galleys. Richard had, according to Ralph of Diceto, left Cyprus with thirteen large ships, 100 transports and fifty galleys[27] and most of those had yet to arrive at Acre.

Richard now completed his journey to Acre, arriving there on 8 June 1191; Ambroise for the first time calling him the Lion-Heart.[28] He milked the applause that greeted him when he arrived to the full; it was said that 'the land shook with the Christians rejoicing'.[29] Just as he had entered Messina in a carefully choreographed show of pomp, he now came into the crusader camp in the same fashion.

Richard was a man who courted publicity, a proud warrior and king who desired nothing more than the adulation of those around him. The bonfires that were lit and the celebratory songs that went up from the crusader camp that night evidenced the euphoria that had greeted his arrival. Ambroise wrote that a huge party took place on the Saturday night of his arrival.[30] Few men went to sleep; torches stayed blazing through the night, wine was drunk in copious amounts and music went up from pipes, trumpets, horns and drums. Above anything else, it was a massive release of pent-up emotion after months of living on the edge.

To the attackers, the arrival of Richard had sealed the deal; Acre was already theirs. He had already boosted the spirits of those besieging the city; after all, he arrived complete with a large army and a burgeoning reputation. On the other hand, those inside the crumbling walls trembled. They could see the size of the newly arrived fleet and realised that they were now cut off from re-provisioning and reinforcements. They looked inland and saw the wax candles and flaming torches burning and it seemed to them as if the whole valley was on fire.[31]

The defenders' morale plummeted. Baha' al-Din wrote that Richard 'was courageous, energetic, and daring in combat.

Although lower in rank than the king of France [a comment that Richard would probably have taken great exception to], he was richer and more renowned as a warrior [a comment that presumably he would have liked much more].' When Richard reached Acre, 'the Franj let out cries of joy and lit great fires to celebrate his arrival. As for the Muslims, their hearts were filled with fear and apprehension'.[32]

All this publicity may have gone to Richard's head for he was soon acting brashly. He hired extra men soon after he arrived; nothing wrong with this in itself, but he very noticeably paid better wages for them than Philip had done when he had first appeared at Acre. He ordered siege engines to be constructed and great battering rams to be built. It was clear that he planned to energetically prosecute the siege and, before long, that he intended to be the dominant partner amongst the two kings.

Philip suggested that the two armies should co-operate. Richard initially agreed but then changed his mind.[33] The result was that the siege then dragged on for months. This was the other side of Richard; vain, selfish, blind to the opportunities offered by co-operation. Great soldier he might have been but he was no team-player. In the short-term, he would benefit from this by becoming the senior player in the Crusading army; in the longer run it would bring him to the verge of oblivion. Richard was even now sowing the seeds of his own destruction.

Power politics were at play too. Richard made an agreement with the Pisan fleet for their help. This was a sensible policy as it strengthened his maritime power. The Pisans had already proved themselves earlier in the siege by prising open a maritime corridor along which supplies could be ferried to the besieging crusaders. He refused to deal, however, with the Genoese, who were friendly with Philip. The French king had in the meantime taken the part of Conrad of Montferrat in his dispute with Guy of Lusignan, who of course was now supported by Richard. Whatever one king decided to do, it seemed that the other must inevitably do the opposite.

Conrad's position had been strengthened when, after the death of Sibylla, Guy's queen, he had married her sister Isabella. This was a remarkable marriage on several counts. It was notable not so much because there was a big age difference between the two – such a situation was by no means uncommon at the time – but rather because both Conrad and Isabella were already married. As Isabella's sister Sibylla had been married to Conrad's brother

William Longsword the marriage was also, according to canon law, incestuous.[34]

Conrad manipulated the situation by obtaining a disputed annulment of his own marriage whilst Isabella was persuaded to part from her young husband, Humphrey of Toron, even though the two were said to be unusually happy together. Humphrey was widely regarded as being something of a pushover; he had been derogatorily described as being 'more like a woman than a man'.[35]

These events were shocking to some; one wrote that they were worse than the Rape of Helen that had led to the Siege of Troy.[36] They happened long before Richard arrived but his archbishop of Canterbury, Baldwin of Forde (who would die soon after, reportedly because he was so shocked at the promiscuity that he had witnessed in the camp[37]), was on the spot at the time and was furious, though it is not clear whether this was on moral or political grounds.

But his threats to excommunicate those who supported these doubtful arrangements were not supported by other important ecclesiastical figures and came to nothing because of his untimely death; Philip, the bishop of Beauvais, duly officiated at the wedding ceremony a few days after. It was later ruled by a papal commission that the annulment of Isabella's marriage with Humphrey was wrong but far too late to make a difference.

Muslim writers had also been forcibly struck by what they considered to be the extreme promiscuity of the women in the crusader camp; injunctions to bring along washerwomen only at the start of the crusade were clearly being ignored (even in fairness by Richard, who had brought along his wife and his sister with him, neither of whom was presumably well-known for their washing skills).

Imad ad-Din wrote of the women in the crusader camp as being tinted and painted, desirable and appetising, bold and ardent. As to what they got up to, in terminology that verges on the pornographic he talks of them bringing their silver anklets up to touch their earrings, of making themselves targets for men's darts, offering themselves against the lance's blows, making themselves shields for javelins. And so it went on; catching lizard after lizard in their scabbards, guiding pens to inkwells, bringing firewood to stoves. He certainly had an extremely febrile imagination when he described these sexual gymnastics;[38] Ambroise also wrote of the sinful lust of the crusaders, though in somewhat more restrained terms.[39]

Conrad had previously joined the Siege of Acre. The unexpected aggression of Guy of Lusignan in launching the attack there had caught him off guard. Men had slipped away from Tyre to join Guy's army and Conrad had little choice but to join in or see his influence dwindle. His arrival had been important in that it had allowed the encirclement of Acre to be completed when he reached the siege along with the Hospitaller knights.[40] But now, with the arrival of Richard, who was clearly in Guy's corner, Conrad decided that it was time to leave. He was back in Tyre soon after.

This was the important backdrop to the situation facing Richard and he would soon find himself involved in the ramifications of this tangled web of deceit and intrigue. In the meantime, Richard turned enthusiastically to warfare, which was after all what he did best. His prefab castle, the Mategriffon, was put together again. Great siege engines were built but the walls stood defiant and largely unbroken. The siege was dragging on for what seemed an eternity.

A different tack was needed and one was duly tried. It was unglamorous and claustrophobic; mining. The thought of men nibbling away at the foundations of a city like so many moles may lack glamour but it required great amounts of courage and the approach had a proven track record. The crusaders had found this out to their cost when one of their major cities, Edessa, had been lost to them due to the effects of sapping on Christmas Eve 1144.

It was also back-breaking work. It required men to tunnel under the walls in cramped, claustrophobic spaces, propping up the ceilings of the passages they had carved out with timbers. When the moment was right and the correct spot had been reached, a great pile of brushwood was heaped up. This was set ablaze and, as it was consumed and the heat intensified, the whole collapsed, bringing the walls down with it.

This was the theory, and it was a good one. But the enemy often knew what was coming. They could often see the miners getting into position. Even if they could not, they could take subtler steps such as putting jugs of water on the ground; if ripples began to appear on the water, then it was obvious that the ground too was moving because of tunnelling. They could then dig their own countermines, into which they could send their own men. Bitter hand-to-hand fighting would then break out in the dark, sweaty, cramped tunnels. Men would hack at each other with everything to hand; daggers, picks, shovels, anything that could maim or kill. There was nothing particularly chivalrous about this arm of warfare.

The attack continued above ground too. The garrison had an advantage at Acre for the crusader lines were overlooked by Saladin's forces. This meant that the defenders could be warned when an attack was imminent. Several methods of communication were used to do so including the use of drums and carrier pigeons. On other occasions, fires were lit to alert Saladin to the fact that a serious assault had been launched. But the crusaders also had some help. There appeared to be spies inside the city who would fire arrows across the walls carrying messages with information that was useful to the besiegers.

And, if Muslim chroniclers are to be believed, the garrison was by now vastly outnumbered.[41] They were under attack for virtually 24 hours a day and they got little sleep and that which they did get was troubled and shallow. On the other hand, the crusaders could use their superior sources of manpower to rotate their men, taking some out of the line to recover their energy whilst rested troops moved up to take their place. The garrison of Acre was starting to suffer from exhaustion.

In addition to the mining, a large array of siege engines was now in place and doing their worst against the walls. They were provided not just by Richard but also by Philip, Hugh of Burgundy, the Knights Templar and the Hospitallers. The siege was now relentless and morale inside the increasingly broken walls of Acre continued to decline. Heroes were emerging on the crusader side: Geoffrey of Lusignan was lauded as a worthy successor to those legendary chivalric paragons Oliver and Roland. In one bitter hand-to-hand fight he brought down ten of the enemy with the mighty axe that he wielded.[42]

Just then the defenders had an unexpected respite. Both Richard and Philip were struck down by disease. It has been suggested that Richard was suffering from an ailment called *arnaldia* (in Latin) or *leonardie* (in French). It was a debilitating condition which caused hair and nails to fall out.[43] It has alternatively been suggested that the condition affecting both Richard and Philip may have been malaria.[44] It was thought to be so serious that the lives of both kings seemed to be in the balance. However, both men would survive the ordeal.

Disease was a great killer in medieval warfare, especially during times of siege which went hand-in-hand with bad sanitation, malnutrition and exposure to extreme conditions. Mortality in the Third Crusade was high, with an estimated 16 per cent of all named clerics dying and 30 per cent of all named nobles.[45] Both Richard and Philip appear to have been struck down by their illnesses within a week of arriving; Richard would not recover fully until early August. William the Breton, a chronicler who was a supporter of Philip, wrote that the French king had been poisoned.[46] The most likely interpretation though was that this was some form of infectious disease and that the loss of hair and nails were due to a general loss of vitality while their bodies struggled to fight it off.[47]

This was a blow to morale and to the momentum of the assault, which ran out of steam. In one Muslim counter-raid several siege engines were set alight. The garrison began to taunt the attackers as the intensity of their efforts slackened and then dropped off altogether. The death of Philip of Flanders soon after was a further blow. The besiegers started to despair; both the kings were suffering from ill-health and the enthusiasm that had been apparent when they had first arrived was rapidly dissipating. However, there was then something of a boost when reinforcements arrived including Robert, earl of Leicester.

Both the kings started to recover, with Philip first to return to health. There was a constant bombardment and counter-bombardment. Philip had a catapult which was named Bad Neighbour but it was often hit and damaged by missiles from one inside Acre called Evil Cousin. Nevertheless, he kept rebuilding it and gaps began to appear in the walls around the Accursed Tower,[48] helped by a reliable supply of suitably sized stones that Richard had brought with him from Sicily. Another device constructed for the Hospitallers which was christened the Catapult of God also caused a good deal of damage. Those in charge of this engine were constantly urged on by a priest who had unofficially adopted it and made himself responsible for collecting funds to repair it when required.[49]

When Richard rose from his sick-bed, he quickly threw himself into the thick of the action in his own inimitable style. He had inherited a good stone-thrower from Philip of Flanders and ordered two more of his own to be constructed. He also had a belfry made, a high, moveable tower covered with wetted hides to make it more resistant to Greek Fire. Two mangonels were also built for him, a form of catapult which flung stones into Acre, causing devastation far in the city streets around the meat-market. One of these was said to be so powerful that it killed twelve men with a single shot.[50] But the defenders were hanging on grimly and continued to destroy some of the siege machines employed against them with Greek Fire and their own stone-throwing machines. The rate of progress being made by the crusaders was still slow.

Richard did not just restrict himself to military action in his attempts to strengthen his position. On 18 June, he sent an envoy to Saladin suggesting a meeting between the two men. Saladin responded cautiously. However, discussions continued and it was agreed that negotiations would continue with Saladin's brother, Al-'Adil, known to the crusaders as 'Saphadin'. Richard was initially restricted from following up through his illness. When he had recovered, he sent messages to Saladin, explaining that his lack of proactivity should not be taken for a sign of prevarication.

Richard soon after despatched an envoy with the gift of a freed Muslim prisoner for Saladin. Other envoys soon followed. Saladin had been courteous to Richard and Philip while he was at Acre, sending gifts of pears, plums and other fruits. These exchanges should not at this stage be considered as a full-blown diplomatic approach but rather an initial feeling-out exercise. There was also undoubtedly some intelligence to be gleaned through the eyes and ears of the envoys and an element of low-level espionage going on. Certainly, the siege carried on regardless and the stones from the siege engines continued to thud into the walls of Acre, causing more damage to them.

The crusaders had help from inside the city where there was a Christian who frequently sent messages to the crusaders, written in Greek, Latin and Hebrew. He was a mysterious individual whose name was unknown to the besiegers (and indeed never would be, even after the eventual capture of Acre) but he assiduously told them of what the next planned move of the defenders was, so he was presumably quite well-connected to those in command inside the increasingly fractured walls.

By now the position of the garrison was deteriorating. Philip's miners brought down a section of the walls. The rubble collapsed into the surrounding ditch. Although tired, the garrison still fought hard and the French who attempted to follow-up on the breach were driven back, suffering heavy losses in the process. Alberic Clement, Philip's marshal, had charged up the hill of shattered stones carrying his king's standard. The defenders threw a great iron hook over the walls and snagged the marshal with it. He was pulled over into the city and killed on the spot.

So many men attempted to climb up siege ladders that they broke under their collective weight. Forty other French soldiers were crushed to death by stones flung down on them by the increasingly desperate garrison. While all this was going on, Richard and his men kept watch in the trenches as he and Philip had agreed that, whenever one of them was attacking, the other would stay on the defensive to guard against a Muslim counter-attack.

Richard was still not well enough to stand and he was carried to the front line on a silken litter (it was said that Philip had also done this when he was ill earlier on). He was even able to shoot dead a Muslim warrior who had donned the distinctive armour of the slain marshal Alberic Clement with a crossbow bolt. His own sappers were now busy and soon after they succeeded in bringing a tower down. Acre was starting to crack. Richard's men went on the attack, attempting to take advantage of the breach. Included in their number was the earl of Leicester, Andrew de Chauvigny and Hubert Walter, bishop of Salisbury.

A vicious fight broke out at 9 o'clock on the morning of 11 July 1191. The English attackers scrambled up the scattered walls to be met by a defence that was as determined as ever. This was hand-to-hand fighting, primeval in intensity with enemies staring each other in the face. The Muslim defenders again deployed their secret weapon, Greek Fire. Once again it was impossible for the crusaders to stand up to and they were soon fleeing for their lives.

But the effort expended in repulsing the repeated attacks took its toll on an already tired garrison who were nearing the end of their stores of endurance. They were deprived of sleep and hungry. However reassuring Saladin might have been in the past, he had been unable to drive the attackers off. Those besieging the city had been hugely reinforced. The naval blockade was doing its part and the future for those inside the city now looked increasingly bleak.

The very next day after the walls were breached an envoy came out from the city seeking terms. He asked that those inside the city should be spared but the discussions, which were with Philip, did not go well and the envoy returned to Acre in a rage. That night, several emirs slipped away in a boat, like rats deserting a sinking ship. Saladin, his armies reinforced and refusing to countenance the surrender of Acre, had launched fierce attacks during the night of

4 and 5 July. The defenders had rushed to the trenches which they defended with great determination and drove the attack off. Saladin was starting to realise that he was losing the battle for the city.

The defenders sought permission to send messengers to Saladin. Their plight was now parlous and without hope unless something could be done to relieve them soon. Saladin encouraged them to hang on. He was expecting significant reinforcements imminently. He pleaded with the garrison to fight on and resist the crusaders for at least another week when he hoped that their situation would be much improved. But his advisers, some of whom had friends and relatives inside Acre, urged him to allow the garrison to seek terms.

The endgame was now being reached. Even Saladin saw that the position was now precarious. He approached the crusaders to offer terms whilst also setting vineyards in the area alight to deprive the crusaders of their use. He offered to return the fragment of the True Cross that had been captured at Hattin; in addition, a prisoner would be released in exchange for each man within Acre. It was not enough. The crusaders scented blood and said that they would only consider terms if all of Saladin's conquests in Outremer were returned along with every *Franj* prisoner that he held.

By now the supernatural had allegedly intervened. A vision of the Virgin had been seen and told the besiegers not to be alarmed for the city would be theirs within four days. News of this timely apparition was greeted with great joy by the crusaders when it was spread amongst them on the following morning. As if to back up the point, the garrison was terrified by an earthquake that soon after struck Acre.

Further discussions over the terms of surrender were held in the tent that formed the headquarters of the Templars outside the city walls. All of Acre, including its provisions and the Egyptian ships that had been trapped within the harbour, were to be handed over. The lives of the garrison and their families with them would be spared in return for a massive ransom, 200,000 dinars, the release of nearly 2,000 prisoners and the return of the True Cross. A particularly significant detail as it turned out was that the Christian prisoners were to be released within one month.

Saladin was not party to these decisions. He was horrified when he heard of the harshness of the terms but it was too late now for him to intervene. The matter of the loss of Acre was now out of his hands. Before long the banners of the conquering crusaders were flying over the shattered walls of Acre. The crusaders moved in and took up residence.

A great deal was lost to Saladin by the fall of Acre. There was not least damage to his reputation but there was also much in the way of material possessions too including seventy galleys. Ibn Shaddad, a Muslim writer, noted that 'he was more affected than a bereft mother or a lovesick girl' by these events.[51]

But as often happens at such moments, it did not take long for infighting to start amongst the victors on the vexed question of the division of the spoils of war. They entered the city on 12 July. A hundred of the richest men in the city were selected and put under guard in one of Acre's towers. Any Muslim who converted to Christianity was to be given their freedom. Some did so. But when they were freed, they allegedly made their way to Saladin and renounced the baptism they had received.[52]

The banners of the kings of England, France and Jerusalem were soon flying over the shattered walls (which, within days, the crusaders started to repair). This was more than just a statement of pride. It signified that the spoils of the city belonged to these men, to do with as they wished. Many were not happy with this assumption. Men had been fighting for Acre long before the kings of England and France arrived, most notably the Germans, who had struggled through to Outremer after the demise of Frederick Barbarossa.

Some of them held a protest meeting outside the walls. Richard and Philip promised to look at their demands but did not do so. Some historians suggest that this was because they had more important things on their minds[53] but this does not wholly ring true. It would not have taken long to at least make an interim gesture. That neither Richard nor Philip did so does not reflect well on them, and it was hardly likely to attract these men to continue serving with them. It was a move entirely in keeping with the Plantagenets' generally imperious attitude towards the rights of kings, one which was being increasingly mirrored by Philip of France too.

This dispute led to an event that was to have profound future implications. Duke Leopold of Austria had become de facto leader of the remnants of the German army when he arrived at Acre as Frederick of Swabia, Barbarossa's successor as leader of the army, had died by then. Leopold had in fact not been in Outremer for long before the two kings arrived, journeying from Venice. On his arrival, as a relative of Barbarossa he was a natural replacement for him. William of Newburgh suggested that Leopold had entered the service of Richard as he was unable to pay for the German army out of his own resources.

Leopold's actions in choosing this moment to raise his banner over the walls of Acre was significant. By so doing, he was staking his claim to a share of the spoils. Before long, his banner was lying in a ditch, thrown there by Richard's soldiers. It is not certain that Richard ordered this move but it would have been no surprise if he had. Whether his actions were legally justified or not, it was an unwise and imprudent move, though it was one that was fully in accordance with his own views on his regal status. It was a classic, and to be frank, foolish exhibition of Richard's pride – his superbia – and he would come to regret it bitterly.

There were other practical issues to attend to. For one thing, up until four years before Acre had been a Christian city whose population was dispersed after its capture by the Muslims. Some of those people now wanted their properties back. Richard initially spent little time on the issue of returning refugees. He was prevailed upon to do so by Philip and they were eventually allowed to return. Some of the churches in Acre had been converted into mosques and they were now restored to their original state and re-consecrated.[54]

On 20 July, there was a discussion between Richard and Philip that was to have massive repercussions, not just on the crusade but also on Richard's future. Philip appeared to be a reluctant crusader, as if he took part through obligation rather than any sense of vocation. He had also been in poor health at Acre and the prospect of a gruelling continuation of the campaign was not an attractive proposition.

Richard suggested that the two kings should issue a joint statement that they planned to stay on crusade for three years. This was probably because Richard had come to realise that Philip was itching to get home. Just two days later Philip announced that he did indeed plan to return to France. His excuse was that with the death of Philip of Flanders he had important business to attend to in territories that were on the vulnerable frontiers of his kingdom; and indeed he would reap significant gains in the late count's territories after his return.

When Richard pushed him to stay, Philip stated that he would only do so if he were given half of Cyprus, showing how much the capture of the island rankled. This again Richard refused to do; in fact, Richard said he would give Philip half of Cyprus if in return he would receive half of Flanders. Philip might well have hoped that such a negative response would be the case as it would give him greater excuse to return to France. Go he would.

News of Philip's decision to return westwards was probably received with mixed sentiments by Richard. On the one hand, he must have been nervous of what Philip would do to his lands in France when he was so far away, despite the French king's vows not to take advantage of Richard's absence; these fears would prove well-founded. But on the other, Richard would no longer have to share the limelight with Philip. Once the French king had left, there was no doubt that Richard would be the leader of the Crusade. Some of Philip's men were shocked at their king's decision and begged him to reconsider what to them seemed a great disgrace.

It was soon time for Philip to leave. He vowed again not to attack Richard's lands in France when he returned; how well he kept that promise we shall soon see. He appointed Hugh of Burgundy to lead the men that he left behind. The half of Acre that was his he gave to Conrad, probably a political gesture to confirm his continued support for him. The Muslim prisoners that had been taken after the capture of Acre were divided between Richard and Philip. Philip then took himself off to Tyre, taking his share of the prisoners with him.

Philip left Tyre for France on 3 August, having left Acre three days before. He had been in Outremer for less than four months. He was probably very frustrated. Richard had been unco-operative throughout much of the expedition. The two kings had fallen out at Messina and Philip had been humiliated by the rejection of his sister Alice. Richard had then refused point-blank to divide Cyprus with him. Richard had often been uncooperative at Acre too and the two men were supporting different candidates for the throne of Jerusalem.

Then there were human factors at work. Richard had been the rising star at Acre. He was outgoing and capable of generous gestures that won men's hearts; all things that Philip generally was not. So it is likely that he left with an inner anger burning within him, determined to make life as difficult as possible for Richard. During the last months of the reign of Henry II, the two men had been close though probably through mutual interest rather than any genuine affection. Those days now seemed a long way off. They would never again return.

Philip's apologists sought to justify his departure by pointing to his illness. Yet this would not have been considered much of an excuse by more devout crusaders. Once the vow to journey to Jerusalem had been made, it was imperative to honour it. Death on crusade through illness was as much a passport into heaven as death in battle was. It was considered a shameful act to withdraw from a crusade with vows unfulfilled. Some who had taken such a vow were later absolved of it by the Church but only if certain conditions were fulfilled.[55]

On his return to France, Philip's itinerary took in Antiochetta, Rhodes and Rome. Whilst in the Eternal City, he held an audience with Pope Celestine. It was said that here he asked to be relieved of his oath to Richard because of the English king's behaviour towards him. Celestine was having none of this. The crusading rulebook was clear on this point; Alexander III, for example, had pointed out back in 1181 that it was strictly forbidden, 'after the assumption of the cross, [that] any claim shall be entertained with reference to the things of which they [i.e. the absent crusader] are in reasonable possession until such time as they return, or certain information shall have been brought of their death'.[56]

That was clear enough. Richard had not returned, neither was he dead. That meant that his rights must be strictly protected whilst he was absent; otherwise how could potential future crusaders feel confident that they would return to their possessions after years away fighting for the cross? The observance of such vows must be maintained. Celestine cajoled Philip into making an even more stringent oath not to take advantage of Richard's absence.[57]

Some of Richard's men went back too, including Roger of Howden. This may have been to ensure that preparations were made to resist Philip should he attempt to stir up trouble. As Richard's ships caught up to Philip's and accompanied them back, there was no attempt to conceal the fact and their visible presence was even then a warning shot from Richard.

Philip's reputation was damaged by his departure. There had not even been the beginnings of an attempt on Jerusalem whilst he was there and this was the ultimate prize for a crusader. It was an outrage to Christendom that the city remained in enemy hands. Hugh of Burgundy, who had been left behind in command of the remaining French, was so short of money that he was forced to borrow funds from Richard. Even the later famous French chronicler, Jean de Joinville, who accompanied Louis IX (Philip's grandson) on his later crusade and wrote a memorable work on the subject, could not resist comparing him unfavourably to

Richard.[58] Philip had claimed in correspondence that he 'burned with desire' to complete his pilgrimage; his actions now did precious little to support such a contention.[59]

Richard's reputation on the other hand was high in many eyes, even amongst those who were not there. A Nestorian Christian writing in Mosul in 1192 wrote of 'the young lion, the king of England, the shining light. He fought without pause, both day and night'.[60] From this moment on, Philip of France, and more especially his reputation, were on the back foot. Richard, on the other hand, made generous gifts to those of the French army who had stayed behind to try to secure their commitment.

Richard had taken up residence inside Acre in the king's palace, where he was joined by Berengaria and Joanna. For the short time he was there, Philip stayed in the headquarters of the Templars. On the same day that Philip left Tyre, 3 August 1191, Richard ordered his ships to load up and prepare to sail down the coast to Ascalon. The army were ordered to follow suit. In the meantime, the walls of Acre were repaired so that they were even stronger than they had been before the siege.

Richard was almost immediately faced with a problem. The time agreed for Saladin to pay over the money to ransom those taken captive at Acre was rapidly approaching and there was as yet no sign of it arriving. It was a large sum and would have taken time to collect. It also served Saladin's purposes to prevaricate as it would enable him to prepare for the next stage of the crusader assault now that Acre had fallen.

Saladin had a month to collect the ransom. He had contacted Richard to say that he was experiencing practical difficulties and it was agreed that for now a first instalment would be acceptable. This would represent half the money, the return of all the prisoners that Saladin had agreed to hand back and, last but certainly not least, the fragment of the True Cross that was in his possession. Richard's envoys were even shown the latter as evidence that it still actually existed; so struck were they at the sight that they prostrated themselves on the ground before it. For the Muslims, it was more an object of contempt; in their view of religion Christ was a leading prophet but it was widely believed that he had not been crucified. Baha' al-Din confirmed that the fragment of the True Cross was in Saladin's camp and that he understandably intended to use it as a bargaining chip.[61]

Time was marching on. Acre had been taken and Richard was anxious to prosecute the campaign further. The delays were becoming frustrating. As the days passed, the frustration welled up within him until dark thoughts started to consume him. Richard was about to commit an act which would leave an indelible stain on his character and his reputation for honour that would haunt his legacy and continues to do so. A new, dark chapter in the legend of the crusader king was about to be written. It marked a fork in the road. Acre would shape Richard's reputation in more ways than one.

11

Arsuf (1191)

'They call him Melec Richard'
Baha' al-Din, Muslim chronicler

The date agreed for the downpayment, 11 August, was reached. In return for handing it over, Saladin insisted that all those held captive after the fall of Acre were to be released with hostages being given for the remaining payment that was due. The crusaders, however, refused to accept this condition and the negotiations rapidly went downhill from this point on.

Richard was also faced with a practical problem. He did not have all the prisoners from Acre to hand as Philip's share had been taken to Tyre when the French king left for home. Hubert Walter, the bishop of Salisbury, had led a delegation that had been sent to fetch them back on 5 August. Conrad refused to co-operate, creating another delay. Now the duke of Burgundy, Philip's representative in Outremer, went to Tyre, accompanied by others including the count of Dreux. They took with them a warning that if Conrad did not hand back the prisoners then the next person he would be dealing with was Richard in person, backed up by an army if necessary. This did the trick and the prisoners arrived back in Acre on 12 August.

The discussions with Saladin dragged on for over a week longer. Many felt that this was part of a deliberate tactic of prevarication on his part. There were occasional skirmishes between the crusaders and Saracen forces during that time, in one of which a prominent knight from Richard's household, Peter Mignot, was killed. Then on

19 August a rumour spread around the crusader camp that Saladin had killed the Christian prisoners he was to hand back as part of the deal. It was not true but that did not matter for it was believed to be true; the story spread alarm amongst the crusader army and in the atmosphere of heightened suspicion and tension tempers began to fray still further.

The crusaders were angry and embittered. The losses sustained by them in taking Acre had been great. Ambroise noted that six archbishops, a patriarch, twelve bishops, innumerable priests and clerics, forty counts and 500 great landowners had perished during the siege along with countless other common folk, not including a queen and her daughters, who for some reason he chose not to mention.[1] Emotions were raw and there was a strong desire for vengeance in the ranks given the losses that had been suffered. The rumours that the captured crusader prisoners had been killed added fuel to the fire and it was now impossible to put it out.

Baha' al-Din, a Muslim chronicler, insisted that Richard had stated that, should the negotiations with Saladin fail, then the prisoners taken at Acre would be enslaved. Possibly the belief that they would not be killed fuelled Saladin's attempts at prevarication. But if so his reasoning had terrible repercussions for the captured garrison. On 20 August 1191, Richard took a fateful decision, one that has dogged his reputation ever since.

On the afternoon of that day, during the time of Muslim prayers, the prisoners were led out onto the plain outside Acre. Although there are small differences in the exact numbers given by various chroniclers, a figure of around 3,000 seems to be the general consensus. Here, in full sight of watching Muslim forces, they were butchered; Roger of Howden even says that they were disembowelled and a remarkable amount of gold and silver was found in their entrails, insinuating that they had swallowed it to stop it being taken from them.[2] From what we can tell, the men delegated to carry out this task did so with enthusiasm. This was the logical extension of the concept of the crusade; the most famous cleric of the twelfth century, St Bernard of Clairvaux, had suggested divine sanction for such acts when committed by crusaders:

> Neither does he bear the sword in vain, for he is God's minister, for the punishment of evildoers and for the praise of the good. If he kills an evildoer, he is not a man killer, but, if I may so put

it, a killer of evil. He is evidently the avenger of Christ towards evildoers and he is rightly considered a defender of Christians. Should he be killed himself, we know that he has not perished, but has come safely into port. When he inflicts death it is to Christ's profit, and when he suffers death, it is for his own gain. The Christian glories in the death of the pagan, because Christ is glorified; while the death of the Christian gives occasion for the King to show his liberality in the rewarding of his knight.[3]

It did not matter that Bernard quickly went on to state that such slaughter should only take place if all other options had been exhausted; the caveat was lost in the atmosphere of Christian fundamentalism that he had helped to create. Bernard was going down a dangerous road and its terminus was arrived at on the plain outside Acre.

Panicked warnings of what was happening had been sent to Saladin by his scouts but by the time that reinforcements arrived it was too late for them to intervene. There was nevertheless a violent confrontation between crusaders and Muslim forces later in the day. It came to nothing but on the next day Muslim forces wandered over the plain, strewn with the already-rotting cadavers of the slain beneath the scorching sun. Many of them were still recognisable as friends and former comrades-in-arms of those who walked the blood-soaked plain in disbelief. As they looked at the mortal remains of those who had been slaughtered in cold blood, they felt the bile rise inside them. Thoughts of vengeance filled them and, for a while afterwards, the fate of crusaders captured in battle was a grisly one. Such is the case following most such massacres, for this is what this was.

Richard was quick to justify his actions. He wrote a letter on 1 October 1191 in which he explained that he had given Saladin full opportunity to comply with the terms agreed.[4] The more important of the prisoners were spared, not for reasons of humanity but because they were valuable in terms of ransom. Yet it cannot be denied that this was a brutal act, standing out by its very scale even by the standards of the time. It was one after all that was committed not in the heat of battle or the immediate aftermath of a siege but as a cold, calculating move weeks after the capture of Acre.

Moralising is a dangerous game nearly a millennium after the events that took place. There was no criticism of Richard from

Christian chroniclers at the time, though Muslim commentators were understandably horrified by the massacre. The fanaticism that underpinned the crusading ethos, which encouraged those taking part to see the enemy as an inferior moral group, was always likely to lead to butchery such as this; for this reason, the capture of Jerusalem in 1099 by the First Crusade had seen equally appalling bloodshed. The action of Richard's men was the logical conclusion of prevailing crusader mentalities.

The chronicler Ambroise certainly had no doubts as to the morality of Richard's actions. He referred to the recent Siege of Acre in which many Christian lives had been lost as a justification for it. To him the massacre was a manifestation of divine retribution; 'Thus was vengeance taken for the blows and the crossbow bolts. Thanks be to God the Creator'.[5] The writer of the *Itinerarium*, who perhaps felt that Richard's actions needed to be defended, says that he did not take the decision alone but after consulting his council.[6]

But both would also have been dismayed that the fragment of the True Cross that was part of the negotiated settlement would now no longer be coming back into Christian hands. Another Muslim writer, Imad ad-Din, said that it was taken back to Saladin's treasury, there to be humiliated rather than honoured. Other delegations from both the Byzantines and the Georgians tried to recover the sacred item from Saladin but failed in their efforts.[7]

Later historians have not been slow to criticise the events at Acre and there is something about the cold-bloodedness of the slaughter that still has the power to disturb. Richard's supporters even now feel compelled to explain away his actions by explaining, for example, that Saladin also killed prisoners, such as the execution of the Templar and Hospitaller knights captured at Hattin in 1187. They also point out that the presence of 3,000 Muslim soldiers would mitigate against the crusaders leaving Acre and moving on to their next target whilst they were still alive.

For all that these may be considered reasons, it is more difficult to regard them as excuses. John Gillingham, Richard's outstanding biographer in the twentieth century, wrote a comprehensive and insightful biography but the pages devoted to the explanation for the massacre are probably some of his least convincing.[8] Gillingham states that in his view Richard did not order the massacre in a fit of Angevin rage but rather as a consequence of a calculated chain of thought. That in some ways makes it worse.

And it does contrast negatively with the actions of Saladin after the capture of Jerusalem in 1187. Then, even though thousands of Muslims had been slaughtered when the city had been taken in 1099, there had been no major blood-letting in the aftermath. Those who could not afford their ransom then had been taken off into slavery; not an easy life no doubt and a bitter existence; but a continued existence nonetheless.

When all is said and done, cold-blooded killing is a rash move. Any short-term advantage it might give in terms of cowing an enemy is counter-productive, for in the long-term such acts merely ignite a burning fire for revenge and a fierce desire to even things up; they also make it pointless to surrender if men believe that they will die in any case. As Mahatma Gandhi said in more recent times, an eye for an eye only succeeds in making the whole world blind. As a case in point, in a story told by Imad al-Din, a Muslim prisoner taken at around this time was burned alive. Very soon afterwards a Christian prisoner was dealt with in the same way. That brought an abrupt halt to the tit-for-tat reprisals; both sides could see that it was foolish.[9]

Acre would fall once more to the Muslims in 1291, virtually the last blow struck in the long epic of the crusades to Outremer. After the city was captured, the blood-letting that followed was horrific. To an Egyptian chronicler of the time by the name of Abu I-Mihasin, this was recompense for the treacherous slaying of the garrison at Acre a century before.[10]

John Gillingham points out that this was a long time after the event but that does not diminish the symbolic impact on Muslim minds of the butchery at Acre unleashed by Richard. Indeed, such moments are what build into mythology, often more powerful than history, and they often increase rather than diminish over time. Martyrs are always a powerful motivator, as we know very well from our own era, and it would be easy for Muslim propagandists to portray those slaughtered at Acre as such.

That those at Acre who were killed were probably in the main no such thing and were really ordinary soldiers who happened to be in the wrong place at the wrong time does not really matter; in this case perception is more powerful than reality as it nearly always is. The fate of the Christians killed in 1291 was equally horrific; yet in its own way this was a striking if harrowing example of the reality of that disturbing concept that in life you often reap what you sow.

With Acre now captured, the key question for Richard concerned his next move. Many of the crusaders wanted to fulfil their pilgrim vows by going to Jerusalem. Once they had visited the city with its holy shrines, the Church of the Holy Sepulchre in particular, they were then free to return home with their crusading vows fulfilled and their remission of sins earned. And that was exactly the problem as Richard quickly came to realise. Although capturing Jerusalem would be a very hard task indeed, holding on to it afterwards would be even more difficult.

This was the perennial challenge, ever since Jerusalem had been captured by the First Crusade in 1099. The Muslims had access to a vast reservoir of resources from lands that surrounded Outremer. In contrast, the crusader states in the region had to rely on new and infrequent injections of manpower from the west and these tended to be short-term in nature. Visiting Jerusalem as a pilgrim was one thing, becoming a settler in Outremer quite another, and the prospect of the latter simply did not interest many crusaders. Most of those who came to Jerusalem went home again soon after.

The military orders in Outremer were an important part of the answer. This perhaps led to the establishment at this time of the Hospital of St Thomas of Acre, an order whose membership was restricted to Englishmen. However, it was at first a non-military body whose duties were to care for sick pilgrims and bury those who perished in battle. Its founder was William, chaplain to the Dean of St Paul's. Only thirty years later would the order be militarised by Peter des Roches, a well-known crusader-cleric who was bishop of Winchester.

Richard realised that he could not stop at Acre for long without his campaign losing momentum. On 22 August, Richard assembled his men outside the walls of Acre, ready to march off. This time, the rules concerning women would be rigorously applied; washerwomen only (Ambroise noted approvingly that 'they were as clever as monkeys at getting rid of fleas').[11] Even Berengaria and Joanna were to stay at Acre, which would be under the command of Bertram of Verdun in Richard's absence.

Three days later, the army set out. Jaffa was to be the first target. The port had biblical connections and featured in the stories of those great Hebrew kings, David and Solomon. St Peter later raised a widow from the dead there. It would be an important symbolic addition to the crusader conquests. But it would also be a valuable strategic gain. It was another port further down the coast than

Acre and it was the one which was closest to Jerusalem. It would be ideally placed as a launchpad for the final assault on the Holy City itself.

But Richard had another objective in mind. Further down the coast again was the crucial prize of Ascalon. This stood astride the main line of communication from Egypt to Jerusalem and was a regular supply route for the city. If he were to take it, it would be very difficult for reinforcements to make their way up from Egypt and attack the crusaders from the rear whilst they were attacking Jerusalem. On the other hand, he feared that if he did not take Ascalon then he would be caught in a trap, with fresh Muslim forces from Egypt hammering him from behind against the anvil of the strong city walls of Jerusalem.

Richard had already taken preliminary measures to put his plans into effect. He appointed Geoffrey of Lusignan as the lord of Jaffa and Ascalon on 28 July. The small problem with this otherwise excellent plan was that neither place was then in crusader hands. Richard aimed to put this right. The choice of Geoffrey was an interesting one. He had been a troublesome vassal in Aquitaine but during the crusade he had fought well and his reputation had been considerably enhanced. As a younger son, he had more opportunities in Outremer than he would have in France, so the crusade gave him a unique chance for advancement.

Richard was now faced by a daunting new challenge. The capture of Acre was a classic example of siege warfare, not so very different than he had experienced in the past though on a much greater scale. Now though he was moving out into the open. It was unthinkable that Saladin would not oppose him as he marched on Jaffa. After all, his army was still intact. His losses had not been so great that they could not be replaced.

Large-scale pitched battles were the exception rather than the rule during this period. There was too much at stake to gamble all on a massive confrontation between two large armies. Even great warrior kings fought only a handful during their career. Henry V, for example, only fought two, at Shrewsbury and Agincourt. Henry II, a very capable strategist, never fought one. Neither had Richard been involved in one so far. This was uncharted territory he was now entering.

The style of warfare now facing Richard was also very different than anything he had experienced previously. The main tactic of the Muslim forces, deployed with such stunning effect at Hattin, was to charge in and out of the relatively static crusader armies who opposed them with their light cavalry. They were particularly famed for their ability as horse-archers, using composite bows. These tactics resulted in the sky being filled with arrows descending on their enemy from many different directions simultaneously.

A favourite trick (soon to also be employed by the Mongols with great effect) was to scatter before their enemies as if retreating in chaos. Thinking that they were on the run, the enemy would then chase after them. In the process, they would lose their discipline and order. Once they were broken up, the fleeing Muslim horsemen would suddenly re-form and turn on the pursuing foe. All too often, this ruse would win the battle. It was frequently employed and should therefore have been a known quantity. Despite this, the crusader forces had over the past century fallen into the same trap on several occasions.

The crusader forces on the other hand had strong advantages if their order and cohesion could be maintained. Their most powerful weapon was their heavy cavalry. A well-co-ordinated charge from these could prove irresistible. The knights and other mounted warriors (for a knight was really a cavalryman from a certain social class, whereas over time the term has become synonymous with any medieval horseman) were well protected in their heavy armour. The momentum that they generated in the charge could be devastating; it was said that they could even smash their way through the walls of Babylon.

But they needed to stay co-ordinated to utilise these advantages. If they lost their discipline and split into small groups, they could be picked off easily by the enemy. Several battles had been lost over the years for this very reason. Spurred on by religious euphoria which they believed gave them moral supremacy over their Muslim opponents, or just by the blood-red mist unleashed in the heat of conflict, battles had been lost because the heavy cavalry of the crusaders had lost cohesion.

Richard, as a student of military strategy, was aware of these risks. He formed his army into contingents of men from different regions; Bretons, Normans, English, Angevins, Poitevins. There was also the French contingent led by Hugh of Burgundy, whose contribution is underplayed by English chroniclers. Then there were the Templars and Hospitallers, the closest that Outremer had to a standing army. They had been formed during the early part of the twelfth century, ostensibly to protect pilgrims making their way to Jerusalem. Subsequently, they took on a wider role in the defence of the kingdom.

They were organised like monastic Orders. Templars and Hospitallers were supposed to practice chastity and renounce all worldly wealth (though ironically the organisations as a whole became immensely rich as they attracted widespread donations, particularly in terms of land). They had significant influence right across Europe. In Britain and Ireland even now the presence of the word 'Temple' as part of a place name often suggests that there were Templar landholdings in the vicinity at one time.[12]

Because of their monastic links, the Orders (others would emerge over time but the Templars and Hospitallers remained the most prominent, at least until the Teutonic Knights evolved in later years) reported not to the kings of Jerusalem but to the Pope. This gave them a dangerous propensity to act unilaterally, not always taking the priorities of the kingdom into consideration. They would also acquire a reputation for excessive pride, greed and even immorality; for the Templars, this would eventually have catastrophic consequences.

Both Orders had been decimated at Hattin. Those of their knights captured were almost all beheaded after the battle, apart from the Master of the Templars, Gerard de Ridfort, a hot-headed and rash leader in battle, often more dangerous to his own side than the opposition; his survival was almost certainly due to the strategic advantages he would give Saladin as a hostage, though he would later be killed at the Siege of Acre. But those that remained of the Orders' knights formed an important part of Richard's army. As professional soldiers in all but name they would take up key roles in his force as it advanced.

In this respect, the appointment in 1191 of a new Grand Master of the Templars, Robert de Sablé, who was an Angevin vassal of Richard's, must have been welcome news to the English king. Robert had accompanied Richard on his journey across the Mediterranean and had been a leading negotiator with Tancred in Sicily, so the two men were well-known and trusted by each other.[13] This made the Templars potentially useful allies of Richard.

Richard realised when making his dispositions for the march that he could expect Saladin to launch heavy raids against his army throughout the journey to Jaffa. He had devised tactics to deal with these expected assaults. The cavalry's armour would protect them against the arrows unleashed by Saracen archers. There were accounts of such men riding on unperturbed with so many arrows sticking in their armour that they looked like porcupines.

Their horses were more exposed as they were not so well protected. Kill a cavalryman's horse and it was like cutting off his legs, or, as one historian noted, like being an admiral without a fleet.[14] His effectiveness would be vastly diminished, indeed in an offensive sense it would be completely destroyed. Therefore, measures needed to be employed to protect against this. Horse-armour was only just starting to develop so this was not yet a viable solution in many cases.

The cost of horseflesh was enormous. A knight would be expected to have several kinds of horse to support him. There was a relatively cheap palfrey to carry a knight on a journey. His baggage was carried by a sturdier sumpter. But his pride and joy was his *destrier*, a great warhorse, immune to the terror caused by the clash of sword in battle, fleet and sure of foot, but enormously expensive; one such horse could cost the equivalent of 4,500 sheep.[15] As far as possible the horses needed protection.

The solution was to have a protective screen of infantry on the flanks of the cavalry. They formed a human wall which it would be very difficult for the enemy to break through; they could prevent the enemy from getting close enough to bring down the horses. But for these tactics to be effective both arms had to work closely together, the cavalry and infantry moving as one with no gaps emerging. This was much easier said than done.

Saladin though had his own problems to think about. The terrain down the coast was not always conducive to his preferred tactics and one flank of the crusader army, that protected by the coast and the navy, was out of reach. But he had done his homework and sent out several emirs to identify places where attacks could be launched. They had returned with positive news on that front.[16]

Richard devised a plan to take advantage of the naval superiority that he now enjoyed. His fleet would sail just offshore as the army advanced, well stocked with supplies such as biscuits and flour, wine and meat. The main benefit of this was that his men could be kept resupplied as it was highly probable that Saladin would launch a scorched-earth policy in front of the crusaders as they advanced. There was also another important advantage to be gained in that he only needed to worry about protecting the flank of his army from the landward side. He could rotate his infantry, one part marching by the sea, protected from attack and effectively taking a breather. From time to time they could change places with those who had been under attack from the raids of the Muslim light cavalry, always keeping part of his force relatively fresh.

The army set off and Ambroise waxed lyrical in describing them in purple prose that would do credit to an Arthurian epic:

> There you would have seen chivalry, the finest of young men, the most worthy and most elite that were ever seen, before then or since. There you would have seen so many confident men, with such fine armour, such valiant and daring men-at-arms, renowned for their prowess. There you would have seen so many pennocels [small pennons] on shining, fine lances; there you would have seen so many banners, worked in many designs, fine hauberks and good helmets; there are not so many of such quality in five kingdoms.[17]

It all sounds like a glorious adventure, but in reality there would be much hard scrapping along the way.

When the march began Saladin closely followed it from a safe distance. He launched raids on the crusader army with his horsemen, taking advantage of the sand dunes that hid his forces from the crusaders as well as the occasional presence of the mist that further concealed them. Richard had commanded that on no account should his men react to these and break ranks, for this is exactly what Saladin hoped that they would do. It became a battle of endurance with the rear-guard especially under attack. At times, they were forced to march backwards to keep their shape in the presence of determined Muslim attacks. But keep it they did and they advanced methodically but inexorably southwards.

Prominent in their army was the king's standard. The name might summon up a mental picture of a flag being carried in the middle of the line but in fact it was far more imposing than this. It was carried on a four-wheeled wooden platform on top of a beam that was similar to a ship's mast. On the top of this flew the banner; in the words of one Muslim writer is was at the top of a tower as high as a minaret. The device was guarded by some of the crack troops in the army, in this case Normans. It served a purpose as a rallying point and as such must not be captured. Those who were wounded in battle were brought here for refuge whilst the fighting was going on, as well as the bodies of the more illustrious men who were killed in battle so that they could later receive the proper funeral rites.[18]

There were alarms along the way. Early on, the duke of Burgundy's men started to lag behind. Seeing an opportunity by the gap created as a result, Saladin unleashed his cavalry to attack the baggage train which was now exposed. It was a dangerous moment but according to the chroniclers the worst consequences were avoided by the heroic actions of one man, Richard himself.

He was at the head of the army but when he heard what was happening he charged back. His presence changed the momentum back in favour of his army. Laying about him with abandon, Richard inspired his men to fight back which they duly did. Richard may have been an imperious and sometimes haughty king but he was in battle a soldier's soldier.

Stragglers were picked off though as the highly mobile Muslim cavalry swooped every time they saw a weakness. In one vicious skirmish, a servant of the bishop of Salisbury named Everard had his right hand lopped off; he simply transferred his sword to his left and carried on fighting. There was a fortunate side-effect from this early scare. As well as Richard, the French knight William des Barres also fought with great gallantry and effect; he that day 'stretched many a Turk on the ground'.[19] Richard noticed this. Previously the two men had not got on well but Richard recognised bravery when he saw it and decided to bury his grudge from this moment on.

The discipline of the crusader army remained strong. After these attacks on the very first day of the march, there was much more provocation to come. The frequent skirmishes took a toll of the crusaders both physically and mentally. To compound their discomfort there was the searing heat, made worse by the need to constantly be arrayed in full armour to protect against the arrows and javelins of the enemy. There were many casualties; Richard himself wrote in a letter of 'a severe loss of men' on the march.[20]

Ambroise stated that men had to be left behind as they were dying of the heat and of thirst.[21] This was not surprising as foot soldiers carrying their personal supplies and ten days of rations might have up to 70 lbs (over 30 kg) on their backs.[22] Earlier on, a Frankish prisoner who had been taken told Saladin that more than 400 horses had been lost and that the price of provisions had already gone up a third; and that would only have got worse with the passage of time.[23]

The march was already reaching nightmare proportions. Taking pity on some of those in the worst condition, Richard had them transferred to the ships offshore to gain some respite. As well as the harsh natural conditions, there were constant attacks from the Muslims. From time to time there was an almost irresistible urge from some of the crusaders to retaliate. But the urge continued to be resisted and the order of the line of march held firm.

Even the enemy were impressed at this stoicism. Baha' al-Din was there and saw some of the crusaders marching along with ten arrows protruding from their armour. Yet still they stayed in the ranks, marching along at the same steady pace, their rhythm and determination both equally unperturbed. He admired their 'wonderful patience', their ability to withstand the aching sense of fatigue that must have been assailing them, sucking the energy out of their bodies but seemingly not out of their souls. Yet he knew that many of them were humble men, who stood to gain little from their exertions.[24]

The army marched on. They passed places of biblical significance along the way, most notably Mount Carmel, famed for its associations for here the prophet Elijah once lived. During the twelfth century a well-known monastic Order, the Carmelites, was formed and took its name from here. The mountain was also sacred to other religions including Islam. Pythagoras had reputedly visited the site, moved to do so by its sacred reputation. The Roman Emperor Vespasian had once journeyed here to consult an oracle.

The road near here was very narrow and the countryside was overrun with tarantulas; the crusaders took to making as much noise as possible, beating pots and pans, helmets, shields and armour to frighten them off.[25] The species of tarantula found in the region is particularly active at night. Its bite, whilst not normally life-threatening to a human, is painful. Several species of viper in the region added their own threat to the crusaders, as did scorpions, of which the yellow variant, *leiurus quinquestriatus*, which is found in the region gives a particularly unpleasant sting.[26]

Nearby was a pass of vital strategic importance from way back in time, long before even Christ had walked the earth. Its name in Hebrew was Megiddo and here perhaps the Egyptian Ramesses II had fought the famous Battle of Kadesh in distant Antiquity. At the other end of the historical spectrum General Edmund Appleby fought a decisive battle here against the crumbling Ottoman army in 1918. This was a place of rare historical resonance though it is now better known from the Hebrew name for the hill of Megiddo, *Har Megiddo*; Armageddon.

But there was no apocalyptic battle here now, perhaps a disappointment to those mystics like Joachim Fiore who tried to peel away the layers of mystic uncertainty that made it so hard to discern the true meaning of the Book of Revelation. Instead the army moved on towards Caesarea, a fine port where Herod the Great had ordered the construction of a harbour more than a thousand years before. But in front of the crusader host, everything had been burned. It was just as well that the fleet was there to keep them provided because the land through which they were passing was scorched earth.

The march became even tougher as the army faced further ordeals. In some areas, their progress was blocked by thorns that tore at their clothes and their bodies as they tried to push their way through. As each day ended, a ritual was played out. As the crusader army settled down to sleep, one man let up a cry: 'Holy Sepulchre, Help Us'. The rest of the camp responded in the same vein. Three times this ritual was repeated before the camp settled down to rest.

Moving out from the Dead River, where they found water by digging down through a dried-up river-bed, they crossed particularly barren territory and were forced up into the mountains as the path by the sea was blocked by thick scrub. They were often under attack still and in one skirmish Richard was wounded in the side by an arrow, though not seriously; in fact, it merely nicked him and sent him into a violent rage which made him fight with even more vigour.

Eventually the crusaders camped by the banks of the Salt River, which – as the name suggests – did nothing to improve their position further in terms of potable water. There was an unseemly scrummage over the cadavers of the dead horses that had died on the march so that the men could get something to eat. So bad did this breakdown of discipline become that Richard offered to exchange a live horse for each dead one handed over so horses were still at least in reasonably good supply despite their losses, even if their quality was diminishing. This solved the problem and there was meat enough for everyone, some of the men even managing to improve the flavour by adding some bacon to the best cuts of horseflesh.[27]

Richard in the meantime continued discussions with Al-'Adil, Saladin's brother. Saladin encouraged Al-'Adil to drag these out for as long as possible. He realised that his strategy for disrupting the crusaders was not working; they were simply too disciplined to fall for the traditional hit and run tactics he was employing. There was now no alternative but to commit his forces in battle and go head-to-head with Richard. We may assume that this was not his preferred tactic; it must have been clear by now that the military skills of Richard were formidable.

Unknown to Richard, the greatest challenge of his military career was looming. His men pushed their way through the forest of Arsuf, relieved to do so unmolested for some feared that this was the ideal place for an ambush. Others were afraid that Saladin would set fire to the forest. But there was nothing and no doubt a few sighs of relief were exhaled, along with a few prayers offered up in thanks for their safe passage.

Beneath Richard's dragon standard, being carried by one Peter of Préaux who had received the honour ahead of Robert Trussebet who said that it traditionally belonged to his family, the army emerged once more into the full light of day. As they exited the trees, scouts were sent out. A sight that must have caused some to tremble met their eyes, for there, drawn up impressively in battle array and blocking their way, was what seemed to be a vast host of the enemy.

Reports came back to Richard and a battle appeared to be unavoidable. That Richard should order a retreat was completely unthinkable; that Saladin should lose face by withdrawing equally so. Saladin had rolled the dice and the game was now in full play with extra high stakes involved for both leaders. The next few days would define Richard and his military reputation more than any other moment of his life so far.

Richard had enough time to ensure that his forces were organised to their best effect; in fact, Ambroise suggests that the army was encamped for several days before battle was finally joined.[28] But then, on 7 September 1191, the day of battle at last arrived. Richard's men rose from their sleep and put on their armour knowing that a fight was now inevitable

In all, there were twelve battalions deployed in the crusader army. The Templars, amongst Richard's crack troops given their experience, local knowledge, armament and training, were deployed in the vanguard, more than capable of brushing aside any force that was rash enough to stand in their way, though that was not the Muslim army's preferred way of fighting. Instead, Saladin would use the flexibility given him by his light cavalry, charging in and out of Richard's lines in what a modern commentator has called a 'war of the wasps'.[29]

Behind the Templars were the men from Brittany and Anjou. Then came those from Poitou led by Guy of Lusignan, one of their own even if he was no longer king of Jerusalem. The English and Normans then marched together in their division; the standard of the king was in their charge. The Hospitallers held one of the key positions, the rear-guard. They were every bit as adept as the Templars; they had jointly formed the backbone of the army of the kingdom of Jerusalem. Henry of Champagne was responsible for protecting the flank on the land-side of the army.

The rear-guard was the Achilles' heel of Richard's force. Hugh of Burgundy had nearly come unstuck earlier on the march when he and his men were positioned there. This was the place where Saladin was most likely to focus his attack, doing all he could to force the Hospitallers to break formation, leading to a disintegration of order in Richard's army. The knights of the rear-guard would have to be at their most patient and long-suffering if a turn of events that could lead to calamitous consequences was to be avoided.

Richard ordered his ranks to close up as tightly as possible. So packed were they that it was said that you could not throw an apple between the men without hitting somebody.[30] Richard and Hugh of Burgundy rode up and down the lines, making sure that close order was maintained whilst also keeping an eye on Saladin and his movements. The advance was slow and deliberate, that of a tortoise making its way along with its sturdy and difficult-to-penetrate armour but pedestrian pace. Most important of all was that the line should not become in the least bit extended or broken.

Saladin was patient. He was a thoughtful, studious man, not prone to acts of sudden decision but sizing up the situation moment by moment, waiting clinically for the right moment to strike. It was about 9 a.m. when he unleashed his cavalry.[31] Ambroise, who was there, describes in awed tones the sight of countless pennons fluttering from their lances as the Muslim cavalry charged ferociously at Richard's extended line of march. He talked of thousands of men, their horses dashing like lightning across the plain. A huge cloud of dust billowed up from the parched ground as their hooves thundered over the ground, creating a thick veil before them and hiding their mass from the crusaders who stood grimly, waiting to take their impact. They could not see the enemy but they heard the growing thunder as the dust-cloud billowed towards them. Some at least must have trembled.

This was a cosmopolitan Muslim force, men from 'Damascus and Persia, from the Mediterranean to the East'.[32] Crusader chroniclers talked of troops who were 'very black in colour', probably Sudanese or Nubians. There were also 'Bedouins', 'savage and darker than soot', resolute infantrymen carrying round shields and bows and quivers. Then there were 'Turks', horsemen carrying lances and billowing pennons (perhaps 20,000 of them according to the chroniclers') who were described as being 'swifter than eagles'.[33]

There was a great cacophony too, of trumpets blaring and of the massive kettle-drums beating out their warlike rhythm, urging the Muslim cavalry on towards death or glory. There were the rhythmic sounds of rattles, there were flutes, there were cymbals, there were tambourines. The creation of as much of a din as possible was a core part of Muslim battle tactics. It was a noise that drowned out every other, that overwhelmed the crusaders with its intensity. It spoke of violence, of hatred, of imminent oblivion. Ambroise, who was there that day, wrote of a ripple of fear spreading through the ranks, starting to affect even the bravest of the Christian warriors. To cap it all, it was a hot, airless day, and the suffocating, dusty air added to the sense of imminent doom. After all, this was the way that Hattin had ended just a few years before.

As they thundered into range, the crusader archers and spearmen launched their missiles at the Muslim cavalry. Their aim was true enough but there were so many of the enemy that the number of those who fell made barely a dent on the great mass that continued to bear down on the crusaders. Their light, fleet-of-foot steeds charged in and out of the ranks, probing for an opening, striking men down here and there, trying to get through to the main body of knights behind the infantry screen to provoke them prematurely to an ill-starred charge. But perhaps the greatest danger was that many horses, less well-protected than the men, fell, struck down by arrows from the enemy horse-archers.

The Hospitallers were, predictably enough, the prime target for attack, for if the rear broke then the flank could be attacked and chaos would quickly ensue. The sky was blackened by the clouds of arrows cascading down on the well-armoured knights of the Order. Although they were well protected in their suits of steel, it galled the Hospitallers no end. It was infuriating to have to take this punishment without fighting back. The knights of the Orders found little glory in the fighting of a defensive action, an imprudent approach that contributed towards the disaster at Hattin.

It began to get too much for the Hospitallers to bear any longer. Many of the men in the rear were crossbowmen and archers but they found that the enemy was now so close that they could not use their weapons properly, so they threw them aside and rushed against the enemy in hacking hand-to-hand fighting. So strong and relentless were the attacks of the Muslim horse that the crusaders in the rear-guard were again forced to march backwards so that they could fight them off.[34]

Several times, the Hospitaller Master, Garnier of Nablus, hurried over to Richard, urging him to give permission to fight back. The Master had frequently cried on St George for aid, but St George was clearly not listening. But Richard urged the Master to be patient; the enemy would grow weary and either retire or could be beaten off more easily. Garnier returned to his men, muttering under his breath; each time his appeals were ignored, the sense of frustration inside him grew. Richard still wanted to wait; he had deployed six trumpeters along the line, two at the rear, two in the middle and two in the van who were to sound the charge when the king felt that the time was right.

But there was no sign that the Muslim cavalry were letting up in their efforts. Increasingly it was not arrows that were taking a toll but close-quarter weapons. Allied to the desiccating heat of the sun, it was Hell. The crusaders 'burned in torment but were given no rest'.[35] At last, it became too much for Garnier to bear any longer. He turned his horse and lowered his lance, scattering the infantry screen before him as he accelerated towards the enemy. Another knight, Baldwin of Carew, taking up the cue charged alongside him. For the other Hospitaller knights there was no question of letting their recently appointed Master (he had only become so in 1190) ride to a heroic death unaccompanied. So they too turned their horses and galloped hell-for-leather towards the enemy. They were joined by other bold knights, men like Henry of Champagne, Robert of Dreux, James d'Avesnes and Robert, earl of Leicester.

Further down the line Richard was soon aware of what was happening. If the Hospitallers were not supported then they could be engulfed and, with their fall, the whole of the army was threatened. It was the moment for a critical decision to be made. Richard might have been inwardly livid at the indiscipline of the Hospitallers but the time for any recrimination was later.

He almost at once ordered his cavalry to charge the enemy and support Garnier and his brave if reckless men.

All of a sudden, the Muslim cavalry saw a wall of steel charging towards them. The force of the charge of heavy horse was renowned throughout the world, and here it was heading in their direction. This was no isolated assault by a small group of cavalry as they had hoped, it was a tidal wave heading towards them with unstoppable power and irresistible force. At the head of that wave, having charged through the Hospitaller line, was Richard, 'as swift as a thunderbolt'.[36]

The Muslim warriors now had a decision to make; stay and fight or retreat. To stay where they were in front of that meant only one thing; death. So retreat it was; but this was not the planned feigned withdrawal for which they were so famous; it was a headlong flight propelled by terror. Baha' al-Din was there and he made unambiguously clear what was happening:

> I was in the centre and when that body fled in the wildest disorder, I tried to take refuge with the left wing which was nearer, but that too was struck with panic. On turning to the right wing I found it in even greater confusion.[37]

In other words, this was threatening to become a rout.

Muslim archers who had dismounted to get a better aim were decapitated where they stood as the wave rolled over them. The fallen dead of the enemy lay as thick as corn reaped at the harvest. Some were forced by the press over some cliffs, falling 60 feet into the sea. Some climbed into trees hoping to escape but they were pulled down from them and slaughtered. But the majority of the Muslim army was able to outrun the crusaders and re-form at a safe distance.

Richard's handling of what could have become a crisis was masterful. It was a glorious moment for which the great knights of chivalry lived; a deadly serious tourney with the knights charging with abandon toward the enemy. But there was also a far more pragmatic and cautious side to Richard which he now demonstrated. Before the charge got out of hand, he reined it in and reformed his line in a defensive fashion. His objective was not to destroy the Muslim army in battle; he would have welcomed that but he was not in a position to do it here. Charging too far might lead to the enemy re-forming and attacking his scattered ranks. His objective remained to get through to Jaffa.

Saladin was no slouch either when it came to warfare. He managed to prevent a complete collapse of his force and committed his reserve to the battle. However, Richard also had uncommitted forces at his disposal in the form of his English and Norman troops. He responded to Saladin's counter-measures by launching these into the fight. Richard was there to receive the enemy, mounted on the famous Fauvel, a trophy taken from Isaac Comnenus, and managed to form a new line around his Standard.

The fighting was hard. As usual, Richard was everywhere in the fight, leading charge after charge. Richard was no fool when it came to the arts of government, he was adept at his strategic decision-making when mapping out a military campaign and he loved the thrill of the chase when he was hunting. But the battlefield was more than anything his natural element, where he could throw himself into the heart of the action and inspire his men through his courageous actions. It required action more than thought. This was no tournament, no sanitised version of warfare. This was out and out conflict, man against man, life or death the prize. This was what Richard did best.

Also prominent in the latter stages was William des Barres, his repaired relationship with Richard now proving invaluable. He too fought heroically. Gradually Saladin's counter-attack began to run out of steam and then it ceased altogether. The battle was over and the road to Jaffa was open. Saladin had lost many men; 'you would have seen so many headless corpses of beardless Turks lying there'.[38] But his army was still largely intact. That said, they were in a desperate hurry to escape to safety and they left a lot of booty behind them, reasoning that their lives were worth more than material possessions.[39]

In some ways, the Battle of Arsuf was indecisive, 'a striking and temporary tactical success but nothing more'.[40] Saladin and his army lived to fight another day. But in other respects, it was seminal. It cemented the image of Richard as the most powerful knight in Christendom, not least in the eyes of Saladin. Richard had gained an upper hand in this respect, which he would never subsequently lose.

Baha' al-Din acknowledged that the impact of the battle was massive in terms of morale.[41] Four years before, Saladin's reputation was at its zenith. The army of Jerusalem had been destroyed at Hattin and the Templars and Hospitallers, the crack troops of the enemy, had been decimated. Al-Quds, Jerusalem, the Holy City had been regained and cleansed, its mosques returned to worship.

But fame and glory were fickle mistresses. First his inability to take Tyre, then the loss of Acre, now this. It was a devastating blow to Saladin's reputation. He was ageing now, and the drive and adrenalin of earlier years was fading. He had a few years before been taken seriously ill, so much so that it was thought he would not survive. When against the odds he revived, he underwent a religious re-awakening and it was this that had led to his determination to recover Jerusalem for Islam in the first place.

He was tired now. He had fought for decades to advance not only Islam's interests but also his own. First, he had managed to make himself the ruler of Egypt and change it from a Shi'a state to one where the Sunni branch of the faith was prominent. Then he had seized control in Syria, forming a Muslim super-state which trapped the crusader kingdoms in a vice-like grip, squeezing with both hands around its neck. Finally, he had brought those kingdoms to the brink of extinction.

All this had taken its toll. He was no longer young and the years of incessant political manoeuvring, diplomatic relationship-building and constant conflict had wearied him. He was already thinking about what, or who, would come after him. Fate was indeed playing a cruel hand.

His opponent on the other hand was young, not even yet at the peak of his powers. The legend of Richard was already taking shape and not just in Western circles. Baha' al-Din paints a vivid scene in which Saladin berated his commanders for the defeat at Arsuf. But one of them answered him back. The battle had been lost he said first of all because of the quality of the armour worn by the enemy. It was so tough that in many cases arrows and sword-thrusts had no impact on them; it was 'as if they were made of flint'.[42]

Secondly, he declared, there was one man who stood out above all others, who inspired his troops to superhuman efforts. 'You never saw anyone like him', he stated. 'He will always be at the front, always at the place of greatest need as a good and tested knight. It is he who cuts so many of us down. They call him Melec [King] Richard'.[43]

A significant aspect of Richard's legend was how it was developed not just by Christian writers. Baha' al-Din also described Richard as an extraordinary warrior. Perhaps Muslim writers wanted to play up the qualities of Richard as a way of helping to explain away Saladin's successive reverses at Acre and Arsuf. Whether these stories are completely true or not does not ultimately matter one iota, for this is how legends grow. The reputation of Richard had now risen to a new high but from this point on it would come under increasing pressure. As Rudyard Kipling so eloquently implied there is never that much of a gap between triumph and disaster as Richard would find out to his cost over the course of the next few years.

12

Facing up to Reality (1191)

'With God's grace we hope to take the city of Jerusalem'
Letter from Richard I dated 1 October 1191

There were inevitably deaths resulting from the brutal fighting at Arsuf though those who died were not just mourned. If a crusader lost his life in battle against the Infidel it was considered the most honourable of ends. To die fighting the enemy would help to remit a man of his sins and ensure a reduced stay in the never-never world of purgatory (still a developing concept at the time and not formally adopted by the Catholic Church until the First Council of Lyon in 1245), allowing a quicker entry into Paradise.

Amongst the fallen was James d'Avesnes, one of the best-known of contemporary knights. He came from a French noble family with its roots in the north of the country. He had taken the Cross almost at once on receiving the bitter news of Hattin. He had been amongst the first to arrive at Acre in 1189, leading a contingent of French, Flemish and Frisian troops as the siege unfolded. At Arsuf, he had been unhorsed and then fought grimly to survive, taking fifteen Muslim warriors down as he was cut off and surrounded. But he was eventually overwhelmed or simply collapsed from his wounds.

His body was recovered from the battlefield after the fighting was over; he was found dead with three of his family by a party of Templars and Hospitallers along with a body of Turcopoles (mounted local auxiliaries who acted primarily as skirmishers and scouts) who searched the battlefield on the following day, a Sunday. He could not easily be recognised for his face was covered by congealed blood; but they washed it off and saw it was him. He was buried with all due honour at Arsuf in a ceremony attended by both Richard and Guy of Lusignan at the Minster of Our Holy Lady (coincidentally and appropriately, it was the Festival Day of her Nativity). A party of nobles carried the corpse on their shoulders and lowered it gently into the earth. But in the aftermath of the battle there would be persistent gossip that he had been abandoned at the end by Robert of Dreux.[1]

That night, the crusader army encamped outside Arsuf. Whilst some dealt with their wounds, others returned to the battlefield in search of loot. Despite the intensity of the fighting, Ambroise suggested that Muslim losses (about 750 bodies were counted on the field, though some may of course have died elsewhere of their wounds) massively outnumbered those incurred by the crusader army.[2] In addition, Saladin's army had suffered heavy losses amongst their horses and camels, which would have a significant logistical impact.

Richard's army completed their march to Jaffa in another three days, arriving there on 10 September with the Templars now forming the rear-guard; perhaps Richard bore a grudge that the Hospitallers had not obeyed his orders during the recent fight or maybe they were exhausted after their exertions there. Even after the Battle of Arsuf, the army was constantly sniped at by the horse-archers of Saladin's army. But Richard's force did not break its line again and the Muslim horsemen were a little less determined in their attacks now.

Saladin had already abandoned Jaffa as it had limited strategic importance though he made sure that the walls had been thoroughly destroyed before he did so. So wrecked was the town that Richard's army could found no useable shelter inside and instead set up camp in some olive groves nearby. But the area was at least fertile and the army helped itself to natural stores of grapes, figs, pomegranates and almonds. And the fleet was now able to ferry down fresh supplies from Acre to Jaffa.

Saladin may well have assumed that Richard would push straight on to Ascalon given its strategic importance. There was a debate amongst Saladin's council about whether both Jerusalem and Ascalon could be protected. The decision in the end was that they could not. It was decided that Ascalon would be abandoned, though only after making sure that the town was so damaged that it would be useless to Richard as a defensive position. Instructions were also given to Saladin's brother Al-'Adil that many of the castles in the region were to be demolished though the walls of Jerusalem and, to the south, Darum were to be kept intact.[3]

This was another crushing blow to Saladin's reputation. Not unnaturally the residents of Ascalon were devastated when told to leave their city. It had strong walls and was extremely defensible and its abandonment seemed an act of despair. There were fifty-three towers dotted along the walls, said to be so old that they had first been constructed by the children of Ham, the son of Noah. For the residents of Ascalon, Saladin's decision was a life-changing one. They were ordered to exchange their life in Ascalon for the uncertain lot of refugees with unclear futures.

But they had no choice. Saladin was on edge throughout the demolition process, fearful that Richard would learn of his plans and rush to intervene; even he, it seems, was distraught at the damage that he felt forced to wreak on the city; as he watched on, he was unable to eat.[4] Al-'Adil had been left to watch Jaffa with his men. Richard did indeed find out what was happening at Ascalon. Geoffrey of Lusignan, its notional lord, was sent down by ship to learn more. With him was a knight, William of L'Éstang, who would later return to England with Richard and witness many of his charters.[5] Rumours were going around the camp that Saladin had already demolished the walls; soon afterwards Geoffrey and William returned with confirmation that this was true.

Richard planned to push on to Ascalon but many of his men wanted to stay in Jaffa and refortify it first. There were several possible reasons for this. The march had been hard if short (80 miles in distance, it had taken nineteen days to make the journey so great were the attacks of Saladin's forces as well as the ravages of nature en route). They were perhaps missing the relatively pleasant life that they had enjoyed after the capture of Acre. For others, more zealous in their motivations, Ascalon seemed to be veering off-course from Jerusalem; the finer points of military strategy were lost on such men.

Ambroise says there were many debates about what to do next. He suggests that to some extent what a man felt was related to their age; presumably, the younger members of the expedition were more ambitious whilst the older showed greater caution.[6] In the end, Richard decided to stay at Jaffa. He was not able to act autocratically in his decision-making even though he was a king. Whilst Richard was undoubtedly commander-in-chief, a crusader's prime motivation was not to be found in any earthly power. And some of the army were not his subjects.

The French contingent was answerable to Hugh of Burgundy and through him Philip of France, even though he was in absentia. The Templars and Hospitallers were under the command of their respective Masters. In the end, Richard was unable or unwilling to force the army on to Ascalon.

An element of uncertainty now entered Richard's strategy. He was forced to compromise and he appeared to lose some of his clarity of thinking. His interventions in Sicily and Cyprus were not planned in advance; they were opportunistic adventures. On arrival in Outremer, the obvious, possibly the only realistic, first target was Acre. In theory, the ultimate objective now was the recovery of Jerusalem; on this most crusaders were likely to agree but it was already clear that this was a very difficult goal to achieve. From this moment on, Richard was forced to compromise.

The march on Jerusalem would raise the risks facing Richard significantly. He would no longer be able to protect his flank from the sea and he would be marching into territory where his supply lines could be seriously threatened. He then needed to be confident that he had sufficient troops to properly lay siege to Jerusalem. These were all legitimate concerns which contributed to Richard's hesitation, so his army stayed at Jaffa for now. Before long Ambroise was caustically criticising the men for once again enjoying the delights of the women who had joined them from Acre despite Richard's efforts to stop them.[7]

There was no cessation of hostilities though. Saladin's scouting parties kept a close eye on Richard's army and from time to time they launched a sudden attack on any group of crusaders who dropped their guard. Richard was active in spying out the land in person, aiming to understand it better before making his next move.

In one such mission Richard himself came under attack. On 29 September, he was identified by watching Muslim scouts when he led a foraging party out of Jaffa (as Richard had a hawk with him there was presumably pleasure as well as business involved). In Roger of Howden's words Richard was literally about to be caught napping as he was having a siesta, unaware that they had been spotted.[8] They soon found themselves under fierce attack and in danger of being overwhelmed.

Richard charged the enemy but was drawn into an ambush. A disaster of the greatest possible magnitude loomed. That the king of England should be killed or captured was an awful prospect; should either of these outcomes occur then the crusade would quickly come grinding to a halt. So fierce was the fight that Richard himself was wounded and in imminent danger of being taken.

He was only saved by one of his knights, William de Préaux, who, seeing the danger, sacrificed himself so that Richard might escape. William's comrades in arms, Renier and Walter of Marun and Alan and Lucas of L'Etable, were killed. The king was in such a hurry to escape (he was again on the swift Fauvel) that he dropped a purse full of gold and precious stones as he hastily mounted his horse, though one of his men saw this and recovered it. Some of the army were alarmed at the risk that Richard had taken by putting himself in such a position in the first place. But for Richard to remove himself from such situations in the future was unthinkable. As a warrior-king, it was part of his role to be in the thick of the action and to take the same risks as his men.[9]

As far as Richard was concerned, this was what was expected of a man in his position. The greatest warrior in history, Alexander the Great, was wounded in the heat of battle on several occasions. A later medieval king, Robert the Bruce of Scotland, fought in single combat on the eve of Bannockburn in 1314. There was little prospect of Richard reining in his adventurous instincts because of this close shave; such risk-taking was part and parcel of all that he was. This was not the last time that Richard would find himself in mortal danger in the thick of the fight, and he would have it no other way: as one chronicler noted, it was impossible for Richard to go against his own nature.

But there was another angle to this incident. Richard and his men were caught totally unprepared. One of those killed, Renier of Marun, was described as being almost unarmed.[10] Alongside Richard's bravery there was his rashness: two sides of the same coin. Saladin would later remark that, much as he respected Richard in many ways, he was too rash in his instincts and his actions. It was an accusation that others would level too. Sooner or later, such rashness would come back to haunt Richard.

The crusaders could not remain indefinitely at Jaffa. They would either become lethargic or impatient. Many intended to return home as soon as they had fulfilled their pilgrim vows by visiting the holy places in Jerusalem. There was great danger that momentum

Above: The ornate West Front of Poitiers Cathedral. Henry II and Eleanor of Aquitaine were married here and later sponsored the building of the magnificent church that now stands in Poitiers. (© W. B. Bartlett)

Below: The castle of Chinon, site of some of the most dramatic events in Angevin dynastic history. (© W. B. Bartlett)

Above: The entrance to the port of La Rochelle, a relatively new town when Richard was Duke of Aquitaine. (© W. B. Bartlett)

Left: The martyrdom of Thomas Becket, Archbishop of Canterbury. (Courtesy of The British Library)

Above: St George in twelfth-century armour rescues a damsel from the dragon. From the exterior of Angoulême Cathedral. (© W. B. Bartlett)

Right: Knights in single combat, with spectators. (Courtesy of The British Library)

The last surviving remnant of the castle at Taillebourg, site of one of Richard's great early triumphs in France. (© W. B. Bartlett)

The marvellous Romanesque columns of the abbey church of St Hilaire in Poitiers, where Richard was made Count of Poitou. (© W. B. Bartlett)

A knight hawking; from Loches. (© W. B. Bartlett)

What remains of Old Sarum Castle, where Eleanor of Aquitaine lived out some of her long captivity. (© W. B. Bartlett)

The great and ancient Umayyad Mosque in Damascus, one of the main cities in Saladin's Syria. (© W. B. Bartlett)

Saladin's castle, one of the major Muslim fortresses in Syria on the borders of Outremer. (© W. B. Bartlett)

Right: The Siege of Acre. (Courtesy of The British Library)

Below: The souls of the dead are weighed in the balance: from the then new front of Nôtre Dame in Paris. (© W. B. Bartlett)

The magnificent Hospitaller fortress of Crac des Chevaliers in Syria. (© W. B. Bartlett)

Christ in Majesty, from the superb baptistery in Richard's Poitevin capital of Poitiers. (© W. B. Bartlett)

The mausoleum of the Angevins; the abbey at Fontevraud was in its day one of the foremost religious establishments in Western Europe.

The fortress at Saumur, another important Angevin town where in 1188 Henry II spent his last lonely Christmas. (© W. B. Bartlett)

The twelfth-century abbey at Les Salles Lauvauguyon, now a quiet backwater but at the time a busy stopping place on the pilgrim trail to Santiago Compostella. (© W. B. Bartlett)

The crucial Normandy border town of Arques, site of bitter fighting in the last years of Richard's reign. (© W. B. Bartlett)

The Route de Richard Coeur de Lion, a modern tourist trail around Richard's Aquitanian lands. (© W. B. Bartlett)

The famous 'Three Lions' emblem of Richard's kingdom, from a window at Fontevraud. (© W. B. Bartlett)

The stout donjon at Loches is a typical example of such tower fortresses during Richard's lifetime. (© W. B. Bartlett)

The tomb of William Longespée, Richard's half-brother; the first tomb in the new cathedral at Salisbury. (© W. B. Bartlett)

Durham Cathedral, episcopal seat of Hugh de Puiset; being a strong supporter of Richard's at times did not stop him from being exploited by the King. (© W. B. Bartlett)

Above: Château Gaillard, Richard's pride and joy above the Seine. (© W. B. Bartlett)

Below: The walls of the town of Loches, site of one of Richard's greatest triumphs during the last years of his reign. (© W. B. Bartlett)

Together in death in a way that they were not in life: Henry II and Eleanor of Aquitaine at Fontevraud. (© W. B. Bartlett)

The face of the Lionheart: Richard's tomb at Fontevraud. (© W. B. Bartlett)

would be lost if the delay lasted indefinitely so Richard turned his thoughts to developing a plan of campaign that might attain his ultimate objective, the recovery of Jerusalem.

There were some major challenges facing him. It was not an easy march to Jerusalem and with winter approaching there was a risk that the weather could turn, increasing the size of the challenge. Saladin would not remain inactive in the face of any advance from Richard. He would do all he could to disrupt the march and interfere with the flow of supplies. He might try and lure Richard into a trap too, just as the unfortunate Guy of Lusignan had been ensnared at Hattin.

Some would be unconcerned. The very name of Jerusalem had a siren-like quality to them as a place of redemption and holiness. Surely God would be at their side in such a venture. And if it was their time to take up the martyr's crown then they were prepared to do so, for death suffered in answering the call of the righteous was a prospect that offered immense spiritual rewards.

The challenges of attacking Jerusalem were real, and were even apparent into modern times. When General Edmund Allenby prepared to attack Jerusalem in 1917, he also became familiar with the obstacles that got in the way of achieving such an ambition. He too – or more accurately his men – had to face the travails of coping with heavy rain as winter approached or of marching along roads that were so stony that they cut even modern boots to shreds. Allenby triumphed because he had moral and material superiority over an increasingly demoralised opponent; Richard did not enjoy the same conditions.[11]

Then there was the terrain that faced an army moving on the city. In an account from the First World War a vivid description was given of the hill country of Judaea; it was 'penetrated by a number of defiles; few are straight; most of them sharply curve. The sides are steep, and often precipitous, frequently with no path save the rough torrent-bed, arranged in rapids of loose shingle, or in level steps of limestone strata, which at the mouth of the defile are often tilted perpendicularly into easily defended obstacles of passage'.[12] This was the country that Richard would have to cross if he wished to take Jerusalem.

But the energetic actions of Richard and his foraging parties were forcing Saladin onto the back foot. So great was their impact that Saladin was forced to withdraw further back towards Jerusalem. As he did so, he destroyed fortifications along the way, depriving

Richard of their use. If Richard wished to benefit from these shattered fortifications on the way to Jerusalem, then he would have no choice but to spend time rebuilding them.

The defences of Jerusalem on the other hand were being strengthened by Saladin. A sixteenth-century Arab historian, Mujir al-Din, wrote that around this time 2,000 Frankish prisoners were deployed to assist in the task and a party of masons were sent from Mosul to widen the ditch that surrounded the city. Many towers were restored or rebuilt. A range of sources was exploited to obtain building materials for this, including several then redundant churches outside the walls of Jerusalem.[13]

From surviving documentary evidence, we have a clear insight into Richard's plans. He wrote a letter on 1 October 1191, in which he stated that 'with God's grace we hope to recover the city of Jerusalem and the Holy Sepulchre within twenty days after Christmas and then return to our own dominions'.[14] This was an ambitious timescale and may have been stated merely for public consumption, yet it might also be the case that at this stage Richard retained some optimism for the enterprise.

But he was worried about certain aspects of the looming campaign even now. He sent a letter to the abbot of Clairvaux, asking for reinforcements to be sent urgently. Other correspondence made it clear that he did not intend to hang around after retaking the city. Many of his men would most probably sail west with him when he left. Who then would defend Jerusalem?

It was the age-old problem of manpower rearing its head again. Richard asked the abbot to use his oratorical skills to stir up religious fervour in Western Europe as others like him had done so successfully in the past. But the reality was that too often such emotional responses did not meet the long-term needs that had to be addressed if a sustainable Outremer was to emerge; the spiritual rewards available to crusaders came from completing the pilgrimage to Jerusalem, not from staying there afterwards. There was therefore a major mismatch between the motivations of the crusaders and the long-term needs of the kingdom.

There was a distinct loss of momentum noticeable by now. Some of the crusaders had already made their way back to Acre: the chroniclers suggest that they had been seduced by its taverns and the promiscuity of its women.[15] Guy of Lusignan was sent to encourage them to re-join the army. To set the right example, Richard summoned the 'Queens' (Berengaria and Joanna) to make their way to Jaffa. But the time it took for the absentees to return delayed the army for several months.[16] But it was not just the Christian army where promiscuity was allegedly a problem. The Muslim chronicler al-Fādil wrote of fornication, sodomy and perjury in the ranks of Saladin's force as well as numbers of them eating openly during Ramadan and drinking wine with Christians in the evenings.[17]

Richard also told the Abbot that he was running out of money, as were other prominent crusaders with him such as the duke of Burgundy. He suspected that this would force him to depart from Outremer at Easter, 1192. This was consistent with the plan to be in Jerusalem by January that year and then leaving for home.

But whether he meant it or not is quite another matter; another prize was now in his sights, one which suggested that Richard was not a glory-driven religious zealot but a practical, deep-thinking strategist. On 11 October, just ten days after committing his thoughts on the conquest of Jerusalem to parchment, he was discussing quite a different objective with the Genoese whose help he now sought despite his reluctance to talk to them at earlier stages in the campaign.

That objective was Egypt and Richard asked the Genoese to prepare a fleet to attack the country during the following summer. He would contribute half the costs involved and would also share out any land that was captured during the subsequent campaign with them; cleverly, he would do this in direct proportion to the size of the fleet that they sent. He also pressured the Pisans to support the expedition, no easy task given their rivalry with Genoa. He persuaded Guy of Lusignan to support the plan.

These conversations give an insight into Richard's thinking. It was a strategic plan that made a lot of sense. Egypt was a crucial source of supplies for the Islamic states further east. Its capture would bring significant extra wealth to the crusaders and deprive Saladin of the same. It would also remove a potential source of reinforcements from that direction.

So convincing was the argument that the major crusades despatched in the thirteenth century would make Egypt rather than Jerusalem their initial target. There were difficulties with it for sure, not the least of which was convincing crusaders whose stated aim was Jerusalem to go along with the plan; this very point contributed to the disastrous turn of events that led to the outcome of the Fourth Crusade in 1204.[18] But the strategy, if implemented successfully, would loosen Saladin's grip around Outremer's neck.

But there was a more sinister aspect of Richard's character in evidence here. On the one hand, he said he was running out of money, on the other he was offering to partially finance an expedition to Egypt. He was telling one party that his target was Jerusalem and another that it was Egypt. He was informing the abbot of Clairvaux that he was returning home at Easter but suggesting to the Genoese that he was headed for Egypt in the summer.

Richard may have thought that he was being clever here. Appeals to the West might generate both the men and the money that he needed, and he had been adept in succeeding with the latter so far. But by being inconsistent, he risked being seen as shifty, dishonest and duplicitous and indeed his critics would accuse him of such. The truth must come out in the end, whatever it was, and when it did then it was unlikely that many would have been pleased. Few men like being played for fools.

Richard's attentions were not solely on military matters at this time. Even whilst he was planning attacks on Muslim-held territory, he continued to reach out to Saladin, not least because there were strong rumours that Conrad of Montferrat was doing the same. The stories about Conrad were true; several Muslim chroniclers provide details of the conversations in confirmation. Conrad was no fool: he knew that Richard, now the most powerful Christian representative in Outremer, was firmly wedded to the cause of his arch-rival, Guy of Lusignan. Therefore, he looked for allies in unlikely places.

An agreement between Conrad and Saladin was not as unlikely an idea as it first looked. Conrad had a certain flexibility of conscience which would allow him to become party to such a deal. And for decades Christians and Muslims had been living alongside each other in the region. Whilst relationships between the two sides had not always been harmonious, a kind of co-existence had been the norm for much of the time.

In contrast, it was the influxes of crusaders from Europe that tended to raise tensions locally. To those who had been exposed to Christian preachers exhorting them to fight for the Cross, Muslims were pagan enemies. It was much more difficult for them to accept that Christians and Muslims should co-exist. Richard was an exception. There was a strong element of pragmatism underpinning his principles, making discussions with Saladin far more acceptable to him than they were to many in his army.

The discussions involving Richard were still with Al-'Adil rather than directly with his brother Saladin. On 17 October Al-'Adil's secretary and one of his favourites, Ibn an-Nahhāl, made his way to Richard's camp at the king's invitation. Richard sent back a message to Saladin, emphasising that both Muslims and Christians in the region were suffering because of the ongoing conflict and suggesting that it was now time to stop this.

But Richard's terms were unlikely to attract Saladin. They were that the relic of the True Cross should be handed over, that Jerusalem should be returned and that all the land on the western side of the River Jordan should be given up to the crusaders. Quite why Saladin should consider these demands is unclear. It is most likely that this was only an opening gambit from Richard who expected further negotiations. He did not want to concede anything when setting out his initial position.[19]

Saladin's reply was courteous but predictable. He pointed out that Jerusalem was even more sacred to Muslims than it was to Christians; it was from here after all that the Prophet had ascended into Heaven. The other lands that Richard referred to had always belonged to the Muslims and had only recently been captured by the crusaders. And the True Cross, whilst it meant nothing to Muslims, was a very strong bargaining chip given its significance to the crusaders; why then should he merely hand it over?

Richard then made an extraordinary offer to Saladin. It was not mentioned by crusader chroniclers, perhaps because Richard considered it to be so sensitive that at this stage it was best kept a secret. But Muslim commentators wrote of it and there is no reason to think they were making it up. The suggestion in question was a very personal one; nothing less than the marriage of Richard's sister Joanna to Al-'Adil.

As part of the plan, Al-'Adil would be made ruler of Palestine and Joanna would be given the coastal cities as her dowry. Christians would be given free access to Jerusalem and the fragment of the True Cross would be handed back. Prisoners would be handed over from both sides. It was a remarkable suggestion and Al-'Adil for one seems to have been seriously interested in it. Saladin, when he heard of the plan, agreed with it at once though it was most likely, he thought, that it was a trick on Richard's part and he had no intention of going through with it.

As Saladin suspected would be the case, the plan came to nothing. Richard later informed negotiators that Joanna was outraged when she heard of the idea; unsurprising as she had presumably been kept in the dark regarding Richard's radical idea. One wonders what Richard's more fundamentalist crusader colleagues would have made of the suggestion that they should abandon their attempts to reconquer Jerusalem too. Richard also said that he would have to write to the Pope to gain approval for such a contentious match and, due to the distances involved, that would take three months to obtain. At one stage, Richard apparently offered the hand of his niece as a substitute but Saladin wanted nothing to do with this plan.[20]

Richard's tactics were aimed at prevarication rather than being meant in earnest; an approach that Saladin himself was very familiar with as he was a master of it himself. Even as these talks were going on and messengers were riding backwards and forwards between camps, Richard was also planning his next military move. On 31 October 1191, he left Jaffa and took possession of two ruined fortresses, the Casal of the Plains and the Casal Moyen. He rebuilt these in two weeks, his energy demonstrating how strategically important they were.

Foraging and skirmishing intensified whilst the crusaders worked on restoring the two castles. On 6 November, some Templars were ambushed whilst escorting a party looking for fodder. Word reached Richard who was supervising operations at Casal Moyen. He despatched a rescue mission under the earl of Leicester and including Andrew de Chauvigny but the situation rapidly deteriorated when they too were ambushed. As the fight went on, more and more of the enemy entered the battle. A full-scale fight loomed – Ambroise talks of an attack by 4,000 men – and Richard spurred to the scene of the fighting accompanied by only a few reinforcements.

He arrived and quickly sized up the situation. Those with him urged him to stay clear of the fight, no doubt remembering his recent close-shave near Jaffa. Richard would not listen. His words, according to Ambroise, tell us much about how he saw himself and why at the personal level he inspired so many of his soldiers: 'I sent those men there. If they die without me, may I never again be called a king'.

Inspiring words indeed (though as they are words that would be expected of a chivalric hero, we cannot be sure that the chroniclers did not make them up). Richard dug his spurs into the side of his steed, charging headlong for the enemy. He smashed through the ring surrounding his men, 'striking out with the power of a thunderbolt'.[21] This again was Richard in his element though one gets the strong impression that Ambroise is doing his best here to ascribe superhuman powers to his subject. But the enemy were beaten off.

Just two days later Richard was again involved in discussions with Al-'Adil. This time they were face to face. Al-'Adil had arrived in Richard's camp on 7 November but was unable to meet the king, who had just been bled and was not up to a meeting. Stephen of Turnham was responsible for laying on a sumptuous dinner for the visiting notable in his honour whilst Richard recovered his strength.

The following day gifts were exchanged; Al-'Adil sent Richard seven camels and an excellent tent.[22] Richard was still taking a hard-line, insisting that he had dynastic rights in Outremer that should be restored to the Christians. He was also keen that the castle of Shaubak (Crac de Montréal) should be destroyed as part of any agreement which Saladin. But Saladin, who currently held the castle which protected the southern approaches to Palestine, demurred. Just in case Al-'Adil was unsure of how determined Richard was, crusader raiding parties would return to camp in full sight displaying the heads of those they had killed.

Saladin was still not convinced by Richard's approaches to his brother. He considered that he could not trust the crusaders to stand by any treaty that was subsequently made. And his opponents were divided; even whilst the Arab-speaking Humphrey of Toron had been negotiating with him on Richard's behalf Saladin was inclined to accept the terms of an agreement offered by Conrad of Montferrat.

The approaches made by Conrad included some incendiary suggestions. They stipulated a condition that, if Saladin supported Conrad, then the latter would be prepared to fight against his fellow Christians. This shows the full extent of the ambition of Conrad which would stop at very little. But Saladin's council was not convinced that Richard's proposals should be dismissed so easily, so negotiations with him also continued.

Conrad might have been untrustworthy in the eyes of some but he was also a shrewd political operator. Many credited him for saving Outremer in the aftermath of Hattin, not just for his sterling efforts at Tyre. He also played an active role in convincing the West that reinforcements were needed. He used a simple propagandistic device to drum up support, a picture of the Church of the Holy Sepulchre in Jerusalem which was passed around Europe. The image showed a Muslim urinating over Christ's grave. It was crude but very effective propaganda.

Once Richard had rebuilt the shattered fortifications of the Casal of the Plains and the Casal Moyen and so protected his lines of communication, he advanced on 17 November to Ramla with a strong force. His horses were now well-fed and his army were keen to go on the offensive. Ramla was a strategically significant point. It stood astride a major crossroads, with the road from Jaffa to Jerusalem running west to east whilst across it went the ancient highway of the *Via Maris* linking Cairo to Damascus. The crusaders called it Arimathea. Once prosperous, it had been badly damaged by an earthquake in the eleventh century and had never recovered its former glory. Nevertheless, this was a vital position for Richard to take in his move on Jerusalem. He was not the last would-be conqueror from the West to set up camp here for Napoleon Bonaparte did the same during his abortive attempt to take Palestine in 1799.

It is not far from Jaffa to Jerusalem. Yet the path ahead was not easy. Saladin abandoned Ramla but destroyed its walls before retreating to Latrun. He was now seriously concerned about a push on Jerusalem itself. Latrun too was strategically important, standing on a hilltop on the road to Jerusalem, less than 8 miles from Ramla in one direction and only about 15 miles from Jerusalem in the other. There was a Templar castle here which had fallen to Saladin in 1187. It remained strategically significant into modern times, for there was a sharp fight here in 1948 between Israeli and Arab forces.

The crusader army was slow to set out. Richard had problems of his own to contend with. The weather was awful and heavy rain turned the paths into quagmires. Stores were damaged, morale battered, the men were fed up and frustrated. Ambroise wrote that the rain and the hail was so strong that the gusts brought tents down, turned biscuits soggy, caused salt pork to go off and made armour rusty. Clothes were ruined and malnutrition started to affect the crusader army. Pack animals died in their hundreds. These problems also affected Saladin though and his men suffered the same gamut of emotions as Richard's army did. His force was not a standing army and men wished to return home rather than wait in a state of nervous agitation for the next move. But this did not stop frequent Muslim attacks on the crusaders.

It was a question of who would blink first, and it was Saladin who did so. With some of his emirs putting him under heavy pressure to disband the army and many of his men increasingly unhappy, he felt compelled to retreat from Latrun, leaving only a defensive position at Beit Nuba, which Saladin had himself used as a forward base for his attack on Jerusalem in 1187. It was only 12 miles from the Holy City.

Richard moved his men forward to the recently abandoned Latrun, where he spent Christmas in 1191 with his wife and sister and Guy of Lusignan. The weather continued to do its worst, raining constantly, threatening to dampen the men's spirits as well as their bodies. Yet if we are to believe the chroniclers, morale was on the up. Jerusalem was at last in striking distance and the enthusiasm of the crusaders soared with each mile covered on the way towards the completion of their pilgrimage. They sang psalms of praise as they advanced further.

The army would not have been happy if it had known the thoughts of some of their commanders. Supply lines were badly exposed and a Muslim raid near Ramla on a caravan on 3 January 1192 succeeded in capturing a significant volume of supplies. Richard's attempts to ambush the raiders on the way back only met with limited success. It was an episode that highlighted the vulnerability of the crusader army and led to some serious soul-searching.

Soon after, just past Epiphany (6 January 1192), there was a meeting of Richard's war council. Those who knew Outremer well – the Templars and the Hospitallers especially, along with the Poulains (European settlers who had made their homes in Outremer) – expressed their deep concern that the army would be attacked from the rear if they laid siege to Jerusalem. This was exactly what had happened at Acre but around Jerusalem, its flanks not protected by the sea as Acre was, they would be far more exposed and annihilation could be the result.

The road ahead was, literally, a rocky one. Jerusalem may have been first and foremost a Holy City but it was also one in a very strong defensive position. The land that the crusaders must cross was full of risk and threat, later described in the following terms; 'everything conspires to give the inhabitants easy means of defence against large armies. It is a country of ambushes, entanglements, surprises, where large armies have no room to fight and the defenders can remain hidden, where the essentials for war are nimbleness and the sure foot, the power of scramble and of rush'.[24]

It was significant that the Templars and Hospitallers were foremost in urging caution for not long before their rashness had led to the catastrophe at Hattin. The outcome of that battle had clearly made them less reckless. They also realised that those of the masses that made up the bulk of the army would be desperate to return home as soon as they had taken Jerusalem and they feared that the city could therefore not be held. Strong tensions were wearing away at the unity of the army.[25]

Richard sought further advice, asking for a map of Jerusalem to be charted so he could see for himself the obstacles in the way of taking the city. It was largely surrounded by steep valleys and was strongly positioned. It was embraced by solid walls. Even the Roman army at its imperial peak had struggled to take it from the Jews who had held it for several years against them over a millennium before.

Richard turned these things over in his mind for a while. In contrast to his impulsive actions in a battlefield environment, strategically he was capable of deeply reasoned caution. He evidenced this now. However much the hurt to his reputation or his pride, the right thing to do was to revert to his first plan and move on Ascalon. It was, as one modern historian asserted, 'an admission of failure, or at least of impotence'.[26]

He may have been guilty of indecisiveness in this change of heart but he also had to consider the difficulties of keeping what was essentially a volunteer army together. Many of those volunteers now cursed him for his abandonment of what was to them a sacred goal. A retreating army is never happy but this one had good reason to complain. The roads which they now marched back down were mud-tracks, churned up by the plodding feet of thousands of dispirited men and over-burdened pack animals. They were further slowed by the large numbers of wounded or sick with them who seemed to have lost all hope. Richard, said the chroniclers, did what he could to look out for them but this was a miserable journey. Ambroise commented that not since God created time had an army been so demoralised.[27]

The practical impact of this sense of demoralisation became clear when the army returned to Ramla. Here, it started to disintegrate.

Some from the French contingent left altogether and made their way to the coast, back to Jaffa, to Acre and even as far as Tyre. The remainder made their way without much enthusiasm southwards to the deserted town of Ascalon. The journey was a nightmare. The road from Ibelin was awful and many horses died from their exertions. The weather continued to be appalling and icy rain blew in the faces of the crusaders as they trudged wearily onwards. Ambroise put it all down to the will of God; if this was the case, then He was surely lacking in mercy.[28]

Whilst it might be a place of great strategic importance, Ascalon did not look much now for when they arrived there all they found was the skeleton of a once impressive town, now just a wreck of broken, crumbling buildings. Saladin's engineers had done their work well and it would take a great deal of effort to restore Ascalon to a defensible bastion. It was a place seemingly as old as time itself. Remains of a Neolithic settlement have been found here. Canaanites, Philistines and Ancient Egyptians had all influenced it. Alexander the Great had marched through and the place had soon become an important Hellenistic town. According to Shi'a tradition it later became a shrine where the head of Husayn ibn Ali, the grandson of the Prophet, was buried.

More recently, it had been one of the last places to fall to the crusaders. Although they took Jerusalem in 1099, Ascalon remained in Muslim hands until 1153, resisting several determined attempts to take it. Until then, it was a thorn in the flesh of Outremer. Raids were launched from here to attack the kingdom. At last, it was captured after a siege led by King Baldwin III though the sacred relic of the Prophet's grandson was successfully extricated to Egypt. But just thity-four years later, after the Battle of Hattin, Ascalon had fallen back into Muslim hands.

The lot of the crusader army at Ascalon was not improved by the bad weather which hampered the ships that were supposed to ferry supplies down to Richard and his army. Set on what the Europeans called 'the Greek Sea' (the Mediterranean), the port of Ascalon was not a good one. Bad weather frequently made it impossible for ships to approach. When at last the weather took a turn for the better after the army had been at Ascalon for eight days, ships were able to anchor. But it soon turned again and several vessels were lost and their crews drowned.

Richard urgently needed help. He sent messengers to encourage the absent French to join him. They agreed to do so but only on the condition that they could leave before Easter if they wished. Whilst this probably did not satisfy Richard, he was not in much of a position to insist on anything more. They started to repair the walls, a formidable task given their generally poor condition and the extent of the destruction that had been wrought. But they eventually managed to dig down to the solid foundation stones so that the walls could be reconstructed.

It took four months to restore Ascalon and make it a formidable obstacle to any would-be enemy. The costs were mainly borne by Richard himself, creating a significant drain on already stretched resources. It was something that strategically had to be done, both for defensive reasons and possibly because Richard planned to use the place as a launch-pad for an attack on Egypt. There was a shortage of skilled labour to rebuild the walls and at the outset it was a case of every man to the pumps. Knights and men-at-arms took part in manual labour, lugging stone and raw materials around although masons did arrive later; even Richard joined in.[29]

Yet it grated with many of the crusaders that they were doing this rather than hammering away at the walls of Jerusalem. Even as they were strengthening Ascalon, the defences of Jerusalem were being reinforced by the enemy. The only consolation for Richard was that Saladin's army was also demoralised. Many of his men had been away from home for four years now. The Muslim forces were mainly quasi-feudal in nature and it was very difficult to keep them in the field for long periods of time.[30]

After the heady triumph of Hattin and then the recapture of Jerusalem, the war in Outremer had turned into a long slog for Saladin's army. The fall of Acre was a desperate loss as it turned a tide of almost unbroken Muslim triumph. Many of their fellows would never return, having died on campaign. They had been exposed to searing heat in the summer and freezing temperatures and heavy rains in the winter.

Saladin's men were now told to return home and come back in May for the next campaigning season.[31] No doubt many were delighted to comply with this order, though less keen to come back again. Even allowing for the hyperbole of crusader chroniclers who probably exaggerated the stories of declining morale amongst the Muslims, there was little doubt that Saladin's stock had fallen even amongst those who were formerly his supporters. Baha' ad-Din wrote that 'the army was tired and openly hostile to a continuation of the war'.[32] In this battle of attrition, both sides were approaching the point of exhaustion.

Richard was able to launch attacks from Ascalon against passing Muslim traffic though. In one raid near Darum he attacked a convoy that was carrying Christian prisoners into Egypt and released them. Other excursions took him to the very borders of Egypt where he captured horses, mares, 700 sheep, twenty asses and thirty camels along with 180 prisoners (men, women and children). His army not unnaturally returned to Ascalon with 'joyful countenances'.[33]

All this contrasted with the much less welcome news that the situation back at Acre was now deteriorating seriously. Fissures were appearing in the unity of the crusaders there, caused by political tremors that threatened to bring the whole fragile fabric of the fragmented kingdom crashing down. Inevitably, Conrad of Montferrat was at the heart of it. His supporters, including the Genoese and some of the French there, sought to seize the city on his behalf.

There was a vicious fight between the Genoese on the one hand and the Pisans who opposed them on the other. It was so bad that the horse of Hugh, duke of Burgundy, was killed beneath him as he tried to stop the fighting. Richard made his way north to try to restore order and to reinforce the Pisans who were mounting a determined defence against Conrad's allies. Richard's arrival persuaded the attacking Genoese ships to back off.

Soon after, a potentially awkward meeting between Richard and Conrad was arranged at Casal Imbert, on the road to Tyre. It was not an easy discussion and Conrad refused to lead his men to Ascalon to support Richard. In a retaliatory strike, Conrad was deprived of the share of the revenues of Outremer that had been allotted to him. But he had many supporters in the kingdom and the situation remained parlous. This disunity was not what was needed if Jerusalem was to be reconquered.

Worse was to follow. Envoys arrived at Ascalon sent by Conrad and Hugh of Burgundy, reminding the French contingent where their loyalties lay. This led to the departure of some 700 French knights, heading north to Tyre. Ambroise berated them for their desertion, noting that when they arrived at Tyre they were tempted by the earthly delights of Conrad's city and that they partied into the night, 'returning with wanton young girls'.[34]

Richard had desperately attempted to persuade them to stay, offering to pay them to do so. But it was of no use. They duly left, marking another serious downturn in Richard's fortunes and providing a further example of the disunited state of the crusaders in Outremer. Ambroise caustically noted that the fateful departure of the French from Ascalon was enacted on Maundy Thursday, the eve of Good Friday, the most sacred day in the Christian calendar.

Saladin attempted to take advantage by re-assembling his army but the response to his summons was not a good one.[35] Though the news was not good for him it was far, far worse for Richard. His crusade, which had begun so brightly when Acre was taken, was now on the verge of falling apart. And the ultimate prize, Jerusalem, seemed as far away as ever.

13

The Forlorn Hope (1191–1192)

'If you leave her without help now, then she is dead and betrayed'
William of Poitiers to Richard I when discussing the king's plans to leave Outremer

Shortly after Easter, a thunderbolt struck in the form of an envoy from England. This was Robert, the Prior of Hereford, who caught up with Richard at Ascalon. He brought with him deeply disturbing news. John, Richard's brother, had deposed the chancellor William Longchamp, an ally of the prior. Longchamp had made himself many enemies and the situation back in England was in danger of running completely out of control.

Longchamp had been involved in a bitter struggle with John. Longchamp managed to keep some power for a while by promising John that he would help him achieve the throne of England if Richard were to die on crusade. But when a dispute arose over the ownership of Lincoln Castle, Longchamp laid siege to it. Gerard de Camville had given his allegiance for the castle to John. Longchamp had also forced Roger Mortimer, lord of Wigmore Castle, to leave England for three years after he had been implicated in a plot with some of the Welsh against Richard. Fortunately for the king, Mortimer did not put up much of a fight before departing.[1]

Walter of Coutances had been sent back by Richard from Sicily when the first suggestions of trouble in England surfaced and had landed at Shoreham on 27 June 1191. He then brokered a conference at Winchester in July that brought John and Longchamp together.[2] It was rumoured that so distrustful of Longchamp was John that he had brought 4,000 Welshmen with him to intervene if the chancellor attempted to seize him; in response Longchamp arranged to be accompanied by large numbers of troops too. It was a tense scenario when all-out civil war seemed just a misstep away. But a deal was patched up. De Camville was reconciled with the chancellor and remained in charge at Lincoln.

But this merely plastered over the cracks. Matters had come to a head when Geoffrey, Richard and John's illegitimate brother, returned to England in defiance of Richard's ruling that he was not to set foot in England for three years. On the other hand, no less a person than the Pope had confirmed Geoffrey in his position as archbishop of York. Longchamp was so nervous when he heard that messages to this effect were on their way from Rome that he gave orders that any letters from the Pope were not to be allowed into the kingdom.[3]

Longchamp was seemingly anticipating Geoffrey's attempts to return, so the news of the plan had clearly leaked. His men (commanded by Longchamp's sister, Richent, who was the wife of the keeper of Dover Castle) seized Geoffrey, dragging him out in rough fashion from his refuge inside the priory of St Martin's in Dover where he had sought sanctuary after he had landed; he had been there for six days.

Geoffrey had been standing in his vestments before the altar of the priory when he was dragged out by two knights, Aubrey of Marney and Alexander Puintel, accompanied by fifteen other armed men. Geoffrey defiantly help up a cross in Becket-like pose when he saw that his arrest was imminent. He was pulled unceremoniously along the muddy streets, even as the populace shouted their disdain at the men responsible for this humiliating scene; Geoffrey excommunicated his captors on the spot.

All this inevitably reminded people of the harsh treatment of another archbishop by the Angevin dynasty; it was another public relations disaster. News of it travelled across England 'more rapidly than the wind'.[4] Matthew of Clare, the constable of Dover Castle, was said to have burst into tears when Geoffrey was brought before him. Geoffrey in reply refused point blank to accept anything from his excommunicated jailers and insisted that all his food, water and even fire be brought to him from the townspeople of Dover.[5]

Longchamp had made an appalling misjudgement in his treatment of Geoffrey and he did not have to look far for enemies; soon after, Bishop Hugh of Coventry took the lead in seeking to depose him. In the meantime, Longchamp was quick to order that Geoffrey should be released from custody.[6] But it was too late to turn back the tide of outraged public opinion. The damage had already been done.

John was incandescent with rage; it suited his political purposes to be so. He ordered Longchamp to stand trial for his actions, the date being set for 5 October 1191. Longchamp failed to arrive at a meeting that had been set up near Reading to consider further action and was then excommunicated by a council chaired by Bishop Hugh. Longchamp's position was untenable and he then tried to escape England. There was a running battle when his entourage came into conflict with some of John's men. Lives were lost and Longchamp took refuge in the Tower of London.

John entered London and held a meeting with its leading citizens in the Chapter House of St Paul's. It was even then a cosmopolitan city. A contemporary wrote of it that 'every race of men, out of every nation which is under heaven, resort there in great numbers; every nation has introduced into that city its vices and bad manners'. Visitors were warned by the writer to avoid the enticement of games of dice and to stay clear of the tavern and the theatre. He painted a vivid picture, of streets full of pickpockets, common beggars, 'effeminate sodomites', 'lewd musical girls', magicians, mimics and the delightfully named 'tatterdemalions' (people dressed in rags).[7]

John treated the citizens respectfully, offering them a degree of self-government. In return, they pledged to help him bring Longchamp to justice; Geoffrey of York had already been working on them and ensured their hostility towards his bitter opponent. He had been released from Dover and had duly made his way to London, ostentatiously stopping at the tomb of Thomas Becket where he stopped to pray for a while en route.

The Londoners were inclined to hand over governance of England to John. A meeting held at the Tower of London found decisively against Longchamp. To all intents and purposes, it looked like a coup – and Richard's crusade had barely started at this stage. But if it was a coup then it was one made possible by Richard's disastrous appointment of Longchamp in the first place. However, those replacing Longchamp, especially Walter of Coutances, could produce the written mandate that Richard had sent allowing Longchamp to be overridden by the archbishop of Rouen; by his own poor decision-making Richard had unconsciously strengthened the power of his potentially troublesome brother against his interests.

Longchamp, seeing that the game was up, had accepted the inevitable and moved to Dover Castle. He made several attempts to flee from there; in one, it was said that he was concealed as a prostitute (dressed in green, then the colour worn by such women[8]) and in this garb he was assaulted by a would-be customer, a fisherman who did not see through his disguise. He received something of a shock when he got too intimate with Longchamp and found out beyond all doubt that this was indeed a man. Roger of Howden positively glowed in his gloating as he told the tale of the chancellor who had become a chancelloress, the priest who had become a harlot, the bishop who had become a buffoon.[9]

Other accounts told of Longchamp's partiality for young boys and the fact that he had dressed as a woman led one commentator to suggest that he had to swallow his pride to do so for he hated the sex. No offence or depravity was beyond Longchamp according to his opponents and a deluge of accusations demolished his reputation, leading to his flight from England. His situation did not improve when he eventually crossed the Channel either as he was robbed when he arrived in Flanders.

John sought to take full advantage of the situation. He travelled extensively around England, making himself known to her people and doling out generous gifts. Patronage was a key part of building loyalty in medieval times, as indeed it has been in most others, and John attempted to turn on the charm to strengthen his position.

This development posed a great threat against Richard's interests in England; if Richard did not return home soon, he might not have a kingdom left to go back to. Fortunately for Richard, Longchamp was replaced by Walter of Coutances, and John was for the moment unable to dominate him. One of Walter's first tasks was to appoint a new archbishop of Canterbury to replace Baldwin of Forde. The post was given to Reginald, bishop of Bath, but he died before he took it up.

Walter assumed leadership of the regency council; he had been given papal superiority over Longchamp during Eleanor's visit to Pope Celestine on her way back from Sicily which helped. The arrangement had previously been kept a secret but the time to reveal it was now at hand. Despite his name and his archbishopric, Walter was Cornish and although he detested Longchamp and encouraged John to overthrow him, he did not overstep the mark and abandon

Richard. He played the part of 'fixer' well, maintaining a delicate balance between supporting the king's interests on the one hand and not completely alienating John on the other.

Roger of Howden enthusiastically recounted the object lesson offered by the fall from grace of Longchamp. He listed his offences in detail; his love of luxury; his excessive gluttony; his delight in lording it over the great men of England; his disdain of all things English (for he was a Norman who liked to be escorted by Frenchmen and Flemings). He saw himself, said Roger, as a latter-day Tiberius, a Roman Caesar. Clearly the chronicler felt that Longchamp, who came from humble beginnings, had risen far above his station. Roger theorised that this was a moral tale of how pride comes before a fall.[10]

Longchamp moved on to Paris before going to Normandy. He was not well received in the duchy on the orders of Walter of Coutances, who was archbishop of Rouen. As soon as he entered a church, any service that was being held there would come to a halt as Longchamp had been declared an excommunicate. Eleanor, who was present at Rouen at the time, also wanted to have little to do with him. Given his isolation, Longchamp decided to appeal both to his spiritual master, Pope Celestine, and his secular lord, Richard.

In response, Celestine sent a letter to England commanding the lords there – including John – to change their attitude towards Longchamp. The Pope did not want to see instability in the kingdoms of those monarchs who were away on crusade. Those who did not step back into line were to be excommunicated. For a man who was eighty-five years old when he was installed as pontiff, these must have been desperately trying times coming so late on in his life.[11]

Soon after, Longchamp contacted Hugh, bishop of Lincoln. He asked him to watch over both his own interests and those of the king whilst he was to all intents and purposes in exile. Strict religious penalties were to be placed on those who continued to persecute Longchamp and harm the king's interests though John was to be exempt for the time being to see if a change of heart would materialise on his part. But for those other 'rebels' as Longchamp would see them, no such leniency was to be forthcoming. No divine services except for baptism were to be allowed on their lands.

There were some prominent names on the list of those so excommunicated, including Walter of Coutances (described as 'the

Pilate of Rouen'), Godfrey, bishop of Winchester; Hugh, bishop of Coventry, and several high-ranking secular lords including unsurprisingly some of John's key supporters. The bishop of Coventry was picked out for special opprobrium for 'the entire subversion of the realm of England, a disturber of the peace, and a public advocate against the royal dignity and interests'. Action needed to be taken quickly so that 'a sheep so diseased may not be able to blemish and corrupt the flock of the Lord'.[12] The bishop had been in violent opposition to his monks at Coventry (quite literally as they had come to blows) and against many of the rest of his flock since Richard's accession.[13]

The response from those on the receiving end of these dictates from Longchamp was in the main to ignore them completely. Some were signatories to a letter composed for Richard in which they complained of how Longchamp had laid waste to England in his absence. In response to being excommunicated, the bishops of England who opposed Longchamp did the same to him which caused considerable hardship to the people of his bishopric. In the meantime, Geoffrey, archbishop of York, took up his post in the north of England in a sumptuous ceremony in the Minster. But he was almost at once at odds with Hugh de Puiset, the bishop of Durham, and another undignified spat loomed.

John's perfidy must always have been regarded as a strong possibility given the fact that Richard knew his brother better than most men. But the plotting of King Philip, who was now back in France, was hard to stomach. Richard and Philip had taken crusader vows and had undertaken further pledges to protect each other's interests whilst they were on crusade. Philip had then come back to France in unseemly haste very early on. He had given every sign of being a reluctant crusader. Now he was taking advantage of Richard's absence to stir up trouble with his own self-interest at heart. It was a disgraceful betrayal and Richard must have felt as if he was being stabbed in the back.

Eleanor tried to intervene. Even though Richard's continental possessions were under threat, she saw her current priority as England and hurried back there, crossing the Channel in early February 1192, a time of year when sea travel was generally avoided. She landed at Portsmouth on 11 February, just as John was planning to leave Southampton to cross the Channel to meet Philip. She summoned four separate meetings at London, Winchester, Oxford and Windsor where she cajoled the leading men of England into renewing their oaths to Richard. She managed for the time being to stop John from leaving England and he retired to Wallingford in a huff. As one modern historian said of Eleanor 'though her reputation derives largely from earlier events in her life, especially her unhappy marriages to two kings, she exercised her greatest political power as a widow'.[14]

Eleanor made her way to Ely, where she was shocked at the damage that had been caused by the interdict hurled at Longchamp and his flock. Unburied bodies lay in the fields and the people of the places through which she passed approached her in tears and in a terrible state. She was so disturbed by what she saw that she persuaded Walter of Coutances to lift the interdict and restore the spiritual rights of the people of Ely.

Richard was caught in a terrible dilemma because of these developments. The result of this shocking news when it arrived in Outremer was to 'throw the whole army into confusion'.[15] With each subsequent message that arrived, his concerns grew. His lands back in Western Europe were now in great danger but he had not achieved the ultimate objective that he had striven for during the crusade, the recapture of Jerusalem. His hand was now forced when many of the leading men in what was left of the army resolved to relaunch the assault against the Holy City.

But in the meantime, the situation between Guy of Lusignan and Conrad of Montferrat needed to be resolved as a matter of urgency, otherwise Outremer would fall apart when Richard left and Saladin could pick off the kingdom as surely as if he was taking a ripe fruit from a tree. Someone must be confirmed as the king of Jerusalem. Richard called a meeting to discuss this.

Guy had fought bravely to try to restore his battered reputation during the crusade but nothing could wipe away the unforgiveable blemish of Hattin from his record. That others were equally, if not more, culpable, really did not matter one iota; in this case perception was all. On the other hand, Conrad was the man who had started the unlikely fight-back in Outremer. He had arrived like a classic hero in the nick of time. Since then he had proved himself extremely resilient. Ironically it probably even helped him to win favour and support that he had been bold enough to stand up to Richard.

It was true that he was manipulative and of dubious morals. It was also the case that he had recently been negotiating with Saladin; one of Richard's envoys, Stephen of Turnham, bumped into two of Conrad's negotiators, Balian of Ibelin (described as being 'more false than a goblin'[16]) and Reginald of Sidon, even as they were leaving Jerusalem.[17] These were perhaps unwelcome traits to Christian moralists; but at the same time, they showed that Conrad had strong political skills, even if they were sometimes of a kind such that later commentator on such matters, Niccolò Machiavelli, was more likely to approve of than anyone else. These again were welcome qualities to many. First and foremost, the next king of Jerusalem had to be a survivor. Conrad had shown time and again that he was just such a man.

Ambroise suggests that the decision to support Conrad was virtually unanimous, an example amongst other things of how Richard's writ did not count in the same way in Outremer as it did in the territories that he ruled directly. Richard seems to have found himself virtually in a minority of one in supporting Guy. Given this outcome, his support of Guy appears to be a strategic mistake that undermined the already fragile unity of Outremer.

And so it was decided. Conrad, closely aligned to the French and the Genoese, was the chosen candidate. Guy, whom Richard would undoubtedly have preferred, had lost the fight for the kingdom of Jerusalem. Richard softened the blow. He had recently arranged to sell Cyprus to the Templars but not all the required payments had yet been made. Their attempts to extort heavy taxes had already led to violent resistance from the Cypriot population. Richard therefore agreed with the Templars that the island would be handed over to Guy. Guy had to pay for it; it was his responsibility to reimburse the Templars for the 40,000 bezants that they had already handed over as a down-payment. But the Lusignans would go on to rule Cyprus for the next three centuries, so presumably this was a price well worth paying.

Richard's nephew, Count Henry of Champagne (he was also the nephew of Philip of France) was sent to Tyre to give Conrad the good news, which he joyfully received. Ambroise says that when he was told that he was after all to be king, Conrad fell on his knees and offered his thanks to God. He asked that if he were not worthy of such a prize then it should be taken from him.[18] His people were overjoyed and prepared themselves to support his coronation. Count Henry then returned to Acre.

For Richard, there were no doubt a bitter taste in his mouth that his preferred candidate had been denied the kingship. Given the fact that a return to England could not be long delayed due to the shenanigans of John, the chance of maintaining some form of distant influence in Outremer when he left appeared to have gone.

Conrad busied himself in Tyre in preparation for his accession as king. On 28 April 1192, he made his way to the house of Philip of Dreux, bishop of Beauvais (the French king's cousin and Richard's bitter enemy), to dine with him. Life was good; his wife Isabella was pregnant and he was to be king, what more could be desired? Isabella though had been late back, having been to bathe, and so the couple had not eaten, hence the impromptu visit to the bishop.

But the bishop had already dined so Conrad decided to return home. As he wandered through the streets of Tyre, he was approached by two men dressed as monks (according to some accounts, they had actually been accepted into his retinue some months before). Whilst one of them engaged him in conversation, the other surreptitiously approached him from his blind side and plunged a knife deep between his ribs.[19]

Conrad fell to the ground, already dying. His attackers were seized but too late to save him. There are different accounts of how long he lingered on before expiring. Some said that he died soon after, either on the spot or in a nearby church. Others have him playing out a deathbed scene in which he said that Isabella should now hand Tyre over to Richard or his representative; there is no proof of this and it seems a distinctly too convenient explanation given its unlikely support for the English king.

The assassination was opportunistic. Conrad's movements on the day were erratic, so this was no pre-designed, well-rehearsed plan put into action. Conrad was simply in the wrong place at the wrong time and the killers seized their moment. They were members of a shadowy Muslim sect known as the Nizaris, part of the Shi'a branch of Islam. They lived in remote mountain fastnesses in both Syria and Persia. They were renowned for their unquestioning obedience to the orders of their leader, Rashid al-Din Sinān, an over-arching mastermind who had been given the exotic name of 'The Old Man of the Mountains'. It was a moniker that summoned up pictures of a mysterious organising presence pulling the strings of the organisation from his remote hideaway in the hills, the inaccessible castle of Masyaf in the north of Syria.

The members of the sect were known for one thing above all; the killing of those who were their political enemies. They did so on what were effectively suicide missions for they almost invariably struck in the full light of day. It was considered a disgrace for any man who was given such a responsibility to return home alive and there were stories of mothers whose sons had managed to escape after their missions had been carried out wearing black as a mark of mourning as a symbol of their shame.

In return for their devotion and sacrifice, the killers would be given access to the delights of Everlasting Life, in a Paradise populated by beautiful virgins whose sole task was to meet their sexual needs. It was a wonderful land, where fountains flowed with streams of refreshing liquid that never ran dry. The killers were only ready to carry out their task after they had gone through months of careful spiritual and physical preparation. Their main targets over the years had been Muslims rather than Christians, often ostentatiously struck down in public after Friday prayers.

The killers' Muslim enemies, of which there were many, scorned them, alleging that they were hashish-takers, the lowest of the low (for the unorthodox practices of the Nizaris led to widespread detestation from mainstream followers of Islam). From this, they were given the derisive name of hashishin, which, in a corrupted form, entered the English language as an everyday word – the Assassins.

Whilst it appeared clear who the killers of Conrad were – devotees or *fida'is* of the Nizaris – the motives behind their actions were much less obvious. There were stories that appeared later that Conrad had seized a ship with supplies bound for the Nizaris and had refused to pass them on. Other suspects were nominated by different writers. Saladin was one candidate; there was good reason for him to wish to be free of Conrad given his qualities as a potential opponent. But Saladin's relationships with the Nizaris were difficult; he himself had once been a potential target. As an orthodox Muslim, he had been a strict punisher of heretics and he considered the Nizaris as such.

Whilst besieging their castle at Masyaf, he had awoken one morning in his strongly guarded tent to find a cake by his pillow of a type for which the Nizaris were famous; no one knew how it had got there. The implication was clear; the cake could just as easily have been a knife, the 'Assassins' were like ghosts in the night, able to materialise out of thin air. No human sentry could guard against them. Saladin had taken the point and abandoned the siege soon afterwards.[20]

Others have suggested that one of the crusaders was behind the plan, for Conrad had plenty of opponents amongst them. One nominee is Humphrey of Toron, a romantic notion based on his true love for his former wife, Isabella, who was now carrying Conrad's child. However, such decisive action would be altogether out of character for the mild-mannered young man who had so easily been cajoled into agreeing to an annulment of his marriage when prevailed upon to do so.

Another candidate was Count Henry of Champagne, who would emerge as the major beneficiary of Conrad's death. He had also been in Tyre not long before the assassination which is interesting circumstantial evidence of his ability to hatch a plan though nothing more than that; anyway, the assassins were more than capable of hatching a plan of their own given their experience. Muslim chroniclers such as Baha' al-Din and Imad ad-Din suggest that they had been living disguised as monks for six months before the assassination.

There was one other candidate who appeared to benefit from the death of Conrad; Richard. Now he could put an alternative nominee forward. It was perhaps inevitable that it would not be long before specific accusations would emerge against him, given the fact that he profited from Conrad's demise as much as anyone. The Muslim chronicler, Imad ad-Din, specifically stated that the captors of the two killers 'asked them who commanded them to commit this murder, and the assassins said it was the king of England'. He also saw it as an unfortunate turn of events for Saladin as Conrad was an opponent of Richard and he noted that the king was more confident in his demands once the Marquis was eliminated.[22]

A replacement for Conrad was soon identified. It was not Guy of Lusignan who was too divisive a figure. Instead Richard's nephew, Henry of Champagne, became the front-runner to succeed Conrad. Some accounts claim that Henry was 'begged' by the people to do so. He said that he would need Richard's approval to go along with the suggestion.

Richard supported his nomination. After all, he was now in a perfect position. Conrad was out of the way and so too, from a different perspective, was Guy. Henry of Champagne was heavily under his influence. It could not have come out better if Richard had planned it – and it is not inconceivable, though probably now beyond proof, that he had. But at the same time, it also suited the French party rather well too, given Henry's connection to King Philip. In many ways, Henry was the perfect compromise candidate.

The nomination was quickly accepted but the practical issue to be dealt with was that the right to the crown emanated from the royal blood that flowed through the veins of Isabella, Conrad's widow. This turned out to be a minor problem. She was now theoretically available but convention suggested a suitable period of mourning for her late husband. Her current pregnancy also argued on the grounds of decency that she should wait.

Given the urgency of the decision, convention and decency went out of the window. Within seven days, Isabella was married to Henry of Champagne. He became *de facto* king of Jerusalem, though he was not subsequently crowned as such, possibly because the traditional coronation church, the Holy Sepulchre in Jerusalem, was now beyond his reach. Henry allowed himself to be persuaded that he should marry the recently widowed Isabella rather easily. Richard was, some said, not so keen that Hugh should marry Isabella as he considered her marriage to Conrad to be bigamous and by implication she was therefore still married to Humphrey of Toron. However, when Richard finally heard that the marriage had taken place, it was effectively a *fait accompli*.

Ambroise, a pro-Richard chronicler which must call his objectivity into doubt, wrote that Isabella locked herself up when the duke of Burgundy attempted to seize her after Conrad's death. He says that she would only discuss the future of the kingdom directly with Richard. But it is highly unlikely that Isabella had much say in the discussions that took place later; after all, she had been bullied into agreeing to the annulment of her marriage with Humphrey of Toron earlier, despite the supposed happiness of their union. Now she was being pushed into her third marriage, at a time when she was only about twenty years old. She was little more than a tradeable commodity, to be passed around from one husband to another as the moment dictated.

One slightly garbled account of the killing of Conrad said that the assassins had been in Tyre for months, dressed in Frankish garb, speaking the Frankish tongue and adopting Frankish customs.[23] The way in which the killers had become an almost unnoticed part of everyday life in the city suggests that they had been there for some time. This argues against this being an act that Richard had commissioned in a fit of pique against Conrad's selection as king of Jerusalem. The Nizaris anyway took orders from no one and were not normally regarded as mercenaries for hire.

But some of the mud thrown at Richard's reputation stuck; in this instance, perception was every bit as powerful as reality. Ambroise tells of messengers being despatched back to France, warning Philip to be on his guard as Richard had sent four Assassins across the Mediterranean to kill him too. Certainly, many said that Richard was behind the assassination. This was an accusation that would cause enormous problems for Richard later.

The power of the Nizari in anything save a local sense have been much exaggerated. The aim of many terrorists, as we well know nowadays, is to sow fear into the hearts of men. It mattered little that the 'Assassins' had never struck outside their core regions in Syria or Persia. Neither did the fact that nearly all their victims were Muslims rather than Christians. Philip may well have believed that they were coming for him; and even if he did not believe it, it was in his interests to pretend that he did as it put Richard in an even poorer light.

A letter would eventually appear, allegedly from Sinān, the leader of the Nizaris, 'The Old Man of the Mountains'. It cleared Richard of any part in the murder, though many historians consider the letter to be a forgery. It concluded with an important punch-line: 'We can tell you in truth that Richard king of England is not guilty of the death of the marquis, and anyone who does him harm on that account does so unjustly and without cause'. It concluded 'and know for certain that we do not kill any man in this world for a fee or money of any kind unless he has first done us an injury'.[24] It was later stated that Philip had written to Sinān, asking him if Richard was involved in the removal of Conrad, to which he received this negative answer. But to some extent the damage was already done.[25]

With these dramatic events being played out in the political arena, Richard turned his attention back to military matters. He launched a raid on the fortress of Darum, about 20 miles to the south of Ascalon. Although he was expecting support from the forces of Henry of Champagne and the French in this enterprise, he was impatient to get on with it and had gone there with only his own household troops to prepare the way for ships to land.

Saladin was struggling to find enough troops to react to the threat and when he did send some under the command of 'Alam al-Din Qaisar to reinforce the garrison they stayed meekly behind the walls rather than face up to Richard. Perhaps the reputation of 'Melec Richard' was doing its work as 'Alam al-Din did not seem at all keen to fight.

Soon after, three siege engines arrived having been shipped down from Ascalon. Richard was prominent amongst those who not only supervised their re-assembly but also put in the hard graft of moving them up from the beach into position near the walls; again, in this instance, seemingly a soldier's general. There were not enough men to surround the fortress and those that were there had to be paid well for their co-operation but Richard, or his engineers, had spotted a weakness in the defences. Soon the steady thud of missiles launched from the siege engines could be heard, crashing into and cracking the walls.

This was not the only line of attack. Miners were also deployed to dig away beneath the foundations. This combined assault soon started to show signs of working. The walls began to crumble and it was clear that a complete collapse was not far off. The garrison sued for surrender, seeking terms that would guarantee them and their families their freedom. Ambroise's account gives the impression that they did not have much stomach for a fight and perhaps had little confidence that Saladin would come rushing to the rescue. But Richard was not having this and soon after a final assault was launched after a tower came crashing to the ground. Darum was taken.

The members of the garrison who survived the assault took refuge in a tower but soon after surrendered unconditionally. They were taken off into captivity whilst about forty Christian prisoners were released. One of the first into the captured town was Stephen Longchamp, William's brother. The banners of other knights there were raised, including the earl of Leicester, Andrew de Chauvigny and Raymond, the son of prince Bohemond of Antioch.

The following day both Henry of Champagne and the French arrived. It must have been a source of great satisfaction to a man with Richard's pride to be able to capture Darum without their help. It also served a useful purpose in restoring his reputation, dented by his retreat from Jerusalem. As such the taking of Darum had positive benefits beyond the purely military.

Richard then played an astute political hand by giving Darum to Henry of Champagne. This was an important gesture which would help to strengthen the credibility of the new lord of Outremer. There were signs of a healthier relationship between the different elements of the crusader army for the French were also buoyed by this development.

At least now the weather was more clement. But Saladin had taken advantage of the lull in the campaign to recruit reinforcements. Richard was still under pressure to return to the attack on Jerusalem. Yet he was still not convinced that such an action was wise. Richard brooded on the subject in his tent for several days until William of Poitiers, one of his chaplains, managed to restore his flagging spirits. William reminded him that God had been good to him so far and this was no time to abandon his faith. Great triumphs awaited Richard if he would only believe.

But the mood in the army was still sour and many had lost confidence in Richard's leadership. It was said that some of the great men with the army had resolved to march on Jerusalem whether he led them or not. William's words to Richard had been strongly expressed, telling him plainly that 'everyone, great and small, everyone who wished to honour you, says that you are father and brother of Christianity, and if you leave her without help now, then she is dead and betrayed'.[26]

Richard was faced with a massive decision that gnawed away at him like some never-ending nightmare. It was there with him for every hour of his waking day as well as torturing his thoughts at night. On the field of battle, Richard was a man capable of making quick and brilliant decisions. Balancing strategic and political considerations on the other hand was a completely different kettle of fish. But now, with the words of William of Poitiers ringing in his ears, Richard decided to have one last throw of the dice. The march to Jerusalem was back on.

14

The End of the Dream (1192)

'Fortune favours the brave'
Aeneas, chronicler of the Trojan War

For all that Richard was accused later of indecision and vacillation, Ambroise's words speak of a king who was greatly vexed by the news that kept arriving from England; he was unsurprisingly 'melancholy and saddened' by it.[1] Richard's anguish is completely understandable; he was faced with a dire dichotomy. Suggestions that Philip of France was going out of his way to fuel John's treachery did nothing to allay his sense of alarm. But he could not yet abandon his quest to retake Jerusalem without a huge loss of face. Perhaps the words of the chaplain had had an effect after all as some of the chroniclers suggest.[2]

Richard decided to return to the attack on the city, to the great joy of those with him (it was said that 'everyone gave thanks as a bird does at the dawn of day').[3] He said that he would stay until the following Easter and that the army should get ready to march on Jerusalem. They moved out of Ascalon and on to Blanchegarde some 19 miles inland though on the way they were plagued by bites from swarms of flying insects that assaulted them. The wildlife of the country was not friendly; when they camped that day a knight and a squire were both bitten by snakes and subsequently died.

The army moved to Latrun where it caught a Muslim raiding party by surprise. The next stop was Beit Nuba, the high-water mark of the last advance on Jerusalem and just a day's march from the Holy City. The major difference was that whereas last time it had taken three months to advance this far, on this occasion it was a five-day journey. The weather was also very different, being fine and clear.

There were few casualties. Henry of Champagne had returned to Acre to collect reinforcements and Richard ordered a halt until he came up with them. There were skirmishes, raids and reconnaissances. In one of the latter, Richard breasted a hill from where those who had been involved in the First Crusade had first seen the distant walls of Jerusalem. The city was now tantalisingly close but still frustratingly far enough away in terms of practicalities for Richard to fear that he would never take it. He was so moved by the sight that he covered his face with his shield and wept. He begged that God would not taunt him with a distant view of the unattainable.[4]

Legend this may be but it has the touch of truth about it. Richard had set off having vowed to do all he could to restore Jerusalem to Christendom and with it gain a large slice of personal glory. But he was by now pragmatic concerning his prospects of achieving this objective. This came as a huge blow to his pride. His tears were probably more of disappointed ambition than anything else.

The army remained at Beit Nuba, waiting for reinforcements which were slow to arrive. Richard stood still for several weeks and once again there was a loss of initiative. The men began to lose their motivation, their sense of momentum dissipated and their energy with it. There were raids from Saladin's men to cope with too. With their highly mobile cavalry, they were perfectly equipped to create maximum discomfort for the crusaders. The latter were almost completely reliant on provisions being brought up from Jaffa and the convoys that carried them were exposed to fierce attacks as they lumbered along towards Beit Nuba.

Morale was lifted temporarily when a relic of the True Cross (not the one that Saladin held, there were many similar objects in circulation) was delivered to Richard by the 'Syrian' bishop of St George. Another part had been hidden away by a local hermit ('the abbot of St Elijah') and he led the crusaders to the spot where he had buried it. The timing was highly convenient given the depths to which morale had sunk; probably too convenient to be accidental. This was not the first time that such a thing had happened during the crusades; a discovery of the Holy Lance when the armies of the First Crusade were struggling whilst besieging Antioch had caused morale to soar. Relics were a very important commodity at the time and there is good reason to doubt their genuineness on many occasions as is evidenced, for example, by the existence of more than one head of John the Baptist.

But on this occasion, these finds had little tangible impact on the long-term spirits of the army. Richard, still unconvinced at the wisdom of making a further push on Jerusalem, called a council meeting to discuss his next steps. The French contingent wished to continue the advance but the rest, dominated by local men and representatives of the Templars and Hospitallers, instead recommended that Egypt should be their target as Richard probably knew and hoped that they would all along.

The French were dead set against the plan; for them, it was Jerusalem or nothing. So were some of the army, who had no interest in the strategic merits or otherwise of Egypt, though others of the 'common people' were starting to lose enthusiasm for the venture altogether. But just as the arguments were growing fierce, the opportunity for a welcome distraction arrived. News came in that a large caravan was making its way from Bilbeis in Egypt to Jerusalem. Richard responded energetically to it, putting together a crack force of 500 knights and 1,000 sergeants to attack the caravan. With him were Hugh of Burgundy's Frenchmen, encouraged to join in by Richard's offer to let them have a third of any plunder taken.

They marched out through the night under the bright moon. Saladin in the meantime had his scouts watching them, and they reported news of the movement back to him. Messengers were sent out to warn the caravan of the fact that Richard and a large body of crusaders were in the vicinity. But the two forces bivouacked on the night of 22 June 1192 just 14 miles apart from each other.

Richard sent out spies in disguise to gain more information. One of them, Bernard the Syrian, was presumably a local man; there were three spies altogether and each of them had received 100 silver marks in advance. Ambroise said that he had never seen anybody look more like the enemy or talk their language so well. What Richard now heard from them convinced him to attack next day. His men ate well, as did their horses, but sleep was absent as they marched through the night. It was with a sense of adventure and a burst of adrenaline that they made their way through the hours of darkness towards their unsuspecting target.

Just after dawn on 23 June 1192, the Muslim caravan was preparing itself to resume its march. Men were readying their horses and camels were being loaded with their heavy burdens whilst the soldiers rubbed the dust of sleep from their eyes and prepared their stiff, unwilling limbs for the day ahead. Then from the blue,2 a dust-cloud descended on them. Richard's force had achieved complete surprise against their opponents. Their horses fell on the camp, a solid wave of cavalry overwhelming it in an unstoppable surge that rolled over everything that got in its way.

What followed was not a battle, it was a rout. Seeing what was coming, the guards escorting the caravan broke without a fight. Some escaped due to the speed of their horses, no doubt aided by the fact that the crusaders wanted to make sure that they secured whatever loot was available. It was said that 500 men, 3,000 camels and as many horses, mules and donkeys were captured. Many of Saladin's men tried to escape into the desert but were either cut down by chasing horsemen or died a long, drawn-out death through thirst. A huge amount of booty was taken, including silk, cloth from Persia, a vast range of spices and a host of other luxury items along with more down-to-earth but even more vital foodstuffs. There was such a surfeit of camels that the crusaders ate the young ones which were said to provide a delicious white meat when cooked in fat.

Baha' al-Din was there when Saladin received the news. A young groom had entered his tent with the unwelcome message. Baha' al-Din saw that Saladin was overcome with grief at the tidings for the caravan's supplies were significant and would have boosted the chances of mounting a successful defence of Jerusalem. Saladin now believed that the way to the city was open.

Those around him had no stomach for a protracted siege of the city. They urged Saladin to fight in open battle in a last, desperate defence. But his heart was not in it, perhaps remembering the mastery of his opponent at Arsuf. On 29 June, Saladin ordered that all the cisterns around Jerusalem should be destroyed to deny water to the enemy. On Friday 3 July, it was decided that Saladin should be moved away to safety. He first went to hear prayers in the great al-Aqsa Mosque. Those there saw that as he did so the tears were pouring down his cheeks.

The door to Jerusalem was now open. But then, a miracle; the crusaders did not come. Saladin's spies told him that the crusader army remained divided and that their movements were confused and indecisive. Morale amongst the Christians was again plummeting. All the old debates about whether Jerusalem could be held if it was taken re-surfaced. Fodder and water for the horses was also in short supply, ironically a situation made worse by the fact that so many had recently been captured. Supply lines were stretched and frequently attacked by hordes of 'Turkish' horsemen.[6]

Henry of Champagne had by now arrived with reinforcements but it made no difference; there was no more likelihood of a push on Jerusalem than there ever had been. The French were furious at Richard's indecision and the duke of Burgundy made up rude songs about him, to which Richard responded in kind. The day after Saladin left Jerusalem, it all came to a head when Richard decided to retreat from Beit Nuba. It was a key decision. It marked a turning-point, not just to the course of the Third Crusade but to Richard's life.

Richard must have known that he would be open to much personal criticism for his decision to withdraw; it went against all the precepts of honour and glory that the Age of Chivalry espoused. It also went against Richard's publicly expressed motivations when he had taken the cross. Justify it as he might try to do on the grounds of military expediency, many would be unconvinced. But it was also a cautious act. His vacillation about the assault on Jerusalem, for such it was, spoke of a huge internal debate going on inside him.

The retreat from Beit Nuba was also a retreat from Richard's dreams. It began on 4 July 1192, five years to the day since the disaster at Hattin. Inwardly perhaps Richard cursed the betrayal of John and Philip which in the end had left him with no real alternative. The demands of England and France had to take precedence (those of France had certainly done so for Philip). John's treachery was expected and Philip's betrayal of a fellow crusader probably equally so; but the sense of hurt and grief was great. It festered away, a malevolent ulcer gnawing at him until grief transformed itself into a deep, burning anger and an overwhelming desire for revenge.

Saladin though was still not convinced that Richard was planning to return to Europe and feared that he would instead move on Egypt. Richard's capture of so many animals during his recent raids meant that he had plenty of beasts of burden to help him. The crusaders also retained control of the sea and held the strategically vital town of Ascalon.

What Saladin did not yet know was that the unity of the crusader army had been smashed as if it were a thin sheet of glass. Many of the men were resolved on an attack on Jerusalem, the sole reason for their committment to the crusade, and now that the opportunity was withdrawn, their morale collapsed. It was an angry, resentful army that Richard now led with an increasingly uncertain grip.

Richard's decision to retreat from Jerusalem left contemporary chroniclers, even those normally supportive of him, struggling for answers. Roger of Howden blamed the situation on the lack of co-operation from the French contingent, an accusation not backed up by much evidence. The later French writer, Jean de Joinville, nevertheless also blamed the retreat on the duke of Burgundy. But at the time other writers, especially in France and Germany, loaded all the responsibility for the decision on the shoulders of Richard. It was a metaphorical burden that he would always struggle to carry.[7]

Richard resolved to do the best he could before leaving Outremer and to this end he reopened discussions with Saladin. Richard told him not to be deceived by his withdrawal, equating it to the movements of a ram before charging. Saladin for his part wanted rid of Richard and his army without surrendering everything of importance in the process. It was agreed that Christian pilgrims would be allowed into Jerusalem and that the crusaders would be able to retain most of the places that they had seized along the coast.

There was one exception to this proposed settlement; Ascalon. Saladin insisted that its fortifications should be destroyed, something that Richard was loath to do given the extensive efforts (not to mention the cost) he had recently expended in restoring them. He refused to concede this point in his initial response to Saladin's overtures. Baha' al-Din cursed Richard for his cunning and considered that 'we never had to face a craftier or bolder enemy'.[8] But Richard did dismantle the defences of Darum on his own initiative for he no longer needed the town and wished therefore to deny it to Saladin.

Richard still planned to continue to make military gestures against Saladin's territories before he departed to get a better deal from the negotiations. He moved back to Acre and from there he planned to attack Beirut, which was in Saladin's hands and would be a useful bargaining chip if he could take it. Saladin, however, seems to have been aware of his plans – the spy network was clearly working well – and planned to respond to Richard's aggressive move by one of his own against Jaffa.

The crusaders were taken by surprise when a large Muslim army, boosted by reinforcements from Aleppo and Mesopotamia, arrived unexpectedly outside Jaffa. By 28 July, missiles from Saladin's artillery were smashing into the walls whilst, beneath the surface, miners scratched away at the ground as they dug out tunnels which they ultimately planned to set ablaze, bringing the fortifications above crashing down.

Soon a stretch of the walls of Jaffa, some 10 metres long, collapsed. When the dust and the smoke cleared away, the besiegers saw that a new wall had materialised in seconds, this time made of human flesh and blood. They saw before them a hedge of lances and bills, behind which were men determined to die if need be and to take as many as possible of the enemy with them if they did so.

However, these brave soldiers were powerless to resist the stones and missiles unleashed against them from Saladin's artillery. They apparently had stone-throwers of their own but did not have the skills to use them.[9] Before long there were gaps in the human wall, inexorably increasing in size as men were crushed to pulp, their bodies battered, their bones smashed as the artillery took its irresistible toll.

Further resistance seemed useless and negotiations began. The English chroniclers said that the constable of the fortress, Aubrey of Rheims, tried to flee for his life on a ship but was prevented by his own men from leaving.[10] Terms of surrender were agreed with the new patriarch of Jerusalem, Ralph, who proved himself a skilled negotiator.[11] The garrison was instructed to hole up in the citadel; an interesting insight into how afraid Saladin was that he would be unable to control his men who might slaughter them otherwise; indeed, Ambroise stated unequivocally that those who were ill (there seems to have been some kind of epidemic in Jaffa at the time) were killed in their beds. If no help arrived by 1 August, then Jaffa and its citadel would be handed over to Saladin with who knew what results for those who were taken captive.

But then worrying news was received from Saladin's scouts outside Acre; a relieving force was on its way. The surrender of Jaffa now became a race against time. Saladin frantically tried to persuade the garrison to evacuate the citadel of Jaffa before they became aware of the imminent arrival of reinforcements. But he also had trouble with his own men, who wanted to take the citadel by force so that they could lay claim to any plunder in line with the rules of war.

As dawn broke over Jaffa on 1 August, the day of the festival of St Peter in Chains, the silence of the lethargic early hours was shattered by the sound of trumpets. This was a dawn chorus that told of imminent conflict; more crusaders had arrived. A land force was advancing on Jaffa led by Henry of Champagne and Templar and Hospitaller troops. The duke of Burgundy's Frenchmen refused to take part in this advance, which spoke volumes of their disenchantment with Richard and indeed the whole crusade.

Richard was not with this army though. He had taken ship with the Pisans and Genoese, for once putting the confrontational politics of the Italian city-states to one side and serving in a common cause. With him were some of his most trusted warriors such as the earl of Leicester and Andrew de Chauvigny. Richard was delayed en route by contrary winds which added to his frustration. When he at last arrived off Jaffa his heart sank when he saw that the banners of Saladin and his emirs were flying over the walls of the town. He had no idea yet that the citadel was still held by the crusaders. Saladin for his part was confident that he had more than enough men to drive any attack launched from the ships back into the sea. He had taken the town and some of the defenders had already been killed as well as many pigs whose presence offended Muslim sensibilities.

Unsure of the situation, the ships stayed offshore without attempting any attack. Some of those inside the citadel lost heart and a few gave up and surrendered their arms and left the doubtful safety of its walls. Some even handed over the financial compensation that was due to Saladin as part of the surrender terms but were beheaded as soon as they had done so. But then an unnamed hero, a priest, emerged. He leapt from the citadel into the sea and swam out to the ships, being picked up partway by a boat sent to do so.

Richard watched on, his eyes fixed on the brave priest like a hawk surveying the landscape before stooping into fatal action. The king was on a galley that was painted in red, flying a red flag – the colour of blood. The rescue boat tied up alongside and the priest scrambled aboard. He gasped out his news; the citadel had not yet surrendered and all was therefore not lost. But it soon would be unless precipitate action was taken.

It was as if someone had set a spark to Richard. He was about to re-enter his element, to journey into a land where only instant action and extreme courage would do; a land populated only by heroes. At once he ordered the ships to move towards the shore.

Another chapter in the legend of Richard the Lionheart was about to be written.

Less than an hour later the men from the ships were charging up the beach, inevitably led ashore by Richard. Even from a distance, he reputedly struck down many of the enemy by practising his crossbow skills. The troubadours of the day said that his personal heroism matched that of the immortal Roland at the pass of Roncesvalles. Richard's troops resisted Muslim counter-attacks with great spirit. Saladin's soldiers even marched into the sea to resist the advance but were pushed back. The crusaders were soon erecting barricades made of all the timber that they could get hold of at short notice; logs, barrels, planks from grounded old ships and driftwood.

They fought off Saladin's attacks and started to advance. Bit by bit, the crusaders pushed their way up the blood-stained sands. Their crossbowmen took a great toll and the Muslims started to retreat before the looming shadow of Melec Richard. He and a small group of his men broke into the town where they fell on the Muslims inside it who were helping themselves to booty. Having overcome them, they hoisted Richard's flag, heartening those left inside the citadel who then launched their own attack.

No doubt Richard's burgeoning reputation weighed down the hearts of some of Saladin's men. One historian has suggested that a key explanation for this turn of events was that 'there were no Muslim troops who fought in expectation of victory'.[12] Saladin's men inside Jaffa were soon in a race to save their lives, a race that they all too often lost.

Richard sent a messenger to Saladin. That same afternoon Muslim envoys visited Richard's makeshift camp on the beach. They found him in the company of some of the important men who had been captured at Acre and had survived the slaughter after its fall. Richard sensed that he held the upper hand. He knew, he said, that Saladin was a mighty man. 'Why then did he run away as soon as I appeared? By God, I was not even properly armed for a fight. See, I am still wearing my sea boots'.[13]

However, Richard was not in a strong position. The land army had been held up by Muslim ambushers along the route; Henry of Champagne had taken a galley to arrive more quickly. Richard's force only had three horses that they had managed to acquire when they got ashore. The walls were shattered in several places and Richard did what he could to improvise running repairs.

Richard moderated his tone, keeping his pride under control. He urged the envoys to go back to Saladin and ask him again for a peace treaty. He explained that he had urgent problems in his homeland to attend to. It was in nobody's interests, he suggested, to let the fighting continue. Saladin soon responded to this approach with a message of his own; he was not prepared to compromise on his demands over Ascalon. Saladin reminded Richard that it was easy for him to stay where he was and bring up reinforcements in contrast to the problems that the king was facing in this respect.

Negotiations therefore foundered once again over the issue of Ascalon. With discussions seemingly going nowhere, Saladin devised a plan to go onto the offensive again. Richard's men were camped outside the broken walls of Jaffa in a vulnerable position, so Saladin decided to attack them, hoping to catch them off guard. The crusader land army had not yet arrived but if they did then it would be difficult for Saladin to beat their combined forces.

Saladin's forces did everything they could to gain an element of surprise. Some of his men crept stealthily forward during the night of 4 August, aiming to take Richard's tent and capture him whilst he slept. They almost succeeded in doing so. At the last moment, as dawn was breaking, an alarm was raised by an alert Genoese guard. The men in Richard's camp stumbled into position, some of them not even having time to get dressed. They arranged themselves in ranks, kneeling behind a wall of shields with their lances pointing forward towards the horses of the enemy, much as Scottish infantrymen later fought in their famous schiltron formation or Henry V's men lined up behind their stakes at Agincourt.

Behind this front line, their lances forming a wall daring the Muslim cavalry to try and break through, were the crossbowmen. The crossbow was a formidable weapon with frightening stopping power. So deadly was it considered to be that at one stage the Church considered banning it as an immoral weapon; attempts were made to do so during the Second Lateran Council of 1139 though with limited success. But it had one major disadvantage; loading it was a time-consuming process. To counteract this problem, Richard ordered that pairs of crossbowmen should work together, one loading whilst the other fired.

But Richard's men were heavily outnumbered. The king strode up and down the lines, a colossus urging his men not to fear and to believe in the righteousness of their cause and their military superiority over the enemy. He was pragmatic but defiant; there was no point in trying to flee for 'there is nowhere to run'.[14] The Muslims charged headlong against the camp, inspired by thoughts of victory against their overmatched opponents. They broke like the waves of the sea against the defensive line.

Richard's army stood as firm as any sea-wall, holding back the breakers which crashed against it time and again. They were unflinching, unmovable, as if their formation was made of solid granite rather than flesh and bone. The Muslim cavalry saw that the line of bristling lances did not budge an inch and were therefore faced with the option of veering away or being skewered on the spears of the crusaders as they charged. Many of them took the first of these options and the force of the attack began to dissipate.

The fighting lasted for nine hours. Richard's army was greatly outnumbered; he had fifty-five knights, about 2,000 foot-soldiers, and had managed to assemble fifteen horses by now.[15] Against this force, Saladin allegedly fielded 7,000 cavalry alone.[16] Heroes emerged, or were rather confirmed, who helped to hold back the Muslim tide until it started to ebb away. Men such as Robert, earl of Leicester, Andrew de Chauvigny, Raoul de Mauléon, William de l'Étang, Hugh Neville, Bartholomew Mortimer, Gerard de Tourneval, Roger de Saci and the German Henry le Tyois, who carried Richard's banner (a single lion rather than three of them at this stage), wrote their names into history by their heroism.

But above all these mighty warriors, Richard was, according to the chroniclers, a giant amongst giants. The *Itinerarium* speaks of Richard swinging about him with his mighty sword, so powerfully that men were cut into two when his blade hit home with such force that it sliced through flesh and smashed through bone (these and other such descriptions were also freely used by Ambroise.).

The writer said that it was as if he were protected by divine powers as he appeared invulnerable to everything that Saladin's cavalry threw at him. There was one word that he used that summed up how Richard appeared that day; 'invincible'.[17] Another writer, Ralph of Coggeshall, kept using the word 'incredible' in his account and referred to the battle as 'the great miracle at which the whole world wonders'.[18] On this day, in the words of Aeneas, the chronicler of the Trojan War, fortune favoured the brave.[19]

In the face of Melec Richard, morale in the Muslim camp was conversely not high. Saladin's men were still fuming at being deprived of the plunder they believed they were entitled to after the town of Jaffa had been taken. Some historians have suggested that the defeat of the Muslim army at Jaffa is as much to do with the low morale of Saladin's men as it was the quality of Richard's leadership.[20] But this was certainly another piece slotting into the jigsaw that is the legend of the warrior king; and it is counter-intuitive to dismiss the strengths of Richard out of hand when his enemies wrote of them too.

It was for his formidable fighting qualities that Richard became known as 'Lionheart'. The lion was the king of the animals, renowned for its ferocity and bravery and the term suited Richard well when also considering his violent streak. The Plantagenet dynasty had appropriated the lion as their emblem; it had been adopted by Richard's grandfather Geoffrey as far back as 1127. Arthurian romance, then approaching its zenith, told romantic tales with the lion as a key symbol too. All these attributes fitted perfectly with Richard.

Ambroise could not resist comparing Richard's actions favourably to those of Roland during his heroic and ultimately futile rear-guard action at Roncesvalles, again painting him as the epitome of chivalric kinghood.[21] In fact, there are several phrases in the accounts of the chroniclers that suggest that this is as much a literary as a historical account. Richard is referred to as a knight and not a king. He is painted as the ultimate knight, the paragon of all chivalric heroes. We have some clues in a few paragraphs in the *Itinerarium* as to what is going on here.[22] So 'he mows the enemy with a sword as if he is harvesting them with a sickle'. At the fight's end, we are told 'this extraordinary knight returned from the contest', as if he is coming back from a tournament and not a battle. The praise is so over the top that the account reads more like the actions of a quasi-Arthurian knightly hero than those of a real-life warrior.

But the Muslims praised him too, perhaps in a self-justifying attempt to explain an otherwise highly embarrassing reverse. Baha' al-Din heard that Richard rode up and down along the lines on one of the few horses that was available and none dared to challenge him; such was the aura of invincibility that surrounded the king. Al-'Adil, who was probably not present at the battle as he was ill at the time, heard such tales of Richard's prowess during the fight that he later sent him a gift of two magnificent Arab horses in honour of his performance during it.[23] Outnumbered and outmatched, this was perhaps the finest moment of Richard's military career. It is a tale that resonates with the English with their traditional love of the underdog and battles won against overwhelming odds; Agincourt, Crecy, the Armada, Trafalgar, the Battle of Britain.

It is likely that a key role was also played by the high number of crossbowmen Richard had with him (a force of about 400 men out of the 2,000 *pedistes*, foot soldiers, that he had available) and in this respect the contribution of the Genoese, who were famed for their skill with the weapon, is likely to have been vital. It was these unnamed men, working in tandem with one man firing whilst his mate loaded his next bolt, who probably secured victory rather than the magnificence of the chivalric knightly heroes that the chroniclers extolled in their works.[24]

Richard now seemed to have a hex over Saladin. The victor of Hattin had been bested once again and his reputation, if not in tatters – after all, he still held Jerusalem – had been badly tarnished. We may surmise that these reverses were draining Saladin of his vitality too, especially as he was now well past the prime of life and had been suffering from a long-term illness. But the reality was that, glorious though it was and magnificently as it reads in the chronicles, the victory at Jaffa changed very little. Richard had avoided defeat and possible capture or even death, which was of course highly important, but he gained little strategic advantage from his triumph.

In the event, the desultory negotiations started up again after this military interlude. And it was about this time that the truth of Saladin's earlier words about the relative ease with which he could be reinforced came home to roost. Saladin could bring up fresh men, from Mosul in Mesopotamia and from Egypt. Ever the gallant adversary, and perhaps more cynically also a skilled spymaster who wished to find out what was going on inside Jaffa, he sent messengers to Richard with gifts of fruit and snow from the mountains (the king was especially fond of pears and peaches).

Richard's position was increasingly parlous. Physically, he was a wreck due to his exertions and he had been ill; Richard of Devizes suggested that he only started to improve at the end of August when he was cheered up by news of the death of Hugh, duke of Burgundy, at Acre.[25] Other accounts suggested that his illness was so serious that his life was feared for. Soon after, Hugh's replacement as leader of the French contingent in Outremer, Philip, bishop of Beauvais, issued the instruction that they were all to return home.[26] Only Henry, the count of Champagne, stayed behind; given his new-found status, he had very good reasons to do so.

It was said that 'the king was extremely sick and confined to his bed; his fever continued without intermission; the physicians whispered that it was an acute semitertian [a form of malarial fever]. And as they despaired of his recovery even from the first, terrible dismay was spread from the king's abode through the camp'; clearly the king's state of health was an ongoing worry.[27] The desertion of many men had left him short of numbers and although he ordered that the walls of the citadel of Jaffa should be repaired, those of the town itself were still in a ruinous state.

Abu Bekr, Saladin's chief negotiator, told his lord that Richard had mentioned in conversation that Ascalon remained the main bone of contention. He wanted to keep it for himself but if he could not then he asked that he be reimbursed for the great expense he had incurred when reconstructing its fortifications. His main purpose was to save face over Ascalon and he was desperately looking for ways of doing so.

Correspondence from Saladin to Al-'Adil suggests that he too wanted peace, as his army was approaching the point of exhaustion despite the new reinforcements; possibly they were not of a high standard compared to the men that they replaced. A deal was struck soon after; Richard could keep most of the gains including Jaffa (though not all of its dependent territories such as Ramla). He could also retain Caesarea, Haifa and Acre although again some dependent territories such as Nazareth would be handed back. But on Ascalon, Richard got nothing; there would not even be compensation for the work that he had paid for there. In the event, it would be abandoned until 1240 when a later crusader, Earl Richard of Cornwall, had the fortifications rebuilt.

Al-'Adil came to Jaffa soon after to seal the deal. Richard was clearly seriously ill (so much so that Al-'Adil was visibly moved) and when he was asked to read the treaty he said that he could not and merely responded by saying 'I have made peace. Here is my hand'.[28] This was perhaps a sign of just how ill Richard was, a mark of resignation to the inevitable. He had been sick for three months and at times some of his army feared for his life. Allied to the extreme stresses of command in this hostile environment, Richard was close to breaking point. A truce was agreed, starting on 2 September 1192 and lasting for three years, three months, three days and three hours. It seems to have taken a long time for Saladin and his councillors to agree it for Al-'Adil had had to negotiate with them for seventeen days before the deal was finalised.[29] But at last it was done.

The truce extended to the crusader territories of Antioch and Tripoli and also covered the lands of the Assassins. There was to be free movement between Christian and Muslim territories. The revenues of Ramla and Lydda, though in Muslim hands again, were to be divided between the two sides. Hubert Walter was instrumental in negotiating this deal; Richard was fortunate to have such a reliable adviser close to hand at this crucial time.[30]

Whilst peace gave neither party what they wanted, it was the lesser of several evils. Morale in Saladin's camp was also low. His men were disheartened at losing so frequently to Richard, who clearly had the upper hand over Saladin in a military sense. Many had been away from their homes for years and they were not a professional army. And in recent days, significant chunks of the territories they had taken after Hattin had been lost.

For Richard, however much his supporters might argue about the useful gains that had been made, the greatest prize – and to many the only one that mattered – remained in Muslim hands. The crusader was a pilgrim whose goal was to take Jerusalem and this Richard had failed to do. To this extent, the negotiations over Ascalon had been a blind. Few of the crusaders cared a jot about the place; to them it was Jerusalem or nothing.

But Richard was left without many choices. He had issues back in England and France that required his urgent attention. He was ill and running short of funds. His army was disunited and he had lost the respect of the French as a leader of the expedition. And, being a good strategist himself, he realised that all the high-value cards were in Saladin's hand; accessibility to large supplies of reinforcements, ease of communications and control of the surrounding territories which would allow his armies to be re-provisioned. He also saw that the crusader kingdoms in Outremer were disunited and lacked real leadership; it was ironic that the strongest candidate for an effective, if not a good, king, Conrad of Montferrat, was dead and that some suggested that Richard was behind the plot to kill him.

Relying on the provisions of the deal, many of the crusaders made their way in peace to Jerusalem, the Holy City, coming unarmed as pilgrims rather than as warriors. Despite fears that they might be attacked they returned unscathed. They were in many cases overwhelmed by the holy sites they saw. They visited them, in the words of one modern commentator, as if they were modern tourists on a package holiday though the pilgrims kissed each site they visited rather than took photographs of them.[31]

The fulfilment of crusader vows was an intensely emotional moment for the pilgrims. Three main parties made the journey, one led by Andrew de Chauvigny, one by Ralph Teisson and one by Hubert Walter. They wandered its streets, the very roads on which Christ had walked. They worshipped at the Holy Sepulchre, the most sacred church in Christendom, and knelt before Christ's empty tomb whilst nearby Muslims worshipped unmolested at the Dome of the Rock and the al-Aqsa Mosque. They visited the room where the Last Supper had been held and they paid their respects with tearful reverence at the spot where the story of the Dormition of the Virgin, her assumption into Heaven, had been played out. They returned with religious souvenirs such as palm leaves and the warm satisfaction of knowing that they had earned the right to religious indulgences which would give them remittance of their sins and a smoother path into the Life to Come.

For Saladin, this was all very useful. Allowing the pilgrims to visit Jerusalem brought in money, which was always welcome, but also diminished their need to fight and conquer. He spoke at length to Hubert Walter, praising Richard's qualities but remarking that he did not wish to emulate his rashness. He even showed him the relic of the True Cross that he held (at around the same time that Richard had been attempting to regain this, so too had the Byzantine emperor Isaac Comnenus, something that must have increased the distrust of Byzantium amongst the crusaders).[32]

Saladin permitted Latin priests to hold services in the Church of the Holy Sepulchre where before only representatives of the Syrian church could do so; similar privileges were granted for the churches in Nazareth and Bethlehem. However, he was duly cautious in his actions. The eastern portal to the Church of the Holy Sepulchre was blocked up so that the flow of crusader traffic into and out of it could be better controlled; so too was the way to Calvary, that most sacred of Christian sites.[33]

Those who visited Jerusalem saw some heartbreaking sights according to Richard of Devizes. As they walked through the streets, they saw 'captive confessors of the Christian name wearing out a hard and constant martyrdom; chained together in gangs, their feet blistered, their shoulders raw, their backsides goaded, their backs wealed; they carried materials to the hands of the masons and stone-layers to make Jerusalem impregnable against the Christians'.[34] They were angered at seeing horses stabled in the holy places of Christendom though the Templars had done the same at the al-Aqsa Mosque when the Christians ruled the roost in Jerusalem. But they were powerless to do anything about it.

Ironically, Saladin's success in holding on to Jerusalem undermined its longer-term economic health. Although pilgrim traffic continued to come to the city from the West, it was in much smaller numbers than had been the case when it was in crusader hands; few liked being allowed to visit the holy sites under the sufferance of Muslim owners. To keep Jerusalem afloat, the Muslim authorities had to eventually supplement its income with some of that of nearby Nablus. The True Cross, later removed from the city, was eventually brought back by Saladin's successors to try to attract more visitors. Eventually Jerusalem would virtually be abandoned by them and briefly restored to crusader hands, largely out of apathy rather than any victory in battle.[35]

Having fulfilled their vows, many of the pilgrims made plans to return home, as Richard knew they would. He had tried without success to insist that only men carrying his passport should be allowed to go to Jerusalem and that they should make any gifts not to the holy places of the city but to the fund to restore the shattered walls of Jaffa. In this respect, Richard – inspiring battle-leader though he was – was not on the same wavelength as most of his men. Saladin's magnanimity had defused the explosiveness of the situation, an object lesson to obdurate politicians of all generations.

The outcome of the crusade was a bitter personal blow to Richard and he had not taken advantage of the chance to visit Jerusalem. Perhaps he was still too ill to travel but more likely he only wanted to see Jerusalem on his own terms, as the man who restored it to what he fervently believed to be its rightful owners. It was said by Richard of Devizes that he was unwilling to receive as a gift from the 'pagans' that which he had not been able to obtain as a gift from God.

On 9 October 1192, Richard set sail for home (wherever that was) in a ship called the *Franche-Nef*. Before he left, he arranged for the ransom of William of Préaux who had gallantly sacrificed himself to save Richard earlier in the campaign. Berengaria, Joanna and the mysterious 'Damsel of Cyprus', the daughter of Isaac Comnenus, had sailed several weeks before; the women would reach Rome by Christmas. Nothing that had happened since the marriage of Richard and Berengaria gives the lie to the suggestion that it was a relationship that was first, foremost and only about politics.

That said, this had been an extraordinary period for the newly married couple. They had been thrown straight into a war zone as soon as they were married. Richard had then been taken seriously ill and had been away fighting for months. It is easy for historians to forget the human emotions that underpin any relationship. If Berengaria and Richard were never to enjoy a particularly close partnership, it is hardly to be wondered at given the start that they had to their married life.

Saladin's response to Richard leaving was highly suggestive; as soon as he heard the news that Richard had gone, he returned to Damascus. It was an unambiguous statement that he knew that there was no threat to Jerusalem now that Richard had departed. Ironically given the way that the story of Richard and Saladin is a core part of the Ricardian legend, the two men never met. That both men respected each other does not seem unlikely but behind the chivalric gestures, there was always the harsh truth of *realpolitik*. Both men inspired respect in later generations: Richard's magnificent Westminster statue, built by public subscription with a subscriber's list led by Queen Victoria and Prince Albert is a good example. On the other hand, the German Kaiser Wilhelm II was so obsessed by Saladin that he felt that his humble wooden sarcophagus was not good enough and therefore gave one of marble to replace it.[36]

The actions of the proud German Kaiser show how little he really understood of Saladin, who was at heart a humble and devout conventional Muslim who disliked ostentation. And he would soon be needing that sarcophagus for on 4 March 1193 he died, worn out by a life of hard work and great achievement. It is a tempting, if largely pointless, speculation to wonder what might have happened if Richard had still been in Outremer at the time of his death, one of the 'what if's' of history. For by that stage Richard had far greater problems of his own to worry about. As one chronicler sagely remarked, echoing the words of the great Roman writer Ovid, 'all human affairs hang by a slender thread'.[37] Richard was about to find out just how true that saying was.

15

Betrayal (1192–1193)

'When they are dead, they will have their remorse
If I am too long here'
Extract from a song written by Richard when a captive

When Shakespeare wrote of the 'slings and arrows of outrageous fortune' in the famous soliloquy from *Hamlet*, he might have had Richard in mind, for he was about to be shot at by them from all different directions. First of all, he would have to deal with the opprobrium of those who felt he had deserted the cause of Outremer, ironically often from the supporters of Philip of France, a man who had sailed back to France at the earliest available opportunity. Others pointed the finger at him for his alleged involvement in the death of Conrad of Montferrat.

A slightly later commentator, the bishop of Acre Jacques de Vitry, put the blame for the relative failure of the crusade – it had after all not retaken Jerusalem which was its prime objective – on the discord and rivalry between Richard and Philip. He said of them that 'they each sought for their own glory and laboured for their personal cause, detesting each other and tearing each other apart, to the very great joy of their enemies and the confusion of the Christian people'.[1] It is an accusation with many elements that ring true.

He added that the Christians, 'covered by confusion and prostrated by grief', had given up all hope of taking Jerusalem despite their great efforts, and were weighed down with the futility of the enormous sacrifices that they had made. Jacques de Vitry bemoaned the fact that Richard had not kept his planned departure secret or delayed it for longer, though this fails to consider the issues that demanded Richard's attention back home and the perfidy of his ostensible fellow-crusader, Philip of France, in his absence. But the mood was bleak and there were many who sought for scapegoats to explain away the failure of the Crusade. Richard was one of their chief targets.

Richard also had his defenders though. The writer of the *Itinerarium* blamed his illness for his departure, along with the fact that he had so little support which gave him little option but to get the best deal that he could. The perfidies of the French come in for particular criticism. He said defiantly that Richard had no choice; and 'anyone who wished to put forward a different opinion of this peace agreement is liable to be labelled a perverse liar'.[2]

This might not have mattered quite so much were it not for the course of events that unfolded when Richard started his journey back home. Richard reached Corfu by 11 November 1192. Which route to take from there posed a conundrum. To travel through France was clearly highly dangerous, given Philip's enmity and the likelihood that he would have to travel through the lands of the count of Toulouse. Further east, if he travelled up through Italy or through the Balkans into Austria, he would be traversing lands controlled by the Emperor Henry VI, still furious given Richard's support to Tancred in Sicily, or even worse those of Leopold of Austria, likely to be smarting after his banner had been unceremoniously dumped in a ditch at Acre.

For those who cared to look – and there were many in those more superstitious times – there were omens that something was about to go badly wrong. Unusually, the Northern Lights had appeared far south in England that year according to William of Newburgh; he described them as 'twinkling with a kind of blood-stained light'.[3] This seemed to suggest that all was not well with the world.

Soon after, people in England started to fret. They believed that the king would be home by Christmas. But as the days passed and he did not appear a sense of alarm appeared, small at first but then growing with the passage of time. In those days of poor communication when news that now would take seconds to travel would then take weeks, his people began to become fearful due to his continuing absence. Candles were lit in churches across the country and prayers offered up for his safe return. Eleanor of Aquitaine kept her Christmas court at Westminster, increasingly concerned for the safety of her son.

Richard had practical issues to contend with when plotting his journey too. Winter was approaching and normally, given the dangers of crossing the Mediterranean in the frail vessels of the time, there would be no sea-going traffic abroad during the season. Taking a ship now posed a real risk of wreck and this could lead either to Richard's death or to him being thrown up on some foreign shore where the local lord was hostile to him and his interests; and there were many such falling into that category.

Richard was faced with a terrible predicament whichever way he went. Most of Europe was allied by now to either Philip of France or the Emperor Henry VI, both men who would like to take Richard captive; the continent had been turned on its head since he left. The countries dotted along the southern shores of what is now France, although nominally independent, were friendly with Philip. Even small states like Piedmont were potentially hostile to Richard as they were linked with Conrad of Montferrat. The eastern coast of Spain was also problematic. And sailing west through the Straits of Gibraltar was a practical impossibility, mainly due to the currents but also because of the proximity of Muslim North Africa.

Richard therefore sought alternatives. There was only one apparently viable route; to head for the Hungarian coast (back then, King Bela of Hungary had several coastal towns such as Zara – now in Croatia – in his possession and he was well-disposed towards Richard). From here he could try and find his way through to lands under the control of King Henry the Lion, his brother-in-law who had been married to Richard's deceased sister Matilda. Henry the Lion was fiercely opposed to the emperor, Henry VI, and his ports at Hamburg and Lübeck were suitable places from which Richard could sail back to England.

As Richard approached Ragusa (now Dubrovnik) there was a change in the detail of the plan. Richard would transfer from his large but slow 'bus' in which he was travelling to a smaller galley. A small flotilla of two or three such galleys set out for the Hungarian coast. They were fast and relatively anonymous unlike Richard's larger, slower ship. But they did not handle well in bad weather and as it was now winter, and past the end of the normal travelling season, they were very vulnerable.[4] We know of some of the men with him; Baldwin of Béthune, a French knight and a great friend of William Marshal, William of L'Étang and Richard's favourite clerk, Philip of Poitou. There was also a small group of Templars escorting him, suggestive of close links between the king and their Order.

The fragile ships of the time hugged the coastline, especially during the winter if they were rash enough to journey then. They routinely put in at night to avoid the perils of travelling in the darkness. The next we know of Richard we find him ashore somewhere between Venice and Aquileia, an ancient Roman city in the very furthest niche of the Adriatic in the north-eastern corner of what is now Italy. The galleys had apparently been useless in the teeth of bad weather and had been forced ashore miles away from where Richard had intended them to be.

Richard now found himself in a region controlled by Meinhard of Görz, a nephew of Conrad of Montferrat. Given allegations against Richard concerning his supposed part in the death of the late marquis it did not take a genius to work out what Meinhard's reaction might be should he find out that Richard was nearby. By this time, Richard had grown a beard and had long hair and was wearing clothes that he hoped would allow him to blend in with the locals or at least appear to be a pilgrim. He had already made generous gifts to the cathedral at Ragusa en route and, good though this might have been for his soul, this was hardly sensible if he wished to merge into the background. *Superbia* made it difficult for him to avoid drawing attention to himself.

There were several practical reasons for Richard to be worried too. It was winter, almost Christmas, and most people were at home or not travelling at this time of year. The mere fact that he was on the road would draw attention to himself. His general state of health would not have been conducive to this sort of arduous travel either. The road system was awful and would take Richard through some wild, unforgiving country.

It seems that Meinhard worked out who the strange pilgrim, who was travelling under the name of Hugo, really was. But then Richard had a stroke of luck. Meinhard sent one of his men out to confirm Richard's identity. The agent, Roger of Argentan, was a Norman though he had not been in the duchy for several decades. He quickly worked out who 'Hugo' really was. Old loyalties died hard and, rather than hand the king over, Roger promised to help him. He returned to Meinhard and told him that the pilgrim was not Richard. Meinhard did not believe him. But by the time he swooped on the place where Richard had been staying, he had already gone.

There was now only one way Richard could travel, towards Bohemia where he might find friends. But he would have to cross the lands of Duke Leopold of Austria to get there. The duke had been insulted when his banner had been flung into the ditch at Acre; however technically correct this action might have been, it was politically inept. Whilst Richard may not have ordered the act (though it is also conceivable that he did) it was unlikely that it would have been done without his knowledge and tacit approval. While Richard perhaps did not envisage the set of circumstances that would lead to him falling into the hands of Leopold, there was little reason to expect friendly treatment if he did.

There are several versions of what happened next. The cat was out of the bag now that Meinhard had worked out who 'Hugo' was and he sent messengers out to warn those ahead that Richard was somewhere in the region. Even allowing for the poor communications in that area at that time of year, the king was in a race against the clock. He was not good at disguise, being prone to extravagant and expensive gestures which did not fit the part that he was supposed to be playing. A Bavarian chronicler, Magnus of Reichersberg, told how Richard's party was attacked; several men were killed or wounded though he himself escaped.

His party probably traversed the valley called the Val Canale which led from lands that were in spiritual terms the responsibility of the patriarch of Aquileia to those answering to the bishop of Salzburg. This brought Richard into Carinthia, an isolated and culturally mixed area.[5] The party probably had little access to local guides and were only aware in a general sense of where they were headed. Their situation was now parlous.

In Roger of Howden's account, Richard realised that his party was coming under suspicion. He broke away from the main group accompanied by just one man, whilst he left the others, including Baldwin of Béthune, in his wake as a decoy. Baldwin was seized at Friesach, possibly as part of a ruse in which he spent extravagantly whilst Richard slipped away. Baldwin, once a keen member of the *mesnie* of the late Young King, had proved his worth in the retinue of his new master, Richard.

There were now only three of them left in Richard's group, including a local boy who had been recruited to guide them to the borders of the lands of King Henry the Lion, now tantalisingly close. Vienna hove into view, then an unimpressive town of hovels where virtually the only stone building was the palace of the Babenberg dukes, the residence of Duke Leopold. They were entering the wolf's lair. They reached a small village called Erdberg, barely in fact a village at all. While the king slept, having fallen on his makeshift bed and almost instantly becoming dead to the world through exhaustion, the boy went to exchange some money; the coins he had on him came from Syria, in itself likely to draw attention.

The boy visited the market several times. On the last occasion, he borrowed Richard's richly made gloves, perhaps lent because the weather was cold. Whilst he was there, he was recognised by one of Leopold's men and seized; rough treatment probably quickly followed. It was only a matter of time before Richard was also taken. Some accounts suggest that when he was discovered Richard would only surrender directly to Leopold. The duke therefore came to the village where he came face-to-face with Richard for the first time since his humiliation at Acre.

Most German accounts of Richard's capture say that it took place in a little hut, effectively a peasant's hovel, though the version told by Otto of St Blasien suggests that the king was trying to disguise himself as a servant in a kitchen; Henry VI thought it very amusing when he heard that Richard had been captured holding a roast chicken. Otto suggests that Richard had been recognised when he forgot to take off an extravagant ring he was wearing.[6] In a letter subsequently sent from Henry VI to Philip, Richard is said to have been taken in 'a despicable house'. Many of these details painted a humiliating picture of the way in which Richard was seized. For this reason, it is perhaps not surprising that English chroniclers do not mention them.

Henry VI wrote to Philip in France informing him that Richard, 'the enemy of our empire and the disturber of your kingdom' was in custody, having been captured on his way back home. He said that he had been denounced by Count Meinhard of Görz after 'calling to mind the treason, treachery and mischief of which he had been guilty in the Holy Land'; this in a letter written by one man who had not even been on the Crusade to another who had hurried back to France as soon as he could.[7]

Henry's letter gives further details. It confirms that the authorities in the region were aware that Richard was in the vicinity long before he was captured. Eight of his entourage were seized earlier on in the journey and a further six when his party was journeying through the bishopric of Salzburg. It was written just days after Christmas, showing that Leopold had wasted little time in passing on the news to the emperor. Henry made great play on the fact that it was Philip's great enemy that had been taken and did not dwell a lot on the emperor's own feelings towards Richard.

Richard had been taken to the nearby castle of Dürnstein ('dry rock'), where he had probably arrived for Christmas, a very different affair with a very different context than the Angevin Christmases of old. It was in a wonderfully romantic position, clinging to the top of a rock high above the Danube. But its current situation, a picture-postcard ruin in an impossibly beautiful location, should not disguise the fact that it was for Richard a prison from which escape would have been very difficult indeed. And it would have been no consolation for the people of England at all to learn that Richard was, or had been, in Austrian hands for they had a low reputation amongst the English, Ralph of Diceto saying that 'they are savages, who live more like wild beasts than men'.[8]

However, even some English commentators saw an element of divine justice in the capture of Richard though for reasons not connected to the crusade. In an age when such missteps were often attributed to the will of God, there had to be an explanation for such things. Ralph of Diceto saw these events as divine retribution against Richard for his rebellion against his father Henry II and his treatment of him in his last days.

The reality was that Richard was guilty, not of any moral misdemeanour which had outraged the emperor, but of getting in the way of his interests in Sicily. Philip was a natural ally of Henry given his desire to undermine Richard in France. There was common interest between the two men in having Richard safely out of the way for a while. This was nothing to do with any moral judgement and everything to do with rather grubby power-politics, of a type with which Richard was also very familiar.

There is evidence that Henry and Philip had reached an understanding when they met in the north of Italy (probably in Milan) whilst the French king was travelling back from Crusade at the end of 1191. Philip needed help if he wished to take advantage of Richard's absence in Outremer when he arrived back in France. The Pope, Celestine III, had already left him with a flea in his ear when he tried to persuade the pontiff to absolve him of his crusader oath so that he could go on the offensive in France. Celestine quite rightly dismissed this idea out of hand, making plain that he would excommunicate Philip if he dared to lift a finger against a fellow crusader in his absence.

There was other grubby gossiping going on too. Philip, the bishop of Beauvais, was a close friend of Conrad of Montferrat; indeed, the marquis was returning home from his house when he was assassinated in the streets of Tyre. The bishop had returned home before Richard and had not missed a chance to berate him for Conrad's death. For good measure, he also threw in the 'fact' that Richard had tried to betray Philip to Saladin. He accused Richard of being 'an extraordinarily savage man, thoroughly unpleasant and as hard as iron, adept at deceit, a master of dissimulation'.[9]

Philip, sensing that he had a powerful weapon in his hands with the story of Richard's involvement in Conrad's death, did not hesitate to thrust it between the ribs of the captured king. He wrote to Leopold, reminding him of Richard's alleged involvement in the assassination, asking him not to release Richard without informing him. A series of actions that amounted to cynical opportunism that went against the moral tenets of crusading (such as they were) was now in train.[10] It was an ideal opportunity for the French king to gain more lands, which he had already done in Flanders by taking advantage of the death of Count Philip. He was inspired by his own chivalric ambition, in his case to restore France to her former glory as last seen in the time of Charlemagne.[11]

The plot thickened early in 1192 when Philip presented William FitzRalph, the seneschal of Normandy, with a demand to hand the Vexin over to him. This strategically important territory on the borders of the duchy was, Philip asserted, due to him because it was a dowry for Alice's marriage which had not gone ahead: The seneschal refused to comply and Philip angrily departed.

Philip had sensed that he had a potential ally, a weak link in the Angevin chain, in the form of John, Richard's brother. A deal was proposed whereby John was to journey to France to discuss matters further with Philip. News of this got out and John was soon faced by two strong opponents who persuaded him to reluctantly think again. One was Walter of Coutances, proving his worth once more; he had seemingly been the first man to pass the news of Richard's capture across the Channel to England, sending copies of his letter to members of the Great Council there in case some did not get through.[12] The other personality was even more terrifying to John; his mother. In a combined attack, they told John that if he dared to go ahead with his plotting with Philip, he would lose all his lands in England. It was enough to persuade him to back off for the time being.

This resistance to the pressure that Philip applied was initially the standard reaction throughout most of Richard's territories in France. Only Aquitaine, predictably enough, proved troublesome and rebellion subsequently broke out there. However even here Richard's seneschal, Élie de la Celle, succeeded in seizing the initiative and dampened down the flames of revolt.

Count Raymond of Toulouse was behind the trouble in the south alongside Philip but now the alliance with Navarre, sealed by Richard's marriage to Berengaria, proved its worth. Her brother, Sancho of Navarre (Sancho El Fuerte, 'The Strong'), brought up a force to help the seneschal and that was enough to swing the balance; some chroniclers asserted that Richard and Sancho enjoyed a kind of chivalric 'brotherhood' and if so it was certainly paying dividends now. This was proof of Richard's underrated political skills and acumen which, if we are to believe some critics, never actually existed. It is true that excessive pride sometimes undermined these attributes but to say that he lacked political awareness is a statement that simply does not stand up to scrutiny.

Henry VI had serious problems of his own to contend with. Germany back then was a state divided into smaller principalities. Henry's authoritarian rule – he had been accused of being directly involved in the murder of Albert of Brabant, a prince of one of these principalities – had led to rebellion in several places. There were rumours that there were plots abroad to replace him. Henry needed something to boost his fortunes and the capture of Richard gave him the perfect opportunity.

When he heard that Leopold (who was Henry's cousin) had Richard in his hands, the emperor ordered that he bring him to his court at Regensburg, for the duke was his liegeman. Despite their family connections, Leopold and Henry were not on good terms. Leopold would certainly not be handing Richard over free and gratis and was determined to drive a hard bargain. When he and his retainer Meinhard of Görz arrived before Henry with their prisoner on 6 January 1193, it was not long before they were returning to Austria with him as they feared that the emperor was prepared to forcibly take Richard from them. Leopold knew how valuable a prisoner he had – how could he not? – and he would not be pushed into handing him over until the price was right.

Contemporary illustrations show Richard lying prostrate at the feet of the emperor in a scene of abject humiliation.[13] It was the first time that the rulers of Germany and England had met in recorded history. Given the nature of this meeting, it is perhaps not surprising that it was another 150 years until the leaders of these countries met again when Edward III visited Germany in 1338.[14]

There was understandable shock when the news of Richard's capture was received in England. Walter, archbishop of Rouen, wrote to Hugh de Puiset, bishop of Durham, when he first heard of it in terms that suggested that even he, who understood that God worked in mysterious ways, was completely baffled as to why this had been allowed to happen to such a loyal crusader. He enclosed a copy of Henry's letter to Philip of France but reminded Hugh that 'there is need not of your tears but of your promptness'. Hugh and others were summoned to a meeting in Oxford to decide what to do next.

By this time, Savaric de Bohun, the bishop of Bath, was already in Germany negotiating with the emperor (who was also his cousin: family inter-relationships in European politics were common at the time). Walter took a strong lead in dealing with the situation but Hugh also reacted vigorously to this alarming turn of events.[15] In the meantime, Berengaria and Joanna stayed put in Rome, not wanting to travel in case they too should be taken hostage. Hubert Walter, one of Richard's closest confidants, had been in Sicily when he heard the news and at once made his way to Rome to consult with the Pope as to what should be done. William of Newburgh says that Hubert then proceeded north towards the lands of the emperor to see if he could obtain more information.

Apart from a small reference, Berengaria played little part in the story of Richard's ransom (Henry's clerks did not call it a 'ransom' in their correspondence; Pope Innocent III was the first to call it such a few years later and by then Henry was dead).[16] One legend that did surface told how Berengaria had been shopping in a market in Rome when she saw a jewelled belt for sale and realised at once that it belonged to her husband. That told her that something was seriously amiss.[17]

Once more, we enter the realms of legend. Richard had a minstrel, a man who loved him and was his loyal and devoted servant. Richard, who loved music, had spent many hours with this man, Blondel le Nesle. There was one song that they had composed together which was unknown by anyone else. Blondel hit on an idea by which he hoped to find out where Richard was incarcerated, as for a time no one knew where he was.

Blondel wandered across Europe. Each time he stood outside the gates of a castle he would sing this song and stop at the end of the verse, waiting for Richard's voice to be heard singing the refrain. Time after time he was disappointed. Then at last he came to Dürnstein. He sang the verse and waited with baited breath for a reply. And now, to his great and total joy, he heard Richard's response. The king had been found, though even if the story is true it did little good in helping to obtain Richard's release. As one of Richard's biographers has said, 'there is not a shred of evidence to indicate that there was any truth in the story – but it was good publicity for minstrels'.[18]

There is good evidence that Richard did indeed have a great love of music though. Several troubadour songs have been attributed to him. This betrayed his origins in several ways. Aquitaine was a region famed for its love of music and indeed many other arts. Richard was directly descended from a famous troubadour, William IX, duke of Aquitaine. It was perhaps appropriate that the duke was a crusader who had written some of his most affecting poetry whilst he was a captive; Richard surely would have empathised.

The story of Blondel is an intriguing one but is first mentioned in the works of the so-called 'Minstrel of Rheims' in about 1260. This reverses the normal storyline and has Richard singing the song first when he catches sight of Blondel through an arrow-slit. The 'Minstrel's' account is not the most reliable of historical sources – it also includes a highly improbable story of Eleanor of Aquitaine having an affair with Saladin – but the story stuck and is now solidly accreted to the veneer of legend that has been overlaid on Richard's story.[19] It is certainly true that there was a contemporary *trouvère* called Blondel de Nesle as some of his works survive.

In the meantime, John managed to make his way to France. In Paris, he did homage to Philip for Normandy. He also promised to marry Alice, who was still in English hands; the longest running soap opera of twelfth-century marriage politics was restarted as a result. The fact that John was already married did not seem to be regarded as an insuperable obstacle. The Vexin and Gisors would be handed back to Philip as part of the deal. It was even said in England that John was prepared to hand over that country to Philip too.

John returned to England and the castles at Windsor and Wallingford were surrendered to him. He then moved to London where he met with Walter, archbishop of Rouen, and others and tried to convince them that Richard was dead. But they refused to believe this untruth. John's attempted coup failed because those in power in England had too much loyalty to be won over. Frustrated in his planned power-grab, John left and set to the task of fortifying his castles and preparing for war.

Soon England was rife with stories that Philip was preparing an invasion fleet. John also started negotiations with King William of Scotland looking for his help. William, to his honour – and there was precious little of that quality being shown in certain other places at the time – refused to have anything to do with such duplicity, remembering the favourable terms that Richard had given him before he had set out on crusade.

John had overstepped the mark and seriously underestimated both Richard's loyal supporters and, not for the first time, his mother. When John spread rumours that Richard was dead, it was realised with alarm that he was now scheming to take the throne for himself; a story that later legends of that semi-mythical outlaw known as Robin Hood mined to the full and which has led to Richard having many a walk-on part in a succession of Hollywood movies on the subject.[20]

Eleanor and the justiciars of England threw their energies into preparing coastal defences against a possible invasion by French or Flemish forces. They were active in other ways too: Ralph of Diceto noted that 'Queen Eleanor, the king's mother, and Walter of Coutances and other barons did their utmost to conserve the peace of the kingdom, seeking to join together hearts which were permanently at loggerheads'.[21]

The fact that negotiations with Henry VI for Richard's release had already started made a nonsense of John's claim that Richard was dead. Walter of Coutances held his meeting of the council at Oxford in February 1193 to discuss the next steps that should be taken. It was decided that two Cistercians would be sent to Germany to clarify the situation. They met with early success, coming across Richard in the town of Ochsenfurt near Würzburg. They were even able to meet him and update him on affairs back in his kingdom. He was distressed to hear of John's treachery after he had made such generous grants to him before setting off on crusade. But then he calmed himself and noted that 'my brother John is not the man to subjugate a country, if there is a person able to make the slightest resistance to his attempts'.[22]

It was a harsh comment perhaps (though much worse could have been expected given John's treason) but essentially an accurate one. John's military record was far from stellar. He had been outclassed by Richard when he tried to take him on before Henry II's death. Military successes would be few and far between for John.

The two abbots accompanied Richard on his next step to Speyer. This was one of the most important places in the Hohenstaufen territories and had served as the royal mausoleum for recent generations of the dynasty. Here Richard was to suffer the indignity of a show trial. This was intended to give the emperor legitimacy. The charges were that Richard had betrayed the Holy Land, that he had been responsible for the death of Conrad of Montferrat and that he had broken agreements with Henry.

This was even though that letter had now allegedly been received from Sinān which said that Conrad had been eliminated because he had killed one of his envoys and that Richard had nothing to do with the act.[23] The thought that such a shadowy figure might actually bother to write this letter, and that it so helpfully exonerated Richard of all involvement in the killing, makes it hard to believe that it was not a forgery crafted to help Richard's cause.

Richard defended himself stoutly and won many of the court over. Even Henry was moved; he dropped the charges and instead gave Richard the kiss of peace. He said he would patch up the differences between Philip and Richard, though of course this would come at a cost; the fee for providing his good offices was in fact a ransom in disguise. In response Philip sent ambassadors making it clear that as far as he was concerned there could not be any reconciliation between him and Richard.

Richard's public performances whilst a captive in Germany were in some ways his finest hour. Here, with no possibility of freedom except on the emperor's terms, Richard defiantly fought his corner. Even his natural enemies were impressed. William the Breton, who took the part of Philip of France, wrote of him that 'when Richard replied, he spoke so eloquently and regally, in so lionhearted a manner, that it was as though he had forgotten where he was and the undignified circumstances in which he had been captured, and imagined himself to be seated on the throne of his ancestors at Lincoln or at Caen'.[24] Not just on the battlefield was Richard a Lionheart in the eyes of his opponents.

The 'ransom' to be paid, 100,000 marks, would place a great strain on the resources of Richard's lands (the emperor had agreed to pay 50,000 to obtain Richard from Duke Leopold so was making a handsome profit).[25] News of the demands was taken back to England after Easter. Richard sent his loyal servant, Hubert Walter, bishop of Salisbury, as his right-hand man to take a lead role in raising these funds; he was accompanied back to England by William, the bishop of London. Hubert had already proved himself during the Siege of Acre and now was the time for his reward. The archbishopric of Canterbury had been vacant since the death of Baldwin of Forde during the crusade and Richard wished Hubert to fill his vacant see. Several other appointments were also made, including making Henry Marshal the bishop of Exeter.

Hubert had journeyed to Germany where he had campaigned assiduously on Richard's behalf. Now he would return to England along with the two Cistercian abbots with orders to send hostages and assemble a flotilla to bring Richard back. But Henry, as devious a man as was Philip, had no intention of letting Richard go until he had extracted maximum advantage from him. He was sent to the castle of Trifels where he would be isolated from events; the popularity he had won during the recent trial possibly unnerved Henry, who was a man with many enemies.

Trifels was one of the most impregnable of the emperor's fortresses.[26] It was in such a formidable position that the Crown Jewels of the Empire were kept here. It was also a place where political prisoners were often held as escape was deemed to be impossible. Well though Richard had performed at Speyer, and friendly as Henry had seemed to be there, clearly the emperor had had a change of heart.

Fortunately, Richard still had loyal friends to support him. One of them was William Longchamp, who had been forced out of England but was still officially Richard's chancellor. Longchamp had already tried to return to England after receiving the support of the Pope but had been unable to get past Dover and had subsequently returned to mainland Europe. He persuaded Henry to allow Richard to return to his court. He also struck a deal with the emperor that Richard should be released once 70,000 marks had been handed over with hostages delivered until the rest was paid.[27]

Then, despite his recent difficulties there, Richard sent Longchamp back to England with orders that the money should be raised as quickly as possible; Roger of Howden's strongly expressed desire that Longchamp should be removed from all public office was clearly falling on deaf ears; Richard needed a proven tax-collector more than anything now. It must have been with some irony, not to say irritation, that Richard's supporters in England had shortly before received a letter in which the king had described Longchamp as 'our most dearly beloved chancellor'.[28] Richard also suggested that the great men of the kingdom should set an example by making generous contributions towards the funds needed to release him; with the hint of a threat he said that he wished to know how much each of them gave so that he could thank them appropriately later.

The council in England energetically set about the task of raising the required money as quickly as possible. A tax on income and moveable goods of 25 per cent was levied. The wool crop from the Cistercian monasteries in the country was appropriated and silver and gold plate taken from churches;[29] no doubt Richard's stated intention that the money owing for this would be repaid later was treated with a generous pinch of salt. Clerics paid over 10 per cent of their tithes. The urgency of Richard's release was accentuated by the fact that conflict had started in several parts of Richard's lands, fuelled by Philip and John.

Henry also sent a letter to England, one with a breath-taking whiff of hypocrisy. He wrote of 'our most dearly beloved friend your lord Richard'. He told the recipients of the letter that he would not take kindly to anyone who sought to take advantage of Richard's enforced absence by attempting to advance their own interests at the expense of his. Longchamp made his way back to England and St Albans, where he met up with Eleanor, Walter of Coutances and other leading officials.

It was a difficult encounter. Longchamp, conscious that some of those present loathed him, explained that he was not there in an official capacity but as a stranger, merely a messenger for the king. It was time to bury differences before the greater interests of the realm. He encouraged some of the leading men of England to accompany him on a mission to Henry's court; these included the bishops of Rochester and Chichester (places that according to Richard of Devizes 'are mere villages and they possess nothing for which they should be called cities but the sees of their bishops'),[30] Benedict, the abbot of Burgh, Richard, earl of Clare, Earl Roger Bigod and several others.

Money needed to be raised, and quickly. It should be passed through the hands of Hubert Walter who would be responsible for looking after it along with others such as Eleanor, the bishop of London, the earls of Arundel and Warenne and the mayor of London. All business connected to the ransom was to take place under the seal of Walter of Coutances and the funds raised were to be stored in the crypt of St Paul's Cathedral. It was essentially to be looked after by a committee with checks and balances built in; however much he thought he knew these men Richard was playing safe and after what had happened in his absence, who could blame him? Money was also raised from Richard's continental territories and in fact it was said that more was raised from Caen than from London.[31]

In the meantime, that background trinity of women, Berengaria, Joanna and the Damsel of Cyprus, had returned from Rome. They had been escorted to Genoa via Pisa and then took ship for Marseille, then in the territories of the king of Aragon rather than France. From here they passed through the county of Toulouse and finally arrived in Poitou. Berengaria then threw herself into the business of collecting the ransom for her husband.

Soon after, Hubert Walter was formally installed as archbishop of Canterbury. Although the monks duly elected him as required, it was not without some opposition. Hubert, archdeacon at Canterbury, appealed to the Pope against the installation saying that it was invalid as the king was out of the country and so were some of the bishops of England who should have been present. It was an appeal on a technicality and it fell on deaf ears. In fact, from this moment on, the power of the archbishop grew from strength to strength.

What made Hubert Walter indispensable to Richard was his superb organisational skill. He was not the most academically brilliant of Richard's bishops, neither was he the most pious. With respect to the latter, he was not of the same stamp, for example, as Bishop Hugh of Lincoln who was renowned for his saintliness. But he knew the law back to front and led men with a sure touch. If Richard's appointment of Longchamp as chancellor was a major misjudgement, making Hubert Walter archbishop of Canterbury would turn out to be a masterstroke.

But in England, civil war now seemed imminent. John had attempted to take power and had raised men to seize it by force if necessary. However, as Richard had accurately predicted, it was unlikely that he would succeed if even a few resisted him. In reality, there were more than a few willing to do so. John's men soon found themselves besieged in the castles of Windsor and Tickhill.

During the manoeuvres to take the latter, Geoffrey, archbishop of York, fought hard on behalf of Richard.

After their earlier disagreements, Geoffrey had been somewhat restored to Richard's good books though the relationship between the two men always remained volatile. He was given a key role in raising Richard's ransom. But Geoffrey remained bitterly at odds with many church officials at York. They locked the door by which the archbishop entered the great church from his palace and suspended services in the building as well as stopping the ringing of the bells, to the great consternation of the people. They also stripped the altars of their sacred objects.

So the tension between Geoffrey and many of his key officials at York remained high.[32] The latter sent a delegation to Pope Celestine, requesting Geoffrey's removal and saying that he was more interested in hawking, hunting and military matters than religion; this may have been true but he was not the only ecclesiastical figure in this period of history who could be so accused. When Geoffrey failed to attend a hearing in Rome to which he was summoned he was suspended from his duties as archbishop. This was the backdrop to the tangled political landscape in England which served to complicate Richard's release still further.

But the situation was complicated. For example, Hugh Bardolf, one of Richard's sheriffs, was prepared to help defend Doncaster against John's forces but was unwilling to attack Tickhill as he was a vassal of John's. Bardolf had started out on crusade with Richard but had turned back at Messina. Now his unwillingness to attack John led to accusations of treason being directed at him. England was a divided country.

The situation had been calmed to some extent when Hubert Walter arrived back in England. He suggested that a truce be called for a six-month period. John was allowed to keep the castles of Tickhill and Nottingham but would hand over Windsor and the Peak into the safekeeping of his mother. Hugh de Puiset, the bishop of Durham, was most upset at this as he was besieging Tickhill at the time and felt that he was about to capture it. John was probably happy to accept these terms given the very limited progress he had made so far and the strength of the opposition to him. But as time went by and Richard had still not been released from captivity, some in England began to despair of his return to England. Perhaps John was right after all and, if not dead, King Richard would never come back to reclaim his country.[33]

This was the backdrop to the negotiations for Richard's release and as the weeks and the months passed the possibilities of his ever being released appeared to become more rather than less remote. Before long, the people of England despaired of ever seeing their king again. The emperor was making the most of his windfall. And John was there waiting to strike once more as soon as the time seemed right.

16

The Long Road to Freedom (1193–1194)

'Look to yourself; the devil is loose'
King Philip of France to Prince John of England on hearing of the imminent release of Richard I

The terms of the ransom were revised shortly after the feast of the Nativity of St John the Baptist (24 June) at Worms. It would cost Richard a great deal. There was a good deal of to-ing and fro-ing whilst terms were hammered out. It would cost 100,000 marks of pure silver ('Cologne weight' it was noted) though some of this was to be dressed up as a dowry for the marriage of Richard's niece, Eleanor of Brittany, to one of Leopold's sons; marriage politics were again to the fore and she was to be delivered within seven months of Richard's release. Richard was to provide both galleys and men with which to help Henry retake Sicily. He should also hand over 200 hostages to the emperor, of which fifty would be passed on to Leopold.

Richard had some important prisoners of his own to bargain with. These included Isaac Comnenus, taken captive in Cyprus. He was related to Leopold and therefore he became part of the ransom package along with his beloved daughter. He was later released; not long after, he was involved in a plot to seize the Imperial Throne in Constantinople. The Byzantine Empire was by this stage on the verge of meltdown, ruled by a succession of weak and ineffective emperors. But Isaac's plotting came to nothing for he died sometime in 1195 or 1196, with his death commonly attributed to poison.

His unnamed daughter still had a part to play in the affairs of Western Europe. Some chroniclers hint that in earlier times, not long after he had married Berengaria, Richard himself may have had designs on her even though according to some accounts she was very young at the time.[1] A few years after her release she found herself at the court of Count Raymond VI of Toulouse. Here she met Richard's sister Joanna, by then married to the count and heavily pregnant with his son and heir. It was not long before Joanna found herself replaced by none other than the so-called 'Damsel of Cyprus'.

But her relationship with the count – it was probably not dignified with a marriage ceremony – came to an end in 1202 and she then married Thierry, count of Flanders. Together they tried to retake Cyprus but failed and ended up fleeing to Anatolia. Though these three women, Joanna, Berengaria and the unnamed 'Damsel of Cyprus' remained largely background figures, what remarkable lives they seem to have led and what events they witnessed.

There were some important conditions attached to the ransom. Whilst it remained outside of the empire, the money raised was to be carried at Richard's risk, so that if it were lost or stolen he would have to replace it. But as soon as it reached the emperor's territories it was to be the responsibility of the emperor to look after it and the risk passed to him; crucial details given the instability of the times.

There were problems in raising the ransom. This was unsurprising; many of Richard's subjects had already paid heavily to finance the crusade, both in his reign and that of his late father. There were attempts to evade payment and suggestions that in some cases tax collectors had run off with the money that they had raised. John too still had supporters and was doing his best to divert money raised to his own pockets. Even the clergy were resisting attempts to extract further taxes from them. The clock was ticking and much remained to be done.[2]

There was no doubt that England was hurting. Peter of Blois wrote a letter in which he complained of the actions of the Germans, saying that 'those children of perdition were levying a treasure that would not be drawn from the royal exchequer, but from the patrimony of Christ, the pitiful substance of the poor, the tears of widows, the pittance of monks and nuns, the dowries of maidens, the substance of scholars, the spoils of the Church'.[3] Though most scholars believe that the legends of Robin Hood belong to a slightly later period, it is unsurprising that they have found a home in this particular time, when England was struggling desperately to raise unprecedented sums of money.[4] Outlawry also had a negative effect on Richard's ransom; Hugh, the bishop of Chester, was robbed by thieves near Canterbury one night, even before he left the country.[5]

Eleanor was given responsibility for organising the hostages. A council meeting at Ely discussed the composition of the list of those to be sent. It was a high-powered one, including Otto, Richard's favourite nephew, William Longchamp, Walter of Coutances, Savaric, bishop of Bath and Baldwin of Béthune (Longchamp's place was eventually taken by Baldwin Wake). Some of those great men of the realm who were required to send their young sons were distinctly unhappy at the thought of putting them under the care of Longchamp given his reputation as a pederast and said that they would feel more comfortable trusting their young daughters with him instead.[6]

Whilst he was still in captivity, Richard received a letter from the Doge of Venice, Enrico Dandolo, a larger than life figure, virtually blind and nearly eighty, who would nevertheless play the leading role when the Fourth Crusade attacked, took and sacked Constantinople in 1204 in one of the most controversial moments in all crusader history. It contained stunning news: Saladin was dead, having expired at the start of Lent. Even now his empire was falling apart, with two brothers contending the succession, one in Damascus and the other in Egypt.[7] Although he did not say as much, perhaps this was a hint that the time for another crusade was ripe. If this was the intention, this must have caused a wry smile from Richard given his incapacity to go anywhere at this precise moment.

There was much worse news for Richard from France, where Philip had succeeded in forcing the crucial border fortress of Gisors to surrender. It had been handed over without a fight, for which its constable Gilbert de Vascoeuil was widely castigated. He had been sent back by Richard from Messina specifically to protect his interests in Normandy, journeying in the company of Eleanor of Aquitaine and Walter of Coutances.[8] Other frontier lords, who held land both from Richard and from Philip, also capitulated.

This left the road to Rouen itself open and Philip duly marched up it. But the defenders of the city were made of sterner stuff than some of the other Norman lords. Led by Robert, earl of Leicester, a crusading companion of Richard's, they stoutly held out. They opened the gates of the city, offering Philip free access, but this was, as Philip realised quickly, a trap.

Philip had demanded the return of Alice to his custody by the citizens. Robert said that he was welcome to come and see her, provided that he entered the city alone and unarmed. Despite having assembled a formidable array of siege engines, Philip decided to retreat, setting fire to them before he left; perhaps his troops were more upset when he emptied his wine casks instead of leaving them behind. He then moved on to take other border castles in Normandy at Ivry and Pacy.

We have a remarkable insight into Richard's plight through his own words. Richard wrote a song, dedicated to his half-sister Marie, the countess of Champagne, which has survived and gives us a deep insight into the sense of betrayal that he felt, accompanied by not a little gloom as the days passed and his freedom seemed to never draw closer.

Included in those words were the following lines:

> No marvel is it that my heart is sore
> While my lord tramples down my lands, I trow;
> Were he but mindful of the oath we swore
> Each to the other, surely do I know
> That thus in duress I should long ago
> Have ceased to languish here.
>
> My comrades whom I loved and still do love
> The lords of Perche and of Caieux
> Strange tales have reached me that are hard to prove;
> I ne'er was false to them; for evermore
> Vile men would count them, if their arms they bore
> 'Gainst me, a prisoner here!
>
> And they, my knights of Anjou and Touraine
> Well know they, who now sit at home at ease,
> That I, their lord, in far-off Allemaine
> Am captive. They should help to my release;
> But now their swords are sheathed, and rust in peace,
> While I am prisoner here.[9]

The sense of betrayal felt by Richard comes down loud and clear across the centuries. The most remarkable thing perhaps is the person who is not mentioned in the song; John. It was as if his treachery was expected and, whilst Richard was disappointed, he was hardly surprised. But Richard's betrayal by Philip cut him to the quick. So too did his abandonment by some of his men in France. As time passed, the sense of outrage inside Richard festered like a sore. He had plenty of time to plan his revenge during these days. These times spent as a prisoner, brooding in captivity far from home, would shape the course of the rest of Richard's life.

There are also suggestions from William of Newburgh that Richard was not well treated at all stages of his captivity. William wrote that the king himself had said that he was at first dealt with with respect but after the arrival of Philip, bishop of Beauvais, who was acting on behalf of the French king, his position grew far worse. He was loaded down with chains so heavy that a horse or donkey would have struggled to move them.

Peter of Blois reported that he was not well fed and looked pale and weak. This happened whilst he was a captive at Trifels though his position improved when he was moved to Hagenau.[10] If this harsh treatment was a direct result of the bishop of Beauvais, then Richard would have a glorious chance for revenge a few years later when he took him prisoner in France. He would not pass up on the opportunity.

Richard had many other difficult moments to contend with. At one stage Philip planned a meeting with Henry, and Richard greatly feared that this would lead to a worsening of his situation. Henry was a man without scruples, motivated solely by his own best interests. If he felt these were best served by keeping Richard a prisoner and throwing his lot in with the king of France, he would surely not hesitate to do so. Fortunately for Richard, the planned meeting never took place.

The emperor has been described as 'pallid, intellectual, coldly inhuman and intensely ambitious'.[11] In Sicily – which he would later conquer – his name became a byword for viciousness and cruelty. Renowned as a superb chess player, Henry was playing the game of his life. His actions throughout this period were devious and manipulative, symptomatic of a calculating brain unrestricted by any moral limitations. If Richard was a man of fire, Henry was one of ice.

Henry's ambitions reflected those of the Hohenstaufen dynasty of which he was a part. Earlier in the century, John of Salisbury had argued strongly for an alliance between England and France against the aggressive imperialism of the Hohenstaufens, asking 'who made the Germans judges over the people of Christ?'.[12] It was Richard's bad luck to find himself as a helpless pawn on the chessboard of European power politics. However, he would play a masterful role in making use of the limited advantages that he had in this situation.

During his time in Germany, Richard played an important part in reconciling Henry VI to some of those who were rebelling against the emperor. This was most likely an attempt to make himself useful as Philip was doing all that he could to prevent Richard's release and possibly even hoped that he would be handed into French custody.

However, Richard's position remained desperate. Henry, sensing that there might be yet more money to be had, upped the ransom payment to 150,000 marks. Pressure was also put to bear to accelerate the delivery of Eleanor of Brittany so that she could be married off to Duke Leopold's son as soon as possible. However, the conditions regarding the provision of military forces to help in the conquest of Sicily were quietly dropped.

Philip sensed that the end-game was approaching. His actions had incurred the wrath of Pope Celestine who had threatened him and his kingdom with severe spiritual sanctions if he did not desist from 'persecuting the king of England'. The emperor had been similarly threatened.[13] Celestine had been under huge pressure. Eleanor of Aquitaine had been unhappy with what she saw as Celestine's inactivity in his efforts to release Richard and had written to him to say so. After all, her son was a crusader who was supposed to have the protection of the Church whilst he was away. Eleanor clearly did not think much of the Church's definition of protection.

The first paragraph of her letter to Celestine ends in terms that make clear what is likely to come next when the writer (who may have been Peter of Blois, Eleanor's secretary, though it seems inconceivable that he would have written it without her knowledge or approval) entreats Celestine 'to show himself to be a father of mercy to a pitiful mother'. She told how 'I am defiled with torment, my flesh is wasted away, and my bones cleave to my skin. My years pass away full of groans, and I wish they were altogether passed away'.

This extraordinary letter carries on in the same vein but turns from self-pity to anger. Eleanor was livid with the actions of John, who was adding 'grief upon grief'. She wanted more than anything else to leave England and go and help Richard but she did not dare to exit the country in case still worse disasters followed in her absence. Henry was 'an impious, cruel and dreadful tyrant'. It rested with the Pope to right these wrongs for 'the Cross of Christ exceeds the eagles of Caesar'.

The letter writer, whether her secretary's words or Eleanor's herself, was clearly warming up and the Pope was the next target. Bluntly the writer asked 'why then do you so long negligently, nay cruelly, delay to free my son, or is it rather that you do not dare? Perhaps you will say that this power is given to you over souls, not bodies: so be it. I will certainly be satisfied if you bind the souls of those who keep my son bound in prison'.

This long letter continues in words that make it clear that Eleanor was as furious with the Pope as she was with anybody else. She wrote, 'alas for us when the chief shepherd has become a mercenary, when he flies from the face of the wolf, when he abandons in the jaws of the bloodthirsty beast the lamb put in his care, or even the chosen ram, the leader of the Lord's flock'. Three times the Pope had promised to send legates and not once had he done so; Eleanor wondered how different this might have been if the king had been free and rich with much wealth to offer the Church.

Now the sentiments being expressed were truly remarkable: she urged Celestine to save his own soul for he would be answerable for his inaction at the Last Judgement. She accused him of making false promises to her and 'mocking the faith of the innocent'. Henry and Philip were destroying her son and at the same time demolishing the credibility of the Church. Eleanor felt that a bitter denouement was coming, though not from any earthly power:

> I declare to you that the time of dissension foretold by the Apostle is at hand, when the son of eternal damnation shall be revealed. The fateful moment is at hand when the seamless tunic of Christ shall be rent again, when the net of Peter shall be broken, and the solid unity of the Catholic Church dissolved. These are the beginnings of sorrows. We feel bad things, we fear worse.[14]

It was an amazing diatribe, insinuating the eternal damnation of Celestine's soul and the destruction of the Catholic Church as it did. It was safe to say that the Pope was probably not used to being spoken to in this fashion. Yet it seems to have done the trick partly because the Church was in a morally indefensible position when a crusader of Richard's stature had been falsely imprisoned whilst returning from his efforts in the Holy Land.

Other letters followed with a similar message.[15] The eighty-seven-year-old Pope was worn down by the frank-speaking and consistent pressure emanating from Eleanor and in time the threat of excommunication was at last raised against Richard's jailors, though much later than Eleanor had wanted. In the event, when Celestine started to act with more proactivity and threatened an interdict against the people of England if they resisted attempts to raise Richard's ransom money, Eleanor wrote a conciliatory letter to him, regretting her previous intemperate language. These apologies should perhaps be taken with a pinch of salt; her earlier messages with their harsh language had done the trick, now it was time for more diplomatic approaches to be employed.[16]

The emperor decided that it was time to begin to draw matters to a close; from now onwards there were only diminishing returns in prospect. Henry had extracted great financial benefit from the negotiations and had managed to force the price upwards through fear of an alternative offer from Philip. He was under pressure from the Church for his imprisonment of Richard and even his own people may have doubted the morality of his actions for on many of these significant events their chroniclers are silent, as if somewhat embarrassed. Even Rigord, who was supportive of Philip, conceded that Richard's imprisonment was unjust.[17]

Richard was already seeing some improvement in his situation, evidenced by the charters that he managed to approve even whilst in captivity during the second half of 1193. Henry for his part saw benefits in having Richard as a future ally and a counterbalance to the French king, whose lands bordered his own. It was now that Philip penned his famous lines to John: 'look to yourself; the devil is loose'. The response from John was that of a man who was with good reason terrified and he took himself out of England and made his way to Normandy.

But it would still be some time yet before Richard was free. No doubt Richard longed for revenge but was not able to do anything about it just yet. That would have to wait for another day. Instead, he swallowed his pride and his agents began negotiations with Philip to patch up matters in France. They were led once more by William Longchamp who still clearly held the king's trust, however disastrous his actions in England had been. With him were William des Roches, an Angevin knight who had once been a diehard supporter of Henry II, in which capacity he had joined the fight against Richard led by William Marshal. Des Roches had since become a loyal adherent to Richard's cause and had accompanied him throughout his recent crusade.

A treaty made at Mantes on 9 July 1193 allowed Philip to keep all the gains that he had made in Richard's absence, no doubt to the chagrin of the English king, who was in a very weak negotiating position. Philip's ally John was not forgotten either; his lands were to be restored to him in full. Richard was also to pay 20,000 marks of silver, 'good and pure, Troy weight' to Philip in instalments. In the meantime, the castles of Loches, Châtillon-sur-Indre, Drincourt and Arques were to be handed over as security.[18]

Probably no one was fooled by this treaty. As soon as Richard was free, it was highly likely that he would do his utmost to recover the lands that had been snatched away from him. But Philip had a trump card to play. He was still a widower and now decided to enter an alliance with Cnut VI, the king of Denmark, by marrying his sister Ingeborg. The Danish king was a distant descendant of Cnut the Great and could therefore claim a very watered-down right to the throne of England, a useful subsidiary point in his favour and one that Philip sought to exploit in the marriage negotiations according to William of Newburgh.[19] The scene was set for a story that has been described as 'one of the saddest in the history of medieval queenship'.[20]

The marriage turned out to be extraordinary for bizarre reasons. In a turn of events that would have done that famous Bluebeard Henry VIII proud, when Philip got out of bed on the morning after his wedding night, he seems to have decided that he had had enough of his new bride already.[21] There were subsequently disputes about whether the marriage was consummated; Philip said it had not been, Ingeborg said that it had; Roger of Howden seems to have adopted the view argued by the queen.[22] Philip eventually declared the marriage invalid as he said he had found evidence that they were too closely related, an argument that certainly did not convince the Pope.

Various reasons were put about for why the king found Ingeborg so repugnant; according to William of Newburgh these included the suggestion that she had bad breath, that she had some secret infirmity that was presumably revealed in the bridal chamber or that she was not a virgin when she came to Philip's bed.[23] Philip's attempts to send Ingeborg back to Denmark failed and she took herself off to a convent in Soissons, from where she protested to Pope Celestine III. He was sympathetic to her predicament but was unable to force Philip to take her back. Philip would later marry a German heiress by the name of Agnes of Merania, the marriage taking place in 1196.

That was far from the end of the story. Pope Innocent III – a formidable figure in the annals of papal history – subsequently conceded that the children born from this later match should be treated as legitimate but refused nevertheless to annul the marriage to Ingeborg even when Philip sought a cancellation of it on the extraordinary grounds of witchcraft.

Ingeborg continued to be a thorn in Philip's flesh and would considerably outlive him. She suffered much. Finally, in 1213 – twelve years after the death of Agnes – Philip gave in to pressure and took Ingeborg back, though with no visible sign of a change in attitude regarding his animosity towards her. It is an indication of Ingeborg's long-suffering nature that she insisted after Philip's death in 1223 in instituting memorial Masses for him.[24]

Richard was now allowed to hold court and received visitors from England and elsewhere. He could go out hunting and enjoyed local wines in the evening and had even asked for his falcons to be sent over from England.[25] There was a steady flow of correspondence and messengers to and from his lands. But whilst he was still inside the emperor's territories and unable to leave he could not of course regard himself as free.

The emperor's envoys visited England in October 1193 and took possession of 100,000 marks, two-thirds of the required ransom. Eleanor was instructed by Richard to journey to Speyer with the remainder of the money and the required hostages. In December 1193, Henry VI fixed the following 17 January as the day on which Richard would be released.

Henry planned to make Richard the ruler of Provence, which would strengthen the English king's position in France. John was in Normandy, finding that few there wanted to hand over their castles to him even though Richard ordered them to do so in an attempt to patch up relations with his errant brother. In a huff, John now offered to hand over a large chunk of territory in Normandy to Philip if he would help him in his efforts to gain a stronger foothold there.

The offer intrigued Philip enough for him to approach Henry VI with a last throw of the dice. He offered to pay £1,000 for each month that Richard continued to be held in captivity. Alternatively, he would pay 80,000 marks if Richard were retained until the autumn; the figure would go up to 150,000 marks if he would hand over the English king into his keeping. Philip and John's scheming carried on in the hope that Henry could still be tempted to change his mind over Richard's release. Henry showed a perturbing interest in this offer and Richard's release was delayed. Instead a meeting was convened at Mainz in February.

A high-powered delegation from England would be present. Eleanor, Walter of Coutances and other leading officials had crossed the North Sea in December 1193 and, no doubt to everyone's relief during this season of hostile weather, it was a straightforward voyage. Also with the party were Eleanor of Brittany and the Damsel of Cyprus. Hubert Walter had been appointed justiciar and would watch over England in their absence. They thought that they were there to simply hand over the remainder of the ransom and return with Richard.

They arrived at Cologne on 6 January 1194, the feast of the Epiphany. Richard was supposed to be released eleven days later, but Eleanor would not meet her son until 2 February. By this time the delegation had learned with alarm of the counter-offer made by Philip, and apparently supported by the treacherous John. But Richard now had other unexpected allies. He had courted the support of many German princes and nobles during his time in captivity and they were greatly angered at the dishonourable actions of the emperor and put pressure on him to respect the agreement he had made.

Richard was no doubt shocked and alarmed when the emperor showed him the letters that he had received from Philip and John. Roger of Howden says that when he read them he 'was very much disturbed and confused, and despaired of his liberation'.[26] It seemed as if his hopes had been raised only to be cruelly dashed. But the concerted action of men like the archbishops of Cologne and Salzburg and the bishops of Worms and Liege who were outraged by Henry's consideration of the approaches made to him at the eleventh hour by Richard's antagonists began to turn the tide.

By now Henry had probably already decided to let Richard go but he was a man who was determined to extract the last ounce of profit from the situation. It was resolved that Richard should do him homage for England, an extraordinary concession and one that was so sensitive that it seems that it was kept a secret from the English people.[27] Roger of Howden mentioned this event but apparently only added it to his account later, as he includes the comment that on his deathbed in 1197 Henry VI had released Richard from his homage so its impact was null and void.[28] Ralph of Diceto considered that the arrangement was scandalous and dishonourable and stated that 'the parties were absolved from the oath because it was extorted unlawfully'.[29]

This public scene, probably stage-managed, clinched the deal at last. The ransom and the hostages were delivered though many were reluctant to allow themselves or their sons to be handed over in this way. One of the first to refuse the 'honour' was Robert de Nonant, brother of the bishop of Coventry, who said that he would not be a hostage as he was a supporter of John rather than Richard. This only resulted in him being thrown into prison for his impudence and disloyalty.[30]

As part of the arrangement, Henry and Richard were now formally allied to each other. Richard had written back to England towards the end of the previous year that 'each of us is bound to aid the other against all living men in gaining his rights and in retaining possession of the same'.[31] Henry would certainly be prepared to call in the promise if and when he invaded the kingdom of Sicily and no doubt Richard would be happy to do the same in France as he attempted to restore his position there.

At 9 o'clock on the morning of 4 February 1194 Richard was handed over to his tearful mother; the devil was loosed at last. One of Richard's first acts was to write to Henry of Champagne telling him that he planned to return to Outremer as soon as possible; but he caveated this with the condition that he needed firstly to recover his lost position in his lands. This was a clear indication of where his priorities now lay.

Henry VI wrote to Philip and John, telling them that he would support Richard to the hilt if they did not hand back the lands taken from him. After all the prevarication, Henry had now firmly thrown in his lot with Richard. Richard had also managed to buy the support of several German princes. Philip, rather than returning lands to Richard, now sought to take more from him before he arrived back in France. He took several towns in Normandy including Evreux and Neubourg, turning John's theoretical surrender of them into a practical reality.

Richard, unable to do much about this state of affairs in the short-term, needed to get back to England so Henry duly gave him a safe conduct. There was a cynically hypocritical moment when Duke Leopold and Richard were publicly reconciled. Eleanor could not wait to get Richard away from Henry's clutches, motivated by complete contempt and distrust of him. In fact, it was even suggested that Henry soon after changed his mind and tried to recapture Richard but he was too late to do so.[32]

Richard's route back to England took him through Cologne where he heard Mass in the great cathedral: the archbishop, Adolf, was a good friend of Richard (and no ally of the emperor) and took as his text 'Now I know truly that the Lord has sent His angel and had rescued me from the hand of Herod'. Eleanor was presumably the angel and, given Adolf's past quarrels with him, the emperor was clearly Herod.

They travelled on to Louvain and then to Brussels. Richard was in no great hurry and it took him two weeks to make the journey from Cologne before finally reaching Antwerp, 'where the Rhine falls into the sea' as Roger of Howden put it. On the way, he took the time to build good relationships with several men in the region who were sympathetic to his cause, especially the archbishops of Mainz and Cologne and the duke of Brabant. He was forging alliances already against his principal enemy; not some Muslim leader in a distant land but a Christian king much nearer to home.

At Antwerp, he found a fleet from England that had been sent to collect him. He sailed down to Zwin, a harbour now on the Dutch-Belgian border which gave access to the great port of Bruges. Worried about his security with the threat of being attacked by French ships to concern him, he spent the day on board a galley but at night he went aboard a large ship that had been sent from England to protect him. It was not until 12 March that he at last set sail for England. The following day, he set foot on English soil again when he landed at Sandwich, initially to a quiet reception, perhaps because Richard wished to keep his return a secret as much as was possible to prevent any French ships from interfering with his safe passage across the Channel.

It was a bright, sunny morning, the Lord of the Sky signalling his approval of Richard's return. There were accounts of great joy at his arrival; though perhaps this was confused with relief.[33] Richard dutifully gave thanks at both Canterbury, where he visited the shrine of his father's nemesis Thomas Becket, and at Bury St Edmunds.

But there was not unconfined joy in all parts of England. It was said that when the constable of St Michael's Mount in Cornwall, Henry de la Pomeroy, a supporter of John, heard that Richard was back he promptly died of shock. Those in authority in England had already in the main disowned John before Richard's return and the bishops had excommunicated him.

The castles of Marlborough and Lancaster also surrendered quickly after declaring for John. All that John had gained for his efforts was a reputation for disloyalty, one which he would always struggle to throw off. He did have a few castles in Normandy that Philip had given him such as that at Arques, a formidable fortification dominating the surrounding area and even now an impressive ruin. John had little option but to seek his brother's forgiveness if he wished to regain his position.

John still had some supporters to fight his corner. One of them, a man named Adam, had been sent to London to try to protect his position. He was a boastful man and when he had dinner with Hubert Walter, the new archbishop of Canterbury, he could not resist telling him how friendly John was with the king of France. Shortly afterwards the said Adam was seized and incriminating documents from John were found on him. When this information was made public, it had the effect of solidifying support against Richard's brother as it was now clear that John was planning a coup.

Like John, Duke Leopold of Austria did not gain very much from his actions. For daring to imprison a crusader Leopold was excommunicated and ordered to repay the ransom money that he had received, though he refused to do so. He still had hostages which he kept pending the arrival of Eleanor of Brittany for her marriage to his son. When she did not arrive, he threatened to execute them.

Finally, Baldwin of Béthune set out with Eleanor and the daughter of Isaac Comnenus, the fallen king of Cyprus. But Pope Celestine had ordered the bishop of Verona to command Leopold to return all his hostages and make reparation for the wrongs that he had committed. Only then would the interdict against him and his lands be lifted; and even then, he would be required to journey to Outremer before he could be forgiven.[34]

In the meantime, Leopold's lands had suffered torments of almost biblical proportions. The Danube burst its banks and flooded, causing extensive damage and killing more than 10,000 people. The crops failed due to unusually hot weather. Fires broke out for no apparent reason and destroyed several towns. The corn was eaten up by a plague of worms. There was a sickness then that had a particularly strong impact on the leading men of the country.

Now further disaster was about to overtake Leopold. On 26 December 1194, Leopold was out riding when his horse fell, crushing his foot in the process. It was a serious injury – the shattered bones apparently protruded some way out of his leg – and within a day the foot had turned black. The only option was to amputate but no one had the courage to do it. In the end, Leopold held an axe to his foot and ordered a servant to drive it through with a mallet. The pain must have been excruciating and it was also in vain. The operation had been left too long and shortly afterwards Leopold died. To many it no doubt seemed just desserts for his treacherous actions.

As he was dying in agony, Leopold sought absolution. His bishops said that this was impossible, given his status as an excommunicate, unless he took steps to restore himself to the good graces of the Church. So Leopold gave orders that his hostages were to be released and that Richard was to be exempted from the money that remained from his ransom. His heir immediately tried to overturn these provisions but this resulted in Leopold's body lying unburied for eight days until the hostages were finally released. He was finally buried dressed in the habit of a Cistercian monk. The delegation with Baldwin of Béthune returned to France, its mission unfulfilled and with the prospective bride still in tow.

Records concerning Richard's ransom have not survived. However, the tally sticks that were used as an aid to the recording process did. They collected dust in the basement of the House of Commons for centuries. Then in 1834 it was decided that they had to go. They were thrown on a fire inside the building but it got out of control. Soon flames were eating up the fabric of the ancient building. Due to the catastrophe that followed, Parliament had to be rebuilt in its present form. Richard's ransom was still causing pain more than 600 years later.[35]

Richard pondered over his next move when he arrived home. England had survived the vicissitudes caused by his imprisonment remarkably well, though the cost had been immense. The same could not be said of his territories in France. Aquitaine had seen several attempts to take advantage of his incarceration but the major challenge had come from Normandy where some of his subjects had changed sides in his absence. Philip of France had seized the moment to increase his power there. Now Richard was free again, it was time for him to restore his flagging fortunes in France and to this aim he would first and foremost devote his energies. The crusades would have to wait their turn for the time being. Other priorities loomed.

17

The Return of the King (1194–1195)

'Then did the citizens, having heard of his approach, take up the oil of gladness instead of weeping'
William of Newburgh on the return of Richard to London

When Richard returned to England, two castles still held out for John. One of them, Tickhill, surrendered quickly but the other, at Nottingham, held out for longer. Those besieging it included Earl David, the brother of King William of Scotland. Richard announced his arrival at the scene with a great show, with trumpets blaring and a sizeable force, obviously wanting to terrify the garrison into a quick surrender. Several men standing close to Richard were struck by arrows launched from the castle battlements so he ordered his force to go onto the attack. He was predictably enough in the front rank and even killed a knight with a crossbow bolt;[1] Richard fancied himself as an expert with the weapon. The outer walls were taken before the sun went down.

At Richard's side was William Marshal, who had been at his castle at Chepstow on the Welsh borders when he heard of Richard's return. He had been careful not to antagonise John too much even during the difficult recent days; after all, he was probably the next king of England and he did not want to burn any bridges just in case. Only towards the end, when it had become clear that John's attempts to usurp power had failed, had Marshal declared for Richard.

But the news that Richard was back could not have come at a worse time from a personal perspective. Marshal had just heard that his elder brother had died and he would ordinarily attend the funeral as one of the chief mourners. But even he could not be in two places at once. He did his best to keep all parties happy. Men were sent to escort his brother's body and he went out to meet it and pay his respects. But when Richard urged him to hurry up and join him he had done so, missing out on the family funeral at Bradenstoke in Wiltshire.

As the sun rose again the following morning at Nottingham, two things could be seen from the castle walls. The first was the array of siege engines that had been brought up. The second sight was even more ominous, for Richard had ordered that gallows be erected. Soon after, several captured rebels were dangling from them. This was an unambiguous message; if the defenders continued to hold out against their rightful king then they could expect no mercy. It did the trick. Two envoys came out of the castle to the camp and returned with the message that it was certainly King Richard leading the assault. Before the day was out the garrison had surrendered unconditionally. Although most were allowed to live, a number would only be released on payment of a large ransom.

Richard visited nearby Sherwood Forest on 29 March which was a place that impressed him greatly according to Roger of Howden. Several administrative decisions were also taken in Nottingham where he stayed for a few days. Once more, the need to raise money was the driving force, in this instance by collecting extra taxes from sheriffs and in the case of Hugh Bardolf, who had been unenthusiastic in the recent campaigning, depriving him of his position. The latter move was more of a money-making measure than a sign of disapproval; Bardolf was not long after given the county of Northumberland. This caused friction with King William of Scotland who wanted it for himself but Richard refused to sell it to him without retaining the right to keep possession of the castles in the region. Other sums were raised from one-off measures similar to those that he had instituted in 1189–1190.

Richard then decided that he would undertake a ceremonial crown-wearing at Winchester with the date for this set as 17 April. This was a significant symbolic gesture. Richard would show himself to his people and remind them who was king (a similar ceremony had been performed when King Stephen had been released from captivity earlier in the century).[2] It was important to publicly reaffirm his right to rule. Ralph of Coggeshall suggests that he was not at all happy with the suggestion. It would take time to set up the arrangements and Richard was eager to get to France as quickly as possible.

Leaving Nottingham, Richard made his way to nearby Southwell, were he met King William of Scotland. Richard had good reason to be grateful for William's support whilst he was imprisoned. Indeed, William and Richard were to spend several weeks together and arrangements would later be made for William's daughter Margaret to marry Richard's nephew, Otto. The scheme would eventually fizzle out but was an innovative attempt to resolve frontier difficulties with Scotland, particularly over Northumberland, Cumbria, Westmoreland and the earldom of Lancaster which the Scottish king laid claim to.

But William did not go away empty handed. Every time he visited England in the future, he was to be met by the bishop of Durham and given safe conduct through his lands until he reached those of the archbishop of York. The archbishop would be required to do the same and hand him over to the protection of the next bishop whose lands he entered and so on until he eventually reached the English court, wherever it might be at the time. But what William really wanted, which above all seemed to be Northumbria, stayed elusively part of England.

William was to receive grants every time that he visited England, even when he reached the court. Here he was to receive gifts including a daily ration of four gallons of wine for his lords and another eight gallons (presumably of inferior quality) for everyone else with him, 2 lb of pepper, 4 lb of cinnamon and significant quantities of wax and candles.[3] The charter confirming these provisions was signed at Northampton. It was witnessed by William Longchamp, the king clearly stubbornly refusing to reduce his influence, however unpopular he was.

Inevitably the subject of what to do with John was a key problem. Some wanted to auction off his confiscated lands but Eleanor, perhaps motivated by a mother's love as much as by concerns of state, suggested that this would only make him an even firmer ally of Philip of France. It was therefore agreed that he should be summoned to England within forty days to explain himself. The bishop of Coventry, a key member of John's party, was commanded to appear before his fellow ecclesiastics to answer for his actions. Richard also ordered that a ransom of 10,000 marks be sent to Germany so that Walter of Coutances, who had been left as a hostage, could be freed. In a move that must have provoked controversy he also commanded that Longchamp should be restored as his chancellor.

From Nottingham, William and Richard made their way south to Winchester. In a splendid ceremony in the cathedral, Richard processed into the church wearing a crown preceded by William of Scotland and two earls carrying swords, having spent the night before in the priory of St Swithun (the place in which the chronicler Richard of Devizes was a monk). His mother watched proudly from the North Transept, perhaps also glorying in her own part in restoring Richard's fortunes.

In a revealing symbolic assertion of who was the leading woman in Richard's life, Berengaria was still in Poitou.[4] It is also significant that there was a stream of letters to his mother from Richard when he was in captivity but none to his wife. Also absent from the ceremony at Winchester was Richard's half-brother Geoffrey who had fallen out with the archbishop of Canterbury about whether he, as archbishop of York, should be allowed to carry his cross during the ceremony or not, a sign of spiritual equality that Hubert Walter was not prepared to countenance. Geoffrey was in a huff and stayed away.

During his time in England, Richard also visited London. Here, in stark contrast to their previous decision to support John, there were enthusiastic scenes in the streets at the return of the king. William of Newburgh wrote how 'then did the citizens, having heard of his approach, take up the oil of gladness instead of weeping, and put on the garment of praise instead of the spirit of heaviness.'[5]

Richard's time back in England would be brief. Practical affairs needed to be attended to; for example, the Great Seal of England had been taken from Richard whilst he was in Germany and a new one had to be made. But affairs in Normandy were serious and demanded his urgent attention. He got together a fleet at Portsmouth but bad weather delayed them from setting out as early as they planned to and they were held up for two weeks. These were frustrating delays, so much so that scuffles broke out between men from Brabant and others from Wales and in the fracas lives were lost. Portsmouth was a relatively new town, though the nearby fortress of Portchester was anything but, its flinty Roman walls still standing defiant against both the enemy and the elements as it had done for nearly a thousand years.

It was ironic that the town had been founded by John of Gisors who had subsequently thrown in his lot with Philip of France in Normandy, so his new town of Portsmouth was duly forfeited. Richard now granted it its first royal charter on 2 May 1194. Much money was subsequently pumped into it during Richard's reign, especially on the palace there, more so than was even spent on Westminster.[6] It would become a crucial royal town and port and it was from here that the armadas of first Edward III and then Henry V would set out in future attempts to conquer France.

There were some interesting diversions to consider during these times. One concerned who owned the carcass of a whale (described as a 'fat fish') that was stranded on the Naze on land that belonged to the canons of St Paul's in London. Richard's officials claimed it belonged to the crown but the canons insisted that it was theirs. This was an argument that for once the king lost and the findings were eventually in favour of the canons.[7]

Richard grew impatient at the delay and, against the advice of his mariners, tried to leave for France though no other ships accompanied him when he sailed. It turned out to be a mistake. The king's ship soon found itself in the middle of a violent storm. Those aboard were terrified and were forced back, first to the Isle of Wight and then into Portsmouth. But they were eventually able to set sail when the winds and the seas at last settled down.

When Richard finally left, accompanied by Eleanor, he could not have known that he would never again be in England. The chief man there in his absence would be Hubert Walter. Walter's reputation had been made in Outremer when he had proved himself to be a loyal supporter of Richard. Honours duly followed; first the archbishopric of Canterbury, then chief justiciar in succession to Walter of Coutances and finally his appointment as a papal legate in 1195. This portfolio of appointments gave him immense power, greater even than that which had been enjoyed by Longchamp.

Such preferment did not go down well with everyone. The saintly and formidable Hugh of Lincoln, who was not averse to putting even Richard in his place if they disagreed on an issue, castigated himself when he was dying for not rebuking Hubert as often as he thought he should have done. The close association of secular power with Archbishop Hubert, though not unique in the context of the times, created a stir.

Hubert Walter issued detailed instructions in 1194 on the back of ongoing financial difficulties for Richard. One of these concerned the recovery of fines that were still outstanding from the massacre of Jews five years before that were still uncollected. Of course, these amounts would not go to the Jews but to the Crown so they were followed up vigorously. This was needed as there were still outstanding ransom payments to be made to the emperor.

There was also a backlog of criminal justice issues to be addressed. Itinerant justiciars were to be sent around the country to judge outstanding cases. Many of those charged with more serious crimes were to undergo trial by water, a process in which the accused was thrown into a river or pond with his hands tied behind his back. If he floated, he was guilty as charged but if he went under then he was innocent. One such man subjected to this harrowing ordeal was Ælfgar of Hollingbourne in Kent, judging by his name a man of Saxon descent. He was accused of stealing some pitchforks and offered to undergo the trial to prove his innocence. He duly went under and therefore was cleared of the charges against him.[8]

As well as introducing customs duties which helped to start the refilling of royal coffers seriously depleted by the payment of his huge ransom, Richard also introduced several innovations in England concerning the regulation of tournaments. There is little evidence that Richard took part in many tournaments himself, unlike his late brothers Henry and Geoffrey, but in 1194 he legalised them in England.[9]

It was a potentially lucrative money-making exercise. Rather than being a lover of the tournament for its chivalric splendour, Richard liked once again the thought of being able to profit from them. Five official tournament sites were set up in England, including the fields between Salisbury and Wilton and those between Warwick and Kenilworth.

Tournaments created a risk of misbehaviour in a way that sounds eerily similar to modern football hooliganism. When eighty exuberant knights arrived for a tournament in Bury St Edmunds, they over-indulged on alcohol and were soon singing their heads off. Their riotous behaviour finally resulted in the town gates being broken down. Abbot Sansom was so furious that he excommunicated every one of them.[10] The Church was not happy at the whole idea of tournaments and as recently as 1193 had issued an edict that told men who wished to fight that they should head off on crusade and not waste their time and even their lives playing at warfare.

There may well be other reasons for Richard's sanctioning of tournaments. Both William of Newburgh and Ralph of Diceto suggested that they offered a useful training opportunity which certainly is an argument not without merit.[11]

Others have suggested that it was a pragmatic move on Richard's part. If these knights could not fight in these tournaments in England, then they would probably do so in France instead. Richard now needed allies and could not afford to be too choosy about how he got them. Allowing them to participate in such events in England might prevent them from being weaned away from his party by Philip as well as helping him to raise funds and giving his knights some useful training opportunities.[12]

Some though were dismissive of the usefulness of these tournaments for training men for war. Ralph of Diceto stated that 'wielding light lances rendered them not so much ready for battle as for sumptuous and luxurious feasts and showed them to be best at obtaining and lighting candlesticks'.[13] Such writers were dismissive of what they saw as the fopperies of chivalric and, as they perceived it, futile adventures. To them, this was not real war and had very little to do with it.

Richard also issued rules concerning the Jews in his kingdom. Every Jew was to register all his possessions, his houses, rents and lands, and any debts and pledges that they held. If they sought to hide any of these details, then they would not be able to enforce payment of any related debts in the future. Loans were to be agreed at six or seven named places where both Jews and Christians were to be present. Indentures were to be made out for the debts concerned. One part of the indenture was to be retained by the Jewish lender whilst another part was to be kept in a common chest which was to have three locks with each key to be held in different hands. A register of all such indentures was to be maintained and another with receipts for all repayments made.

Steps were put in place for a body of twelve knights in each hundred in England to enquire into all the holdings and seizures made by the bailiffs of the king since the time of his coronation. These men were to establish why the seizures had been made and by whom. They were also to find out who had received any items seized. This suggests that some of the bailiffs had been exceeding their authority, presumably causing a good deal of angst to those who had suffered as a consequence. Richard took personal responsibility for sorting out bailiffs who had overstepped the mark in Anjou and Maine.

Affairs in England were distractions from Richard's main field of interest now, which was undoubtedly to be found in France. For the rest of his reign, in effect his court was there, not in England. Any who misbehaved in England were summoned to appear before him across the Channel. His lands were under threat; in Aquitaine, in Anjou and most of all in Normandy. His position had been compromised during his extended absence in Outremer and then in captivity. It was now time to put this right.

Richard could afford to concentrate on affairs in France precisely because he now had such a reliable lieutenant in Hubert Walter watching his back in England. Yet there is plenty of evidence that Richard kept a close interest in what was happening across the Channel whilst he was in France.[14] This rather goes against the notion of Richard as an absentee, disinterested king. This does not mean that we should rewrite the story of Richard as a king who really loved England; probably more to the point he loved its wealth and the power it brought him, something that could also be said of many a monarch before and since.

Eleanor now took herself off to the sanctuary of Fontevraud. She was around seventy-two years old and understood that the end of her life was much closer than its beginning. She did not take the veil but she spent much of the rest of her life in her guest apartments at the abbey. She would occasionally emerge to advise Richard but she now started to retreat from public life. Richard had taken some key advisers with him to France. These included Walter of Coutances and William Longchamp, bitter enemies in the past but serving their king well now. Longchamp would also never return to England; he had burned too many bridges there.

Richard and an accompanying army arrived at Barfleur. The biographer of William Marshal described how enthusiastically he was greeted but what faced Richard now was little short of a full-blown crisis. In contrast to the relatively secure position he returned to in England, in many parts of his French lands he had lost significant ground. Marshal's biographer also wrote of how Richard suffered from tortured nights, unable to sleep given the many great challenges that faced him.

East of the Seine in Normandy, key positions had been lost at Arques and Eu as well as the sea-ports of Dieppe and Triport. Philip had also made incursions, though smaller in extent, on the western bank of the river. The Norman capital, Rouen, the key-point of the whole duchy, was itself under threat. Along with strengthening his position further north in Flanders, the French king had taken full advantage of Richard's extended absence. The scales that weighed the balance of power had shifted firmly in Philip's favour.

Further south, important positions had been lost to Richard at places such as Loches and Touraine. Key frontier lords had changed sides and gone over to Philip's party. In many cases, it was likely that they felt they had no real option; continuing to side with Richard when he was locked up in a German prison probably meant the inevitable loss of all that they owned as invading French forces descended on them with little prospect of meaningful resistance. In Aquitaine too the situation was deteriorating and many of the lords of that region were also up in arms. The only saving grace there was Richard's alliance with Berengaria's brother Sancho who was well positioned to intervene. But that had not prevented two leading lords from Aquitaine, Geoffrey de Rançon and Bernard de Brosse, from paying homage to Philip at Sens.

Even Richard's imminent arrival on the scene did not stop Philip's advance. A truce had been arranged that was supposed to last until Whitsun. But Philip asserted that it had been broken and laid siege to the important castle of Verneuil. The garrison there assumed that Richard would arrive at any moment to rescue them and mocked the French king, confident in the belief that they would soon be relieved. In fact, the bad weather in England had delayed Richard's departure and the garrison was therefore made to sweat as days passed without a sign of him.

Richard did arrive eventually in Normandy though and was concerned at the potential loss of Verneuil. It was now that his brother John changed sides again. Richard spent some time at Lisieux with John of Alençon, the archdeacon there, who approached him one evening with his face drawn and looking generally very distressed. Richard guessed at once what the problem was; his brother had arrived. Terrified by the imminent return of Richard, with whom he had not yet made his peace, John had made his way to him. He now threw himself on Richard's mercy.

Richard's reaction was, if the chroniclers are to be believed, surprisingly mild. He told John that he was still a child and had merely got into the wrong company. It was his plan, he said, to wreak vengeance not on his brother but on those who had led him astray. Perhaps Richard understood very well from his own experience why John had done what he had; after all, he was not renowned for family loyalty either.

It has been plausibly suggested that this reconciliation was stage-managed by Eleanor, a reasonable enough suggestion of a mother trying to restore amity between two quarrelling sons.[15] John was hungry after his journey and, in a symbolic sign of forgiveness, Richard had a large salmon that had been presented to him by the citizens of Lisieux served up. John of Alençon bluntly told John to his face that if the roles had been reversed Richard would have been treated far more harshly. But there were limits to Richard's forgiveness. It would be some time before John's confiscated lands were returned to him and even then key castles would be held back. John had forfeited Richard's trust and would never fully win it back again. But for the rest of Richard's reign he would act as a loyal lieutenant to him.

Now the tide of the war started to turn. John had occupied the town of Evreux and, keen to prove his new-found loyalties, brutally executed the French garrison there. This forced Philip to move away from Verneuil and, although he ordered the siege of the town to continue in his absence, it quickly fizzled out. His troops at Verneuil now had full knowledge that Richard was on his way. They did not wish to be around when he arrived for a reckoning. Richard's luck may have taken a downward turn in recent times but his military reputation was still apparently intact. He also had some unexpected support; the Norman Pipe Rolls suggest that he had a small number of 'Saracens' with him when he attacked Domfront in Maine.[16]

Soon after, Philip's siege train at Verneuil fell into Richard's hands. In a fit of pique Philip sacked Evreux, an act that was so thorough that even churches and relics went up in flames. He spared neither age nor sex; it was a harsh warning against any of his subjects who contemplated the idea of deserting his cause. This act could not prevent Richard's final relief of Verneuil. He entered the town and kissed each and every one of the defenders as a token of his gratitude for their supreme efforts. The king had returned.

But the turnaround would not be easy. Philip was a resolute opponent and his position was strengthened soon after when the earl of Leicester was captured in a rash sally against Hugh de Gournay. Such a prominent prisoner gave Philip an advantage and he suggested to Richard that a three-year truce should be agreed. After giving the appearance of thinking about it, Richard finally rejected the proposal.

A truce was of little use to Richard as it would enable Philip to keep the lands he had already conquered. This he would not countenance and renewed fighting broke out. The earl would offer to pay a sizeable ransom for his release but Philip, with good reason, was in no hurry to take him up on it. He finally relented and let the earl go in 1196 after he paid 2,000 silver marks for the privilege and had given up his claims to the castle of Pacy.

In the intense conflict which followed, several places were recovered by Richard. Loches was taken with the co-operation of Navarrese allies who were already there when he arrived. They had been led by Berengaria's brother though he had been forced to return home when news was received of his father's death. They had been laying siege to Loches for some time without success, possibly because they were poorly supplied with the necessary engines of war. They were also short of food and reading between the lines morale was not high.

Loches was a key town and of deep symbolic resonance for those associated with the Angevin dynasty. One of its greatest early figures, Fulk Nerra ('The Black') had made his base there and was buried in the shadow of the hill on which Loches was built just across the Indre River in Beaulieu. Loches was considered to be impregnable; its citadel area had more than a mile of thick walls which were built on a solid rock outcrop. But almost as soon as Richard arrived, a violent assault on the town was initiated. After a brief fight, it fell; a feather in Richard's cap which led to widespread astonishment from those who heard of it.

Richard was now hot on the tail of an army that was led by Philip which was threatening to cause chaos in Aquitaine. Richard, soon not far behind him, decided to block any potential retreat by taking up position astride the road at Vendôme. The two sides were so close that they could almost touch. Philip reacted boldly to the news. He told his men that he would take on Richard in battle on the following morning; but come that following morning, the French army was in headlong retreat.

Richard got wind of this and was determined to do all that he could to capture Philip. He was assisted by his loyal mercenary captain Mercadier who did his best to keep him provided with spare horses when he tired one out. The pursuing group passed by Philip when he was sheltering in a church; some said he was praying though it also made a convenient hiding place. Richard did not catch the French king but he did obtain a valuable consolation prize in the shape of his wagon train. This included horses, tents, siege engines and a sizeable amount from Philip's treasury. He also took a chapel in which were stored records of those who had changed over to Philip's side in the recent past.

It was the greatest day that Richard had enjoyed for several years. He celebrated into the night. Special praise was reserved for William Marshal. He had been deputed to hold position in case the French had counter-attacked and he had carried out his instructions to the letter. Richard commented approvingly on the way in which Marshal had carried out his orders; he knew full well that success in war depended not just on glorious actions, heroic charges on the battlefield or single combat but on his commanders doing what they were told to do.

The road to Aquitaine was open. God help those who had chosen to rebel against Richard there now. Chief amongst them had been his old adversary, Geoffrey de Rançon. Richard crushed them underfoot. Key cities and castles fell to him, with Angoulême the greatest prize of all. The work already put in by Sancho of Navarre in advance of his return proved vital.

It was a campaign that deserves to be remembered as one of Richard's greatest. Surviving details of it all are sketchy, which from a historical perspective is something of a tragedy. In terms of what had been done in such a short time though, it was a great achievement. The war in France had been turned on its head.

But the reality was that the losses suffered by Richard in his absence had been extensive and even now they were far from being completely overturned. The main issue was to be found in Normandy which had been the primary focus of Philip's attention. Philip's hasty retreat from in front of Richard's army may have been not so much from panic (though the loss of his wagon train suggests that this is not an impossibility) but from strategic considerations. He was quite happy to distract Richard's attentions with forays further south but this was not where his priorities lay. Normandy was above all what Philip desired.

Richard of course could not be in two places at once. He had left his brother John and the earl of Arundel to lay siege to the crucial castle of Vaudreuil back in Normandy. This was strategically vital as it guarded a crossing across the Seine just 10 miles to the south of Rouen. It seems the besieging force was complacent for it was caught completely off-guard when Philip forced marched his men more than 100 miles in three days. Philip's triumph was total and those from the besieging army who could, mainly cavalry, were soon fleeing for their lives. They were in such a hurry that they left their siege engines behind them.

This was war at its most frenetic and it could not continue at this pace for long. It probably came as a surprise to no one when shortly afterwards a truce was agreed, to last from 23 July 1194 to 1 November 1195. Under the terms of the agreement, Philip and Richard were to keep what they currently held. Restrictions were also put in place to prevent Richard from reconstructing fortifications that had previously been destroyed by Philip. It was far from a perfect situation for Richard but it was much better than it had been just a few months before.

In Richard's absence, there were tensions back in England. Hugh de Puiset, the bishop of Durham, had refused to hand over Northumberland to Hugh Bardolf as he had been instructed to do by the king. The bishop would not take any notice of the king's instructions. Richard was furious at his opposition and gave orders that the lands involved were to be seized from de Puiset.

In 1195 Alice, the sister of Philip, was at last released and returned to her brother after over three decades in English custody. It had been an unbelievably long period away, treated as a faceless pawn in an ongoing political game where the rules changed with bewildering frequency. She had barely time to re-acquaint herself with Philip before she was at last married. Her husband was the count of Ponthieu and he was given Eu and Arques as a gift, though they would both turn out to be difficult towns to hold. From this point on, Alice virtually disappears from the historical record.

Unsurprisingly the truce between Richard and Philip was far from the end of the war and many men would have been greatly surprised if it had held for the agreed duration. If this had been a boxing bout, this was just a breathing space between rounds, a chance for two tough, obdurate opponents to take a breather to recover their strength before fighting hammer and tongs again. As many have found out the hard way, an absence of war is very different from peace.

In the event, it was Philip who blinked first. He considered the truce to be at an end when he found out that Emperor Henry VI was encouraging Richard to attack France, something for which the English king needed little encouragement. Henry and Richard were unlikely allies, given Richard's imprisonment and the enormous ransom paid, but the arrangement suited the English king as he needed allies to restore his position in France and who better than Henry given his vast resources?

Philip went on the attack, deciding to demolish key fortifications in Normandy rather than give Richard the chance to take them. This treatment was meted out to Vaudreuil whose walls came crashing to the ground even as Philip was negotiating with Richard. Richard was furious and swore to create devastation amongst his French enemies but Philip managed to escape and the English king was unable to make good on his vow. Instead he took possession of the shell of Vaudreuil.

Richard attempted to rebuild alliances in Normandy to counteract the presence of Philip and his garrisons. One way he did this was to seek the further assistance of the Lusignan family as payback for the support he had given to Guy and Geoffrey in the East. Another of the family, Ralph of Exoudon, was given the hand of the heiress of Eu, a crucial town close to the sea port of Triport where Richard was responsible for building the massive walls that surrounded it. Baldwin of Béthune, a close confidant of Richard, was also involved in such alliance-building, being married to the countess of Aumâle, a match that the king was so interested in that he even paid for the wedding.

There was an irony to all this in that both Richard and Philip claimed to hold Eu and Aumâle and the latter was the man in possession. This of course gave Ralph and Baldwin an incentive to recover those territories which was Richard's main reason for making these moves. Neither was Richard's ambition limited to Normandy. Further south in Berry, Richard and his allies seized Issoudun and Graçay, long a target of his. Now he was making a point; if Philip felt he could take territory in Normandy with impunity, then he was wrong.

Whilst at Chinon, Richard came under threat from assassins. It was said that about fifteen of them had made their way there to try and kill him. However, the plot was discovered before it could be put into effect. When questioned, some of the plotters said that they were there by order of Philip. Richard however played down the accusations pending the receipt of further information.

The death on 3 March 1195 of Hugh de Puiset removed a problematic figure in England from the scene. His recent disagreements with Hugh Bardolf confirmed him as a man who could be obstinate and proud and excessively aware of his own importance. He died at Howden and was buried in the great cathedral at Durham soon after. But the demise of the bishop did allow those disputed lands in Northumberland to be handed over to Bardolf at last.

De Puiset's demise gave Richard's finances a boost. Many of his possessions were taken by the Crown, probably in distinct contrast to what the will of the late bishop stated. Huge amounts came to Richard as a result; £3,050 was taken from his estate. Relations between king and bishop had been strained lately and Hugh was a man who enjoyed the good life (he had allegedly died of over-eating). Nevertheless, it was a shabby end to the life of a man who had often come to the king's aid in the past.[17]

Richard had another long-running dispute to worry about, albeit at a distance. The friction between Geoffrey, archbishop of York, and his canons continued to run and run. When a new dean sought to take up his position at York, Geoffrey's men seized him and prevented him from doing so. They were quickly excommunicated for their pains. Pope Celestine wrote to Geoffrey soon after in no uncertain terms commanding him to punish them for their actions. A panel set up to arbitrate decided that the losses suffered by the canons at the hands of the archbishop amounted to a value of 1,000 marks of silver.

On 4 April 1195, Easter Sunday, Richard was taken ill. It was not surprising. He had suffered bouts of ill health before, notably during the Siege of Acre. He had been under enormous stress for years for one reason or another which may have affected his natural defences. This was an era when medicine was undeveloped and when many ailments that could be dealt with in modern times could easily kill.

Roger of Howden, seeing the hand of God in everything, viewed this as a punishment; 'the Lord visited him with a rod of iron'. Richard's sin, he said, had been sexual immorality. This suggestion of some kind of sexual misbehaviour reinforced a story from the same year of a hermit who had approached Richard and warned him to 'remember the destruction of Sodom and Gomorrah and abstain from illicit acts for if you do not God will punish you in fitting manner'.

Whilst John Gillingham has argued forcefully that this should not be taken as an allusion to any homosexuality on Richard's part, a close reading of the Bible story concerning Sodom and Gomorrah[18] makes it crystal clear that the cities were punished by God when some of the men there planned to rape two male visitors to the city. And it has been shown by historians that by 1300 the term sodomy referred specifically to an 'unkindly sin that is not twix man and woman'.[19] The Chapter House of Salisbury Cathedral, near-contemporary with Richard's time, houses carvings representing the destruction of Sodom. Not for nothing was Dante's Seventh Circle of Hell populated with blasphemers, sodomites and money-lenders.

That homosexual relationships did exist at the time we should regard as a certainty. This was in many ways a man's world when men were away from sexual relationships with women for months and even years at a time. Romantic writers of the time often talk of 'love' between men though this should not necessarily be seen as sexual in nature but rather composed of a deep sense of comradeship, almost sentimental in its basis, typical of warriors in many ages. But being in each other's company for such a long period may well have led to sexual relationships forming.

There is strong evidence from the period that homosexuality was practised. The Knights Templar, wiped out at the beginning of the fourteenth century, were accused of indulging in homosexual practices. Other circumstantial evidence strengthened the argument, for example Richard's long and ultimately broken engagement to Alice and his frequent absences from Berengaria. Then there was his close and intimate relationship at one time to Philip before their relationship had gone sour.

None of this in isolation means that Richard was definitely homosexual. Even taken as a package the evidence is inconclusive. The unconsummated relationship with Alice is easily explained away if Henry II, Richard's father, had taken her as his mistress. In such circumstances, Richard's reluctance to marry her would be understandable, especially if as some gossips said children had resulted from the relationship. Richard might also not have found Berengaria attractive; Henry VIII's relationship with Anne of Cleves was famously not consummated because of physical repulsion. Closer to Richard's time, any sexual attraction towards Ingeborg of Denmark from Philip II did not survive their wedding night.

There were also stories about Richard's relationship with women. As a younger man in Aquitaine, he was accused of seducing women and then passing them on to his men to enjoy as they wished. There was also an illegitimate child by the name of Philip. Even stories in later life and in fact beyond into the next century associate Richard with energetic trysts with the fairer sex.

One of them concerned a nun at Fontevraud, a woman of great beauty. Richard was besotted and made advances towards her. She was a virtuous woman and resisted him determinedly. When he continued to harass her, she asked him what he most liked about her. He said her eyes. The nun then cut them out and sent them to Richard as a present. This is a moral tale, not one based on fact. But its purpose was to emphasise the chastity of the nun contrasting with the worldly desires driving Richard on. In Flori's analysis, Richard was a hedonist and, using a memorable turn of phrase, 'a versatile lecher'.[20]

Most probably Richard was bisexual.[21] It was not until comparatively recently that the first overt suggestions of homosexuality were made, in 1948 when JH Harvey stated that Richard's sexuality took this form. Other historians in earlier times hinted at this but did not state it openly. But it is an interpretation that has gained some currency.

Homosexuality was subject to condemnation in medieval Europe. At times during the period, sodomy was punishable by death. Thomas Aquinas (1225–1274), a renowned theologian, condemned homosexuality whilst his female counterpart, Hildegard of Bingen (1098–1179), made her negative views on lesbianism very clear. Edward II, the later English king, was accused of a homosexual relationship with his close adviser Piers Gaveston though both men had children with their wives. The truth is that homosexuality almost certainly was a part of life in the period but was largely kept obscured from public view because of the condemnation that it would lead to from conservative Church circles.

We must also remember that the twelfth century was one of significant cultural development. Not only did it witness the first beginnings of what would become as the Age of Chivalry, it was also a period of remarkable artistic development. There were vigorous building programmes in much of Western Europe. What was known as Romanesque architecture reached its final glorious flowering to be replaced by that fantastic form known as Gothic.

In literature too, there was an explosion of creativity. Though perhaps most famously known for the development of Arthurian literature, with the work of writers such as Chrétien de Troyes whose fertile imagination gave birth to the character and chivalric paragon known as Lancelot, there was a great deal of poetry produced. Not for nothing did this period later become known as the twelfth-century Renaissance.

As part of this creative development, there was a relaxing of the strictly conservative attitude against homosexuality, though elements of the Church fought this tooth and nail. The writer Marbodius of Rennes wrote of the ideal male form; 'A handsome face demands a good mind and a yielding one... this flesh is so smooth, so milky, so unblemished, so good, so slippery, so handsome, so tender'.[22] Whilst it would be perhaps too much to call this homo-erotic, it would have been unthinkable that this could have been written at an earlier time. Such liberalism did not last for long. There was a conservative reaction in following centuries and serious serial 'offenders' could be executed for their 'crimes' so the twelfth century was a short interlude during which the practice of homosexuality was judged in some quarters less harshly than in other times during this epoch.

The hermit who had berated Richard for his behaviour shortly before had not made a great impression on the king (although he may not have existed at all, but may have been a caricature invented to make a point in a story). Although Roger of Howden does not go into detail on the subject, the implication of his account is that he was dishevelled and unclean, the classic image of a hermit of the time. That said he was brave to broach the subject with Richard but his words did little good.

Richard's illness though gave credence to what he said. Richard had not slept with Berengaria for a while and at times he seemed to go out of his way to avoid her. Now this changed; it was said that 'rejecting illicit couplings he joined with his wife, and they were both one flesh; the Lord restored health to his body as well as his soul'.[23]

This was a significant development in terms of their personal relationship, for the phrasing used in the chronicles suggests that Richard had abstained from sexual relations with Berengaria for some time. It seems most likely that she had been leading a life of seclusion in Beaufort en Vallée, a quiet spot close to the road between Angers and Le Mans. That Christmas was spent together at Poitiers. The area had been hit by a serious famine and the warm-hearted Berengaria prevailed upon Richard to help the people by making generous gifts to them.

The king also became noticeably more fastidious in his attendance at church services. According to Roger of Howden, he began to take much greater care of the poor and needy. Chalices of gold and silver were distributed generously by the king amongst the churches. All this is suggestive of a man who was seriously worried by his illness and had become acutely aware of his own mortality. But it does not seem to have been long before Richard and Berengaria were leading separate lives again. The reunion was brief and fleeting and Richard was soon back on the battlefield. Richard's brief flirtation with domesticity did not last for long. It was time to resume the war.

18

A Never-Ending War (1195–1198)

'Their direful fury immediately blazed forth'
Roger of Howden on the resumption of hostilities in 1198

Richard decided that it was time to restore John's lands to him, which he duly did though he kept the castles that had previously been in his brother's hands for himself. Clearly John was still effectively on trial. But Richard did grant him the sum of 8,000 pounds Anjou to keep himself. He also forgave Hugh, the bishop of Coventry, for his support for John. This was not however a move motivated by Christian forgiveness; the bishop would have to pay 5,000 silver marks for the privilege. In the event, Hugh took himself off into voluntary exile and when he lay dying a few years later it was difficult to find a priest who was prepared to give him the last rites.

Richard also forgave his half-brother Geoffrey, a measure that he seemingly came to regret almost at once. Geoffrey's tactlessness and arrogance were so great that soon after Richard deprived him of his archbishopric. Roger of Howden castigated Geoffrey for the sharpness and indiscipline of his tongue, sermonising that it might be one of the smaller members of the body but it could do the greatest damage.[1]

Geoffrey's dispute with his church officials continued seemingly *ad infinitum*. Roger of Howden, to whom these events were local, goes into almost tedious detail on the subject. The Pope wrote several letters and appointed a panel to investigate the alleged abuses of Geoffrey and in 1196 he gave orders that he should be suspended from his office. Simon of Apulia, the Dean of York, was appointed to take over some of his role. By that time Geoffrey had made his way to France to present his case to Richard; he would not return to England during his brother's reign.

Pope Celestine wrote an open letter to the bishops of England in 1195 dealing with the problems in York. In it, he confirmed the appointment of Hubert Walter as archbishop of Canterbury and his position as papal legate in England. Shortly after, Hubert made his way to York to symbolically affirm his authority and show the argumentative factions in York who was in charge. He held a synod in the city which resulted in the crafting of a number of rules that the clergy there were to follow. Their content was revealing; it was emphasised that clergymen were to abstain from the taking of bribes, which suggests that this was exactly what they had got used to doing. Nuns were reminded that they were not to leave the sanctuary of their abbey without being accompanied by their abbess or prioress; again, suggestive that some form of impropriety had been taking place.

Priests were not exempt from the criticisms either. They were reminded not to keep harlots in their houses. They were to be suspended from their duties if they did not desist, though those who repented of their sins were to be looked upon favourably.[2] All in all, the impression given is that the Church in England, or perhaps more specifically that at York, was a veritable den of iniquity.

Hubert Walter was a no-nonsense administrator. When he fell out with Robert, abbot of Tournai, the unfortunate man found himself clapped in irons in a prison in Gloucester for a year and a half whilst he appealed to the Pope for relief. The people of England were required to take an oath to keep the peace and abstain from being thieves and robbers, nor to harbour them. Instead they were to hand them over to the king's sheriffs. They were required to join in the 'hue and cry' when a criminal was being pursued. Every person of the age of fifteen and upwards was required to take the oath before knights appointed for the purpose, a number of whom were appointed and were soon busy arresting people who had failed to comply with the requirements of law and order.[3] This talk of sheriffs, posses and a breakdown of law and order all makes the England of 1195 sound rather similar to the Wild West of America in the nineteenth century.

Disturbing news came in from Spain that Almohad Muslim forces were making advances there and had defeated King Alfonso VIII of Castile at Alarcos on 18 July 1195. Soon after, Alfonso found himself under siege in the city of Toledo. Both Richard and Philip wanted to be seen as being loyal to the Christian cause, whatever their personal differences, and in the face of a renewed Islamic threat to Europe itself desired to present a united front, even if this was mainly for public consumption; fortunately for Alfonso, he was not forced to rely on such untrustworthy allies and himself led an army that defeated the invaders later that year. But a peace of sorts was patched up between the English and French kings and it was even suggested that Richard's niece Eleanor of Brittany, now free to marry after the death of Duke Leopold, should wed Louis, Philip's son. In return Philip would hand back most of the territories he had seized in Normandy.

Richard explained that he would have to clear the arrangement with Henry VI as he was now nominally the vassal of the emperor. Philip even publicly exonerated Richard from any involvement in the death of Conrad of Montferrat. It promised a thawing of relations but nothing came of these discussions; in fact, it seemed as if the emperor had no interest in an outbreak of peace between Richard and Philip. War soon threatened once more and at the end of August a large English army arrived at Barfleur.

Richard had been encouraged in his warlike tendencies by Henry who had sent him a magnificent crown, encouraging him to stay on the offensive. Richard was however not sure of Henry's true intentions; not unreasonably he did not have a great deal of trust in him. William Longchamp was sent to Germany to find out more. Hearing of this, Philip tried unsuccessfully to seize Longchamp as he passed close to his territories. Longchamp returned with news that Henry felt that the proposed peace was a dishonourable one; more likely it served his purposes better to have Richard creating chaos in France.

The death of Tancred of Sicily in 1194 had encouraged Henry to attempt to take his lands as he had long threatened to do. With an army financed in part by the huge windfall he had enjoyed from Richard's ransom, he entered Apulia and took Salerno where he dealt with the citizens harshly, putting some of them to death and sending others into exile. The city was levelled to the ground and a vast amount of treasure was taken. Amalfi was also captured. The island of Sicily soon afterwards fell to him with a great amount of money being taken in the process.

Henry was crowned in Palermo on Christmas Day 1194. He was vindictive towards his former opponents. The bodies of the late

Tancred and his son, King Roger, were dug up and despoiled of the royal regalia that had been buried with them. King William III, the son of Tancred, was blinded and castrated whilst many of his close supporters were burned alive. These were savage acts and Richard must have breathed a sigh of relief that he had managed to escape unscathed from the clutches of the emperor. Richard might have justifiably been regarded as being ruthless on occasion but the brutality of the emperor was on a different level and ultimately even alienated his own people. Henry's triumph seemed to be complete when, just over a month later, his wife Constance gave birth to a son who was named Frederick. But fortune was fickle. Unknown to anyone at the time, these events marked the high-water mark of the late medieval Holy Roman Empire.

In France, Philip launched a surprise attack on Dieppe, which Richard had only recently established, leaving the town in flames. Even the ships in the harbour were set ablaze with Greek Fire. Richard in return besieged Arques, trying to take back that key strategic point. Philip took advantage of his strong internal line of communications to recapture the town of Issoudun further south, though the castle held out. Messages were despatched frantically to Richard further north, who demonstrated his usual rapid response when he received them. He set out at the greatest possible speed to Issoudun where he succeeded in breaking through the French lines and making his way into the castle.

To the casual observer it might seem that Richard was trapped but in fact exactly the opposite was the case. More and more of Richard's troops came up behind Philip and threatened to ensnare him. In the end, Philip was forced to seek a truce. When this was finally ratified in January 1196, most of the territories that Philip still held in Normandy were handed back. Only the long-disputed Vexin and a few other castles were retained by him, though that would no doubt have rankled greatly with Richard. But the Peace of Louviers also enabled Ralph of Exoudon and Baldwin of Béthune to take possession of the territories that they had previously only nominally held.

This 'peace' was yet again only a breathing space. It gave Richard a chance to attend to another problem area in France. Brittany had enjoyed an increasing amount of autonomy in recent years. The duchy was nominally the possession of Duchess Constance. She was married to Ranulf, the earl of Chester, but it was a long-distance relationship as she remained in Brittany and Ranulf lived in England. Richard as duke of Normandy saw Brittany as rightfully belonging to him, a point he demonstrated on several occasions by his use of Eleanor of Brittany in the marriage game. But now he wanted more.

What he now sought was custody of the heir of Brittany, his nine-year-old nephew Arthur. The matter became complicated when Constance was seized, by her husband of all people, whilst visiting Normandy. Her council in Brittany were alarmed at this action and blamed Richard for it; there was no firm evidence for this but it was not in the least unlikely on a circumstantial basis. They therefore appealed to Philip to intervene on their behalf.

Richard would not tolerate this and launched a vigorous assault on Brittany. In a military sense, it was a one-sided battle, fought by Richard with great determination and ferocity. Brittany was overwhelmed. But what Richard most desired was denied him. Arthur was smuggled out and ended up at Philip's court where he was well received. He was a useful counterweight to Richard and Philip was delighted to have custody of him.

The cost of Richard's war in France was biting heavily by now. This was a long, gruelling conflict and the financial consequences of waging war were piling up. In England, people were starting to groan under the strain. Resentment against heavy taxes was building up and, to compound these hardships, famine was abroad in the land which was followed by a 'great mortality'.[4]

The famine lasted several years and caused much hardship along with the cold weather. There were reports of people dying of hunger; specific cases are known from several parts of the country and these were likely to be just the tip of the iceberg. Interestingly these cases were recorded as 'murder' in the court records of the times and the hundreds from which the victims came were fined collectively in punishment.[5]

This was suggestive of a distant, uncaring king who cared little for his people and it did not help that he complained that, despite these heavy burdens, nowhere near enough money was being collected. His obsession with recovering lost ground in France was now his supreme driving force to which everything else came a distant second.

The common people found a leader to harness their disapproval of Richard's policies in the shape of William FitzOsbert who had the nickname 'Longbeard'. He was a striking figure who the later chronicler Matthew Paris – who never saw him – described as being 'tall, vigorous and intrepid'.[6] He was also a prominent member of the London contingent that went on crusade in 1190.[7]

Disenchanted taxpayers from what we would now call the working classes flocked to his side, numbering according to some sources 50,000. Many were unhappy at the levels of taxation: Ralph of Diceto writes of a harsh process, 'which many said was unfairly arranged'.[8] They protested against the injustice of the exactions placed upon them and the country seemed to be on the verge of revolt. Longbeard insisted that he was a loyal subject of Richard and went to Normandy to see him but the tension continued to increase.

A riot broke out in the church of St Paul's. Hubert Walter was greatly angered and ordered that any of the common people of London found outside of the city should be arrested. Some officials tried to grab Longbeard when he was unguarded but he resisted and killed one of them with a hatchet.

This unleashed the authorities in full force. Longbeard was forced to seek sanctuary in the church of St Mary-le-Bow. He was soon after burned out on the orders of Hubert Walter and captured after being stabbed in the stomach by the son of the man whom he had killed. The monks of Canterbury, whose church it was, were outraged at the actions of the archbishop for violating the sanctuary. Richard, showing what he thought of this, wrote to Hubert to commend him for his actions.[9]

The terrible penalties made available by the law as punishment for Longbeard's crimes were exacted with full force. He was to be 'stripped with his hands tied behind his back and his feet tied by a long rope, and dragged by a horse through the middle of the city to the gallows near Tyburn. There he was hanged, in iron chains so that he would not die too quickly'.[10]

He died on 6 April 1196 along with nine other conspirators. It is noticeable, and rather chilling, to see how special steps were to be taken to prolong his dying agonies. The rebellion fizzled out but a strong undercurrent of unhappiness at the ferocity of taxation in England continued to build. Longbeard came to be regarded by some as a martyr and crowds flocked to take away the dirt from the spot where he died as if it were some kind of holy relic. So many of them did so that a pit was formed in the ground.

These events were a useful reminder that, even whilst he was in France, Richard could not afford to completely forget domestic affairs on the other side of the Channel. Negotiations continued with a view to arranging a marriage between Margaret, daughter of the king of Scotland, and Otto, Richard's nephew. There was a suggestion that William of Scotland should give Lothian with its castles to Otto as a wedding gift and that Richard should do the same for Margaret with Northumberland and the county of Carlisle. However, William was not keen on the idea; his wife was pregnant and he hoped that she would provide him with a son who would give him a stronger bargaining chip in the marriage stakes.

There was another development in the long-running saga of Geoffrey, archbishop of York, in 1196. He at last arrived in Rome to plead his case before Pope Celestine. The pontiff was not at all happy with the archbishop but his opponents, who had journeyed from York to argue against him were unable to provide decisive evidence to prove their case. Celestine therefore lifted the suspension on Geoffrey.

But this put Richard at odds with the Pope. He had already decided that Geoffrey should be deprived of his authority and gave orders that Geoffrey was to have no say in the management of the church in York. This dissuaded the increasingly problematic archbishop from returning to England and instead he was soon back in Rome. By now, both Pope and king must have desperately hoped that the controversial prelate would just go away. But he would not; and when later that year his clerk Ralph de Wigetof lay dying, he admitted that he had forged letters in support of Geoffrey's case.

That was not even the worst of it. A clerk, Roger of Ripon, was taken in London, carrying not just letters but poison. He said that this had been given to him by Ralph. The target for this poison was Simon of Apulia, the Dean of York, as well as other canons of the church there. Hubert Walter handed the evidence over to Simon to show him what he was threatened with. Roger was thrown into prison to await his fate.

So the problem of Geoffrey continued; and the subject of the crusade would not go away either. Hubert Walter issued instructions in 1196 to the officers of the archbishopric of York commanding them to instruct those who had taken crusader vows but had not yet fulfilled them to do so at the earliest opportunity. If such a person was physically incapable of fulfilling them, then they were to provide a substitute to go in their stead.[11]

This was a direct command from the Pope and a reminder that there was much unfinished business to attend to in the East. It was backed up by firm action from Hubert Walter. He ordered that all those who had failed to fulfil their vows should wear the sign of the cross as a mark of their commitment to do so in the future. Those who proved obdurate were to be denied communion if they had not taken decisive steps to fulfil their vows by Easter 1196.

This was though unlikely to lead to much whilst all the major rulers in western Europe were constantly at each others' throats. The pull of Jerusalem was well evidenced that year when Margaret, once the wife of the Young King Henry, Richard's elder brother, was widowed once more when her present husband, King Bela of Hungary died, and she took the cross and set out for Outremer. She would live out the rest of her days in Acre.

Hubert Walter was struggling to keep his roles as both head of the Church in England and that of acting head of state in balance and in 1196 he offered to give up his position as chancellor. Richard was unenthusiastic; Hubert had been hugely effective in raising money from England; some eleven hundred thousand silver marks having been collected in the last two years.[12] But it was a demanding task for an ageing and increasingly weary man, and Hubert felt that he could not continue with these dual roles for much longer.

In July 1196, Philip launched a major attack on Aumâle. He had managed to keep his allies together very well. They included the count of Flanders and Hainault, Baldwin IX, a powerful lord indeed. The counts of Ponthieu and Boulogne were also in his camp. Richard responded with vigour and took Nonancourt. But his subsequent attempt to relieve Aumâle failed, though English chroniclers suggest that he decided instead to take his men elsewhere.

Aumâle surrendered a week later and Richard was forced to pay a ransom of 3,000 marks for the garrison that in some ways he had let down. Philip's losses in taking it had been significant and the damage to Aumâle was great, so much so that he decided to demolish what was left of the walls rather than repair them. But it was a very unwelcome reverse for Richard whose performance in the defence of Aumâle had been untypically unconvincing.

It was an unusually bad summer for Richard, who also lost Nonancourt. In an event that later seemed like an ominous portent, he was wounded in the knee whilst besieging the castle of Gaillon, hit by a crossbow bolt fired by the castellan, a mercenary named Cadoc. It knocked Richard out of action for a month and slowed the campaign down as a result. These were painful reminders that Richard was still far from final victory in France, however much progress he had made. It was proving to be a long slog and any thoughts he might have had about returning to Outremer to fulfil his Crusading vows were further away than ever.

About 25 miles to the south of Rouen the River Seine meanders its way towards Paris. There is a particularly strategic point where the settlement of Les Andalys now stands. Now it is a pleasant spot for a summer vacation, a small but pretty place replete with charming old houses and riverside walks. Nothing could be more sublimely peaceful. Look up to the sheer cliffs that are close by though and there is a reminder that at one time this was one of the most significant spots in France; evidence in fact that this area was once at the heart of the battle for Normandy.

On top of those cliffs is a ruined castle, still impressive even though parts of it are well past their prime. It does not take a military genius to work out why the castle was built there in the first place. It completely dominates the river and whoever held it would be in a strong position to interfere with ease with any river traffic that sought to move up or down the watery road, a thoroughfare that stretched from the stormy seas of the Atlantic at one end to the very heart of Paris at the other.

That was not the only reason for its importance though. It also helped to protect Rouen from attack from the direction of the east of Normandy where Philip still held stubbornly on to land that he had not handed over as a result of the Peace of Louviers. Conversely it was also a perfect stepping off point for any army making its way from the west of Normandy to assault those lands further east, especially those disputed territories of the Vexin, and this perhaps was the main reason that Richard ordered the castle to be built in the first place.

The castle here became known as Château Gaillard (popularly translated as 'Saucy Castle') and it was Richard's military masterpiece; he spoke of it lovingly as 'his daughter'. Even now, it is the most impressive surviving military monument that can be directly connected to Richard. It speaks of power, of grit, of resolution; all attributes that Richard possessed in abundance. Everyone recognised the importance of the site at the time, so much so that recent treaties had expressly forbidden the building of any kind of fortification there. The fact that Richard now chose to do so suggests that regardless of truces, peaces or the like, the gloves were truly off. The building of Château Gaillard was the clearest possible symbol that for Richard his war with Philip was about to enter another aggressive stage.

Since his return from captivity, Richard had resolutely been rebuilding his position. He knew that to get it back to the state that it was in in 1189 would take time. This was why there had been a succession of truces in France; on each new occasion one was agreed, he was in a slightly better position than before. They bought him time, and he used this time to build up his forces.

Richard's determination to recover his position in France was an all-embracing ambition, greater even than that to return to Outremer. It consumed him; the thought of retribution against the French king who had in his eyes committed an act of supreme treachery was perhaps an even stronger motivator than issues of *realpolitik* which required that he needed to recover his lost lands to preserve his reputation and credibility in the eyes of his contemporaries.

Château Gaillard spoke eloquently of his intent far more than any words would do. Its strategic position was vital. From here he could launch a renewed assault against Philip. It was crucial given the fact that the castle at Gisors, only 20 miles off, was now in Philip's hands. The French king for his part was unlikely to meekly accept this challenge without responding against it vigorously. To protect against any attack from him, the castle was designed to be, as far as was humanly possible, impregnable.

The cost of the castle was enormous (£12,000) and it was built in double-quick time, taking just two years to complete when in many other cases a decade would have been the norm. It incorporated some of the latest thinking in castle design and some experts see similarities between features of the castle's machicolations and those of the great crusader fortress in Syria, Crac des Chevaliers, so ideas had seemingly been brought back from the East with Richard.[13] To put the cost into perspective the amount spent on all castles in England during Richard's reign was £7,000.[14] So determined was Richard to build Château Gaillard that the decision to do so led to a major falling-out with Walter of Coutances, the archbishop of Rouen, for it was located on his manor which was a profitable one.

Walter, who had been a major ally of Richard over the years, was outraged by the king's actions and he did not pull his punches in letters that he wrote to Ralph of Diceto. He felt that the excuses that Richard had put forward in support of his actions were 'worthless and irrational'. Walter approached the king several times on the subject. There had also been a falling-out with William, the bishop of Lisieux, who had taken the king's part in the dispute. Walter intended to set out for Rome so that his complaints could be heard by the highest church authority of them all: 'his [Richard's] intolerable behaviour leaves us with no alternative but to find a condign punishment for him'.[15] This incident gives us a valuable illustration of how Richard was forceful in pursuing his own interests even if it brought him into opposition with men who had been key supporters.

Richard took a very close interest in the progress of construction of the castle and the surrounding fortifications which were built below it by the Seine. It seems likely that he himself took on the role of master builder, even if of course he relied on the assistance of hundreds of masons and labourers as well as a range of other specialist workers with their own discrete tasks. Richard was a driven man, just as much as if he had been on a military campaign. Nothing would be allowed to get in the way of the completion of his masterpiece; William of Newburgh wrote that if an angel came down from heaven to tell Richard to stop, then they would promptly be sent away with a flea in their ear.

The castle incorporated the latest in design, taking care to ensure that there were no blind-spots from which siege engines could launch their missiles against the walls without a violent response from within. Richard asserted that it was so perfectly conceived and sited that it would repulse an attacker even if its defences were made of butter. In the event, the castle would not long survive Richard, being taken by Philip in 1204. So much for hubris (though in fairness the castle was only captured after the isolated garrison had held out for six months).

As part of a diplomatic initiative, there was a surprising development. Richard's sister Joanna, at one time a potential bride for Saladin's brother Al-'Adil, found a new husband after all. Her groom was unexpected; Raymond VI, the recently installed count of Toulouse. The new count was much more accommodating than his late father and he was extremely tolerant, so much so that Pope Innocent III would later sanction a crusade against heretics in his lands, the so-called Cathar Crusade.

This new alliance was a political coup for Richard as the counts of Toulouse were traditional rivals of the dukes of Aquitaine. The marriage took place in Rouen in October 1196 with Berengaria in attendance. Richard made generous concessions, including dropping his claim to be the overlord of Toulouse. It was a price worth paying as Richard could now focus his attentions on the real enemy, Philip. But the marriage would not be a happy one as Raymond was a serial philanderer.

That later brutal extended conflict which became known as the Hundred Years' War was characterised as much by savage raids, the *chevauchees*, as it was by the great pitched battles of Crecy, Poitiers and Agincourt. Richard was also an effective exponent of these as he was about to demonstrate. Out of the blue in April 1197 he swooped on the port of St Valéry. Later made largely irrelevant by the emergence of the nearby port of Fécamp, at the time it was a significant harbour which formed part of the territories of Baldwin IX, the count of Flanders and a close ally of King Philip.

The raid on St Valéry achieved complete surprise. The town was taken and sacked. Much treasure was taken away including the remains of the eighth-century saint after which it was named. A grim fate awaited some English ships that were found in the harbour. The sailors taken when the town fell were promptly hanged, a grim reminder of the ruthlessness of Richard to any who dared cross him, especially those that he regarded as traitors. The ships were burned and their cargoes seized and distributed amongst Richard's men on 15 April.

Shortly afterwards there was another event that would have given Richard great personal satisfaction. A man he detested more than any other, or so said William Marshal, was Philip, the bishop of Beauvais. He had not hesitated to blame Richard for Conrad of Montferrat's death to whoever might listen to him. He was also, not uniquely for the time by any means, a warrior-bishop who felt as comfortable with a weapon in his hand as he did a crozier.

The bishop was captured in the guise of a warrior by Richard's mercenary captain Mercadier, an event that fully supported the assertion made by a contemporary that Philip was 'a man more devoted to battles than books'.[16] This may have been true; but the chroniclers who commented negatively on this did not feel inclined to similarly criticise Hubert Walter who was once described as playing an honourable role at the Siege of Acre; 'his virtues made him a knight in battle, a leader in the camp, and a pastor in ecclesiastical matters'.[17] Both the bishop and William of Merle were captured when they sallied out of the city and many of the common folk with them were killed. The raiders then attacked the bishop's nearby castle at Milli and burned it to the ground.

The bishop was thrown into jail in Rouen and Richard made it clear that he had no intention of releasing him anytime soon. Complaints that he was a churchman cut little ice with Richard, who was easily able to rebut such criticisms by the unanswerable argument that he was not acting like one when he had been taken. Shortly after Richard also captured Dangu, a castle just 4 miles away from Gisors.

The bishop took up his plight with the Pope. He explained to Celestine that he was acting in a righteous cause when he took part in the defence of his city. As he explained it, 'fortune, that step-dame of human counsels, brought my intended purpose to an unhappy result'. Fortune in other words had turned against him; on where God stood on the issue, the bishop suggested that 'the king of England has not dreaded to rage against Christ, our Lord, after the manner of a wolf'.[18]

Celestine replied with a letter of admonition. It was unsurprising that matters had turned out badly when 'throwing aside the peaceful bishop, you have assumed the warlike knight'. In the letter, the Pope made clear that he took the part of Richard in his fight against the perfidy of the king of France. As he put it regarding the bishop's predicament, 'into the pit that you have made you have deservedly fallen'. Despite himself, Celestine concluded by telling the bishop that he would intervene on his behalf; after all, it was not good for the prestige of the Church if a leader of one of its flocks was rotting in jail in such embarrassing circumstances.[19]

This was a very successful raid for Richard and the war seemed to be moving in his favour again. It was a development that seriously unsettled the count of Flanders. Trade between Flanders and England was traditionally strong, with wool from the latter a particularly prized commodity. Richard put pressure on the count; he would lift the trade embargo that had been placed on Flanders and dangled the carrot of generous monetary gifts in front of him too. It was a clever strategic ploy that gives the lie to any perception that Richard was only capable of winning success through victory in battle.

That Christmas was spent by Richard in Normandy. It was not a happy one though. Richard's dispute with Walter of Coutances over the ownership of the land at Les Andalys where Château Gaillard was being built had turned bitter. The interdict placed by the archbishop of Rouen was biting hard. As Roger of Howden put it, 'the bodies of the dead were lying unburied through the lanes and streets of the cities of Normandy'.[20]

William Longchamp was sent to the bishop of Lisieux to plead Richard's case whilst Philip, the bishop-elect of Durham, was to go to Rome. But when they arrived in Poitou, Longchamp fell ill and soon after he died. It was said that a wooden statue of Saint Martial, in the cathedral of Poitiers, wept streams of tears down its face whilst Longchamp lay dying. In recognition of his sterling efforts in support of the king, Longchamp – who had of course been a very controversial figure during recent years – was remembered. Richard gave his brother Robert the abbey of St Mary in York.

In the end peace was patched up between Richard and Walter and the interdict was repealed by Pope Celestine. Richard argued expediency as his motive, as the land in dispute was frequently crossed by Philip's forces on his raids into Normandy. Richard gave substantial compensation to the archbishop, granting him two manors as well as the port of Dieppe, allowing Walter to recover some at least of his lost revenues. But the whole event was an example of how Richard's high-handedness and determination to ride roughshod over the rights of others in his own interests could lead to him falling out with people who he would be better off having on his side.

Richard's campaign for new allies met with success though. Baldwin, count of Flanders, was won over (a gift of 5,000 silver marks presumably helped) and the Bretons also took Richard's part. The delegation to Flanders had been led by Peter des Préaux, a Norman baron, and William Marshal who held land from the count at St-Omer. Marshal continued to provide valuable service and shortly before had played a key role in the Siege of Milli near Beauvais. He had climbed a scaling ladder to get over the walls and, when confronted by the constable of the castle, had promptly knocked him unconscious with a blow to the head. This energy, coming from a man who was now more than fifty years old, impressed Richard who nevertheless chided Marshal for getting too close to danger; if ever there was a case of the kettle calling the pot black, this was it.[21]

In the summer of 1197 the count of Flanders journeyed to Normandy where he agreed a formal truce with Richard. Under the terms of this, neither man was to make peace with Philip without the agreement of the other. It was a great diplomatic triumph for Richard, won by a combination of the politics of war and other more peaceful policies. Each man would be bound to the other and must come to their aid if attacked by the French. The chief witness to this on the English side was Richard's brother John, now becoming a more-trusted lieutenant.[22] This was a development that caused huge headaches for Philip.

The new alliance quickly paid dividends. The count of Flanders descended on Artois whilst Richard attacked Berry. Philip though held his nerve and retook Dangu. He then turned his attention to the count of Flanders further north. At first, he met with success. He managed to relieve Arras from the besieging Flemish forces. Sensing total victory, he chased after Baldwin in hot pursuit. But he lost control of his forces. Baldwin and his men cut down the bridges behind some of Philip's army, leaving them cut off. Philip was amongst those caught on the wrong side of the river.

He tried to negotiate his way out, offering Baldwin the same generous terms that Richard had given him. However, the count was not to be bought off so easily. He insisted that he intended to honour his arrangement with Richard and the arrangements for a conference between the three men were duly agreed. From promising beginnings, Philip's campaign had turned into a fiasco.

A meeting was arranged between Richard, Philip and Baldwin near Les Andalys. Richard agreed to a truce for a year on condition that each side held on to what they had, that trading relations were renewed and that prisoners were exchanged. Again, it was a tactic to buy more time, and once more Richard was in a better position than had previously been the case having made some useful gains further to the south in Berry.

Hubert Walter had been summoned over from Canterbury to add his considerable skills to the negotiations taking place in France. He was instrumental in resolving the conflict between the king and Walter of Coutances at Rouen. His influence was decisive in finally reaching a deal over Les Andalys. He also added clauses to the treaty between Richard and Philip of Flanders. He was away from his palace at Lambeth for nearly twenty-one weeks. He then returned to England where he was tasked with raising yet more money for Richard's campaigning.[23]

During 1197, there was an expedition to Outremer mainly composed of German crusaders. A truce had been in place there for some time but their arrival brought this to an end. Al-'Adil, Saladin's brother, was infuriated by the attack and reacted violently, laying siege to Jaffa. The Christian leadership summoned a council to decide how to respond to this. Their king, Henry of Champagne, was present at this. But when he was leaning against a pillar in an upstairs room, it broke and he fell out of a window to his death in the courtyard below. Jaffa fell soon afterwards with a great loss of Christian life.

But crusader fortunes in Outremer soon turned around. In a great battle against the Muslim army, Al-'Adil was mortally wounded. Many prisoners were captured and Sidon was taken by the Christians. The Muslims soon after abandoned Beirut, being caught by surprise when a fleet from Cyprus led by Aimery of Lusignan (who had taken over on the island after the death of Guy) attacked. Aimery soon after took a wife; none other than Isabella, the widow of both Conrad of Montferrat and Henry of Champagne as well as the former wife of Humphrey of Toron who was yet again proving herself to be a valuable tradeable commodity.

The emperor had by now made himself extremely unpopular in Sicily where his actions became a byword for cruelty. There was a revolt against him led by his own wife Constance (perhaps inspired by the example of Eleanor of Aquitaine?). The people of Sicily rose up in support. There was a mass cull of the Emperor's supporters and Henry was forced to flee to save himself. But the roads leading back to his heartlands were closed and he was forced to seek safety in a fortress.

A reconciliation was brokered between the emperor and his wife as well as his rebellious Sicilian subjects. But then in September 1197 there was upheaval in Europe when Henry died suddenly at Messina. It was said that on his deathbed he was full of remorse and made a request that Richard be compensated for the ransom he had paid over. As Henry was only 31, perhaps he felt that God was punishing him for his sins. Not long after, a bitter succession dispute broke out over who should take his place which 'came to be seen as the turning point from which the Reich never recovered'. German historians later came to see the death of Henry as a catastrophe for his empire.[24]

There was a problem regarding what to do with Henry's body; despite the pleas of the archbishop of Messina, Pope Celestine refused permission to bury him in consecrated ground until the ransom money was repaid. But the money did not return to Richard. Henry's body was left unburied for eight months until a new Pope, Innocent III, ordered that it should be respectfully interred.[25] Henry was buried in Palermo Cathedral, where his large sarcophagus now abuts that of his wife Constance and their son, Frederick II, who was one of the most extraordinary of all medieval rulers, known as *stupor mundi* – the wonder of the world.

Richard had built useful alliances in Germany, such as that with Adolf, archbishop of Cologne. Richard was invited to take part in the election of a new German king but was reluctant to journey to the region in person, fearing that he might once more be held hostage. There were even rumours that he himself was offered the position but turned it down. In any event, he supported his nephew, Henry of Brunswick. Henry however was away on a long-term basis and so his younger brother Otto was put forward in his place.

Otto of Brunswick was close to Richard, having spent some time at the Angevin court, and so was an ideal candidate from his perspective. Richard was one of the main drivers behind his succession and contributed financially to his election. German historians later remarked 'in this way England was directly involved in weakening and destroying the power of the Staufer, and thus in the decline of the empire and Germany's position of power in Europe'.[26] Whether this was Richard's intention or not is not clear; but presumably it may have given him a certain satisfaction if he had known of this outcome. It certainly strengthened Richard's position in Western Europe considerably.

Otto had been brought up in England during the reign of Henry II and Richard had appointed him earl of York when he left on crusade in 1190. Otto was duly elected king and crowned at Aix-la-Chapelle; he would eventually become Holy Roman Emperor in 1209 though not before suffering many vicissitudes in between. This was a very good outcome for the English king. Philip tried to take counter-measures by seeking an understanding with Philip of Swabia, a fierce rival of Otto, but it did him little good. On this occasion Richard had outmanoeuvred him. But Philip of Swabia refused to take his rejection lying down and was soon at war with Otto.

Richard also formed an alliance with Renaud, the count of Boulogne. Renaud's loyalty had been suspected by Philip for some time and now he openly formed an alliance with Richard. The count was soon raiding French territories with great enthusiasm. Other allies joined Richard too, almost a procession of them including Hugh of St Pol, Louis of Blois and Geoffrey of Perche. Richard was reportedly so confident of his position that he even threatened

Paris. The chroniclers of the time largely agreed that Richard could turn so many heads because of his wealth and generosity, an insight into the depth of his financial resources.

Seemingly at around this time Richard changed the emblem used on his royal seal. Lions had appeared in Norman heraldry but now Richard chose to adopt three of them as his royal emblem. One represented England, one Normandy and the other Aquitaine. The symbol has since stood the test of time and remains the royal standard, though Normandy and Aquitaine have long ceased to be territories of the British Crown.[27]

In 1197, Richard issued orders that funds were to be raised in England to pay for the services of 300 knights for one year. This was a departure from feudal norms which required the services of knights for forty days a year. This was a relic of the old system of the *fyrd*, one which dated back to Anglo-Saxon times and was of little use for the extended period of support that Richard required as it was primarily for local defence and it was not intended to provide men for months at a time.[28]

When a meeting was held at Oxford to discuss the issue amongst the clergy, Hugh, the strong-willed bishop of Lincoln, refused to pay the contribution demanded of him. He recognised that the Church was honour-bound to support the king's military actions but only when he was in England. There were angry words exchanged between Hugh and Hubert Walter who completely lost his temper in the debate. Word was sent to Richard of Hugh's intransigence.

Whilst this may appear to be an attempt on the part of a grasping king to squeeze as much money as he could from his bishops, there was nevertheless evidence that what he was asking of them was only to provide the funds that had always been levied on them in the past. Examination of several sets of accounts for the time show that the abbot of St Edmunds and the bishops of Salisbury and Lincoln were behind with the payments that had been required of them in the past two years.[29]

Richard was furious. He ordered that all Hugh's possessions should be confiscated, as should those of Herbert, bishop of Salisbury, who had supported him. But Hugh was no pushover. No one wanted to carry out the king's orders for fear of being excommunicated. Hugh later journeyed to France to present his arguments to Richard in person. He found him at Château Gaillard. When Richard saw Hugh, he turned his back on him. Hugh was not intimidated. Grabbing his cloak, he demanded the kiss of peace as he had travelled a long way to see him. Richard resisted him at first but gave in at last. He confirmed that peace had been restored between them by making a present of a pike to Hugh for his dinner (the bishop did not eat meat).

This did the trick. Richard accepted Hugh's arguments. Hugh and Richard seem to have had something of a mutual affection for each other. Perhaps the king appreciated the virtues of this straight-talking and brave man who sometimes acted in a confessorial role with regard to him. Hugh told him off as he was reportedly 'not faithful to your marriage bed' and also because he had abused his powers in the appointment of bishops.[30]

All this was a prelude to a renewal of all-out war against Philip, something that was perhaps predictable from a downpour of bloody rain falling on the heads of some of Richard's men working on improving the defences at Château Gaillard.[31] In the meantime Geoffrey, the suspended archbishop of York, had made his way to Richard to plead his case. In this he was successful.

But it was one thing to restore his position at York in theory, quite another to do so in practice. Richard also summoned the argumentative canons from York to appear before him but they failed to comply. There was little that could be gained by Geoffrey going back to York without support for his case from the papacy. There was by now a new pontiff in Rome, Innocent III, and it was to him that Geoffrey went next to gain support. Ironically, shortly after he left, the delegation of the canons from York arrived at Richard's court and convinced him that he should not insist on the recognition of Geoffrey's rights until he had come back from Rome with a firm judgement from the Pope.[32] The dispute rumbled on and on, seemingly interminably.

Innocent III would become the most formidable pontiff of the age. He had written to the bishops in England following his election early in 1198, explaining that occasionally God picked for his purposes a younger, inexperienced man (he was in his early thirties) and that 'this is the Lord's doing and it is marvellous in our eyes'.[33] He had demonstrated already that he planned to be a vigorous and proactive pope who would take no nonsense from anyone; one of his first acts had been to dismiss the janitors and doorkeepers at the Vatican so that complainants might have easier access to him.[34] His reign as pontiff would not overlap with that of Richard for long, due to the death of the latter; one wonders what might have happened if two such strong-willed men had to deal with each other over a long period of time.

Richard spent Easter at Le Mans that year in the company of his sister Joanna and her husband Raymond, count of Toulouse. On Good Friday 1198, Hugh de Nonant, the bishop of Coventry, breathed his last not far away to the north at Bec in Normandy. His relationship with Richard had been complicated, as had that with the monks at Coventry whom he had replaced with secular canons, thus creating a controversy that rumbled on for years. The writer of the *Annals of Winchester*, who may well have been Richard of Devizes, wrote enthusiastically that 'after a long illness and unbearable suffering he closed his miserable life by a well-deserved death'.[35]

Richard persuaded Innocent to intervene in a domestic matter. When he married Berengaria, he had been given as her dowry two small castles at Roquebrune and St-Jean-Pied-de-Port but they had never been handed over. This rankled with Richard. Innocent now wrote to the king of Navarre, Berengaria's brother Sancho, threatening him with sanctions if he did not do what was required, though there is no evidence that the castles were ever handed over or that spiritual penalties were imposed because of this non-compliance. It was a rather grubby episode given Richard's general coldness towards his wife, and suggested again that the relationship was merely a business arrangement.[36]

Both Richard and Philip could not wait to get back on the battlefield. The truce that had been agreed between them was due to expire as soon as the harvest had been gathered in. As soon as this was done, 'their direful fury immediately blazed forth, and, all conferences being put an end to, each entered the kingdom of the other in hostile form, and depopulating the lands, carried off booty, took prisoners, and burned towns'. There was also, according to Roger of Howden, tit-for-tat mutilation and blinding of prisoners on both sides.[37] These were terrible times for those caught up in the middle of this savage warfare.

Richard's attack in France that year was spearheaded by Baldwin of Flanders, who felt that he had been unfairly deprived by Philip of Artois. Baldwin was joined by Renaud of Boulogne. He laid siege to St Omer. The citizens begged Philip for help but he was detained elsewhere and St Omer fell. Richard in the meantime was active in Normandy, leading a raid on the French Vexin. Dangu was retaken by him and a tightening noose placed around the key fortress of Gisors.

Philip, alarmed at these developments, led a force towards nearby Courcelles, not realising that it had already been captured by Richard. Richard was out patrolling when he got news that Philip was nearby. Richard and his men fell on the French. The action ended with Philip once more fleeing for his life, or at least for his freedom, making for Gisors, the only place within reach that appeared safe.

Frantically Philip charged over the bridge leading into Gisors. So great was the press of the panic-stricken French on it that it collapsed under their collective weight. Philip himself fell into the River Epte, reaching the surface gasping for air, though managing to extricate himself. Twenty French knights with him were not so lucky and drowned; one of them was John, the brother of William des Barres, that old opponent of Richard who had later won his friendship by his gallantry in Outremer. To the knowledge of William Marshal, 100 were taken prisoner, several being prominent French knights; these included Matthew of Montmorency, Alan of Rusci and Fulk of Gilervalle. Mercadier took another thirty captive.[38]

Two hundred horses were also taken, 140 of them covered in splendid armour.[39] It was a resounding victory for Richard and a humiliation for Philip, even though he escaped from the debacle. French chroniclers explained that Philip's men were caught by surprise by a much larger army and put up a brave fight but could not disguise the fact that this was a serious defeat. Richard on the other hand was described as being at the heart of the action, taking down three knights with a single lance.

Even Philip's supportive chronicler Rigord was unable to gloss over the defeat. In an act which speaks eloquently of the mores of the time, he blamed it on Philip's 'sin' in letting Jews return to Paris as he had recently done. There were other strange omens around too; for example, stories of a knight who had died but had been miraculously resurrected. There was strange weather with stones as large as nuts falling from the air. It was even said that the Anti-Christ had been born in Babylon.[40]

Philip was soon raiding in the south of Normandy again, sacking Evreux. The town was home to a magnificent cathedral, which was damaged during this period of fighting between Richard and Philip. It had only been rebuilt earlier in the century after having been destroyed in 1119 by Henry I, king of France, during a rebellion that had broken out in Normandy. It was in an unfortunate position, being right on the front-line in the ongoing battles between the kings of France and the dukes of Normandy.

Richard had only a few men with him to fight off this renewed attack on Normandy. An all-out attack was unthinkable, even for a man with his risk-taking personality. Instead he stayed close behind Philip's army, shadowing him until he had more men with which to launch an attack. He was soon joined by another 200 knights and Mercadier and some of his mercenaries. They attacked the French near Vernon and caused them to flee. Roger of Howden suggested that Philip fled in disgraceful fashion, on an old dark brown horse that he had owned for a decade, leaving everything of value behind him and accompanied only by three or four knights and a single man-at-arms.

Another round of fighting then broke out in this bitter and seemingly never-ending war. Despite the improvement in Richard's position he still had not recovered all the lands in Normandy that had been lost to Philip during his period of captivity. There did not seem to be an end in sight and the possibility of a return to Outremer to complete his crusade appeared to be further away than ever. Richard had proved himself a determined opponent and a formidable warrior; but so too, much to his chagrin, had Philip of France. It seemed that this must be a fight to the death; but just how close death was, none yet knew. As it happened, Richard's time was running out.

19

Last Rites (1198–1199)

'How brief is the laughter of earth, how long are its tears'
Geoffrey of Vinsauf on the death of Richard

Although the records do not give a blow-by-blow account of every confrontation that took place, there were clearly many smaller-scale skirmishes in France in the last years of Richard's reign. For example, Roger of Howden describes a lightning raid launched by Mercadier and his mercenaries on the town of Abbeville, which he attacked whilst a fair was taking place; he returned to Normandy with a great deal of booty.[1]

It was not all one-way traffic though; whilst attacking the castle of Pacy, the right to which he had previously foresworn, Robert of Leicester was almost captured when the garrison launched a counter-strike. But the collective result of these actions was to force Philip back to the negotiating table. He wished to be free to recover his position in Artois and offered to hand back all his gains in Normandy with the important exception of Gisors. But Richard refused to countenance a deal which did not include his ally Baldwin of Flanders.

Richard could not afford to forget England completely. In 1198, he issued a ruling against those who had been illegally hunting venison in his forests. They were to be visited with the full force of the law as it had been carried out during his father's reign. In other words, those caught committing such an offence were to be blinded and castrated. Men were not allowed to roam in the forests with bows and arrows, nor were they allowed to take dogs into them.

Knights were to be appointed to assist the king's foresters in the protection of his rights. It was a bitter irony that the draconian forest laws whose repeal had caused such joy at the start of his reign were back again. It was also a metaphor for how out of touch Richard was becoming with the English people. He was increasingly autocratic, even vicious, as his obsession with raising money to reconquer his territories in France took over.

Common rights were to be restricted; for example, no domesticated pigs were to be allowed to wander in the forests during the fawning season. Those who farmed lands that had been turned from forest to cultivated ground were required to present the king with a proportion of the crop yielded from them, whether it be wheat, oats or barley or pulses such as beans and peas.[2] If there was indeed a man called Robin Hood around at this time, it is a fair bet that he would have been an opponent of actions such as these.

This was a king ruthlessly reasserting his rights. Not only did this potentially bring him into conflict with the common folk of England but he was also increasingly at odds with the Church. Members of the religious Orders in the country refused to pay the taxes that he had ordered them to. In retaliation, the king ordered that anyone who committed a crime against a churchman should not be required to make satisfaction to him; but if it were the other way around, then the member of the clergy was required to make recompense.[3]

These were dangerous moves which resonated rather too much of Henry II's actions against Thomas Becket. Richard at least had an excellent relationship with his current archbishop. But Hubert Walter was under attack from other directions, perhaps because other clerics thought that he was rather too secular.

A delegation of monks from Canterbury had made their way to Rome to complain that their archbishop was involved in some unseemly secular matters including 'passing sentences of blood' (that is, of mutilation or execution) and that this was not appropriate for a man in his position in the English Church.

Pope Innocent III was no pushover, unlike the previous incumbent of the Papal throne, the octogenarian Celestine. He wrote to Richard demanding that Hubert Walter should be removed from his position as justiciar. Richard reluctantly agreed though it is very likely that Hubert continued to play a leading role as an unofficial adviser in England.[4] Hubert on the other hand may well have been happy with this turn of events as he had previously tried to resign as justiciar but the king would not let him.

The Canterbury monks were unhappy that Hubert had built a new church at Lambeth in London and transferred there some of the rights they had previously held. Pope Innocent soon after wrote to Hubert, expressing his amazement at his actions and giving him thirty days to demolish the church that had caused such offence. Innocent also instructed the bishops in England to ignore the commands of the archbishop if he did not do as he was told. Although he resisted the demands for a time, Hubert eventually caved in and had the controversial building pulled down.

Innocent was determined to launch another crusade to recover Jerusalem. In 1198, he wrote to his officials in the archbishopric of York. He reminded them of the words of Psalm 137: 'if I forget thee, O Jerusalem, let my right hand forget her cunning. If I do not remember thee, let my tongue cleave to the roof of my mouth'. He mourned the fact that the inheritance of Christ's people had been taken by Muslims. The Sepulchre of Christ had been profaned by the unrighteous. The kings of Europe, he said forcefully, were abusing their luxuries and their wealth, 'harassing each other with inexorable hatred'.

One of them – clearly Richard – was using all his endeavours to avenge himself for the wrongs done to him by the other, Philip, said Innocent. Because of this, the enemies of Christ mocked the Christians at their apparent powerlessness to do anything meaningful to recover Jerusalem. Innocent was clearly fed up with the constant warfare between the two kings and wished it to be brought to a prompt close.[5] He had only been pope for a few months but he was already frustrated with the rulers of Western Europe. To make matters worse, the crusade recently launched by the Germans had fizzled out with few tangible results to show for it.

But crusade fever was taking hold again. A preacher, Fulk of Neuilly, was gaining considerable support for his fire and brimstone brand of preaching. He almost seemed to have access to divine powers; Christ-like he cured the blind, the lame and the dumb. He converted harlots and usurers to the Christian cause. He also suggested that one of the kings of France and England would die soon if they did not desist from the constant fighting against each other.

Fulk appeared before Richard and warned him to desist from his three major vices; pride, avarice and sensuality. It was then that Richard made his famous reply that he had given his Pride to the Templars, his Avarice to the Cistercians and his Sensuality to the Princes of the Church. Fulk left the audience disappointed.

That Christmas was spent by Richard in Normandy; Philip also spent it in the duchy whilst Roger of Howden notes that King Otto celebrated it in Westphalia. Not long afterwards,

Otto launched an attack on several cities owned by Philip of France; the alliance that Richard had fostered with his nephew Otto was already starting to pay off.

But the war in France in the meantime had started to exhaust the resources of both Richard and Philip. A peace deal in France suited both men as it gave them breathing space and on 13 January 1199 Richard sailed up the Seine to meet Philip; so little did the men trust each other that Richard shouted over his comments from a boat whilst Philip stayed on the riverbank on horseback. But they did at least agree on a date on which they should formally meet to discuss a truce.

No doubt this was intended to be yet another temporary cessation of hostilities, whatever both men might have said publicly. There was a papal legate present when the negotiations took place, Peter of Capua, and other important nobles were there to hammer out a deal; another legate, Stephen, had been sent to Venice on a similar mission. At the end of the discussions, a five-year truce was tabled; Innocent wanted an end to the fighting for at least this length of time to enable a new crusade to be launched. He further wanted forces to be ready to set out by March 1199, a very ambitious timetable indeed.

It was not an easy conversation with the legate though. Peter attempted to get Richard to soften his demands, which were that all the territory taken from him by Philip should be returned. He was roundly rebuffed by an angry Richard, who reminded him that his lands had been seized unjustly from him whilst he was fighting to recover Jerusalem and then imprisoned when attempting to return home. The actions of his fellow crusader, Philip, had been an outrageous breach of his crusading vows.

This was in line with the views expressed by the writer of the *History of William Marshal* who launched a blistering attack on the corruption prevalent in the Church, when any visitor to Rome who wished to seek justice should go armed with the benefits of those two persuasive saints, 'St Gold and St Silver'.[6] It was as if years of pent-up resentment against the Papacy was coming out and the legate was directly in the firing line.

Richard was eventually persuaded to moderate his demands, with William Marshal, who spent a lot of time in France with his king during the last years of his reign, being the man largely responsible for calming tensions along with his friend Baldwin of Béthune.[7] But then the legate, who does not seem to have recognised when he was onto a good thing, unwisely pushed his luck too far. He asked

Richard to release the still-captive bishop of Beauvais, who was imprisoned in Château Gaillard. The bishop had previously written to Pope Celestine asking for him to intervene but had received a cold reply; 'into the pit you have made, you have deservedly fallen'.[8] On a previous occasion, when being pressured by Innocent to set him free, Richard had replied by sending back the hauberk that the 'bishop' had been wearing when captured and asked the pontiff if he recognised it.

Even Richard's mother had appealed for the bishop's release but for once Richard did not listen to her. His mood regarding the recalcitrant and aggressive bishop was probably not helped when he tried to escape. Whilst being escorted to a meeting with Eleanor, the bishop had broken free from his guard and rushed to a church he was passing in an attempt to seek sanctuary. He hammered the knocker on the door and demanded access: 'I seek the protection of God and of the Church,' he shouted. He had been dragged away and taken back to his prison. Shortly afterwards he was moved to Chinon where Richard could keep a closer eye on him. Not until the reign of Richard's brother John would the bishop be released in exchange for the bishop-elect of Cambrai who had been taken prisoner by King Philip.[9]

This latest approach from the legate, evidencing a change of heart from the papacy, caused Richard to display that famous Angevin temper to fine effect. Furiously he told the legate that the 'bishop' was taken in the guise of a knight and he deserved to be de-consecrated. Richard, working himself up into a lather, now let rip at the legate and his master at the personal level, saying what a hypocrite and a fool Peter was:

> Never did the pope raise a finger to help me when I was in prison and wanted his help to be free. And now he asks me to set free a robber and an incendiary who has never done me anything but harm. Get out of here Sir traitor, liar, trickster, corrupt dealer in churches and never let me see you here again.[10]

The legate, in fear for his life, (or at least, William Marshal's biographer suggested, of being castrated) hastily retreated and Richard in a sulk shut himself in his room on his bed. Only the smooth talking of William Marshal could calm him down – at least according to his contemporary biographer who was unlikely to underplay his brilliance. But there was a real doubt that any truce was ever going to hold for very long, a situation that probably suited Richard rather well as he held the upper hand in the ongoing fighting in France.

There were several incidents that threatened to lead to a renewal of violence before very long. One of them occurred when Mercadier led a force to restore some order amongst recalcitrant subjects in the region of Limoges and Angoulême. On the way, they were ambushed by what might have been a band of out-of-control mercenaries; a breed of soldier who would terrify France on and off for centuries. Philip denied any involvement in planning the action but he naturally enough came under suspicion.

But the other incident was incontestably Philip's responsibility. He took the decision to build a castle on the Seine, in the same way that Richard had done with Château Gaillard. But he was not confident enough yet of his position to go through with the plan. Richard's chancellor, Eustace, bishop of Ely, warned him unequivocally that if he continued, then the truce was off. Philip can hardly have been surprised at this assertive reaction but nevertheless thought discretion to be the better part of valour and backed down.

Further steps were taken to patch up the quarrel between Philip and Richard. The French king had long laid claim to rights over the church in Tours. A deal was tabled. In return for Philip giving up his claim to this, Richard would surrender his to Gisors. There would also be a marriage, making use of that other popular tool for keeping the peace during the medieval period. Richard's niece would marry Philip's son Louis and would come with a dowry of 20,000 marks. Philip would also break his agreement with Philip of Swabia and help Otto of Brunswick secure his crown.

Richard hesitated before responding. He had other business to attend to. Philip's allies in Aquitaine, especially the count of Angoulême and the viscount of Limoges, were not included in any truce. At the end of March 1199, Richard laid siege to the castle of the latter at Châlus-Chabrol, close to Limoges. He was attracted to the site, it was suggested by Roger of Howden, Ralph of Coggeshall and others, by the rumoured discovery of some buried treasure there.

It was Lent, a holy time when the sword was supposed to be laid aside, but Richard was in no mood to miss the chance to put matters right, treasure or no treasure. But the siege was no walkover. Three days passed and the castle continued to stubbornly refuse to yield despite not having a large or noticeably professional force to resist him. This was going to be an arduous siege and Richard instructed his sappers to get to work undermining the walls.

Parts of the fortifications started to collapse but the mining went on. Richard's crossbowmen let off flight after flight of their bolts to keep the heads of the defenders down. But the garrison hurled large chunks of stone down onto the heads of the attackers and refused to yield. These did not harm the besiegers who were well protected with their various siege engines but created a substantial din that alarmed them.

But at last it seemed that the end was near and that the small garrison would be forced to surrender; there were two knights, Peter Bru and Peter Basil, and thirty-eight others, both men and women, inside.

Twilight approached on a late March evening in 1199. Richard had taken supper in his tent and decided to take one last walk around the siege lines and maybe even to practice his skills with a crossbow. He wore a helmet and carried a shield (or had one carried before him by one of his men) but he wore no armour. He had the place pretty much to himself. There was just one lone crossbowman manning the castle walls, not particularly well armed as he needed to use a frying pan as a shield. He had been defying the attackers all day, something that must have been an insult to their pride as much as anything else.

Then this lone crossbowman, a man named Bertrand de Gurdon according to some sources (although others think it more likely to have been Peter Basil)[11] took careful aim with his bow and let loose a bolt. Richard was slow to react and raised his shield too late. The bolt struck home deep in his shoulder. He managed to walk back to his tent, not wanting his men to make a fuss or worry about him. Once he got inside he tried to pull out the bolt but only succeeded in snapping it with the head of the bolt still inside him.

A surgeon was summoned, a man from Mercadier's entourage.[12] Working as well as he could as the shadows of night drew in, the tent dimly lit by a candle flame, the bolt was eventually removed but much butchery was involved in the process. Underneath the bandages that were tied around the wound, the flesh started to go gangrenous and infection began to spread. Richard had seen men die of such wounds and he knew well enough what was happening. According to the later chronicler Matthew Paris the king was by now in 'unbearable pain' as his wounds festered and the bacteria ate away at his body.

He summoned his mother to come to him as quickly as possible, realising that his death was now only a matter of time; this was one foe he could only fight for so long. She came at once from Fontevraud. Significantly there was no last-minute plea for Berengaria to join him. Only four trusted men were allowed to enter his tent so that as few as possible would know what was happening and would not lose heart whilst the siege was unfinished.

Richard lingered on for days, during which time the castle was at last taken whilst orders had been given from his sick-bed that other castles belonging to Viscount Aimar should also be attacked, supporting the suggestion that this was no isolated treasure hunt but rather a strategic mission that Richard was on. The crossbowman who had given him his mortal wound was summoned to his tent after his capture.

In the version told by Roger of Howden, Richard asked Bertrand (if indeed it was he) what he had done to earn his hatred. The crossbowman responded that with his own hand Richard had killed his father and his two brothers. He no longer cared what fate Richard had in store for him. Impressed by his bravado, the dying king ordered his release. If Roger is to be believed, the king's orders were not carried out. Instead that loyal captain Mercadier had him skinned alive (though the *Annals of Winchester* suggest that this was at the insistence of Joanna, Richard's sister).[13]

At last, as evening approached on 6 April, it was clear that the end was nigh. It was a Tuesday, the day of Mars, an appropriate day for such a warrior to die as Ralph of Diceto noted.[14] Peter Milo, a Cistercian abbot from an establishment near Poitiers and Richard's almoner, was at his side. He heard Richard's final confession and granted him absolution. As he whispered the last rites, the king took his ultimate breath. Milo closed Richard's eyes and his mouth in a tender final act of kindness. A monk from Limoges, Bernard Itier, said that his demise was 'to the joy of many and the sorrow of others'.[15] It was a good summing up; Richard was a man who certainly divided opinions. To some extent he still does to this day.

Messengers carried the news post-haste to all corners of Richard's territories. It arrived at Rouen when it was night. William Marshal had retired to bed, having left Richard just a few days before the king's fatal encounter. He was journeying back to England on the king's business. Now, half-dressed, he discussed what was likely to happen next with Hubert Walter, the archbishop of Canterbury, who was also in the city at the time. This premature end to the king's life came as a shattering blow when so much was left to be done. Marshal argued in favour of John taking the throne, a situation in which he presumably felt he could protect and even improve his own position. Hubert took the opposite view and warned Marshal that he would regret his opinion.[16] But in the end Marshal won the argument.

The truth of Richard's death has been the subject of wide debate. Was he at Châlus-Chabrol as part of a treasure hunt or were more pragmatic and less romantic reasons at the heart of his thinking? The irony of all this, as has been pointed out by the French historian Jean Flori, was that the best analysis of the situation has been undertaken not by modern historians but by a nineteenth-century French cleric, the Abbé Arbellot, who examined the evidence meticulously.

He concluded that it seemed highly probable that down to earth reasons regarding the reassertion of his rights as the duke of Aquitaine were the main reason for Richard being at this relatively obscure castle at this particular moment in time. However, he thinks that it is not impossible that treasure was subsequently found in the vicinity of the castle and in particular suggests that some Roman statues representing an emperor with his family seated at a table were found (the details being based on the account of the French chronicler Rigord).[17]

The carving up of Richard's body was undertaken after his death according to the gruesome rituals of the time. Richard's brain and entrails were buried at the nearby abbey of Charroux whilst his heart – as large as a pomegranate said Gervase of Canterbury – was taken to Rouen, there to be solemnly entombed next to his elder brother Henry, something of a bitter irony given their shattered relationship. The rest of him was buried at that favourite Angevin site at Fontevraud, close to his father, again in its way deeply ironic.

Matthew Paris explained this division. Richard wished his body to be buried at the feet of his father at Fontevraud because of the guilt that he felt at betraying him. His heart was to go to Rouen in recognition of the incomparable loyalty he felt for Normandy. His entrails were to be buried in Aquitaine for rather different reasons; it was because they were the receptacle of his excrement and he felt that this was all that the duchy deserved.[18] If true it was an interesting insight into where Richard's affections lay at the end of his reign. Significantly there was nothing of him bequeathed to England.

In 2013, the results of some fascinating scientific research were unveiled by Dr Philippe Charlier, a forensic scientist from

Raymond Poincare University Hospital in France. Forensic investigation had been undertaken on remains said to be Richard's heart. They had badly decayed and were now little more than a grey-brown powder. Whilst it was not possible from this very fragmentary residue to establish for sure a cause of death, the scientists were able to state that a poisoned arrow was not the cause as some had suggested.

The remains included pollen from poplar and bellflower, both consistent with a time of death in April or May. Perhaps most intriguingly, traces of frankincense were also found. This has been valued for thousands of years for its use as incense, especially in burial rituals. Most famously, it was one of the gifts of the Magi to the Christ Child at the time of the Nativity. Its presence in the tomb was possibly a deliberate remembrance of this event, emphasising Richard's Christian virtues. There were traces of myrtle, daisy, mint and possibly lime, perhaps to give a pleasant aromatic counterbalance to the stench of decay. Mercury was also present, possibly as a preservative.[19]

Adam of Eynsham, biographer of the saintly Hugh of Lincoln, noted that the bishop visited Berengaria and held mass for her as soon as he heard of Richard's death, travelling through wild forests to get there. Despite his recent differences with Richard, Hugh was much distressed when he heard the news of his death. He 'groaned aloud' and hurried to Fontevraud to officiate at the funeral. It was a dangerous journey. The violent times had led to an upsurge in banditry and travellers were at great risk of being robbed. Some of Hugh's men were robbed of forty silver marks.

Hugh responded to suggestions that he should not make the journey with scorn. He said that 'it seems to me much more to be feared that I, like a coward, should deny my attendance to my former lord and king on this occasion, and fail to pay to the dead the honour and homage I always faithfully rendered to the living'. In a revealing passage, Ralph of Diceto suggested that, however much the king had fallen out with Hugh in public, in private he always treated him with the utmost respect. Despite it all, the saintly Hugh seems to have felt a genuine attachment to the king and deep sorrow at his passing. This is a significant insight into Richard's character and his ability to encourage attachment from those who knew him best.[20]

The internment at Fontevraud took place on 11 April 1199; just ten years after Richard had shed crocodile tears over his dead father's corpse in the same spot. Berengaria, the wife who seems to have played such a small part in Richard's life and was at Beaufort en Vallée when she heard of his death, was heartbroken. One wonders what emotions lay behind her tears; whether it was a sense of love or one of missed opportunity.

Hugh completed his journey to Fontevraud in time to meet the funeral cortege at the door of the abbey. It was a particularly holy day, Palm Sunday, the commemoration of when Christ had entered in triumph into Jerusalem, an honour that had been conspicuously denied to Richard. Once the ceremony was over, Hugh stayed on for three days. He spent the time assiduously conducting Masses in which he 'prayed for the pardon and the bliss of everlasting life for the souls of the kings buried there and of all the faithful who had fallen asleep in Christ'.[21]

Fontevraud was becoming an Angevin mausoleum. It had been a great favourite of both Henry II and Eleanor of Aquitaine who had subscribed generously to it and the latter had spent much of her later life there. An Order of Fontevraud had developed, encouraging the foundation of churches in its honour in places as far apart as Tickhill in Yorkshire and Amesbury in Wiltshire. Fontevraud had been transformed by Angevin patronage from a house for the dregs of society including prostitutes who had fallen on hard times to a foundation that the rich and famous, royalty and aristocracy alike, were keen to have their daughters associated with. During its heyday, it had one of the largest monastic networks in Europe. There were four separate establishments at Fontevraud alone, three for women, one for men.

And yet for all that, the location was revealing. It was not in Westminster that Henry or Richard were buried; it was in the heart of Anjou, close to Chinon, that they chose to be interred. This is a strong symbolic clue as to where their priorities lay. England was just part of an extended Angevin federation. The territories in France meant as much to them if not more than England did. They were dependent on the wealth of England to finance their ambitious schemes, but their true affections lay more in the Loire region than in London, in Anjou more than Anglia.

Even in death the Angevins did not find peace. A visit to Fontevraud now reveals a place of tranquillity and calm, an out of the way spot off the beaten track. But it was not always so and in Richard's time it would often have been a hive of activity. The Angevin tombs that lie in the main body of the church,

Henry II next to Eleanor in one cluster and Richard and Isabella of Angoulême (John's second wife) in the other, were once tucked away out of sight in the crypt. But during the French Revolution, with its anti-monarchical fervour, the tombs were vandalised and damaged (that of Richard's sister Joanna was lost altogether).

The bones of those inside were scattered. The tombs were later reassembled in their current site though what became of the human remains inside is unclear. Between 1806 and 1963 the abbey served as a prison and it was even the silent witness of French Resistance fighters executed by firing squad there by the Vichy regime during the Second World War. The decline and fall of Fontevraud was something of a metaphor for the decline and fall of the Angevin federation.

Richard's mother, Eleanor, was present at his funeral at Fontevraud and took control of the secular side of the ceremonies. It was said that she uttered a moving elegy for her son: 'I have lost the staff of my age, the light of my eyes'.[22] Also present was Milo, the abbot of Le Pin, who had heard Richard's last confession and Lucas, abbot of Turpenay. It almost goes without saying that Berengaria was conspicuous by her absence. Eleanor donated the pool at Langeais to the church in return for an annual remembrance of her son; this agreement was at least subsequently witnessed by Berengaria.

Hugh then celebrated Easter with Berengaria at Beaufort in the presence of the new king, John. The timing of this is surely significant; when Christians celebrate not just the Resurrection of Christ but also remind themselves of the promise of life everlasting for those who die as true believers. It was a message of hope to Berengaria who was devout in her faith and would no doubt have found comfort in it.[23]

Richard's forgotten queen made her own gift to the abbey in Le Mans so that the anniversary of her husband's death might be remembered.[24] There is very little evidence to go on when assessing how close Berengaria and Richard were. But what there is leads one to speculate that she felt a genuine affection for her larger-than-life husband but that he, for his part, was so busy trying to fulfil his grandiose ambitions that he had little time for her. Whether that was due to a lack of time, a lack of interest or a lack of love is a conundrum.

The memorial Masses she ordered should not be seen as a sign of romantic attachment but are more likely to have been a formal compliance with social conventions at the time; Berengaria seems to have been punctilious in her actions and took care to ensure that she was seen to be 'doing the right thing' though this does not necessarily mean that she did not also have strong and genuine emotions impelling her to do so. She would later bequeath a house that had been built for her and Richard at Thorée to the Hospitallers; but as several commentators have pointed out there is no evidence that they had ever lived there together.[25]

There is some tantalising evidence though that later in his reign Richard planned to involve Berengaria more in his life than he had in the past and indeed may have already done so. Shortly after the king's death, Gerald of Wales, who had been involved in an ongoing and bitter row about whether he should become the new bishop of St David's, appeared at Chinon before King John to present his case. Also present was Eleanor of Aquitaine and, at the instruction of her late husband, Berengaria.[26]

Richard's death during the siege of a minor castle was a squalid end to an extraordinary life. It was an inglorious conclusion to a tale that was generally regarded as glorious and many of the chroniclers who took his part struggled to account for this. There was no treasure found and, if we follow the arguments of Richard's most prominent twentieth-century biographer, that was not anyway the reason he was there.[27] He was instead on the spot to bring Viscount Aimar, a long-time opponent, to heel; Richard died, in this interpretation, in prosecution of his rights. Tradition (and Roger of Howden) asserted that Richard's death was avenged by his bastard son, Philip of Cognac, who killed Aimar. The shadowy Philip himself fades completely out of view shortly after this, having been last noted in the Pipe Rolls for John's reign in 1201.

Richard's supporters struggled to find an explanation for the king's death. Ralph of Coggeshall, a Cistercian who lauded Richard for his support of his Order, could only think it was a punishment for his sins which, like all men, he had too many of. It was easy enough perhaps to think that this was a judgement from on high on the crusader *par excellence* who had failed to fulfil his solemn vows.

Perhaps the last word on his death should go to a contemporary poet by the name of Geoffrey de Vinsauf, a man prepared to take the potentially blasphemous step of criticising God for the premature death of his hero. The last line of his memorial verse contains an elegy of timeless beauty:

> O Lord, if it is permissible to say it, let me say – with your leave – you could have done this more graciously, and with less haste, if he had bridled the foe at least (and there would have been

> little delay, he was on the verge of success). He could then have departed more worthily to remain with you. But by this lesson you have made us know how brief is the laughter of earth, how long are its tears.[28]

At Richard's side when he died was his trusted captain of mercenaries, Mercadier. There is something apposite that the major military presence with Richard at his end was not a king or a prominent crusader but a hired hand, for such men characterised much of Richard's military career, the majority of which was spent outside of the crusading arena. Yet Mercadier himself clearly felt a deep attachment to Richard as well as, perhaps unexpectedly, a sense of honour. A certain pride shines through in a quote attributed to Mercadier with regards to Richard: 'I fought for him with loyalty and strenuously, never opposed his will, [was] prompt in obedience to his commands; and in consequence of this service I gained his esteem and was put in command of his army'.[29] An Aquitanian lament said of him that 'never was there a king so faithful, so valiant, so fearless, so generous'.[30] It was an epitaph of which many kings would have been justifiably proud.

Few deaths can be regarded as 'timely' but in the context of Richard's reign and future reputation the timing was especially unfortunate. It means that assessments are made of Richard when his reign was cut short, before he could really prove that he was not only capable of crusading and fighting wars in France but also of being an effective peacetime king. Perhaps he never would have been but the inconvenient truth was that no one ever had a chance to find out.

If critics are quick to castigate Richard for his ineffectiveness when judged as a king of England, one wonders what they make of the chaos that followed when John took over from him. The war had reached stalemate: Bertran de Born said that the eagle and the falcon had been at each other's throats in a war that neither could win.[31] Now, with the death of Richard, that would all change. As is so often the case, men did not appreciate the greatness of what they had until it was no longer there.

20

Epilogue

'In a death so great the whole world fell'
Roger of Howden on the death of Richard

'Legend is the live part of history. The past, as such, is dead'. So said the writer Vladimir Volkoff. Richard the man was soon engulfed by Richard the legend, and in the process the man was much changed. He became a controversial, complex and divisive figure. Despite his dashing image, he did not even merit a Shakespeare play of his own, that honour being given to his brother John, a far lesser mortal, instead – though in fairness Richard is often referred to in that work in its earlier scenes.

Roger of Howden, who was by no means afraid to criticise Richard, nevertheless wrote that 'in this death, the lion by the ant was slain. O evil destiny! In a death so great the whole world fell!' But the chronicler was a fair man and he knew that his views were not unanimous. He also told of the words of another writer; 'Valour, avarice, crime, unbounded lust, foul famine, unscrupulous pride, and blind desire, have reigned for twice five years; all these an archer did with art, hand, weapon, strength, lay prostrate.'[1] If Richard can divide our modern world, he also had the ability to do the same with his own.

But even some of his enemies, whilst unafraid to point out his faults, also found much to praise in him. Baha' al-Din said of Richard that he was 'a man of wisdom, experience, courage and energy'.[2] Whilst many commentators would recognise the last three qualities easily enough, the first might come as a surprise.

But Richard was a clever man, even if his pride and quick temper could lead to him acting rashly, even foolishly, on occasion.

Richard's passing marked a turning point in Angevin dynastic history. Joanna followed Richard to the grave only a few months later. Her marriage to Raymond of Toulouse was not happy but it had produced a son and heir. She fell pregnant again but soon after her husband found himself at war with some of his subjects. Joanna took an active role in supporting his cause but whilst laying siege to the castle at Cassée on his behalf she was burned in a fire that broke out in her camp. This had occurred even as Richard lay dying and it was only when she went to ask for his help that she heard the shocking news of his demise.

Eleanor arranged for Joanna to be sent to Rouen to be nursed back to health by nuns but soon after she moved to Fontevraud. Despite her status as a pregnant wife, she was exceptionally allowed to take the veil. It was clear that she was dying. To compound her misery the birth was premature and the child died soon afterwards. Poignantly and significantly, one of the last acts of Joanna's complicated life was to have the boy baptised and given the name of Richard.

Joanna died soon after as a member of the Cistercian Order.[3] Her feckless husband, the count of Toulouse, was soon after in a relationship with the unnamed Damsel of Cyprus, though whether that ever became a formal marriage or not is unclear. Suffice to say, that relationship did not last for very long.

John was in the event to be Richard's successor after all whilst his nephew Otto was to inherit most of the late king's jewels. It seems that Richard nominated John personally and the younger brother, virtually the last man standing of the Angevin brood, was formally elected at Chinon. Eleanor was delighted with this; she had little time for Arthur of Brittany and, when all was said and done, John was her natural son. In fairness to John, since his great disloyalty during Richard's absence, he had been on his best behaviour for the last five years of Richard's life and had made amends for what had gone before.

John began his reign well. Philip invaded Normandy almost at once and took Evreux but John reacted with speed and strength. Philip was forced to the negotiating table and a truce was arranged. Arthur of Brittany, John's main rival for the throne, fell into his custody. It was a good start.

But it was not to last. Arthur soon disappeared, probably murdered on John's orders, maybe even by his own hand.[4] Although there were a few military successes in the early days, they became increasingly rare and John was eventually given the unflattering nickname of 'Softsword' by chroniclers. Equally notable was how the alliances that Richard had forged on the Continent, with the counts of Flanders and Boulogne and Otto, for example, quickly began to unravel. Long-term supporters of Richard such as Andrew de Chauvigny within a few years had switched to Philip's side. This may have been cause and effect – as John became increasingly unsuccessful men decided to change their allegiance – but John in every way appeared to be a pale imitation of his late brother.

To compound John's problems some prominent potential opponents of Philip in France started to show interest in a new crusade, momentum for which was starting to build. They duly departed, leaving Philip with a freer hand in France. John also found it easy to fall out with people. He treated Berengaria shamefully and she was constantly forced to ask for his support with very limited success. Eleanor of Aquitaine appears to have shown little interest in her affairs either; she was now old, quite possibly frail and certainly retired from public life.

Eleanor can be forgiven an inward despair at witnessing the dramatic and rapid disintegration of the Angevin dynasty, the unravelling of her life's work. All that she had striven for began to evaporate, as if she had woken from a magnificent dream and found to her shock that none of it was real. If she chose to retreat from the world through disillusionment, no one could blame her, especially as she had seen most of her children die before her.

Pope Innocent III later intervened on Berengaria's behalf. Berengaria's struggles to receive what was due to her from England continued even into the reign of John's successor, Henry III.[5] She lived out much of the rest of her life known as the Lady of Le Mans. The city had been part of her marriage settlement. In her role as its custodian, she showed herself to be a resilient and determined participant in an ongoing battle with some of the Church authorities in the city where she proved a resolute opponent.

Whatever else Berengaria was, on this evidence she was certainly no doormat. If she is a shadowy figure, it is only in the context of her role as a wife of Richard, in which part she was largely airbrushed, or perhaps more accurately ignored, by the chroniclers. Her reputation has suffered because she was the wife of one of the most intriguing kings of medieval England and daughter-in-law of one of the most formidable women of the age. She was in reality as much over-shadowed as shadowy.

Berengaria never remarried and, whilst this was unusual for noblewomen of the time, it was by no means unique in her family. Her sister Blanca (normally called Blanche) married Thibaut, count of Champagne, nephew of Richard through his half-sister Marie of Champagne. Blanca's husband died after just two years of married life (though two children were produced from the marriage in this short time); she did not remarry. Neither did Berengaria's father, Sancho VI, who was apparently heartbroken on the death of his wife Sancha of Castile.

Berengaria lived to see the accession of, and actually met, King Louis IX of France who was destined to gain as much renown as a crusader as her late husband and to whom she, as well as Richard, was related.[6] In fact, the young Louis (who also had a formidable mother in the form of Blanche of Castile, who was Richard's niece through his sister Eleanor) wrote letters to Berengaria in far more affectionate and kindly terms than her husband ever did if the surviving records are a guide.

Louis supported her generously in her efforts to build a Cistercian abbey at L'Epau on the edge of Le Mans. It was complete when she died in Le Mans, being nursed by members of the Cistercian Order, in December 1230, though the papal bill formally recognising it was not confirmed until shortly afterwards. An eye-witness to her funeral said that it was a sight wonderful to behold and many there were in tears; she had been a generous benefactress despite her own struggles for money.

This affinity with the Cistercians provides one of the frustratingly few examples of a common interest held by both Berengaria and Richard. Despite his occasional sniping at them, Richard was much fonder of the Order than any other religious body. Two of his closest confessors, Milo of St Marie du Pin and Adam of Perseigne, were Cistercians. In 1219, the Chapter-General of the Order instructed that annual anniversary memorials be held in remembrance of Richard and in 1223 they instructed that the same should be done for Berengaria after her death.[7] There was clearly a shared affinity here, a rare glimpse of something that might have to some extent been a source of mutual comfort to both king and queen.

Berengaria was buried at L'Epau. A magnificent tomb was erected in her memory. It was an appropriate resting place for a woman who had lived a difficult life, full of unfulfilled promise, for she was never crowned and never set foot in England during Richard's reign. Perhaps the most fitting epitaph on her end and her internment in the monastery for which she had striven so hard was from the pen of a modern writer who, quoting an old Navarrese saying, wrote that 'you come at last to the place where your heart is'.[8]

Human remains found at the abbey in 1960 are widely, though not universally, believed to be hers.[9] One item of evidence for this is that the cranium had been damaged post mortem and there were signs of a metal object having been there once such as a crown. At some stage, the tomb may have been clumsily opened and the crown, if such it was, may have either been robbed or removed in a rescue when the abbey was burned down in the fourteenth century.[10]

The tomb itself is intriguing. Berengaria is described on it as 'most humble former queen of the English'.[11] She is shown with long, flowing, loose hair; at the time, hair worn this way signified virginity and was often the way that a bride would appear on her wedding day. Her feet rest on two animals. One is a hound, an animal conventionally associated with domesticity and loyalty; perhaps this is a symbolic representation of Berengaria herself. The other animal is a lion; it takes little imagination to think who that might possibly represent.

One commentator said that 'Berengaria was unlucky to have had Eleanor as a mother-in-law and perhaps, unable to compete, she chose to withdraw'. It has been speculated by the same historian that, once she failed to produce children, Eleanor excluded her from affairs of state and Berengaria opted to stay out of the way.[12]

Eleanor was without a doubt the dominant woman in Richard's life and someone he was often in awe of. It would have been crystal-clear to Berengaria from the start that there was no real room for another woman in her husband's life. Both women though in their different ways exhibited some of those qualities which, in the words of modern gender historians, were so necessary for a woman to make a way in the medieval world; 'pleasing, manipulating, enduring, surviving'.[13]

Eleanor of Aquitaine died in 1204, an event that must have shaken her world in the same way that the death of Queen Victoria did in 1901. Eleanor was by then old, of course (in her early eighties, though her exact date of birth is unknown), but she had up until the end still been working to protect her feckless last surviving son from his inadequacies. She had been the greatest female influence on Richard's life, much as her mother-in-law, Matilda, had been with Eleanor's husband Henry II.

Of the ten children that she had brought into the world, only John and a daughter, also named Eleanor (wife of Alfonso VIII, king of Castile), survived her. To many, it must have seemed that Eleanor was immortal. Of course, no one is, as her departure from this world forcefully reminded everybody. She was taken from Fontevraud for her interview with the Almighty to explain her actions in this world. One wonders who was in control of that particular conversation.

During the same year, the crusading movement veered violently off course. A major expedition set off from Western Europe but from the start it was hampered by huge financial difficulties. A large fleet had been built by the Venetians but the crusaders were unable to pay them for it. So instead the crusading army helped the Venetians against rivals in the Adriatic to pay off their debt.

Then they set off, not for Outremer but Egypt, in which Richard had identified a strategic weakness in the Muslim defences of the region. But it would not get there. Instead it was talked into helping an ejected Byzantine emperor recover the city of Constantinople. But then trouble broke out and the crusaders finally sacked and took the city for themselves in an orgy of blood and looting. The recovery of Jerusalem seemed further away than ever; crusaders were too busy fighting other Christians to devote themselves to what seemed a lost cause.

But two decades later, Jerusalem would for a short time be in crusader hands again. Ironically, it was handed over almost as an irrelevance to the Holy Roman Emperor Frederick II; this was doubly ironic because he was at the time excommunicated. It would fall soon after to the Muslims, never to be in crusader hands again. The later crusade led by King Louis IX of France to Egypt at great expense was a debacle; the saintly king and those of his army who survived were taken captive and ransomed at enormous cost. It was an abject humiliation.

Acre itself was almost the last place in Outremer to go, falling to Egyptian Mameluke forces in 1291. Nothing could contrast more with the absence of blood-letting after Saladin took Jerusalem in 1187. This time, decades and centuries of frustration and anger bubbled up and, remembering Richard's slaughter of prisoners there in 1191, there were cataclysmic scenes as the port fell. It was destroyed soon after so that it could not be used as a base for renewed crusader attacks in the future. After the morale-shattering reverses of the thirteenth century, the Third Crusade looked like a triumph in comparison.

In Western Europe, John lost Normandy and many other parts of the Angevin federation in France; he came dangerously close to losing England as well. After the fall of Château Gaillard, Rouen was taken in 1204 and the following year Chinon went too. When the siege of the castle became too difficult, John took himself off to England; that Richard might have done the same in similar circumstances is unthinkable. The English position in Normandy collapsed.

Civil war broke out in England and led in 1215 to the acceptance of the Magna Carta from a cowed king who was desperately hanging on to the last vestiges of power. His rebellious lords in England fought alongside armies from France who had crossed the Channel to bring the English king down and even perhaps to put a Frenchman on the throne. John died soon after, his treasure having been lost in quicksand whilst his baggage train was crossing the Wash in East Anglia; all of this in less than two decades. If some historians regard Richard as a bad king, then what, one wonders, does that make John? It might be a cliché to regard the latter as one of England's worst kings but based on the 'achievements' of his reign it is one that is well justified.

The death of Richard, premature as it was – for he was not old, even by the standards of the time – changed European history. It is difficult to imagine that so much of the Angevin federation would have been lost if Richard had lived on as an adversary of Philip. On the other hand, the territories held by the French crown would not have grown to the extent that they did. For both England and France, the passing of Richard ultimately led to a significant change in direction.

It did not take long for historians to form sweeping judgements about Richard. Roger of Howden was originally sympathetic to his cause but after the chronicler returned from crusade and took up residence in Yorkshire he became increasingly disenchanted. There are several possible explanations for this. One was Richard's determination to tax the Church. Bringing the Church into line with the treatment of secular bodies and individuals was something that Richard's father Henry II had staked a great deal on and in the end his policies came to grief over the traumatic affair of Thomas Becket.

Richard was essentially a chip off the same block as his father and this aroused Roger's ire. But Roger was a churchman who saw the world through the prism of the religious juggernaut to which he was attached. He and others were disappointed at Richard's insistence in resolving matters in France before returning to Outremer. Whilst understandable from the king's perspective it was not so easy to see it that way from the viewpoint of the Church. The return of Jerusalem to its 'rightful ownership' was unfinished business as far as Roger and his ilk were concerned and they were not prepared to let Richard excuse himself on the grounds of strategic priorities closer to home. Their view of the world was essentially different to his.

Richard may have inherited more of his father's traits than he would care to admit. Henry II was said to have 'jealously watched over the royal interests'. A modern historian said of Henry that one of his main aims was 'judiciously increasing the wealth and prestige of the crown whilst curbing the power of his barons'.[14] Such could also easily have been said of Richard.

Given the fact that strong centralised monarchy was a relatively recent phenomenon in England, there was a real danger that it might slip away if not protected jealously. The uncertain balance between king and nobility (full democracy was still a long way off), complicated by the equally volatile equilibrium between king and church, is probably the greatest factor in medieval politics (and not just in England either). It was not until the advent of constitutional monarchy in some parts of the world and republicanism and state authoritarianism in others that these conflicts were resolved.

Yet Richard was a man with strange ideas of family loyalty. His unreliability regarding his father is a core part of the legend, the duplicitous Richard, scheming and plotting, being forgiven time and again only to play the part of Judas once more. But he was on the other hand extremely forgiving of John, perhaps because he saw in his actions something of a mirror-image of his own. In this case, blood was certainly thicker than water.

His forgiveness did not extend to those outside his family who let him down. His lieutenants who did not do their jobs properly suffered significant personal penalties as a result. Robert de Ros was one such man. He was given custody of a French prisoner in 1196. But the man escaped, allegedly with the help of one of Robert's sergeants. The sergeant was hanged for his part in the incident and Robert was imprisoned and fined the enormous sum (for him) of 1,200 marks.[15]

Some of Roger of Howden's comments following Richard's death were almost vehement and did not paint a pretty picture of his character, using the following terms:

> Poison, greed, murder and monstrous sexual urge,
> Shameful appetite, exaggerated pride, blind cupidity
> Reigned twice times five years. A crossbowman
> By his skill, his arm, his bolt and his strength laid it all low.[16]

There are some significant allegations included in this rather judgemental summing up. The suggestion of shameful appetite may refer to his sexual proclivities, which in modern times have become a particularly significant topic of conversation. But it might also refer to Richard's love of the good life and in particular eating well; there were suggestions in accounts of Richard's death that the fat on his body prevented the surgeon from extracting the crossbow bolt from his body easily. There were many who accused Richard of greed though it is far from clear that this was through an excessive love of wealth for its own sake and was probably because Richard desperately needed it to pay for his high ambitions.

That greed may therefore have been inspired by pragmatism rather than a miser's addiction to wealth. With so many ambitions to achieve, funding had to be found from somewhere. There is documentary evidence, for example, that the amount of money obtained from sources in Normandy escalated dramatically between 1180 when Henry II was king and 1195. It went up still further between 1195 and 1198. Those historians who take a positive view of Richard's reign may argue that the taxation was still affordable even in 1198 but this misses an essential point; taxpayers in any generation do not like to pay more than their predecessors did, particularly when they do not see much personal benefit in return.[17]

The common people were particularly harshly affected by the financial consequences of Richard's policies in the later years of his reign, precisely because of course they could least easily afford it. Richard turned to them as a source of revenue because the richer elements of society had already been significantly milked in earlier parts of his reign and he was desperate to recover all his lands in France, something that had become an all-consuming obsession. There were harsh penalties for those commoners who attempted to evade the taxes too, with those who did so liable to lose their finest ox. For some, this might bring them to the edge of oblivion. There was a heavy price to be paid for Richard's wars, both in England and in his French territories too.

The response of commentators like Roger of Howden to increased taxation was predictable from an economic and human perspective. But some have pointed out that the amounts raised by Richard in the final years of his reign were much less than those raised by his successor John. However, Richard courted unpopularity by the measures he took to raise taxes, for example by introducing revenue collection methods such as fines for infringing the technicalities of forest law, which no Englishman ever liked. That said, some English commentators grudgingly accepted that this was the price that had to be paid for a justified war against the immoral and grasping actions of Philip Augustus; in other words, the increased taxation was a permissible means towards achieving a worthy end.

But others were critical of Richard's exploitation of the wealth of his territories. William of Newburgh bemoaned his actions on taking power in 1189 and Ralph of Coggeshall, whilst praising Richard's actions earlier in his reign, criticised his exactions later on. But these were common criticisms of the time and were also levelled at Henry II and John. To exploit his people was to a large extent what came naturally to a medieval king.

Ralph of Coggeshall opted in the end for a moral explanation of Richard's inglorious demise; he was being punished by God for his vices. Ralph was a Cistercian and his Order had been one of those sponsored by the late king. Ralph too was unhappy that the Church was required to pay its taxes to support secular causes. He also criticised Richard for fighting during Lent, a holy time of the year when war was supposed to be off the menu as much as rich food was.

Underlying the heavy taxation of Richard's reign were three main elements that forced costs to be high. First of all was the cost of crusading. Then there was Richard's ransom. The third element driving up costs were those involved in attempting to protect and recover his possessions in France, something which

Edward III and Henry V also spent a large amount of money on, and indeed for which they became English heroes. These were core parts of Richard's territories and it was unthinkable that he would meekly accept their loss without attempting to recover them.

The cost of recovering those lost lands was inevitably massive given the scale of the enterprise. And, once Richard had decided to commit to a crusade and then the recovery and protection of his enormous French territories, there was little doubt who was going to pick up the financial strain. As one leading historian has remarked, 'it was of course the case that it was only because the state found ways extracting substantial sums of money from its subjects that it was possible to recruit large armies and sustain expensive wars'.[18]

Richard is often remembered for his supposed obsession with crusading but it is an accusation that does not totally stand up to scrutiny. If England suffered it was ultimately in comparison with his interests in France, not those in Outremer. Criticisms that Richard was obsessed by the crusades have something of a lazy ring about them.

It was war in France that in reality defined Richard's reign. Aquitaine in particular was a thorn in his side, though in the latter years of his life Normandy took over as the predominant battleground thanks to the efforts of Philip of France. But Aquitaine was constantly in revolt it seemed. Historians note nine instances of significant uprisings there between 1168 and 1199.[19] At times, this must have had a *Groundhog Day* feel about it.

Warfare in Aquitaine did not consist of splendid chivalric confrontations like glorified tournaments or of major, heroic set-piece battles. It was characterised by pillage and robbery, of the laying waste and plundering of lands, of the impoverishing of peasants and the taking of castles in sometimes drawn-out sieges.[20]

There was something rather squalid about this style of warfare, yet it is what really typified the so-called Age of Chivalry. And to make matters worse, such wars had to be fought time and time again, often against the same opponents who had already been defeated in the past. Given all this, there is something poignant yet appropriate in the fact that Richard died besieging a small and insignificant castle in the backwaters of France.

When considering whether Richard was a great general or not, we could do worse than recall the words of Socrates, wiser than most of us:

> The general must know how to get his men their rations and every other kind of stores needed in war. He must have imagination to initiate plans, practical sense and energy to carry them through. He must be observant, untiring, shrewd, kindly and cruel, simple and crafty, a watchman and a robber, lavish and miserly, generous and stingy, rash and conservative. All these and many other qualities, natural and acquired, he must have. He should also, as a matter of course, know his tactics; for a disorderly mob is no more an army than a heap of building materials is a house.[21]

Judged as a general Richard scores well against most of these criteria. It is a less clear-cut picture when we judge him as a king of England. It is not a coincidence that Richard was the last king of England for 500 years to be buried outside of the country.[22] This reflected the fact that he was responsible for the maintenance of a vast cross-Channel federation and not just the English part of it. John, Richard's successor, was buried in England, partly because during his reign the bulk of the federation in France, apart from territories in the south-west, had been lost.

The crusades were though of course still hugely important in Richard's life, especially in terms of creating his image, leading one historian to make the tantalising remark that 'he remains the only king of England who personally played a leading role on the world historical stage'.[23] It is for his crusading involvement that he is by and large best remembered in popular imagination. He was an inspiration to the equally legendary T. E. Lawrence, 'Lawrence of Arabia', who once remarked that his closest ally, Feisal of Mecca, looked 'very like the monument of Richard I at Fontevraud'.[24]

Neither was Lawrence alone in being so inspired. Lieutenant-Colonel Guy Powles, who also fought in the Palestine Campaign in the First World War, came across an old village there and speculated that it was 'most likely the "Darum" of the crusaders of King Richard the Lionheart'. He even felt as if 'we were fairly launched on the Tenth Crusade'.[25] No less a person than David Lloyd George, Prime Minister in the last years of the war, was inspired by the thought of recapturing Jerusalem as Richard had failed to do.

What of Richard and chivalry? That he was inspired by heroic thoughts seems beyond dispute and this must be a part of his motivation and his overwhelming drive to be a crusader. His was the heroism of Achilles, won in battle, a man who did not draw back from mutilating and dishonouring the corpse of his fallen and gallant rival Hector. Defeat meant dishonour and that for Richard was the unforgiveable sin. His was the chivalry of the battlefield, not the playground bravado of the tournament so beloved by his brothers Henry and Geoffrey.

Honour was what Richard craved more than anything, or so said the troubadour, one-time opponent and later supporter Bertrand de Born.[26] Richard's personal heroism in battle, something that both friend and foe commented on, was an extension of this desire for honour. The actions of a leader in sharing the front-line exposure of his soldiers, the danger and the thrill of battle that they lived through (or often died in), inspired the men of Alexander the Great in the fourth century BC as they did those with Colonel 'H' Jones at Goose Green in 1982. Such was an eternal truth and Richard understood it better than most. His supporters were quick to recognise heroic virtues in him and play them up for all they were worth. One said of him that he 'had the valour of Hector, the heroism of Achilles; he was not inferior to Alexander nor less valiant than Roland'.[27]

Richard was living in an age when key developments were taking place in the concept of chivalry and he may even be thought of as being an inspiration for them. The evolution of knighthood had many ingredients pushing it forward. Some were technological, such as the development of the stirrup and of deeper harnesses which enabled a mounted warrior to have a firmer platform from which to strike with his lance. The weapon itself was a new development. It was now held firmly to the body when charging, in contrast to the way that the spear was used by cavalry at Hastings just over a century before. Horses too were stronger and more durable and the mounted knight had become a formidable warrior.

But knighthood was more than just a military concept. It was also increasingly linked to social status and the greatest knights were expected to be men of wealth and prominent social standing. Indeed, given the escalating cost of warfare, weapons, armour and the mighty destriers, the warhorses on which they rode into battle, they had to be. They were also expected to fight according to the formal rules of war. Knighthood was not yet restricted to men born into the highest ranks of society but by Richard's time it was increasingly going that way.

All this developed alongside the growth of a vision of idealised knighthood, when those who were involved in the concept were expected to be paragons. The growth of the Arthurian legend during the course of the twelfth century and the stories of other 'ideal' knights such as Charlemagne's faithful Roland developed an impossible expectation of how such men should fight and act. Eleanor of Aquitaine's court was a centre of such idealism, even if historians might argue that its part in the development of chivalry has been overplayed.

Richard cannot have failed to be influenced by such ideals. He played out a part as king; one which has been described by Jean Flori as that of the *roi-chevalier*; the king-knight.[28] But he played it in a real-life environment, not in tournaments and jousts. He was as likely to use mercenaries as properly dubbed knights. His tourney ground was the battlefield, drowned in blood, pockmarked by hacked-off limbs and heads. Somehow, he managed to see glory still, even in the midst of all this carnage.

Like many idealistic concepts there was a world of difference between what chivalry exhibited in practice and what it espoused in theory. John of Salisbury was a great exponent of the concept and writing in 1159 he said that 'the function of the ordained knighthood is to protect the Church, to fight treachery, to venerate the priesthood, to defend the weak from injustices, to cause peace to reign in the country and – as their oath instructs – to shed blood on behalf of their brothers and to give up their lives for them if necessary'.[29] It was a noble vision, even if it was one that was still based primarily on warfare though ironically it was to be exercised in the cause of, amongst other things, peace; and it would be a hard-hearted individual who would fail to be moved by some of the principles it promulgated.

Over time the association of Richard with this idealised vision of chivalry strengthened rather than diminished. The Minstrel of Rheims, who is strongly associated with the growth of the legend of Blondel half a century later, wrote of Richard's death in the following terms; 'Oh Chivalry, how will you fade away? Alas, poor ladies, poor knights, what will become of you? Who will now uphold chivalry, generosity and courtesy?'[30] This rose-tinted view emerged through the passing of time, which diminished Richard's faults and foibles. Objectivity faded away, not helped by the disastrous turn of events in England and France in the reign of John which followed and which made those of Richard and Henry II look like a utopian Golden Age. But as Jean Flori points out there is strong evidence that even nearer the time of Richard's death he was regarded as a chivalric paragon.[31]

In later times, Richard would occasionally emerge in art in one form or another. A French writer, Marie-Jeanne L'Héritier de Villandon, wrote a story called *The Dark Tower* which resurrected the story of Richard and his loyal minstrel Blondel. An opera opened in Paris in 1784 called *Richard Coeur de Lion* but its association with brave and valiant kings proved to be out of its time when the French Revolution broke out five years later and it was banned in 1791 (it was also banned several times in the nineteenth century).

In the early decades of the nineteenth century, Richard appeared in several works by the romantic novelist Sir Walter Scott. Richard plays a role in both *The Talisman* and *Ivanhoe*. In *The Talisman* Richard is portrayed as both warlike and generous, capable of both cruelty and violence. He is shown as a monarch who is an unfavourable contrast to the more sagacious Saladin, a bold and radical analysis for the time. The background landscape is the dying days of the Third Crusade, when many of Richard's men have lost faith in the king's leadership abilities and his overall prospects; not an unreasonable portrayal of those trying times for Richard.

There is a dark undercurrent to this Richard. There are even stories of cannibalism when Richard has the heads of Muslim prisoners fed up on a plate to visiting envoys from Saladin. The ambassadors refer to him as 'the devil's brother', something that plays up to the king's mythical demoniac dynastic roots. Richard is also described as a man of 'stern resolution and restless activity', something that fits well with what we know of him from history.[32] This is a mixing of dark legend and historical fact; a potent literary cocktail.

Richard's part in *Ivanhoe* is a much smaller one as the work takes place when Richard is in prison after being captured on his way back from the Holy Land. Where he does appear it as a chivalric alter-ego, rushing in to rescue warriors who are having the worst of it in combat or rescuing damsels in distress. Scott also puts Richard in the company of the outlaw troop of Robin Hood, reinforcing connections between the king and the quasi-mythical forest bandit in a way that helped to secure it in the minds of readers (and viewers of television and film aficionados) ever since.

Whilst in some eras, Richard was seen as a heroic king (Baden-Powell referred to him glowingly when the modern Scouting movement was formed),[33] in other times there has been much more criticism of him. A strong critic was Bishop William Stubbs who lived in the nineteenth century when Queen Victoria's power was at its zenith. He called Richard an unscrupulous and impetuous soldier who had too great a love of warfare.[34] This is an interesting example of Victorian hypocrisy; during the queen's reign of sixty-three years, there was only one of them when the British army was not involved in a war somewhere around the globe. And whilst Richard could be personally impetuous, he was often a cautious strategist, as his actions on crusade affirm, so he was much more a thinker than a plain glory-seeker with a gung-ho attitude to conflict. But Stubbs's criticism stuck and the reputation of Richard went downhill for a while afterwards.

Stubbs was withering in his comments; sometimes bluntly, on other occasions more obliquely. Stubbs said of Richard that 'he was a bad king: his great exploits, his military skill, his splendour [*sic*] and extravagance, his poetical tastes, his adventurous spirit, do not serve to cloak his entire want of sympathy, or even consideration, for his people. He was no Englishman…'

Stubbs also made no attempt to understand the era in which Richard lived and instead represented what we might now see as the rather petty nationalism of his day. He was writing when the concept of nation states had developed significantly. The idea of nationhood was very different in the twelfth century. England had only been added to the domains of Richard's Norman ancestors just a century before; Normandy was almost as important in the scheme of things as England was. So too were Aquitaine, Poitou, Maine and Touraine.

Whatever else might be said of Richard's reign, even Stubbs accepts that it was effective. He wrote that, 'The reign of Richard is marked by no outbreak of insubordination: had there been any such, the strength of the administration would have been sufficient to crush it'. Many of the great nobles were, like the king himself, engaged abroad; the ones that were left at home had learned the lesson of submission; they saw themselves surrounded by a new body of equals. Richard was not a man afraid to reward loyalty amongst his supporters, even if it meant disadvantaging others who had previously held the upper hand. Conversely, he was not slow to punish those who let him down.[35] To that extent, he was meritorious in his actions.

One more modern assessment of Richard sums him up in the following terms; an attractive man and a thoroughly bad monarch. War, it is alleged, was his one delight and his only interest in England was as a source of funding to enable him to set out on his ambitious adventures.[36]

This assessment would be perfectly correct if Richard was a twentieth-century monarch. Unfortunately for such commentators he was not. There is even some irony here; in the twelfth century, when Richard actually lived, he would not have been universally regarded as an attractive man and was more likely to have been thought of as a good king; if not one who inspired love, he certainly demanded respect. This was a warrior society after all and from this perspective Richard could be seen as an outstanding figure.

One assessment of Richard says that 'although a man of knightly prowess, a writer of courtly poetry, patron of culture, cunning politician, and diplomat, Richard exhibited qualities regarded today as repulsive. Even by contemporary standards, he could be less than humane, vengeful and beastly; however he was the ideal martial king and a masterful leader of men'.

The same writer noted in his concluding remarks assessing Richard's life that at the time 'wars were not viewed from a modern perspective, nor were their aims to be construed in terms of the goals of modern war. Richard was highly regarded by his contemporaries; perhaps they knew better than we what it meant to be a chivalric hero'.[37] Here is perhaps is the key to any assessment of Richard; it should be arrived at after looking at him through the prism of his own times, not ours.

Another twentieth-century historian confirmed this analysis. Whilst certainly not being afraid to criticise Richard as a king from a modern perspective, he noted that 'to the men of his time he was almost an ideal king, a perfect knight, a hero, bold, fearless, and courageous, a born leader of men in battle, quick to avenge an insult or to reward a friend, recklessly generous, wildly extravagant, dazzling in his person, and utterly tenacious in defending what was his'.[38]

He concludes that England was fortunate to survive his absence. Certainly, at times a vacuum of power threatened to emerge and men like his brother John attempted to fill it. But others stepped in to protect his interests as well as no doubt their own. And in the end the balance between the king and his people shifted. It was a change in direction that led to a meeting of the barons and a beleaguered King John at Runnymede in 1215 leading to the signing of a document called Magna Carta.

Another writer remarked of Richard that he was 'a legend in his own time and still, in ours, surrounded by an aura of glamour and romance which neither the solemn strictures of nineteenth-century historians nor any amount of fashionable revisionism can ever quite dispel'.[39] But in the modern legends of Richard, he tends to be in the shadows.

Hollywood does not know quite what kind of a man he was. In the Errol Flynn version of *Robin Hood*, for example, he is very much a background figure for much of the film. Robin fights on Richard's behalf to protect his kingdom from the grasping clutches of Prince John. In this version, Richard is portrayed as a protector of the Saxon commoners from the predatory Normans. It is arguable whether this unusual interpretation would have come as a greater surprise to the real-life Lionheart or his Saxon subjects.

Richard returns from captivity in disguise. He is shocked at the state of the country and the heavy yoke being borne by his Saxon subjects, so much so that he regrets ever leaving England. John, hearing of his brother's return, takes steps to have him assassinated. Maid Marion, who is Richard's royal ward, is caught trying to help her rightful king and is sentenced to death. Robin waylays Richard in the forest not recognising who he is but Richard reveals himself just at the right time. Marion is rescued from her prison cell in Nottingham Castle at the last possible moment, just before John is going to be made king.

Richard then restores Robin Hood to his rightful position. John on the other hand is exiled from England for the rest of Richard's life and the restored king promises that from now on justice will return to England, and Saxons and Normans will live together equally as Englishmen. All very entertaining and barely one iota of historical fact to be found anywhere. But Richard is at least a significant figure, cutting a fair bit of dash.

More recent Hollywood movies that include a role for Richard tend to make him very much a bit-part player, as if unsure what to make of him and therefore giving him the most minor of parts. In *Kingdom of Heaven* he appears right at the end of the largely fanciful film trying to persuade Balian of Ibelin (Orlando Bloom) to journey back to Outremer with him to recover it for Christendom. In *Robin Hood: Prince of Thieves*, Richard appears for about a minute at the end as a marriage broker. Here, the king of England, who probably spoke barely a word of English, delivers his lines in a distinctive Scottish brogue, the part being played by Sean Connery.

Richard in other words has, in the eyes of Hollywood, now become a nonentity. The issues that he was at the heart of are embarrassing ones in the modern world. The crusades are now seen as something to be forgotten and Richard because of his part in them should ideally be forgotten too. All this is a bit of a travesty given the part that he played in world history, more a player on the global stage than most other English monarchs before or since. If recent historians have done their bit in rehabilitating Richard from the biting accusations of those who went before them, the rest of the modern world has been less kind to him. Richard in the public consciousness is now a man who should largely be ignored. It is hard to think of anything that would have hurt him more.

Notes

Prelude

1. Interview with Al-Jazeera correspondent Tayseer Alouni in October 2001, shortly after the terrorist incidents that took place in New York and elsewhere in the USA. Bin Laden described George W. Bush's military campaign as a continuation of the crusades, a perception that was not dispelled when the US President used that precise word in his attempts to form an alliance in response to the attacks.
2. Turner and Heiser, 2.

1 The Third Nesting

1. Poitiers Cathedral was substantially rebuilt in dramatic Gothic style about a decade later. However, the magnificent and extant East Window in this wonderful building is a gift from Eleanor and Henry.
2. Although the word perhaps has assumed derogatory connotations in more recent times, its origins are less so. It is from the Greek *sarak nos* which merely meant someone who comes from the East: Miller, 28.
3. At this period in history, the excuse of previously unrecognised close family relationships was a popular way of ending marriages: both kings and nobles adopted this approach, such as William Marshal's father John, who successfully argued his case on these grounds so that he could subsequently marry Marshal's mother: see Crouch, 15.
4. Weir, xvi, 1.
5. Ibid., 146.
6. Ibid., 153.
7. DeAragon, 103.
8. Boyd, 17.
9. The term 'Capetian', after the founder of the dynasty, Hugh Capet, did not gain currency until the eighteenth century: see Weir, 22.
10. Warren, *Henry II*, 3.
11. In Gillingham, *Richard I*, 24.
12. In Warren, *Henry II*, 3.
13. Ibid., 2.
14. In Gillingham, *Richard I*, 32.
15. Warren, *Henry*... 5.

16. See Turner and Heiser 21. Chapter 2 of this work, 'The Character of the Angevin Empire', presents a very convincing analysis of the structure of the Angevin 'federation'.
17. Gillingham, *Richard I*, 28.
18. From the chronicle of Robert de Torigni, abbot of Mont St Michel in Normandy. Quoted in Weir, 170.
19. Bradbury, 2.
20. Ibid., 3.
21. Sometimes known as the Empress Maud, a name by which she is called in a poem by the nineteenth-century poet Alfred, Lord Tennyson.
22. These castles were also evolving from wooden-palisaded motte and bailey castles, typical constructions of the initial decades after the Norman Conquest, to much stronger stone-built fortresses which increased the scale of the threat they posed as they were much better positioned to resist a siege. See Weir, 113.

2 The Winter of Discontent

1. Asbridge, 82.
2. Crouch, 35.
3. From the biography of William Marshal, quoted in Flori, 237.
4. Asbridge, 178.
5. Weir, 185.
6. Asbridge, 178.
7. In Warren, *Henry* ... 112.
8. The dower and dowry were different things. The 'dower' was something given to the bride in a marriage that could be used as a source of income if she was later widowed; the right to do this was legally called a 'usufruct'. The 'dowry' was the gift bestowed on a newly–married couple by the bride's father. The politics of the 'dower' and the 'dowry' were a fundamental part of medieval marriage alliances.
9. *Itinerarium*, 146.
10. In Hallam, 124.
11. Gillingham, *Richard I*, 47.
12. Ibid., 42.
13. Asbridge, 107.
14. There has been a settlement at La Rochelle before this but it was in the twelfth century that it began to achieve prominence as a port and trading centre.
15. The attachment of a monastery to a cathedral, as was the case at Canterbury, was a characteristic of some of England's great churches.
16. Ralph of Diceto in Hallam, 136.
17. Gillingham, *Richard I*, 53.
18. McNeill, 29.
19. Weir, 227.

3 A Family at War

1. Roger of Howden, 23.
2. Asbridge, 113–14.
3. In Weir, 228.
4. Flori, 45.
5. The contemporary chronicler Robert de Torigni in Warren, *Henry*... 571.
6. Gillingham, *Richard I*, 61.
7. In Hallam, 154.
8. Warren, *Henry*... xxv.

9. See, for example, Boyd, 90.
10. Gillingham, *Richard I*, 64.
11. Turner and Heiser, 23.
12. Crouch, 34.
13. Ibid., 28.
14. See Turner and Heiser, 3.
15. Ralph of Diceto in Hallam, 272.
16. Roger of Howden, 23.
17. Gillingham, *Richard I*, 68.
18. Roger of Howden, 23.
19. Ibid., 25.
20. Ibid., 26.
21. Ibid., Marshal fulfilled this commitment, remaining in the Holy Land for more than two years.
22. Asbridge, 170. In the event he would not need this for more than thirty-five years.
23. Roger of Howden, 27.
24. Most historians view the Young King as something of a wastrel. For an alternative view, if briefly expressed, see Asbridge, 95.
25. In Flori, 52.
26. Weir, 236.
27. In Flori, 53.

4 Crisis

1. Roger of Howden, 64.
2. Flori, 57.
3. Weir, 243.
4. Roger of Howden, 47.
5. *Itinerarium*, 23.
6. Tyerman, *God's War*, 342.
7. In Warren, *Henry…* 605.
8. Roger of Howden, 49.
9. Ibid., 51.
10. Ibid., 56.
11. Warren, *Henry…* 601.
12. Trindade, 31.
13. For a synopsis of the arguments in favour of a date somewhere in the 1180s, see Trindade, 66–9.
14. Trindade, 43. Her work is the best of modern accounts of Berengaria's life, being well researched and presented.
15. In Boyle, 29. A *trouvère* was a poet-minstrel who wrote in the dialects of northern France.
16. Flori, 62.
17. See, for example, the views of Gillingham, *Richard I*, 84.
18. Boswell, 231–2.
19. Trindade, 71.
20. Roger of Howden, 63.
21. Ibid., 90.
22. Ambroise, 29.
23. Roger of Howden, 70.
24. Barber, 117.
25. Tyerman, *England and the Crusades*, 55, *God's War*, 388.

26. Tyerman, *God's War*, 376.
27. Ambroise, 31.
28. Roger of Howden, 98.
29. Ibid., 103–4.
30. Ibid., 82.
31. Tyerman, *England and the Crusades*, 77–8.
32. Tyerman, *God's War*, 434.
33. Ibid., 434.
34. Tyerman, *England and the Crusades*, 67.
35. See https://legacy.fordham.edu/halsall/source/cde–privs.asp for details of the exemptions given by Philip of France. See Howden, 80–1, for details of the terms laid out by Henry II.

5 *The Bitter Inheritance*

1. Roger of Howden, 83.
2. See Asbridge, 122.
3. In Gillingham, *Richard I*, 93.
4. In Flori, 66.
5. Asbridge, 98.
6. Crouch, 55.
7. Gillingham, *Richard I*, 99.
8. Ibid.
9. Roger of Howden, 110.
10. Flori, 70.
11. Roger of Howden, 110, suggests that Henry found out about John's treachery during the parley at Ballan.
12. Asbridge, 203.
13. Roger of Howden, 111.
14. Appleby, 8.
15. Roger of Howden, 111.
16. Crouch, 20.

6 *Long Live the King*

1. Ralph of Diceto in Hallam, 195.
2. Crouch, 59.
3. Ibid., 60.
4. Roger of Howden, 112.
5. Appleby, 2.
6. Crouch, 61.
7. Ibid., 11.
8. Ibid., 66.
9. Ibid., 2.
10. Roger of Howden, 114.
11. Ibid., 111.
12. Richard of Devizes, 6.
13. Roger of Howden, 116.
14. Ibid., 117–20.
15. Richard of Devizes, 59–64.
16. Ibid., 5.
17. In Hallam, 208.
18. Pipe Rolls I, Richard I, 21, 30, 216.

19. Ambroise, 32.
20. Roger of Howden, 119.
21. Richard of Devizes, 5. As the chronicler was a monk in Winchester he had perhaps good reason to emphasize the virtues of the city.
22. Ibid., 61. In fairness, the writer is trying to extol the virtues of Winchester compared to everywhere else in England.
23. Roger of Howden, 120.
24. Appleby, 45–6.
25. See www.historyofyork.org.uk/themes/norman/the–1190–massacre
26. Howden, 115.
27. Richard of Devizes, 7.
28. Appleby, 6.
29. E.g. Boyd 140: 'Richard would have done better to have locked John up for the duration'.
30. Turner and Heiser, 91.
31. Ibid., 106.
32. Appleby, 16.
33. Richard of Devizes, 11.
34. Crouch, 69–70.
35. Appleby, 20.
36. Ibid., 187.
37. Roger of Howden, 3.
38. Turner and Heiser, 95.
39. Unfortunately, this was not a permanent solution. Richard of Devizes, 26, noted that the following March the monks of Canterbury dismissed the prior that Baldwin had appointed and installed their own choice in his place.
40. Turner and Heiser, 107.

7 The Crusade Departs

1. *Itinerarium*, 23.
2. A very good summary of the background to the writing of the *Itinerarium* can be found in the Introduction to Nicholson's translation of the work. The translation is based on 'IP2'.
3. *Itinerarium*, 310 – this is one episode that is not included in Ambroise.
4. Ibid., 48.
5. These were five ports in Kent and Sussex, namely Hastings, Romney (later changed to Rye when the channel silted up), Hythe, Dover and Sandwich.
6. Details from Gillingham, *Richard I*, 114.
7. Flori, 83.
8. Richard of Devizes, 10.
9. Turner and Heiser, 106.
10. In Gillingham, *Richard I*, 115. Gillingham discusses a number of specific examples of how Richard took advantage of these one-off measures and also the reaction of contemporary writers to them: 115–22.
11. Stenton, 167.
12. Roger of Howden, 4.
13. Roger of Howden, 101–2. The letter, and a supposed reply from Saladin, can be found in the *Itinerarium*, 49–54.
14. This is the evidence of Baha' al-Din in Maalouf 206: the chronicler was himself one of the ambassadors sent to drum up support.

15. *Itinerarium*, 65.
16. Gabrieli, 210.
17. Ambroise, 78.
18. Hallam, 206.
19. Roger of Howden, 448.
20. Flori, 86.
21. The fact that Ida was William's mother only became known in 1979 when some charters relating to Bradenstoke Priory were discovered: these included a reference by William to '*comitissa Ida, mater mea*' – 'countess Ida, my mother'. Before 1979 it was assumed that Rosamund Clifford was William's mother. Despite confusion over the identity of William's mother, there was none over his father as Henry II publicly acknowledged him as his son.
22. Roger of Howden, 141.
23. *Itinerarium*, 150.
24. See Szarmach et al., *Medieval England* – under 'Richard I'.
25. Ambroise, 34.
26. This is the version according to Ambroise: the *Itinerarium* says that Richard solved the problem by making a temporary pontoon bridge by tying small boats together.
27. Ambroise, 36.
28. In Gillingham, *Richard I*, 129.
29. Richard of Devizes, 68.
30. *Itinerarium*, 142.

8 Mayhem and Matrimony

1. Flori, 245.
2. Roger of Howden, 9.
3. Richard of Devizes, 16.
4. Ambroise, 40.
5. De Camville and de Sablé had sailed with some of the ships from the mouth of the Loire. Tyerman, *God's War*, 436.
6. Roger of Howden, 149.
7. Ibid., 154.
8. Ibid., 146, Richard of Devizes, 12.
9. Tyerman, *England and the Crusades*, 65.
10. The work of Roger mainly referred to in this current book is his *Chronica*, which was translated from Latin into English in the nineteenth century by H. T. Riley (volume 2 in particular).
11. Introductory notes in Ambroise, 2–3.
12. Ambroise, 37.
13. Richard of Devizes, 18.
14. Ambroise, 37; the author of the *Itinerarium*, possibly using Ambroise as his source, says largely the same thing (157).
15. *Itinerarium*, 157.
16. Ambroise, 38.
17. Richard of Devizes, 19.
18. Ambroise 40; *Itinerarium*, 158.
19. One son had been born from the relationship but had not survived infancy.
20. See Gillingham, *Richard I*, 132.

21. Ambroise, 41.
22. Richard of Devizes, 23.
23. Ambroise, 42–3.
24. Even in modern Sicily, there is an annual festival celebrating a Norman woman and an Arab man who fell in love. Their names are Mate and Griffon. Whilst it is difficult to definitively argue any connection between these events and those of 1190, perhaps the names are a distant and confused remembrance of Richard's time in Messina.
25. Ambroise, 43.
26. *Itinerarium*, 168.
27. Appleby, 57.
28. Ambroise, 46.
29. Gillingham, *Richard I*, 137.
30. Roger of Howden, 80.
31. Ambroise 46; *Itinerarium*, 170.
32. Roger of Howden, 176.
33. Roger of Howden, p177–87.
34. See Flori, 101–4.
35. Roger of Howden, 173.
36. Ibid., 191.
37. Weir, 267.
38. Ambroise, 47.
39. Gillingham, *Richard I*, points out (143) that Roger was more likely to have seen her than the other commentators so was in a better position to judge on such matters. Ambroise almost certainly saw her too.
40. Trindade, 84.
41. See Mitchell, 16.
42. Flori, 372.
43. Trindade, 74.
44. Ibid., 52.
45. In Flori 378, quoting from the 2002 translation from the original French by Molden, Gregory and Crouch. The translation is somewhat vulgarised, perhaps in the interests of making it more accessible to a modern audience; a more literal translation of the original French would be that Marshal was 'doing it with the Queen'.
46. Trindade, 77.
47. See Bradbury, 54.
48. Weir 270. We know of the meeting with Henry because Eleanor witnessed a contract that the emperor made with the bishop of Trent.
49. Taormina remains a haunt of the rich and famous, in recent times a popular spot with Elizabeth Taylor and Richard Burton; one of the nicer spots visited during the research for this book was the *Wunderbar* in the town which was a favourite haunt of theirs. Taormina hosted a summit of world leaders in 2017.
50. Richard of Devizes, 25.
51. Roger of Howden, 195.
52. Richard of Devizes, 25.
53. Flori, 400.
54. Roger of Howden, 174.
55. Weir, 271.
56. Richard of Devizes, 27.
57. Trindade, 95.

9 The Taking of Cyprus

1. Ambroise, 48. Richard of Devizes, 27, notes that there were 156 ships, 24 busses and 39 galleys; i.e. 219 vessels in total.
2. *Itinerarium*, 177.
3. Tyerman *England and the Crusades* 67, quoting Richard of Devizes.
4. *Itinerarium*, 182.
5. *Itinerarium* 179, Ambroise 50. Gamalon was the traitor who betrayed Roland during the retreat of Charlemagne's rear-guard at Roncesvalles.
6. Gillingham, *Richard I*, 146.
7. Roger of Howden, 201.
8. Tyerman, *England and the Crusades*, 66.
9. Ambroise, 52.
10. Flori, 310.
11. Roger of Howden, 202.
12. Ambroise, 54.
13. In Maalouf, 203.
14. *Itinerarium*, 188.
15. From the works of Geoffrey de Vinsauf in Weir, 274.
16. Tyerman, *England and the Crusades*, 62.
17. Richard of Devizes 45. There were rumours that she would remain so, at least until the couple reached Acre. See Mitchell, 65.
18. Mitchell, 52. The Order, it has been suggested, may have been the inspiration for the later Order of the Garter. See The Edinburgh Topographical, Traditional, and *Antiquarian Magazine*, Vol. 1, 1848.
19. Ambroise 58, *Itinerarium*, 192.
20. Ambroise, 59.
21. Trindade, 54.
22. A bezant was a gold coin. The first models were minted in Byzantium and it was from this name that the term 'bezant' was derived.
23. Ambroise, 61.

10 High-Water Mark

1. Warner, 81.
2. Ambroise, 71.
3. *Itinerarium*, 83.
4. Ibid., 73.
5. Ibid., 83.
6. Ibid., 75.
7. Ibid., 133. No doubt modern survival experts would say that they should have eaten the maggots as an added source of protein.
8. Ambroise, 76.
9. *Itinerarium*, 104, 109, 110.
10. Ibid., 71.
11. Gillingham, *Richard I*, 155.
12. Nicolle, *Third Crusade...* 33.
13. Ambroise, 83.
14. Roger of Howden, 172.
15. Ambroise, 77.
16. Ibid., 79.
17. Roger of Howden, 187–8.

18. Tyerman, *England and the Crusades*, 71.
19. Ibid., 72.
20. Ibid., 73.
21. Ambroise, 91–2.
22. Richard of Devizes, 48.
23. Note 173 in Ambroise, 63.
24. Namely Baha' al-Din and 'Imad al-Din; *Itinerarium* 199, Footnote 150. 'Imad al-Din also suggests that five English ships and one galley had been taken and carried off to Beirut; in other words, not a one-sided fight as the English chroniclers suggest.
25. Ambroise, 64.
26. Flori, 120.
27. Gillingham, *Richard I*, 159.
28. Note 183 in Ambroise 65 states that the term had first been used by Gerald of Wales in his *Topographia Hibernica* in around 1187.
29. *Itinerarium*, 202.
30. Ambroise, 66.
31. *Itinerarium*, 203.
32. In Maalouf 208. A slightly different translation is given in Gabrieli, 213.
33. This is one version, according to the hostile (to Richard) Rigord. An alternative told by Ambroise was that Richard wanted to delay until all his siege engines had arrived. Whichever version is true, the disagreement was yet another nail in the coffin for the relationship between Richard and Philip.
34. Footnote 279 in Ambroise, 89, quoting Riley-Smith Feudal Monarchy, 116.
35. *Itinerarium*, 122.
36. Ibid., 123.
37. Ibid., 126.
38. In Gabrieli 206. The risqué nature of these comments makes quotations from this excerpt from Imad ad-Din something of a favourite amongst crusader historians.
39. Ambroise, 110.
40. *Itinerarium*, 81.
41. Baha' ad-Din in Gabrieli, 216.
42. Ambroise 96. The allusions frequently made by the chronicler to heroes of the Romances of the day strongly suggest that he wanted to paint Richard in a similar light; see the work of Jean Flori in which Richard's connection to the stereotype of the chivalric hero forms a significant part of his thesis. Therefore, we should avoid interpreting Ambroise's work too literally.
43. Ambroise, 95.
44. Flori, 122.
45. Wagner and Mitchell, 24.
46. Ibid., 28. William and Rigord were both connected to St Denis in France and were unsurprisingly largely supportive of the French king. They provide a useful antidote to the Angevin chroniclers who were, perhaps equally unsurprisingly, largely hostile to him.
47. Ibid., 44.
48. So-called allegedly because the thirty pieces of silver that had been given to Judas Iscariot for betraying Christ were minted here: see *Itinerarium*, 83.
49. Ambroise, 98.
50. *Itinerarium*, 209.
51. In Tyerman, *God's War*, 453.
52. Roger of Howden, 215.

53. Gillingham, *Richard I*, 163.
54. Flori, 125.
55. Wagner and Mitchell, 43.
56. Roger of Howden, 5.
57. Flori, 128.
58. Joinville, 304–5.
59. Bradbury, 188.
60. Quoted in the introduction to Ambroise, 16.
61. *Itinerarium*, 229, Footnote 3.

11 Arsuf

1. Ambroise, 109.
2. Roger of Howden, 220.
3. See www.christianhistoryinstitute.org/incontext/article/bernard/
4. Gillingham, *Richard I*, 168.
5. Ambroise, 108.
6. *Itinerarium* 231.
7. Flori, 135.
8. Gillingham, *Richard I*, 169–171.
9. In Flori, 360.
10. In Gillingham, *Richard I*, 171.
11. Ambroise, 110.
12. For example, the Temple area off the Strand in London is named after their church which still stands there, whilst Templecombe in Somerset was granted to the Templars in 1185, the same year that the church in London was consecrated.
13. Barber, 119.
14. Crouch, 33.
15. Asbridge, 48.
16. Lyons and Jackson, 334.
17. In Flori, 136.
18. *Itinerarium*, 237.
19. Ambroise, 111.
20. Roger of Howden, 222.
21. Ambroise, 112.
22. Miller, 23.
23. Lyons and Jackson, 335.
24. In Gillingham, *Richard I*, 175.
25. Ambroise, 113.
26. It is often referred to as the 'deathstalker'. It will not normally kill an adult human though men who were run down through their exertions in wartime may perhaps be more vulnerable.
27. Ambroise, 115.
28. Ibid., 115–16.
29. See Faulkner.
30. Ambroise, 116; *Itinerarium*, 246.
31. *Itinerarium*, 247.
32. Ibid., 250.

33. Ibid., 248. Note that the racial attributions made by the writers do not necessarily correspond with modern interpretations. Geographical knowledge and racial sensitivity were not high up the list of virtues of Western chroniclers at the time.
34. Ibid., 249.
35. Ibid., 250.
36. Ibid., 253.
37. Gillingham, *Richard I*, 177.
38. *Itinerarium*, 254.
39. Ibid., 259.
40. Smail 165.
41. Gillingham, *Richard I*, 178.
42. *Itinerarium*, 260. Mayer, 378, suggests that this man was Sonqor al-Halabi.
43. Ambroise, 124.

12 Facing up to Reality

1. Ambroise, 122; *Itinerarium*, 258.
2. Ambroise, 121. The writer of the *Itinerarium*, 257, suggests that 7,000 'Turkish' corpses were counted on the battlefield and that many more must have died elsewhere. He further suggested that Richard's losses were less than a tenth of this number. But medieval chroniclers are notoriously unreliable when it comes to numbers and such disparities in losses between the 'right' and the 'wrong' sides in a battle is a frequent motif; see, for example, the alleged tiny English losses at Agincourt versus the massive mortality of their French opponents.
3. *Itinerarium*, 261.
4. Lyons and Jackson, 340.
5. Footnote 450 in Ambroise, 126.
6. Ambroise, 126.
7. Ambroise, 127.
8. Roger of Howden, 224.
9. Ambroise, 128–9. William was exchanged for ten prominent 'Saracens' when Richard was about to leave for England at a later stage. See Ambroise, 192.
10. *Itinerarium*, 267.
11. Allenby's forces would later cross the battlefield of Arsuf during their advance north.
12. Faulkner, 355.
13. Boas, 18.
14. Key letters from around this time are reproduced in full in Roger of Howden 222–4.
15. *Itinerarium*, 265.
16. Ambroise, 128. Richard was in Jaffa from 10 September to 30 October 1191.
17. Lyons and Jackson, 341.
18. The crusade ended up sacking the Christian city of Constantinople rather than fighting Muslims.
19. For the letter from Richard and Saladin's response see Baha' ad–Din in Gabrieli, 225–6.
20. Lyons and Jackson, 344.
21. Ambroise, 131.
22. *Itinerarium*, 273.
23. Imad ad-Din: Gabrieli, 208.

24. Wavell, 187.
25. *Itinerarium*, 280.
26. Flori, 143.
27. See also *Itinerarium*, 285.
28. Ambroise, 138–9.
29. *Itinerarium*, 289.
30. Smail, 75.
31. Ambroise, 138.
32. Gabrieli, 234.
33. Ambroise, 143: *Itinerarium*, 294.
34. Ambroise, 145.
35. *Itinerarium*, 297.

13 *The Forlorn Hope*

1. Richard of Devizes, 29.
2. There is some confusion over the correct date of this agreement with other accounts dating it back in April; but this seems to be a mistake – see Appleby, 67.
3. Ibid., 71.
4. Richard of Devizes, 35.
5. Appleby, 75.
6. Richard of Devizes, 35.
7. Ibid., 60.
8. Allegedly when King Henry VIII was involved in the composition of the famous ballad 'Greensleeves' in the sixteenth century it was not a romantic lament, as we might now think, but a satirical skit about a prostitute.
9. Roger of Howden, 236.
10. Ibid., 233.
11. Rather like the recent pontiff Pope Benedict XVI, Celestine later tried to resign though on this occasion his cardinals did not permit it. He died in office in 1198 at approximately 91 years of age – his exact birth date is not known.
12. Roger of Howden, 245.
13. Richard of Devizes, 9.
14. Turner, 77.
15. *Itinerarium*, 301.
16. Ambroise, 149. In a largely fictional form, Balian, played by Orlando Bloom, is the main hero of the Hollywood epic, *Kingdom of Heaven*.
17. *Itinerarium*, 304.
18. Ambroise, 150.
19. See Harari, 103.
20. For further information, see Bartlett; *Assassins*.
21. Gabrieli, 239.
22. For a rehearsal of the possible motives for the various suspects, see Harari 95.
23. See Harari, 98.
24. In Hallam, 238.
25. Gillingham, *Richard I*, 200.
26. Ambroise, 160–2. Footnote 613 makes the interesting speculation that, as William of Poitiers has never been reliably identified, this may be a pseudonym for Ambroise himself.

14 *The End of the Dream*

1. Ambroise, 159.
2. *Itinerarium*, 325. The writer suggests that 'the king's heart was completely changed by the speech'.
3. Ibid., 326.
4. Gillingham, *Richard I*, 205.
5. Ambroise, 172.
6. *Itinerarium*, 331–2, has an account of a particularly large attack on a supply train from Jaffa where disaster was only narrowly averted by the intervention of the earl of Leicester. For Richard's concerns on the vulnerability of the supply line see, for example, *Itinerarium* 335. He was also worried that there were not sufficient numbers in the army to properly lay siege to Jerusalem.
7. Gillingham, *Richard I*, 210.
8. Ibid., 211.
9. *Itinerarium*, 350.
10. Ibid.
11. Ralph would be handed over as a hostage along with others including Aubrey of Rheims. They were taken to Damascus as prisoners.
12. Gillingham, *Richard I*, 213.
13. Baha' al-Din in Gillingham, *Richard I*, 214.
14. *Itinerarium*, 362.
15. Ibid., 359.
16. Ibid., 363.
17. The events described are discussed in *Itinerarium*, 361–8.
18. In Gillingham, *Richard I*, 216.
19. Quoted in the *Itinerarium*, 146, when talking of Richard generally.
20. Smail, 74.
21. Ambroise, 180.
22. *Itinerarium*, 367–8.
23. Though the chroniclers suggest that he actually sent them during the battle. See *Itinerarium*, 364.
24. Smail, 189.
25. Richard of Devizes, 73.
26. Ibid., 75.
27. Ibid., 68.
28. Gillingham, *Richard I*, 218.
29. Richard of Devizes, 73.
30. Ibid., 68, 73.
31. Nicholson in *Itinerarium*, 376, Footnote 91.
32. Boas, 33.
33. Ibid., 18.
34. Richard of Devizes, 78.
35. Boas, 18–19.
36. Both sarcophagi still sit side-by-side in the great Umayyad Mosque in Damascus.
37. *Itinerarium*, 372.

15 Betrayal

1. In Flori, 151.
2. *Itinerarium*, 372.
3. See Boyle, 106.
4. Roger of Howden, 269.

5. For Richard's route, I have followed that suggested by Boyle's *Blondel's Song*, which is well argued with regards to this topic.
6. Gillingham, *The Kidnapped King*, 11.
7. Roger of Howden, 278.
8. In Weir, 288. See also Hallam, 224, in which Ralph describes the Austrians as 'stinking of barbarism'.
9. In Gillingham, *Richard I*, 226.
10. Bradbury's biography of Philip Augustus does a fine job in counteracting the anti-Philip bias of English chroniclers. But his defence of Philip for his actions at this time (see, for example, 101) is perhaps the least convincing part of his work.
11. This is Bradbury's conclusion.
12. Boyle, 164.
13. Gillingham, *The Kidnapped King*, 5.
14. Ibid., 6.
15. Roger of Howden, 280.
16. Footnote 64 in Gillingham, *The Kidnapped King*, 20.
17. In Trindade, 111.
18. Gillingham, *Richard I*, 233.
19. For further discussion see Boyle, 167.
20. The semi-mythical stories of Robin Hood were not set in the time of Richard I until the 16th century Scottish writer John Major wrote his work *The History of Great Britain*. See Weir, 306.
21. Weir, 290.
22. Roger of Howden, 281.
23. *Itinerarium*, 385.
24. Gillingham, *The Kidnapped King*, 21.
25. Ralph of Diceto in Hallam, 226.
26. See Ralph of Diceto in Hallam, 224.
27. Roger of Howden, 291.
28. Ibid.
29. Ibid., 292.
30. Richard of Devizes, 61.
31. Weir, 301.
32. Roger of Howden, 303.
33. Ibid., 289.

16 The Long Road to Freedom

1. Weir 274, Mitchell 86, for example.
2. Weir, 303.
3. Boyle, 226.
4. For a summary of the Robin Hood legends and their links or otherwise to Richard's reign see Boyle, 228–30.
5. Ralph of Diceto in Hallam, 228.
6. Boyle, 222.
7. Roger of Howden, 294.
8. Ibid., 289.
9. Translated by Kate Norgate, quoted in Gillingham, *Richard I*, 243. The song is also quoted in full in Boyle, 301.
10. Gillingham, *The Kidnapped King*, 23.
11. Boyle, 180.

12. See Boyle, 195.
13. Roger of Howden, 290.
14. The letter is reproduced in Weir, 291–5. It should be noted that some historians see this as a rhetorical exercise by Peter of Blois and not as letters that were sent to the Pope. See Lees, 78–93.
15. Another later letter is reproduced in Weir, 297–9.
16. Weir, 301.
17. Gillingham, *The Kidnapped King*, 31.
18. Roger of Howden, 299–301.
19. William of Newburgh, Book Four, Chapter 26.
20. Trindade, 114.
21. Henry famously could not bear to spend more than one night with his fourth wife, Anne of Cleves, either.
22. Roger of Howden, 304.
23. William of Newburgh, Book Four, Chapter 26.
24. Trindade, 116.
25. Appleby, 118.
26. Roger of Howden, 310.
27. Gillingham, *Richard I*, 248. It is also important to note that Henry immediately handed England back to him; it was notional rather than actual suzerainty he was after plus an annual tribute that further added to his treasury.
28. Gillingham, *The Kidnapped King*, 26–7.
29. In Hallam, 232.
30. Roger of Howden, 311.
31. Ibid., 291.
32. Boyle, 244.
33. Asbridge, 237.
34. Ralph of Diceto in Hallam, 234.
35. Boyle, 238.

17 The Return of the King

1. Roger of Howden, 315.
2. Appleby, 139.
3. Roger of Howden, 320.
4. Trindade, 112, has suggested that this does not necessarily have to be seen evidence of an estrangement. However, there was adequate if not ample time for her to reach Winchester in time and surely this would have been an ideal opportunity to formally present his queen to her subjects? The fact that Richard never chose to do so on any other occasion either is curious to say the least.
5. William of Newburgh, Book Four, Chapter 41.
6. Gillingham, *Richard I*, 273.
7. Ralph of Diceto in Hallam, 234.
8. Appleby, 164–6.
9. Weir, 113.
10. Boyle, 252.
11. Ralph of Diceto in Hallam, 234.
12. Flori, 304.
13. In Hallam, 234.
14. Summarised in Gillingham, *Richard I*, 276.
15. See Weir, 308.

16. Footnote 120 in *Itinerarium*, 386.
17. Appleby, 172–3.
18. Genesis, 19.
19. Weir, 312. See also Trindade, 123, who notes that 'the terms sodomy and the "sin of Sodom" refer unambiguously and consistently to male homosexual intercourse'.
20. Flori, 393.
21. The conclusion arrived at in Flori, 393. See also Trindade, 59. She points out (72) that if Philip and Richard did become lovers at some stage, then the king of France must also have been bisexual as he fathered children and was well known to be sexually involved with women during his life.
22. Crompton, Louis, Homosexuality and Civilization, Harvard University, 2003. Pages 178–9
23. In Flori, 388.

18 A Never-Ending War

1. Roger of Howden, 356.
2. Ibid., 364.
3. Ibid., 369.
4. Ibid., 394.
5. Appleby, 189.
6. In Flori, 268.
7. Tyerman, *England and the Crusades*, 73.
8. In Hallam, 240.
9. Appleby, 192.
10. Ralph of Diceto in Hallam, 240.
11. Roger of Howden, 385.
12. Ibid., 394.
13. Nicolle, *Crusader Castles*… 27.
14. Gillingham, *Richard I*, 304.
15. In Hallam, 240.
16. *Itinerarium Peregrinorum*, 76.
17. Ibid., 119.
18. Roger of Howden, 401.
19. Ibid., 402–3.
20. Ibid., 397.
21. Crouch, 75–6.
22. Ralph of Diceto in Hallam, 244.
23. Ibid.
24. Gillingham, *The Kidnapped King*, 7.
25. Boyle, 264.
26. Willi Radzcun, quoted in Gillingham, *The Kidnapped King*, 7.
27. Though in the Channel Islands the British monarch is still known as the 'duke of Normandy' so perhaps after all a small portion of the duchy still remains in British hands.
28. Poole, 369–70.
29. Appleby, 209. The writer points out that in 1196 there were still payments outstanding from the bishop of Salisbury that were thirty years overdue.
30. In Hallam, 250.
31. Ralph of Diceto in Hallam, 250.
32. Roger of Howden, 419.

33. Psalm 118:23. It was a popular saying: Queen Elizabeth I of England later used the same phrase when she heard of her accession to the throne.
34. Roger of Howden.
35. Appleby, 214.
36. Mitchell, 87. The author suggests here that this was the only time that Richard ever mentioned his wife in a letter.
37. Roger of Howden, 427.
38. Roger of Howden, 431. In what appears to be a slip of his quill, Roger seems to describe the same incidents at Gisors twice within a few pages of each other, perhaps a sign of a man whose attention was distracted or who, alternatively, was getting old and tired. Roger died just a few years after these events that he was describing.
39. Ralph of Diceto in Hallam, 252.
40. In Flori, 192.

19 Last Rites

1. Roger of Howden, 431.
2. Ibid., 434–6.
3. Ibid., 437.
4. Appleby, 221.
5. Roger of Howden, 441–3.
6. Asbridge, 248.
7. Crouch, 75.
8. Bradbury, 122.
9. Ibid., 133.
10. From the *History of William Marshal* in Gillingham, *Richard I*, 319.
11. See Flori, 200–215, for a detailed discussion of the arguments. Different chroniclers nominate different individuals as being responsible for the death of Richard.
12. Roger of Howden, 453, suggests that Mercadier himself undertook this action.
13. Weir, 319.
14. In Hallam, 252.
15. In Gillingham, *Richard I*, 326.
16. Crouch, 77.
17. Summarised in Flori, 200–15.
18. In Richard, 211.
19. BBC website: 'Richard the Lionheart's mummified heart analysed', www.bbc.com/news/science-environment -21609783, 28 February 2013.
20. In Hallam, 256.
21. Ralph of Diceto in Hallam, 256.
22. In Bradbury, 127.
23. Trindade, 134–5.
24. Mitchell, 92, 96; Footnote 2.
25. Ibid., 108.
26. Trindade, 131.
27. Gillingham, *Richard I*, 327–9.
28. In Gillingham, *Richard I*, 321.
29. Quoted in Turner and Heiser, 61.
30. In Turner and Heiser, 3.
31. Bradbury, 129.

20 Epilogue

1. Roger of Howden, 454.
2. Gabrieli, 214.
3. See Mitchell, 95–6.
4. So says the *Margam Annals*. See Luard, HR (ed.), *Annales Monastici 1, 36, Rolls Series*, London, 1864.
5. Henry was only nine at the time he came to the throne in 1216. But to the credit of at least some of those involved, the large unpaid arrears were settled a few years later. See Trindade, 153.
6. See Bartlett, *The Last Crusade.*
7. Trindade, 184.
8. Mitchell, 129.
9. Trindade, 11.
10. Ibid., 189.
11. Ibid., 147.
12. Ibid., 63.
13. Ibid., 16.
14. The original quote is from William of Newburgh. The modern historian is Weir, see 127.
15. Gillingham, *Richard I*, 262.
16. Reproduced in Flori, 206; alternative translation of the words of Roger of Howden, 454.
17. Gillingham, *Richard I*, 341.
18. Prestwich, viii.
19. Turner and Heiser, 60.
20. Ibid., 61.
21. Quoted by Field-Marshal Viscount Wavell in *Allenby* as his preface.
22. Though the heart of Henry III, who died in 1272, was buried at Fontevraud with his family, his body was interred in Westminster Abbey. James II died and was buried in Paris in 1701 but he had by then been deposed and was in exile.
23. Gillingham, *The Kidnapped King*, 15.
24. Faulkner, 202.
25. Ibid., 225.
26. Gillingham, *Richard I*, 260.
27. *Itinerarium Peregrinorum*, 145. Achilles and Hector were both heroes from the Trojan War. The writer also credited Richard with Nestor's tongue and Ulysses' wisdom; two more heroes of the same war renowned for their sagacity and cunning respectively.
28. This is a key part of the thesis laid out by Flori.
29. In Flori, 251.
30. Ibid., 238.
31. Flori, 240.
32. *The Talisman*, 52.
33. Boyle, 296.
34. Turner and Heiser, 4.
35. Quotes from *Constitutional History*.
36. Painter and Turner, *Western Europe in the Middle Ages*, in Turner and Heiser 5.
37. See Szarmach et al., article by James W. Alexander, under 'Richard I'.
38. Appleby, 233.
39. Trindade, 10.

Bibliography

PRIMARY SOURCES

Ailes, Marianne (trans.), *Ambroise: The History of the Holy War*, Boydell, Woodbridge, 2003

Brewer, John Sherren (trans.), *Giraldus Cambrensis De Instructione Principum Libri III*, Biblio Life, Charleston

Edbury, Peter W. (ed.), *The Conquest of Jerusalem and the Third Crusade*, Ashgate Publishing Ltd, Hampshire, 2002

Gabrieli, Francesco (ed.), *Arab Historians of the Crusades*, University of California Press, Berkeley and Los Angeles, 1984

Giles, J. A. (trans.), *The Chronicle of Richard of Devizes*, FB&C reprint 2015, original London, 1841

Hallam, Elizabeth (ed.), *Chronicles of the Crusades: Eye-witness Accounts of the Wars Between Christianity and Islam*, Bramley Books, Surrey, 1996

Hallam, Elizabeth (general editor), *The Plantagenet Chronicles*, Salamander Books Ltd, London, 2002

Madden, Frederic (ed.), *Matthew Paris: Historia Anglorum*, Cambridge University Press, Cape Town, 2012

Mayer, H., *Das Itinerarium Peregrinorum. Eine zeitgenössische englische Chronik zum dritten Kreuzzug in utsprünglicher Gestalt*, Antonn Hiersemann, Stuttgart, 1962

Nederman, Cary J. (trans.), *John of Salisbury – Policraticus*, Cambridge University Press, Cambridge, 2007

Nicholson, Helen J. (trans.), *The Chronicle of the Third Crusade*, Ashgate Publishing Ltd, Surrey, 2010

Riley, Henry T. (trans.): *The Annals of Roger de Hoveden*, H. G. Bohn, London, 1853

Shaw, M. R. B. (trans.), *Joinville and Villehardouin: Chronicles of the Crusades*, Penguin Group, London, 1963

Stevenson, Joseph (trans.); *The Church Historians of England, volume IV, part II*, Seeleys, London, 1861 (this includes the works of William of Newburgh; the translation can also be found online at http://sourcebooks.fordham.edu/basis/williamofnewburgh)

Stubbs, William, *The Historical Works of Gervase of Canterbury*, Eyre and Spottiswoode for Her Majesty's Stationery Office

SECONDARY SOURCES

Appleby, John T., *England without Richard, 1189–1199*, G. Bell & Sons, London, 1967

Asbridge, Thomas, *The Crusades: The War for the Holy Land*, Simon & Schuster UK Ltd, London, 2010

Bibliography

Asbridge, Thomas, *The Greatest Knight*, Simon & Schuster, London, 2015

Barber, Richard, *The New Knighthood: A History of the Order of the Temple*, Cambridge University Press, 1998

Barber, Richard, *The Devil's Crown*, Book Club Associates, London, 1978

Bartlett, Robert, *England under the Norman and Angevin Kings, 1075–1225*, Oxford University Press, Oxford, 2013

Bartlett, W. B., *Assassins: The Story of Medieval Islam's Secret Sect*, The History Press, Stroud, 2009

Bartlett W. B., *God Wills It! An Illustrated History of the Crusades*, Sutton, Stroud, 2009

Bartlett, W. B., *The Last Crusade*, Tempus, Stroud, 2007

Bartlett, W. B., *The Road to Armageddon: The Last Years of the Crusader Kingdom of Jerusalem*, Sutton, Stroud, 2007

Boas, Adrian J., *Jerusalem in the Time of the Crusades*, Routledge, London and New York, 2001

Boase, T. S. R., *Kingdoms and Strongholds of the Crusaders*, Thames & Hudson Ltd, London, 1971

Boswell, John, *Christianity, Social Tolerance and Homosexuality*, Chicago, 1980

Boyd, Douglas, *Lionheart: The True Story of England's Crusader King*, The History Press, Stroud, 2015

Boyle, David, *Blondel's Song: The Capture, Ransom and Imprisonment of Richard the Lionheart*, Penguin, 2006

Bradbury, Jim, *Medieval Warfare*, Routledge, London, 2004

Bradbury, Jim, *Philip Augustus, King of France 1180–1223*, Addison Wesley Longman Ltd, Harlow, 1998

Bradbury, Jim, *The Medieval Siege*, The Boydell Press, Suffolk, 1998

Bridge, A., *Richard the Lionheart*, London, 1993

Bronstein, Judith, *The Hospitallers and the Holy Land: Financing the Latin East, 1187–1274*, The Boydell Press, Woodbridge, 2005

Brundage, James, *Law, Sex and Christian Society in Medieval Europe*, Chicago, 1987

Clayton, Joseph, *Pope Innocent III and His Times*, Mediatrix Press, 2016

Crouch, David, *William Marshal: Court, Career and Chivalry in the Angevin Empire 1147–1219*, Longman, London and New York, 1990

DeAragon, RáGena, 'Wife, Widow, and Mother: Some Comparisons between Eleanor of Aquitaine and Noblewomen of the Anglo-Norman and Angevin World,' in *Eleanor of Aquitaine: Lord and Lady*, ed. John Carmi Parsons and Bonnie Wheeler, *Palgrave* MacMillan, New York, 2002

De Vries, Kelly; Dougherty, Martin; Jestice, Phyllis G., Jorgensen, Christer: *Battles of the Medieval World 1000–1500*, Amber Books, London, 2006

Erbstosser, Martin, *The Crusades*, David & Charles, Newton Abbot, 1978

Faulkner, Neil, *Lawrence of Arabia's War: The Arabs, the British and the Remaking of the Middle East in WW1*, Yale University Press, 2016

Flori, Jean (translated from French by Jean Birrell); *Richard the Lionheart: King and Knight*, Praeger, Westport and London, 2006

Gillingham, John, *Richard I*, Yale University Press, New Haven & London, 2002 edition

Gillingham, John, *The Kidnapped King: Richard I in Germany*, German Historical Institute London Bulletin Bd. 30, 2008

Harari, Yuval Noah, *Special Operations in the Age of Chivalry, 1100-1550*, The Boydell Press, Woodbridge, 2009

Hillenbrand, Carole, *The Crusades: Islamic Perspectives*, Edinburgh University Press Ltd, Edinburgh, 2006

Hooper, Nicholas and Bennett, Matthew, *Warfare: The Middle Ages 768–1487*, Cambridge University Press, Cambridge, 1996

Hyland, Ann, *The Medieval Warhorse: From Byzantium to the Crusades*, Sutton Publishing, Gloucestershire, 1996

Jotischky, Andrew, *Crusading and the Crusader States*, Pearson Education Ltd, Harlow, 2004

Lees, B., 'The Letters of Queen Eleanor of Aquitaine to Pope Celestine III,' *The English Historical Review 21, no. 81*, 1906

Lord, Evelyn, *The Knights Templar In Britain*, Pearson Education Ltd, Harlow, 2004

Lyons, Malcolm Cameron and Jackson, DEP; *Saladin*, Cambridge University Press, 1982

Maalouf, Amin, *The Crusades Through Arab Eyes*, Saqi, London, 2006

Mayer, Hans Eberhard, *The Crusades*, Oxford University Press, Oxford, 1990

McGlynn, Sean, *By Sword and Fire*, Weidenfeld & Nicolson, London, 2008

McNeill, John, *Old Sarum*, English Heritage Guide, 2006

Miller, David, *Richard the Lionheart: The Mighty Crusader*, Weidenfeld & Nicolson, London, 2003

Mitchell, Mairin, *Berengaria: Enigmatic Queen of England*, A. Wright, East Sussex, 1986

Nicholson, Dr Helen and Nicolle, Dr David, *God's Warriors*, Osprey Publishing Ltd, Oxford, 2005

Nicolle, David, *Crusader Castles in the Holy Land 1097–1192*, Osprey Publishing, 2004

Nicolle, David, *Crusader Warfare: Volume I, Byzantium, Western Europe and the Battle for the Holy Land*, Hambledon Continuum, London, 2007

Nicolle, David, *Crusader Warfare: Volume II, Muslims, Mongols and the Struggle against the Crusades*, Hambledon Continuum, London, 2007

Nicolle, David, *Hattin 1187: Saladin's Greatest Victory*, Osprey, 1998

Nicolle, David, *Medieval Warfare Source Book: Volume I, Warfare in Western Christendom*, Book Club Associates, London, 1996

Nicolle, David, *Medieval Warfare Source Book: Volume 2, Christian Europe and its Neighbours, Arms and Armour Press*, London, 1996

Nicolle, David, *The Third Crusade 1191: Richard the Lionheart, Saladin and the struggle for Jerusalem*, Osprey Publishing Ltd, Oxford, 2006

Norgate, Kate, *Richard the Lionheart*, London, 1924

Oldenbourg, Zoe, *The Crusades*, Book Club Association, London, 1998

Oman, Sir Charles, *A History of The Art of War in the Middle Ages: Volume I, 378–1278 AD*, Greenhill Books, London, 1991

Phillips, Kim M., *A Cultural History of Women in the Middle Ages*, Bloomsbury Publishing Plc, London, 2013

Poole, A. L., *The Oxford History of England: Domesday Book to Magna Carta, 1087–1216*, Oxford University Press, Oxford, 1987

Prawer, Joshua, *Crusader Institutions*, Oxford University Press, Oxford, 1998

Prawer, Joshua, *The Crusaders' Kingdom: European Colonialism in the Middle Ages*, Praeger Publishers, New York, 1972

Prestwich, Michael, *Armies and Warfare in the Middle Ages: The English Experience*, Yale University Press, Yale, 1999

Read, Piers Paul, *The Templars*, Weidenfeld & Nicolson, London, 2003

Regan, Geoffrey, *Lionhearts: Saladin and Richard I*, Constable & Company Ltd, London, 1998

Richard, Jean, *The Crusades*, Cambridge University Press, Cambridge, 1999

Riley-Smith, Jonathan, *The Feudal Monarchy and the Kingdom of Jerusalem, 1174–1277*, Archon Books, The Shoestring Press, 1973

Riley-Smith, Jonathan (ed.), *The Oxford Illustrated History of the Crusades*, Oxford University Press, Oxford, 1995

Runciman, Steven, *A History of the Crusades: Volume 2*, Penguin Books Ltd, Middlesex, 1990

Runciman, Steven, *A History of the Crusades: Volume 3, The Kingdom of Acre*, Penguin Books Ltd, Middlesex, 1971

Saunders, J. J., *A History of Medieval Islam*, Routledge and Kegan Paul, London, 1996

Scott, Sir Walter, *Ivanhoe,* Wordsworth, Ware

Scott, Sir Walter, *The Talisman*, General Books LLC, 2009

Smail, R. C., *Crusading Warfare, 1097–1193*, Cambridge University Press, 1996

Stapleton, Rachel F., *Motherly Devotion and Fatherly Obligation: Eleanor of Aquitaine's Letters to Pope Celestine III*, University of Iowa, 2012

Stenton, Doris Mary, *English Society in the Early Middle Ages*, Penguin Books, Middlesex, 1976

Stevenson, T. G., *The Edinburgh Topographical, Traditional and Antiquarian Magazine*, 1848

Strickland, Matthew and Hardy, Robert, *The Great Warbow: From Hastings to the Mary Rose*, Sutton Publishing Ltd, Gloucestershire, 2005

Stubbs, *Constitutional History of England, Volume 1*, Barnes and Noble Inc., New York, 1967 edition

Szarmach, Paul E., Tavormina, M., Teresa, and Rosenthal, Joel T. (ed.); *Medieval England: An Encyclopaedia*, Garland, New York & London, 1998

Trindade, Ann, *Berengaria: In Search of Richard the Lionheart's Queen*, Four Courts Press, Dublin, 1199

Turner, Ralph V. and Heiser, Richard R.: *The Reign of Richard Lionheart: Ruler of the Angevin Empire 1189–99*, Pearson Education, Harlow, 2000

Turner, Ralph V., 'Eleanor of Aquitaine in the Governments of Her Sons Richard and John', in *Eleanor of Aquitaine: Lord and Lady*, (ed.) John Carmi Parsons and Bonnie Wheeler, Palgrave MacMillan, New York, 2002

Tyerman, Christopher, *England and the Crusades 1095–1588*, The University of Chicago Press Ltd, Chicago, 1996

Tyerman, Christopher, *God's War: A New History of the Crusades*, Penguin, London etc., 2007

Wagner, Thomas Gregor and Mitchell, Piers D., *The Illnesses of King Richard and King Philippe on the Third Crusade: An Understanding of arnaldia and leonardie*, Society for the Study of the Crusades and the Latin East, 2011

Warner, Philip, *The Medieval Castle: Life in a Fortress in Peace and War*, Book Club Associates, London, 1973

Warren, W. L., *Henry II*, Yale University Press, 2000

Warren, W. L., *King John*, Book Club Associates, 1974 edition

Wavell, Field-Marshal, *Allenby: Soldier and Statesman*, Harrap and Co., London, 1960 edition

Weir, Alison, *Eleanor of Aquitaine: By the Wrath of God Queen of England*, Vintage Books, London, 2007

Acknowledgements

I would like to acknowledge the help and support of those who have helped me get the book to this stage. Especially to Angela for an enjoyable road-trip around Richard's haunts in France and to Deyna for helping me with research and proofreading; thanks very much to you both. I would also like to thank Jonathan Reeve for his help and support in the past and wish him good luck in whatever pastures new he is headed for. I would also like to thank others such as Matilda Richards and Alex Bennett at Amberley who have helped to get the book over the line; I look forward to working with you both on future projects.

Index

Acre, Outremer 129, 134, 151, 154, 161, 163, 190, 195, 196, 198, 210, 211, 213, 214, 215, 218, 225, 227, 229, 230, 238, 247, 251, 252, 258, 259, 265, 268, 269, 324
    besieged by crusaders 121, 155, 167–189, 212, 277, 312, 328
    captured by Saladin 74
    crusader infighting in 228
    crusader losses in capturing 191
    massacre of Muslim prisoners at 192, 193, 194, 254
    recaptured by Muslims (1291) 358
Abbo of Fleury, cleric 131
Abraham ibn Ezra, philosopher 101
Abu Bekr, Saladin's negotiator 259
Abu I-Mihasin, Egyptian chronicler 194
Accursed Tower, Acre 180
Achilles, mythical hero 365
Adam of Eynsham, biographer of Hugh of Lincoln 348
Adam of Perseigne, Cistercian monk 356
Adela of Champagne, wife of Louis VII 29, 48
Adémar of Angoulême 53, 85
Adolf, archbishop of Cologne 294, 333
Ælfgar of Hollingbourne 303
Aeneas of Troy 256
Agincourt, Battle of (1415) 196, 255, 258, 328
Agnes of Merania, wife of Philip II 291
Aimar V, viscount of Limoges 39, 40, 49, 53, 55, 59, 346, 351
Aimery of Lusignan 332
Aixe, Aquitaine 54
Aix-la-Chapelle 333
Al-'Adil, brother of Saladin 213, 214, 259, 331
    and battle at Jaffa 257
    death of 332
    marriage proposals regarding Joanna 221, 327
    negotiations with Richard 181, 203, 223, 260
Alam al-Din Qaisar, Muslim commander 243
Alan of L'Etable, knight 216
Alan of Rusci, French knight 337
al-Aqsa Mosque, Jerusalem 249, 261, 262
Alarcos, Battle of 318
Alberic Clement, marshal of France 181, 182
Albert of Brabant 272
Albert, Prince Consort of Queen Victoria 263
Alençon, Normandy 88
Aleppo, Syria 251
Alexander III, Pope 44, 120, 187
Alexander of Necham 14
Alexander the Great 33, 157, 216, 227, 365
al-Fādil, Muslim chronicler 219
Alfonso II of Aragon 56, 126
Alfonso VIII of Castile 32, 318, 319, 358
Alice of Maurienne 37
Alice, fiancée of Richard I 37, 44, 67, 69, 73, 77, 83, 86, 88,126, 151, 162, 271, 285, 310, 313
    alleged relationship with Henry II 39
    as a possible bride for John 72, 274
    betrothal to Richard 28, 29, 63, 70, 123, 147
    repudiated by Richard 150, 186
Alix, daughter of Louis VII and Eleanor of Aquitaine 10
Allenby, General Edmund 217
Almeria, Spain 134
Almohad Muslims 318
Alnwick, England 37
Al-Quds *see* Jerusalem

Amalfi 319
Amboise, Touraine 84
Ambroise, chronicler 116, 129, 175, 193, 195, 201, 214, 215, 222, 224, 226, 227, 229, 230, 238, 242, 244, 246, 248
  at battle at Jaffa 252, 256
  in Cyprus 165
  in Sicily 137, 139, 141, 142
  on Berengaria 147
  on Richard's coronation 102
  on the Arsuf campaign 200, 204, 205
  on the Siege of Acre 168, 170, 171, 173, 177
  views of Richard 223, 257
Amesbury, Wiltshire 349
Anatolia 283
Andrew de Chauvigny, Poitevin noble 124, 182, 222, 244, 253, 256, 261, 355
Angers, Anjou 15, 22, 45, 52, 59, 96, 315
Angoulême, Aquitaine 40, 46, 309, 344
Anjou 6, 26, 29, 43, 52, 60, 65, 66, 84, 88, 124, 125, 129, 205, 285, 304, 305, 349
  ducal powers in 16, 22
Annals of Winchester 336, 346
Anne of Cleves, wife of Henry VIII 313
Antalya, Gulf of 156
Antioch 10, 16, 121, 158, 159, 260
  in First Crusade 247
Antiochetta 187
Antwerp 294
appares 107
Appleby, General Edmund 202
Apulia 319
Aquileia 267, 268
Aquitaine, Aquitanians 1, 6, 11, 23, 27, 28, 29, 32, 33, 34, 35, 36, 39, 43, 45, 46, 48, 50, 52, 59, 65, 66, 67, 73, 80, 81, 84, 107, 124, 125, 129, 158, 196, 305, 308, 309, 313, 334, 344, 347, 368
  characteristics of 9, 21, 22, 49, 54, 363
  Henry II seeks to gain power in 12, 63
  uprisings in 26, 49, 55, 56, 59, 61, 272, 274, 297, 306, 363
Aragon 56, 70, 134, 135, 279
Argentan, Normandy 38
Armageddon, Outremer 202
arnaldia 179
Arques, France 290, 295, 305, 310, 320
Arsuf 204, 209, 211, 212, 213, 249
Arthur of Brittany, nephew of Richard I 69, 141, 142, 321, 354
Arthur, mythical British king 14, 35, 111, 148
Artois 331
Ascalon, Outremer 188, 196, 215, 226, 228, 229, 230, 231, 243, 246, 250
  abandoned by Saladin 213, 214
  captured by Saladin 74, 158, 227
  negotiations over 251, 255, 259, 260
Asia Minor 9, 26, 117, 120, 121
Assassins *see* Nizaris
Aubrey of Rheims, constable of Jaffa 252
Audita Tremendi, Papal bull 75
Aumâle, Normandy 311, 324
Austria, Austrians 265, 270, 272
Auvergne, France 44

Babenberg dukes 268
Babylon 197, 337
Baden-Powell, Robert 368
Baha' al-Din Qaragush, Muslim commander 170
Baha' al-Din, chronicler 188, 191, 228, 241, 249, 257
  on Arsuf campaign 202, 208, 209
  on Richard I 175, 210, 251, 353
Baldwin II, king of Jerusalem 18
Baldwin III, king of Jerusalem 227
Baldwin IV, king of Jerusalem 64, 73
Baldwin IX, count of Flanders and Hainault 324, 328, 329, 330, 331, 336, 339
Baldwin of Béthune, French knight 284, 295, 296, 311, 320, 342
  with Richard on his journey back from Outremer 266, 268
Baldwin of Carew, knight 207
Baldwin of Forde, archbishop of Canterbury 63, 93, 95, 104, 234
  at Richard's coronation 98, 99
  career of 110
  death of 172, 277
  dispute with Canterbury monks 111, 112
  on crusade 158, 177
  preaching tour in Wales 111
Baldwin V, king of Jerusalem 73
Baldwin Wake 284
Balian of Ibelin, baron of Outremer 238, 370
Ballan, Touraine 88
Bannockburn, Battle of (1314) 216
Barcelona, Aragon 134
Barfleur, Normandy 18, 96, 305, 319
Bartholomew Mortimer, knight 256
Basques 21, 42
Bath, England 15
Bayeux, Normandy 30
Bayonne, France 42
Beaufort en Vallée, France 315, 349, 350
Beaulieu, Anjou 308
Beaumont Palace, Oxford 13
Beauvais, France 330
Bec, Normandy 25, 336
Becket, Thomas, archbishop of Canterbury 20, 36, 48, 80,

106, 110, 135, 232, 233, 295, 340, 359
Henry II's penance for 37
killing of 30
Bedfordshire, England 172
Beirut 74, 173, 174, 175, 251, 332
Beit Nuba, Outremer 225, 246, 247, 250
Bela III. king of Hungary 117, 149, 266, 324
Benedict, abbot of Burgh 278
Benedict, Jewish victim of massacre 103
Benjamin of Tudela, traveller 101
Berengaria of Navarre, queen of England and wife of Richard I 69, 101, 123, 126, 144, 152, 154, 272, 283, 313, 346
in Outremer 188, 195, 218
in widowhood 355, 356, 357
journey to join Richard 149, 150
marriage to Richard 153, 162, 336
memorials for Richard 348, 350
on Cyprus 155, 156, 158
on return from Outremer 262, 273, 279, 301
possible early meetings with Richard 70
relations with Richard 263, 315, 316, 349, 351
Bernard de Brosse, baron of Aquitaine 306
Bernard Itier, monk of Limoges 346
Bernard of Clairvaux 20, 191, 192
Bernard the Syrian, spy 248
Berry 44, 71, 81, 124, 311, 331
Bertram of Verdun, commander of Acre 195
Bertran de Born 33, 49, 57, 83, 128, 352
Bertrand de Gurdon, crossbowman 345, 346
Berwick, Scotland 113
Bethlehem, Outremer 261
Bigorre, France 125
Bilbeis, Egypt 248
Biscay, Bay of 135
Blanca ('Blanche'), wife of Thibaut of Champagne 356
Blanche of Castile, mother of Louis IX 356
Blanchegarde, Outremer 246
Blois, France 22
Blondel of Nesle, minstrel 70, 273, 274, 366, 367
Bloom, Orlando, actor 370
Blue Thong, Order of the 163
Bohemond of Tripoli 158
Bolsover, England 104
Bonaparte, Napoleon 224
Bonsmoulins, Normandy 83, 84
Bordeaux 11, 21, 42, 45, 147
Brabant, Flanders 42, 301
Bradenstoke, England 299
Brindisi, Italy 136, 150
Brittany, Bretons 29, 55, 62, 63, 65, 66, 67, 69, 85, 86, 197, 205, 321, 330
Bruges 294
Brussels 294
Bucard, treasurer at York 109
Buffavento, Cyprus 164
Bures, Normandy 30, 122
Bury St Edmunds, England 113, 303
'Butchery of Malmorte' 43
Buza di Luna, ship 155

Cadiz, Spain 133
Cadoc, mercenary 324
Caen, Normandy 52, 276, 279
Caesarea, Outremer 259
Cahors, Toulouse 80
Caieux 285
Cairo, Egypt 224
Calabria 136
Calais, France 121
Canterbury, England 30, 37, 47, 110, 113, 284, 340
Carinthia 268
Carlisle, England 323
Carmarthen, Wales 113, 114
Carmel, Mount 202
Carmelite order 202
Cartagena, Spain 134
Cartmel, Lancashire, England 96
Casal Imbert, Outremer 229
Casal Moyen, Outremer 222, 224
Casal of the Plains, Outremer 222, 224
Cassée, castle 354
Castile 70
Catania, Sicily 143
Cathar Crusades 21, 327
Cathars 33
Celestine III, Pope 153, 291, 295, 329, 330, 332, 340
and Geoffrey, archbishop of York 280, 312, 318, 323
and Philip, bishop of Beauvais 343
and William Longchamp 234, 235
letters from Eleanor of Aquitaine about Richard's captivity 287, 288, 289
meets Philip of France in Rome 187, 270
Châlus-Chabrol, castle 344
chansons de geste 116
Chansons des Lorrains 82
Charente, River 46
Charlemagne, Holy Roman Emperor 271
Charlier, Dr Philippe, forensic scientist 347
Charroux, Aquitaine 347
Château Gaillard, castle 325, 326, 329, 334, 335, 343, 344, 359
Châteauroux, Berry 71, 72, 81
Châtillon-sur-Indre, Anjou 83, 290
Chepstow, England 298
Chester, England 102
Chichester, England 278
Chinon, Anjou 29, 32, 34, 36, 53, 72, 88, 106, 127, 311, 343, 349, 351, 354, 359
death of Henry II at 89
Chippenham, England 15
Chrétien de Troyes, writer 148, 314
Christ Church, Oxford 13
Chronicle of Meaux 44

Chroniques de Saint-Denis 100
Churchill, Sir Winston 4, 5
Cinque Ports 117
Cirencester Abbey, England 14
Cistercian Order 110, 123, 275, 277, 278, 294, 341, 346, 351, 354, 356, 362
Clairvaux, Poitou 53, 54
Clement III, Pope 75, 109, 136, 139, 153, 154
Clerkenwell, England 65
Clifford's Tower, York 103
Cnut the Great, king of England and Denmark 290
Cnut VI, king of Denmark 290
Collioure, France 134
Cologne, Germany 292, 294
Conan IV, duke of Brittany 29
Connery, Sean, actor 371
Conrad III, Holy Roman Emperor 9
Conrad, Marquis of Montferrat 190, 229, 237, 240, 241, 242, 243, 266, 267, 271, 332
  and the Siege of Acre 173, 178
  arrival in Outremer 160
  assassination of 239, 240
  marriage to Isabella 177
  negotiations with Saladin 220, 223, 238
  relations with Philip of France 176, 186
  Richard accused of involvement in his assassination 260, 264, 276, 319, 328
Constance of Castile, wife of Louis VII 28
Constance, queen of Sicily 139, 320, 332, 333
Constance, wife of Geoffrey II of Brittany 37, 69, 321
Constantinople 120, 133, 160, 282, 284, 358
Corfu 136, 265
Cornwall, England 104
Courcelles, France 337
Coventry, England 236, 336
Crac des Chevaliers, Crusader castle 1, 326
Crecy, Battle of 328
Crete 136
Crete 154, 155
Cumbria, England 300
Cyprus 155, 156, 163, 164, 165, 166, 175, 215, 282, 283, 332
  Philip claims half of 185, 186
  sold to Guy of Lusignan 238

Damascus, Syria 9, 206, 224, 263, 284
Damsel of Cyprus' 262, 279, 283, 292, 354
Dandolo, Enrico, Doge of Venice 284
Dangu, Normandy 331, 336
Dante Alighieri 49, 313
Danube, River 296
Darius, Persian King 157
Dark Tower, story 367
Dartmouth, England 133
Darum, Outremer 214, 229, 243, 244, 251, 364
David, Biblical King 195
David, Earl of Huntingdon, brother of William the Lion 99, 298
Dax, France 42
Dead River, Outremer 203
Denise de Déols, heiress from Berry 124
Denmark 168, 291
Derby, England 104
Dieppe, Normandy 30, 305, 320, 330
Dome of the Rock, Jerusalem 75, 261
Domfront, Maine 307
Dormition of the Virgin 261
Dorset, England 104
Dover, England 121, 232, 233, 234, 277
Dreux of Mello, Constable of France 163
Drincourt, France 290
Dublin, Ireland 61
Durham, England 312
Dürnstein, castle 270, 274
Edessa, Syria 178
Edmund, Saint and King 158
Edward I, king of England 6
Edward III, king of England 273, 302, 363
Edward the Confessor, king of England 98
Egypt, Egyptians 175, 183, 194, 196, 227, 229, 258, 284, 358
  jointly ruled with Syria 44, 64
  Richard's strategic designs on 219, 220, 248, 250
El Cid 70
Ela, countess of Salisbury 127
Eleanor of Aquitaine, queen of England 5, 20, 26, 35, 41, 47, 58, 63, 68, 100, 105, 123, 127, 235, 236, 237, 270, 274, 300, 302, 307, 332, 343, 350, 366
  and captivity of Richard 275, 278, 284, 287, 288, 289, 292, 294
  as ruler of Aquitaine 27, 28, 29, 66
  and Henry II 11, 23, 25, 32
  and Louis VII and Second Crusade 9, 10, 12, 13
  at Richard's funeral 351
  captivity of 37, 38, 39, 60, 94, 106
  in later life 305, 354, 355, 357
  journey to Sicily 147, 148, 151, 152, 153
  relations with Richard I 61, 122
Eleanor of Brittany 282, 287, 292, 295, 319, 321
Eleanor, sister of Richard I 14, 358
Elie count of Périgord 53
Elijah, Biblical prophet 202
Ely, England 237, 284
Epte, River 337
Erdberg, Austria 268
Etna, Mount, Sicily 137
Eu, France 305, 310, 311
Eustace, bishop of Ely 344
Everard, servant of the bishop of Salisbury 201
Evesham, England 110

Evreux, Normandy 294, 307, 337, 354
Excalibur, sword 111, 150

Famagusta, Cyprus 163
Fauvel, horse 157, 158, 164, 209, 216
Feisal of Mecca 364
Feversham, England 110
First Council of Lyon (1245) 212
First Crusade 247
Flanders, Flemings 168, 185, 234, 235, 306, 329, 330, 331
Flori, Jean, French historian 61, 148, 314, 366, 367
Flynn, Errol, actor 370
Fontevraud Abbey, Anjou 93, 314, 354, 358
  Eleanor of Aquitaine retires to 305, 346
  internment of Henry II at 91
  Richard's funeral and burial at 347, 348, 349, 350, 364
Forde Abbey, England 110
Forest of Dean, England 118
Fourth Crusade 123, 133, 219, 284
Franche-Nef, ship 262
Franj, settlers in Outremer 115, 159, 160, 176, 183
Frederick Barbarossa, Holy Roman Emperor 64, 98, 117, 139, 184
  marriage proposals regarding Richard 63
  on crusade and his death 120, 121
Frederick Grimaldi 136
Frederick II, Holy Roman Emperor 320, 358
Friesach 268
French Revolution 30
Fulk Nerra 308,
Fulk of Gilervalle, French knight 337
Fulk of Neuilly, Crusade preacher 77, 123, 341
Fulk, king of Jerusalem 16, 17, 18, 76, 77

Gaillon, castle 324
Galahad, Arthurian knight 149
Gallipoli 120
Gamalon 155
Gandhi, Mahatma 194
Garnier of Nablus, Master of the Hospitallers 163, 207, 208
Gascony, France 21, 32
Gaugamela, Battle of 157
Gawain, Arthurian knight 116
Genoa, Genoese 136, 146, 176, 219, 220, 229, 238, 253, 255, 258, 279
  Philip II at 128, 129, 135
Geoffrey de Rançon 45, 85, 306, 309
Geoffrey de Vinsauf, poet 115, 351
Geoffrey fitzPeter, official 107
Geoffrey Hose 172
Geoffrey II, duke of Brittany, brother of Richard I 5, 23, 34, 37, 48, 50, 52, 53, 59, 64, 66, 69, 303
  character of 55
  death of 67, 68
  given Brittany 29
  in conflict with Richard 54, 56, 62
Geoffrey of Lusignan, Aquitanian knight 27, 36, 53, 85, 158, 171, 179, 196, 214, 311
Geoffrey of Monmouth, chronicler 14
Geoffrey of Perche, ally of Richard I 333
Geoffrey Plantagenet, father of Henry II of England 8, 15, 17, 18, 57, 90, 257
Geoffrey, archbishop of York, half-brother of Richard I 90, 127, 301, 317, 318, 335
  at Henry II's death-bed 90
  dispute with church officials at York 108, 236, 280, 312, 323
  exiled from England 126
  made archbishop of York 109
  returns to England 232, 233
Geoffrey, brother of Henry II of England 11
George, David Lloyd, Prime Minister 364
George, Saint 206
Georgians 193
Gerald of Wales, chronicler 12, 23, 33, 55, 66, 68, 78, 89, 90, 197, 119, 128, 351
Gerard de Camville 231, 232
Gerard de Ridfort, Grand Master of the Templars 161, 198
Gerard de Tourneval, knight 256
Germany, Germans 168, 251, 272, 273, 287, 300, 301, 319, 331, 333
Gervase of Canterbury, chronicler 85, 347
Gesta Henrici II et Gesta Regis Ricardi 134
Gilbert de Vascoeuil, constable of Gisors 284
Gillingham, John, biographer of Richard I 193, 194, 312
Gisors, Normandy 63, 77, 81, 274, 284, 326, 329, 336, 337, 339, 344
Glastonbury, England 110, 111
Gloucester, England 78, 318
Godfrey de Lucy, bishop of Winchester 109, 236
Gomorrah, Biblical town 312
Grandmont, France 57, 91
Graçay, Berry 311
Greek Fire 169, 171, 173, 174, 180, 181, 182, 320
Gregory VIII, Pope 75
Grimaldo Grimaldi 135
Guinevere, mythical British Queen 35, 111
Guy de Laval, French baron 98
Guy of Lusignan, king of Jerusalem 36, 85, 160, 166, 167, 168, 176, 218, 219, 220, 225, 237, 238, 311

and Battle of Hattin 159, 161, 217
and siege of Acre 168, 169, 178
and the campaign on Cyprus 162, 163
attacks Eleanor of Aquitaine 27
becomes king of Jerusalem 73
on Arsuf campaign 205, 213

Hackington, England 110, 111, 112
Hagenau, Germany 286
Haifa, Outremer 259
Hamburg, Germany 266
Harold Godwinson, king of England 98
Hattin, Battle of 74, 75, 76, 115, 120, 128, 138, 158, 159, 160, 161, 183, 193, 196, 198, 296, 207, 210, 212, 217, 223, 226, 227, 228, 237, 150, 158, 160
Hector, mythical hero 365
Henry de la Pomeroy, supporter of John 295
Henry I, king of England 13, 17, 24, 39, 56, 62, 105
Henry I, king of France 337
Henry II, king of England 5, 8, 18, 19, 22, 24, 25, 26, 27, 32, 33, 34, 36, 42, 43, 48, 50, 52, 53, 57, 59, 62, 67, 76, 77, 78, 79, 80, 83, 85, 87, 93, 94, 95, 96, 97, 104, 105, 106, 111, 117, 127, 129, 132, 134, 140, 151, 196, 290, 361, 367
and Alice, Richard's fiancée 29, 70, 313
and Aquitaine 12, 23, 39, 49, 54, 55, 56, 63, 66
and Eleanor of Aquitaine 11, 28, 35
and Louis VII 9, 38, 44
and Philip II 71, 73, 81, 86, 118, 128
and Richard 40, 41, 47, 60, 61, 64, 68, 72, 82, 84, 89, 92, 270
and Thomas Becket 20, 31, 37, 110, 359
birth of 13
last days of 88, 90, 91
Henry III, king of England 96, 355
Henry le Tyois, German knight 256
Henry Longchamp, brother of William 103, 114
Henry Marshal, brother of William, bishop of Exeter 109, 277
Henry of Champagne, king of Jerusalem 170, 238, 243, 244, 247, 250, 293
and Saladin's attack on Jaffa 253, 254
becomes king of Jerusalem 241, 242
death of 332
on the Arsuf campaign 205, 207
Henry the Lion, German King 25, 52, 98, 266, 268
Henry 'The Young King', brother of Richard I 5, 14, 23, 29, 33, 44, 52, 56, 60, 63, 67, 69, 149, 303, 324
and Richard 40, 50, 54
and William Marshal 27, 94, 96
becomes King 30
character of 51, 55
death of 57, 58, 62, 68
disagreements with Henry II 34, 61
Henry V, Holy Roman Emperor 17
Henry V, king of England 123, 196, 255, 363
Henry VI, Holy Roman Emperor 139, 149, 150, 153, 265, 266, 272, 277, 287, 310
and captivity and ransom of Richard 269, 275, 276, 278, 303
and Philip II 270, 273, 286, 288
and Sicily 142, 282, 319, 320, 332, 333
Henry VIII, king of England 24, 105, 152, 290
Heraclius, Patriarch of Jerusalem 64, 65, 66, 73, 75, 76, 77, 120, 172
Herbert, bishop of Salisbury 334
Hereford, England 102
Herod 31, 144, 203, 294
Hilaire, Saint 30
Hildegard of Bingen, medieval abbess 314
History of the Kings of Britain 14
History of William Marshal 93
Hodierna, midwife of Richard I 14, 15
Hohenstaufen dynasty 276
'holocaust'; first use in connection with anti-Semitic massacre 101
Holy Lance, relic 247
Holy Sepulchre, Church of the, Jerusalem 17, 65, 195, 218, 224, 242, 261
Holy Trinity, London 116
homosexuality 72, 144, 151, 312, 313, 314, 315
Hospital of St Thomas of Acre 195
Hospitallers, military order 17, 141, 215, 225, 226, 248, 351
and Saladin's attack on Jaffa 253
at Hattin 74, 193, 210
at siege of Acre 178, 179, 180
on Arsuf campaign 197, 205, 206, 207, 208, 212, 213
role of 73
House of Commons, London 296
Howden, Yorkshire 312
Hubert Walter, archbishop of Canterbury 292, 295, 301, 302, 305, 318, 322, 323, 324, 331, 334
and the crusade 134, 158, 182, 190, 260
becomes archbishop of Canterbury 279

becomes bishop of Salisbury 109
criticised by Pope Innocent III 340
during Richard's captivity 273, 277, 278, 280
on death of Richard 346
visits Jerusalem 261
Hugh Bardolf, sheriff 280, 299, 310, 311
Hugh de Gournay, French knight 307
Hugh de Puiset, bishop of Durham 66, 106, 107, 108, 236, 273, 280, 310, 311, 312
Hugh III, duke of Burgundy 127, 141, 242, 248, 251
at siege of Acre 179
death of 258
friction with Richard 250
in command of French after Philip leaves Outremer 186, 187, 190, 197, 201, 219, 229, 253
on Arsuf campaign 205
Hugh Neville, knight 256
Hugh Nonant, bishop of Coventry 232, 233, 236, 300, 317, 336
Hugh of Beauchamp, English knight 76
Hugh of St Pol, ally of Richard I 333
Hugh, bishop of Chester 184
Hugh, bishop of Lincoln 235, 279, 302, 334, 335, 348, 349, 350
Humphrey of Toron 158, 177, 223, 240, 242, 332
Husayn ibn Ali, grandson of Mohammed 227

Ibn al-Athir, Muslim chronicler 121, 160
Ibn an-Nahhāl 221
Ibn Shaddad, Muslim writer 184
Ida de Tosny, mother of William Longespée 127
Ida, Mount 154
Indre River, Anjou 308
Ingeborg, wife of Philip II 290, 291, 313
Innocent III, Pope 273, 291, 327, 332, 335, 336, 340, 341, 342, 343, 355
Irbil, Mesopotamia 120
Ireland 61, 62, 65, 67, 113, 198
Isaac Angelus, Byzantine Emperor 261
Isaac Comnenus, Cypriot Emperor 155, 156, 157, 163, 166, 209, 262, 282, 295
capture of 164, 165, 168
Isabel de Clare, wife of William Marshal 93, 95
Isabel of Gloucester, wife of John 104
Isabella of Angoulême, wife of King John 350
Isabella, queen of France 124
Isabella, queen of Jerusalem 177, 239, 241, 242, 332
Issoudun, Berry 311, 320
Itinerarium Peregrinorum 33, 70, 115, 163, 256, 264
Ivanhoe, novel 367
Ivry, Normandy 285

Jacques de Vitry, bishop of Acre 264
Jaffa, Outremer 195, 196, 198, 209, 214, 215, 216, 219, 222. 224, 227, 247, 251, 259, 262, 332
abandoned by Saladin 213
Saladin attacks at 251, 252, 253, 255, 257, 258
James d'Avesnes, knight 168, 207, 212, 213
Jean de Joinville, Crusade chronicler 187, 251
Jerusalem 48, 57, 66, 73, 77, 86, 117, 119, 184, 186, 187, 196, 198, 225, 228, 237, 238, 248, 249, 250, 258, 262, 263, 264, 341, 349, 360
conquered by First Crusade 16, 64, 193, 247
Crusader propaganda concerning 224
during Second Crusade 9
pilgrim visits to during Third Crusade 195, 216, 260, 261
Richard and 217, 218, 219, 226, 246, 251
taken by Saladin 74, 75, 76, 129, 159, 168, 194, 210, 358
Jerusalem, kingdom of 64, 65, 74, 119, 205, 238, 245
Jews 78, 100, 101, 102, 103, 104, 118. 132, 133, 226, 303, 337
Joachim of Fiore, abbot of Corazzo 144, 145, 203
Joanna, sister of Richard I 14, 283, 346, 350, 354
as wife of Raymond VI of Toulouse 336
death of 354
in Cyprus 155, 156, 158
in Outremer 167, 188, 195, 218
in Sicily 139, 140
marries William II of Sicily 29, 40
on way back from crusade 262, 273, 279
proposed marriage to Al-'Adil 221
John 'Lackland', Prince (later King) of England 5, 6, 14, 23, 34, 36, 38, 49, 60, 63, 80, 96, 113, 119, 126, 135, 232, 235, 289, 291, 292, 293, 294, 298, 300, 301, 317, 331, 353, 358, 360, 364, 369, 370
and his nephew Arthur 69, 141, 142
and Ireland 61
as king of England 343, 346, 350, 351, 352, 354, 355, 359, 362, 367
attacks against Richard in early years 62
betrayal of Henry II 89, 90
character of 19, 20
grants in England to 104, 105
in England whilst Richard was on crusade 231, 233, 234, 274, 275, 279, 295

in Normandy after Richard returns 306, 307, 309
plots against Richard 236, 239, 246, 250, 271, 278, 290
suggested marriage to Alice of France 72
John Marshal, brother of William 99
John of Alen?on, archdeacon 306, 307
John of Anagni, papal legate 86, 112, 122
John of Salisbury, philosopher 287, 366
John the Baptist, Saint 248, 282
John, bishop of Evreux 136, 142, 162
John, bishop of Norwich 134
Jones, Colonel 'H' 365
Jordan, River 221
Joscius, archbishop of Tyre 138
Judaea 217
Judas Iscariot 31, 89, 136, 155, 360
Juhel de Mayenne, French baron 98

Kingdom of Heaven, Hollywood film 370
King's Standard 200, 209
Kipling, Rudyard, poet 211
Knoyle Hodierne, Wiltshire, England 15
Kyrenia, Cyprus 164

La Baniare, priory 140, 152
La Rochelle, Poitou 37, 45
Lacock, England 105
La-Ferté Bernard, Maine 86
Lambeth, England 112, 331
Lancaster, England 104, 295
Lancelot, Arthurian knight 116, 314
Langeais, France 350
Last Supper 261
Latrun, Outremer 224, 225, 246
Laugharne, Wales 113
Lawrence, TE ('Lawrence of Arabia') 364
Le Mans, Maine 52, 57, 315
Berengaria at 350, 355, 356
fight with Henry II at 86, 87
issue of crusade ordinances 143
Lebanon 16
Leon 70
leonardie 179
Leopold V, duke of Austria 271,294, 319
and Richard's ransom 272, 276
captures Richard 268, 269
death of 295, 296
insulted at Acre 167, 184, 185, 265
L'Epau, Cistercian Abbey 356
Les Andalys, Normandy 325, 329, 331
Limassol, Cyprus 155, 156, 162
Limoges, Aquitaine 32, 54, 55, 56, 57, 59, 344, 346
Lincoln, England 66, 102, 231, 232
Lincolnshire, England 172
Lisbon 133, 135, 139, 170
Llanstephan, Wales 113
Llawhaden, Wales 114
Loches, Anjou 81, 290, 306, 308
Loire, River 8, 15, 22, 349
London, England 37, 41, 64, 78, 233, 236, 301, 302, 322, 323, 340, 349
Lothian, Scotland 323
Loudun, France 34
Louis IX, king of France 187, 356, 358
Louis of Blois, ally of Richard I 333
Louis VI, king of France 18
Louis VII, king of France 9, 13, 24, 29, 36, 37, 47, 48, 122, 148, 151
and death of Thomas Becket 31
and Eleanor of Aquitaine 10, 11, 12, 14, 20
and Henry II 23, 28, 38, 44, 76
and Richard 32, 33, 34
Louvain 294
Louviers, Peace of 320, 325
Lübeck, Germany 266
Lucas of L'Etable, knight 216
Lucas, abbot of Turpenay 350
Lucius III, Pope 64, 67
Luggershall, England 104
Lydda, Outremer 260
Lyon, France 128

Machiavelli, Niccolo, political writer 238
Maghreb, North Africa 120
Magna Carta 359, 370
Magnus of Reichersberg, Bavarian chronicler 268
Maid Marion 370
Maine 29, 66, 368
Malaga, Spain 134
Mantes, France 290
Marbodius of Rennes, medieval writer 315
Margaret, daughter of Louis VII and wife of the 'Young King' 29, 37, 44, 57, 324
Margaret, daughter of William the Lion 300, 323
Margarita, queen of Sicily 148
Margat, Outremer 168
Marie of Champagne, half-sister of Richard I 148, 285, 356
Marie, daughter of Louis VII and Eleanor of Aquitaine 10
Marlborough, England 104, 295
Marseille, France 128, 132, 134, 135, 279
Martel, Aquitaine 57
Martial, Saint 330
Mary Magdalene 127
Masyaf, Syria 239, 240
Mategriffon, 'pre-fab castle' 141, 146, 178
Matilda, Empress and mother of Henry II 17, 18, 24, 25, 98, 149, 358
Matilda, sister of Richard I 14, 23, 52, 266
Matthew of Clare, constable of Dover 232
Matthew of Montmorency, French knight 337

Matthew Paris, chronicler 118, 321, 345, 347
Matthew, count of Boulogne 36
Megiddo, Outremer 202
Meinhard of Görz 267, 268, 269, 272
Melisende, queen of Jerusalem 16, 18
Melusine 19
Mercadier, mercenary captain 62, 308, 328, 337, 338, 339, 344, 345, 346, 352
Merlin, seer 14, 58
Mesopotamia 251
Messina, Sicily 128, 134, 136, 137, 139, 154, 166, 175, 186, 280, 284, 332
  Philip arrives at 138
  Richard in 141, 145, 146, 150
Milan 142, 270
Mileta 137
Milli, near Beauvais, France 330
Mirabeau, France 34, 52
Mohammed, Prophet 144, 159, 221, 227
Monaco 136
Mongols 197
Monreale, Sicily 137
Montlouis, Treaty of 38
Montmirail, Treaty of 28
Mortain, Normandy 97
mortality in the Third Crusade 180
Mosul, Mesopotamia 120, 188, 218, 258
Mujir al-Din, Arab historian 218

Naples 136, 149, 150
Navarre, Navarrese 21, 69, 70, 101, 125, 126, 147, 148, 272, 308, 357
Nazareth, Outremer 259, 261
Naze, England 302
Nelson, Admiral Horatio 133
Nero, Roman Emperor 144
Nestorian Christians 188
Neubourg, Normandy 294
Nicosia, Cyprus 164
Niketas Choniates, Byzantine chronicler 165
Nizaris 239, 240, 242, 243
Noah's Ark 173
Nonancourt, France 122, 324
Norgate, Kate, historian 70
Normandy, Normans 8, 22, 23, 25, 26, 29, 52, 60, 62, 63, 64, 65, 73, 81, 84, 87, 88, 93, 95, 98, 102, 121, 124, 125, 126, 135, 235, 274, 297, 302, 305, 341, 347, 354, 359, 361, 363, 368
  and Third Crusade 66, 129, 197, 200, 209
  attacked by Louis VII 11
  attacked by Philip 71, 294
  John in 289, 291, 292, 295
  in Sicily 137
  records from 6, 43
  Richard's post-crusade campaign in 301, 306, 309, 311, 319, 320, 321, 322, 325, 329, 330, 334, 336, 337, 338, 339
Northampton, England 103, 300
Northern Lights 265
Northumberland, England 134, 299, 300, 310, 312, 323
Norwich, England 102
Nôtre Dame, Paris 69, 124
Nottingham, England 42, 104, 280, 298, 299, 300, 301, 370
Nubians 172, 206
Nur al-Din, Muslim leader 44, 45

Ochsenfurt, Germany 275
Oliver, chivalric hero 117
Order of Fontevraud 349
ordinances 127, 129
Ostia, port of Rome 136
Otto of Brunswick, King and (later) Emperor 284, 300, 323, 333, 341, 342, 344, 354, 355
Otto of St Blasien, chronicler 269
Outremer 9, 44, 45, 64, 65, 72, 76, 79, 86, 117, 119, 120, 121, 122, 123, 128, 129, 134, 138, 143, 145, 146, 151, 153, 158, 161, 165, 166, 167, 169, 172, 183, 184, 186, 190, 194, 195, 197, 218, 219, 225, 228, 229, 230, 237, 238, 244, 251, 260, 263, 264, 270, 293, 295, 302, 305, 324, 331, 332, 337, 358, 360, 363, 370
  established by First Crusade 16
  links with Angevin dynasty 17, 18, 19
Ovid, Roman writer 263
Oxford, England 13, 113, 236, 273, 275, 334

Palermo, Sicily 41, 143, 319, 333
Papal indulgences 79
parage 50, 53
Paris, France 23, 32, 34, 36, 44, 64, 65, 69, 72, 86, 100, 124, 235, 274, 325, 334, 337, 367
Paris, University of 14
Patrick, Earl of Salisbury 27
Perche, France 98, 285
Persia 206, 239
Peter Basil, knight 345
Peter Bru, knight 345
Peter des Roches, crusader-cleric 195
Peter Milo, Cistercian abbot of Le Pin 346, 350, 356
Peter of Blois, secretary to Eleanor of Aquitaine 283, 286, 287
Peter of Capua, papal legate 342, 343
Peter of Préaux, standard bearer 204
Peter Préaux, Norman baron 330
Philip I, count of Flanders 36, 72, 106, 121, 127, 149, 150, 180, 185, 271
Philip II ('Augustus'), king of France 25, 49, 55, 63, 64, 73, 78, 79, 81, 88, 100, 125, 130,132, 190, 238, 243, 264, 265, 266, 288,

295, 300, 306, 310, 321, 326, 328, 331, 333, 335, 336, 354, 362
and campaign in Normandy 284, 285, 297, 302, 305, 307, 311, 320, 324, 327, 330, 337, 338, 339, 342, 363
and Henry II 68, 83, 90, 118
and King John 355
and marriage of his half-sister Alice 67, 150, 162
and Richard 71, 72, 77, 82, 84, 86, 112, 114, 122, 128, 151, 166, 167, 185, 242, 319, 341, 344
and the crusade 76, 120, 129, 135, 188
at siege of Acre 169, 170, 172, 173, 176, 182
birth of 24, 29
coronation of 47, 48
during Richard's captivity 269, 270, 271, 272, 273, 274, 275, 276, 277, 278, 289, 293
in Sicily 138, 139, 140, 141
marriage to Ingeborg of Denmark 290, 291, 313
narrowly evades capture 308, 309
plots against Richard 236, 246, 250, 286. 292
returns from crusade 186, 187
Philip of Cognac, illegitimate son of Richard I 351
Philip of Dreux, bishop of Beauvais 163, 177, 239, 258, 271, 286, 328, 338, 343
Philip of Poitou, clerk 266
Philip of Swabia, German king 333, 344
Piedmont 266
Pipe Rolls 102, 307, 351
Pipewell, England 105
Pisa, Pisans 146, 149, 279
Plantagenet origin of name 15
Poitiers, Battle of 328
Poitiers, Poitou 8, 27, 28, 30, 38, 78, 315, 330, 346
Poitou 37, 53, 55, 64, 72, 102, 149, 205, 279, 301, 330, 368
Pons, Aquitaine 45, 46, 47
Portsmouth, England 96, 236, 301, 302
Powles, Lieutenant-Colonel Guy 364
Premonstratensian Order 123
Provence 291
Pythagoras, Greek mathematician 202

Quercy, Toulouse 80

Ragusa (now Dubrovnik) 266
Ralph de Tilly, English knight 171
Ralph de Wigetof, clerk 323
Ralph of Coggeshall, chronicler 123, 256, 299, 344, 351, 362
Ralph of Diceto, chronicler 34, 36, 47, 48, 102, 175, 270, 275, 293, 322, 326, 348
and coronation of Richard 99
and prophecies of Merlin 14
on tournaments 303, 304
Ralph of Exoudon 311, 320
Ralph of Fougères, French baron 98
Ralph Teisson 261
Ralph the Farter, court jester 31
Ralph, Patriarch of Jerusalem 252
Ramesses II, Pharaoh 202
Ramla, Outremer 224, 225, 226, 259, 260
Ranulf de Glanville, chief justiciar 106, 109, 134
Ranulf, Earl of Chester 320
Raoul de Mauléon, knight 256
Rashid al-Din Sinān, 'Old Man of the Mountains' 239, 243, 276
Raymond V, count of Toulouse 32, 33, 35, 67, 71, 80, 81, 125, 272
Raymond of Antioch 158
Raymond of Poitiers, prine of Antioch 10
Raymond VI, count of Toulouse 283, 327, 328, 336, 354
Raymond-Berenguer IV, count of Barcelona 23, 28
Reading, England 64
Regensburg, Germany 272
Reginald de Dunstanville, Earl of Cornwall 39
Reginald of Sidon, baron of Outremer 238
Reginald, bishop of Bath 99
Renaud, count of Boulogne 333, 355
Renier of Marun, knight 216
Revelations, Book of the Bible 144, 203
Reynald de Chatillon 159, 161
Rheims, France 48
Rhine, River 294
Rhodes 136, 155, 187
Rhône, River 129, 134
Rhys ap Gruffydd (Rhys of Deheubarth) 95, 113, 114
Richard Coeur de Lion, opera 367
Richard de Templo, chronicler 116
Richard fitzNeal, bishop of London 109
Richard I, king of England 1, 2, 7, 16, 28, 40, 41, 42, 48, 51, 52, 53, 58, 59, 60, 62, 69, 78, 93, 98, 115, 120, 130, 132, 138, 146, 153, 154, 155, 161, 166, 180, 187, 189, 232, 233, 234, 235, 236, 237, 238, 239, 242, 244, 252, 262, 264, 268, 269, 275, 280, 281, 283, 284, 305, 306, 318, 328, 329, 334, 343, 344, 355, 363, 364
alliances in Germany 333, 342
alliance with count of Flanders 331
ancestors of 26
and Arsuf campaign 196, 197, 198, 199, 200, 201,

203, 204, 207, 208, 209, 213, 214, 215, 216, 217
and Ascalon 226, 227, 228, 229, 230, 231, 251
and assassination of Conrad of Montferrat 243
and battle at Jaffa 253, 254, 255, 256, 257
and Berengaria 147, 148, 150, 162, 263, 316, 336, 351, 356, 357
and Château Gaillard 325, 326, 327
and chivalry 116, 365, 366
and dispute with monks at Canterbury 112, 113
and Hugh, bishop of Lincoln 335, 348
and hunting 49
and Jerusalem campaigns 218, 224, 225, 245, 248, 249, 250
and Jews 103, 104
and mercenaries 43, 352
and Philip II 25, 151, 186, 319
and Pope Innocent III 341
and Toulouse 67
and William Marshal 91, 92, 94, 96, 299
appointment of officials in England 106, 107, 108, 109, 110
appointment of officials in France 124, 125
as duke of Aquitaine 31, 32, 39, 45, 66
at siege of Acre 167, 168, 170, 172, 173, 176, 177, 178, 182, 185
becomes count of Poitou 30
betrothal to Alice 29, 44, 63, 70, 86
birth of 8, 13
campaign in Aquitaine (1179) 46, 47
campaign in Normandy (1195 onwards) 310, 311, 320, 321, 322, 324, 337, 338
captivity of 269, 270, 271, 273, 274, 275, 276, 277, 286, 287, 288, 289, 291, 293
character of 19, 20, 33, 354
conflict with the Young King 54, 55, 56
contemporary assessments of his reign 360, 361, 362
coronation of 99, 100, 102
death of 345, 346, 347, 359
departs Outremer 265, 266
designs on Egypt 219, 220
difficult relationship with England in later reign 339, 340
dispute with Walter of Coutances 330
early opposition to Henry II 34, 36, 37, 38
flight across Europe 267, 268
formative years of 15, 23
funeral and burial of 347, 349, 350
illnesses of 179, 180, 258
in France en route to the crusade 121, 128, 129, 134
in Cyprus 156, 157, 163, 164, 165, 166
in films 370, 371
in literature 367
in Sicily 139, 140, 141, 142, 143, 144, 145, 146, 152
journey to Sicily 135, 136, 137
later tensions and conflict with Henry II 61, 64, 68, 72, 73, 80, 81, 82, 83, 84, 85, 87, 88, 89, 90
'Lionheart' 175
massacre of Muslim prisoners at Acre 191, 192, 193, 194
modern views of 368, 369
near-capture of Philip II 308, 309
negotiations with Saladin 181, 221, 222, 223, 259, 260
poetry of 285
policy with Scotland 113, 323
policy with Wales 113, 114
preparations for crusade 117, 118, 119, 126, 127
ransom of 278, 279, 282, 292, 296
regulation of tournaments 303, 304
relations with Eleanor of Aquitaine 22
relations with John 4, 5, 6, 105, 246, 307, 317
relations with Templars 123
reputation of 188, 210, 211, 353
return to England after captivity 294, 295, 297, 298, 300, 301, 302
sexuality of 149, 312, 313, 314, 315
succeeds to throne of England 93, 97
supports Henry of Champagne as King 241
takes crusader vows 76, 77
truce with Philip II (1194) 310
Richard of Canville 165
Richard of Clare, English knight 172
Richard of Devizes, chronicler 107, 118, 139, 151, 258, 301, 336
and Jerusalem 261, 262
and massacre of the Jews 101, 102
views on Berengaria 147, 162
Richard, Earl of Clare 278
Richard, Earl of Cornwall 259
Richemont, Aquitaine 45
Richent, sister of William Longchamp 232
Rigord, French chronicler 24, 88, 100, 174, 289, 337, 347
Robert de Nonant, brother of the bishop of Coventry 293
Robert de Ros 360
Robert de Sablé, Grand Master of the Templars 133, 198
Robert Guiscard 136
Robert Longchamp, brother of William 330

Robert of Dreux, knight 206, 213
Robert of Turnham 163, 165
Robert of Whitfield, official 107
Robert the Bruce, king of Scotland 216
Robert Trebusset, standard bearer 204
Robert, abbot of Tournai 318
Robert, brother of Henry I of England 105
Robert, Earl of Leicester 99, 180, 182, 207, 222, 244, 253, 256, 285, 307, 339
Robert, prior of Hereford 231
Robin Hood Prince of Thieves, Hollywood film 370
Robin Hood, Disney movie 6
Robin Hood, Hollywood film 370
Robin Hood, mythical hero 275, 283, 340, 367, 370
Rochester, England 278
Roger Bigod, Earl 278
Roger de Saci, knight 256
Roger Guiscard 136
Roger le Pole, English knight 172
Roger Malcheal, Keeper of the King's Seal 89
Roger Mauchat, Vice-Chancellor 155
Roger Mortimer, lord of Wigmore 231
Roger Norreys, Prior of Canterbury 111
Roger of Argentan, Norman agent 267
Roger of Howden, chronicler 54, 55, 57, 73, 75, 86, 106, 127, 150, 156, 187, 215, 251, 268, 290, 292, 294, 299, 315, 317, 341, 351
- background to his writing
- on accession of Richard 97
- on Berengaria 147
- on campaign in Normandy 330, 336, 338, 339
- on coronation of Richard 99
- on death of Henry II 89, 90, 91
- on death of Richard 344, 346
- on Geoffrey of Brittany 62, 67
- on Joachim of Fiore 145
- on massacre at Acre 191
- on massacre of the Jews 102, 103
- on Richard's sexuality 48, 72, 144
- on William Longchamp 234, 235
- retrospective on Richard's life 353, 362

Roger of Mowbray, English knight 76
Roger of Ripon, clerk 323
Roger, king of Sicily 320
Roland, chivalric hero 116, 179, 254, 257, 365, 366
Rome 134, 145, 153, 154, 187, 232, 262, 273, 279, 280, 323, 327, 330, 335, 340, 342
Roncesvalles, pass 254, 257
Roquebrune, castle 336
Rosamund Clifford, mistress of Henry II 35
Rouen, Normandy 25, 57, 96, 106, 123, 126, 235, 284, 305, 309, 325, 327, 329, 331, 346, 347, 354, 359
Roxburgh, Scotland 113

St Albans, England 14, 278
St Elijah, abbot of 247
St George, Syrian bishop of 247
St Hilarion, Cyprus 164
St John's College, Oxford 13
St Mary-le-Bow, London 322
St Michael's Mount, England 295
St Paul's, London 233, 279, 302, 322
St Saviour, Sicilian monastery 140
St Swithun's priory, Winchester 301
St Vincent, Cape 133
St Mary's Abbey, York 330
Saintes, Poitou 37, 38, 45
Saladin Tithe 77, 78, 79, 112, 118
Saladin, Muslim leader 64, 120, 145, 156, 166, 191, 196, 220, 241, 258, 261, 262, 263, 271, 274
- abandons Ascalon 214
- and Nizaris 240
- and defence of Jerusalem 217, 224, 225, 230, 250
- and Hattin campaign 73, 74, 159, 198
- assessment of 160
- attack on Jaffa 252, 254, 256
- at siege of Acre 174, 179, 182, 183, 184, 190
- captures Jerusalem 74, 194, 358
- death of 284
- first becomes Muslim ruler 45
- negotiations with Richard 181, 203, 221, 222, 251, 255, 259, 260
- on Arsuf campaign 199, 200, 201, 205, 209, 210, 211
- views of Richard 216

Salerno 136, 142, 153, 319
Salic law 24
Salisbury, England 40, 124, 127, 313
Salt River, Outremer 203
Salzburg, Austria 269
Sancho I, King 133
Sancho VI, king of Navarre 126, 356
Sancho VII, king of Navarre 149, 308, 309, 336
Sandwich, England 294
Sansom, abbot of St Sansom 303
Santiago de Compostella 21, 42, 70, 125
Saphadin; *see* Al-'Adil
Sarum, England 40, 58
Saumur, Anjou 85
Savaric de Bohun, bishop of Bath 273, 284
Scott, Sir Walter, novelist 367

Second Crusade 9, 117, 122, 153
Second Lateran Council (1139) 255
Seine, River 305, 309, 325, 327, 342, 344
Selby, England 110
Seljuk Turks 120
Sens, France 306
Shaubak Castle 223
Sherborne, England 110
Sherwood Forest, England 299
Shi'a Islam 210
Shoreham, England 231
Shrewsbury, Battle of 196
Sibylla, queen of Jerusalem 73, 158, 161, 168, 172, 176
Sicily 41, 128, 136, 143, 144, 146, 147, 148, 149, 150, 151, 152, 153, 155, 180, 198, 215, 231, 234, 273
attacked by Richard 140, 141
Emperor Henry VI and 142, 265, 270, 282, 286, 293, 319, 332
historic background of 137, 138
Sidon 74, 238, 332
Simon of Apulia, Dean of York 318, 323
Simon of Odell, English knight 172
Socrates, Greek philosopher 364
Sodom, Biblical town 312, 313
Solomon, Biblical King 195
Somerset, England 104
Southampton, England 40, 78, 236
Southwell, England 300
Spain 21, 42, 70, 120, 125, 266, 318
Speyer, Germany 276, 277, 291
Stamford, England 102
Stephen Longchamp, brother of William 245
Stephen of Blois, king of England 24, 105, 106, 132
Stephen of Tours, seneschal of Anjou 87, 97
Stephen of Turnham 223, 237
St-Jean-de-Port, castle 336
Straits of Gibraltar 132, 133, 266
Straits of Messina 136, 137, 138
Stubbs, Bishop William 368
Suger, abbot of St-Denis 13
Sunni Islam 210
Swansea, Wales 114
Syria 1, 16, 44, 64, 210, 239, 243, 269, 326

Taillebourg, Aquitaine 45, 46, 47
Talisman, novel 367
Tancred, king of Sicily 111, 137, 138, 138. 139, 140, 141, 142, 143, 150, 152, 198, 265, 329, 320
Taormina, Sicily 150
tarantulas 202
Tarragona, Aragon 134
Templars, military order 141, 198, 224, 253, 262, 313, 341
and Cyprus 165, 238
at siege of Acre 179, 183, 188
cautious strategy in Outremer of 225, 226
in Hattin campaign 73, 74, 193, 210
on Arsuf campaign 197, 204, 205, 212, 213, 215
Richard and 123
role of 17
Temple Church, London 64, 65
Teutonic Knights, military order 198
Thibaut, count of Champagne 356
Thierry, count of Flanders 283
Thomas Aquinas, medieval mystic 314
Thomas Cromwell, Tudor official 152
Thomas Wolsey, Cardinal 152
Thorée, France 350
three lions 334
Tiber, River 136
Tiberias, Lake 74
Tiberius, Roman Emperor 235
Tickhill, England 279, 280, 298, 349
Titanic 18
Toledo, Spain 319
Tortosa, Outremer 168
Toulouse 33, 71, 80, 83, 126, 279, 328
Touraine 66, 285, 306, 368
Tours, Touraine 76, 126, 127, 344
Tower of London 124, 233
Trenchmere, galley 168
Trifels, Germany 277, 286
Tripoli, Outremer 16, 138, 158, 159, 168, 260
Triport, France 305, 311
True Cross, relic 74, 183, 188, 193, 221, 247, 261, 262
Turcopoles 212
Tyburn, gallows, London 322
Tyre, Outremer 121, 134, 161, 167, 173, 178, 186, 188, 190, 210, 223, 227, 229, 238, 239, 240, 242, 271
Saladin attacks at 159, 160

Urban II, Pope 131
Urban III, Pope 67, 75

Val Canale, road 268
Valencia, Spain 134
Valerie, Saint 31
Vatican 135, 335
Vatican 335
Vaudreuil, Normandy 309, 310
Vendôme, France 309
Venice. Venetians 136, 144, 184, 267, 284, 342, 358
Verdun, France 173
Verneuil, France 306, 307
Vernon, Normandy 338
Vespasian, Roman Emperor 202
Vexin, Normandy 67, 271, 274, 320, 325, 336
Vézelay, France 112, 127, 128
Via Maris, road 224

Victoria, British Queen 263, 357, 368
Vienna, Austria 268
Vienne, River 34
Villandon, Marie-Jeanne L'Héritier 367
Volkoff, Vladimir, historian 353
Vulgrin of Angoulême 49

Wales, Welsh 65, 95, 111, 113, 114, 231, 301
Wallingford, England 13, 237, 274
Walter Map, chronicler 30, 58
Walter of Coutances, archbishop of Rouen 136, 153, 302, 305
after capture of Richard 271, 275, 279, 284, 292, 300
and William Longchamp 233, 234, 235, 237, 278
dispute with Richard over Les Andalys 326, 329, 331
in dispute with monks of Canterbury 112
returns to England 231
takes the Cross 66
Walter of Marun, knight 216
Warren, WL, historian 20
washerwomen on crusade 177, 195
West Knoyle, Wiltshire, England 15
Westminster, England 63, 95, 98, 100, 263, 265, 302, 349
Westmoreland, England 300
Westphalia, Germany 341
White Ship 18, 24, 96, 117
Wight, Isle of, England 302
Wigmore Castle, England 231
Wilhelm II, German Kaiser 263
William Brewer, official 107
William de Beauchamp, knight 114
William de Mandeville, Earl of Essex 99, 106, 107
William de Préaux, knight 216
William des Barres, French knight 81, 146, 201, 209, 337
William des Roches, knight 87
William fitzAlan, knight 114
William fitzOsbert ('Longbeard') 321, 322
William fitzRalph, seneschal of Normandy 271
William I, king of England 50, 62, 108
William I, 'The Lion', king of Scotland 36, 37, 78, 106, 112, 113, 275, 300, 301, 323
William I, 'The Bad', king of Sicily 148
William II ('The Good'), king of Sicily 29, 40, 41, 138, 139
William II, king of England 50
William III, king of Sicily 320
William IX, duke of Aquitaine 26, 274
William Longchamp, chancellor of England 86, 103, 124, 234, 235, 236, 302, 305, 319, 330
appointed bishop of Ely 109
appointed Justiciar of England 107
dispute with John 231, 232, 233
during Richard's captivity 277, 284, 290
restored by Richard 301
unpopularity of 151, 152
William Longespée, half-brother of Richard I 127
William Marshal, English knight 93, 95, 99, 124, 149, 266, 290, 298, 305, 328, 330, 342, 343, 346
and Henry II 84
and Richard 87, 91, 92, 94
and the Young King 57
and tournaments 51
appointed official in England 107
defends Eleanor of Aquitaine 27
responsibilities in Wales 114
with Richard in Normandy 309, 337
William of L'Étang, knight 214, 256, 266
William of Newburgh, chronicler 107, 147, 154, 184, 265, 273, 286, 290, 291, 301, 303, 327, 362
William of Poitiers, chaplain to Richard I 78
William the Breton, chronicler 180, 276
William VI, count of Angoulême 36, 40, 53
William X, duke of Aquitaine 20
William, archbishop of Reggio 142
William, bishop of Lisieux 327
William, bishop of London 277
William, prince of England and infant brother of Richard I 5, 13
William, prince of England and son of Henry I 17
William. archbishop of Monreale 142
Wiltshire, England 40, 172
Winchester, England 40, 63, 68. 96, 101, 102, 106, 109, 151, 231, 236, 299, 301
Windsor, England 64, 274, 279, 280
Worms, Germany 282, 292
Würzburg, Germany 275

York, England 78, 102, 103, 104, 108, 109, 118, 280, 323, 335
Yorkshire, England 134, 172, 359

Zara, Hungary (now Croatia) 266
Zwin, port 294